D1126399

WINNIPEG

Alan F. J. Artibise

Winnipeg

a social history of urban growth 1874-1914

McGill-Queen's University Press   MONTREAL AND LONDON 1975

© McGill-Queen's University Press 1975
ISBN 0 7735 0202 5
Legal Deposit Second Quarter 1975
Bibliothèque nationale du Québec
Designed by Mary Cserepy
Printed in Canada by John Deyell Co.

This work has been published with the
help of a grant from the
Social Science Research
Council of Canada,
using funds provided by the
Canada Council.

to my Mother and
the memory of my Father
Henry Damian Artibise
1909–1964

acknowledgements

This study has developed over a period of time longer than I sometimes care to recall, and in the process I have incurred many debts. Research and writing are essentially lonely occupations made bearable only by the many friends one makes along the way. My first obligation is to Professor Norbert MacDonald of the University of British Columbia in whose graduate seminar the idea for this project was first formulated. He has been a sympathetic critic and a good friend. Without his valuable support this book might never have been completed. A number of other historians have aided me at one time or another, especially by encouraging the publication of a study that began as a doctoral dissertation. These include J. M. S. Careless, W. L. Morton, John Taylor, and, in his own special fashion, Gilbert Stelter.

This study has received financial support from the Central Mortgage and Housing Corporation, the Canada Council, and from the J. S. Ewart Memorial Fund. To all I am much indebted.

Chapters 7, 9, and 15 have been published in slightly amended form in *HSSM Transactions*, *Canadian Historical Papers*, and *Western Perspectives 1*, ed. David J. Bercuson. For permission to reprint these sections my thanks are due to the Historical and Scientific Society of Manitoba, the Canadian Historical Association, and Holt, Rinehart and Winston.

Like all historians, I have been dependent on a large number of librarians and curators of manuscripts. My research was greatly facilitated by the cooperation of the following: the staff of the City Clerk's Office, City of Winnipeg; the Provincial Library and Archives of Manitoba; and the Public Archives of Canada.

I owe a particular obligation to my brother-in-law, Anthony E. Kowaluk, who spent long hours applying his considerable cartographic skills in drawing the maps included in this book.

I cannot adequately thank my wife Irene, who typed, read proof, untangled footnotes, and earned rent money with skill and efficiency. She also lived with this project in its various stages without complaining.

Finally, I should say that the stylistic crudities and errors of fact, judgement, and interpretation that may appear in this book were achieved single-handedly.

contents

illustrations

All plates except numbers 17 and 18 come from photographs in the Manitoba Archives

MAPS

FIGURE

tables

introduction

This history of the City of Winnipeg during the period 1874–1914 is set in a particular framework. I have regarded Winnipeg as a special kind of social environment, set in a particular place and time, and with unique internal patterns and organization. I have stressed the city-building process and attempted to relate it to the various factors that went into the creation of Winnipeg's social and physical structure. This approach accepts the necessity of dealing with the so-called ecological complex: the key variables of population, organization, environment, and technology. But while the ecologists take the aggregate as their frame of reference, I have tried to emphasize the human and accidental, the contingencies of events and personalities.[1]

This study in consequence provides a reasonably detailed social history of Winnipeg: a description—or reconstruction—of the evolvement of an urban area. It endeavours to identify and describe the events, personages, trends, and movements which have played a key role in the development of Winnipeg. This "biography," it must be emphasized, makes no attempt to be definitive; such subjects as economic development and metropolitanism, for example, are given but scant attention.[2]

It is hoped that this study of Winnipeg will provide useful material to other historians, enabling them to compare the development of Winnipeg with that of other Canadian cities. Accordingly, while I have not been unaware of Winnipeg's own distinctive character, I have tended to stress sequential and comparative aspects: to deal with the beliefs, experiences, and problems that the residents of Winnipeg probably had in common with other urban residents.

Some work, of course, has been done in what may be loosely termed "urban history."[3] But these efforts have tended to be almost exclusively descriptive in nature and the work has most often been antiquarian rather than historical. Moreover, far too few cities have been studied and the time span is too full of gaps.

This is not to say these efforts are somehow useless. Many writers on the city have succeeded in catching the tone of a particular city—a tone that is elusive to define and difficult to trace historically through successive periods. What many of these works lack, however, is any attempt at a systematic, analytical approach. This has resulted in a series of disconnected local histories that render the goal of a comparative history and synthesis impossible.[4]

The reasons why the Canadian historical profession has not produced many urban histories are numerous and varied. Urban history is most often thought of as "local" history and Canadian historians, like their counterparts elsewhere, have simply neglected this field. They have neither encouraged nor appreciated the labour involved in writing local history. Instead, they have attempted to write history from the top down, usually from a political viewpoint. But with the increasing recognition of social history as an equal to political history it is being found that this practice must be reversed if we are to arrive at a reasonably complete understanding of the past.[5]

There are, however, other factors besides a distaste for local history that have worked against urban studies. As J. M. S. Careless has noted, "Cities, perhaps, could not gain much attention in the long-dominant French-Canadian tradition of 'les enfants du sol,' which largely viewed them as homes of temptation, corruption and the English; nor in the equally traditional English-Canadian concern with wilderness expanses, near-endless frontiers for pioneers to open."[6] Similarly, the division of Canadian historians into two distinct language and cultural groups, each fostering its own particular approach toward the study of the past, has tended to keep the study of urban history in its infancy.[7] The Quebec historians have been concerned with the events of the French regime and the problem of the survival of a French identity. The English-speaking historians, largely Ontarians, have tended to concentrate on such subjects as Canada's gradual progress towards autonomy and the development of a Canadian identity. In short, in the Canadian experience there were numerous topics that were considered to be far more important than urban development.

But whatever the reasons for a lack of urban history in the past, most present-day historians recognize the need for such studies today and many are actively encouraging such work. With the development of a kind of history that goes beyond a description of major political events and personages to an analysis of society of all levels, cities have been recognized as fundamental units that can no longer be ignored. It is now accepted that it was cities that organized the frontiers of the country, and cities that served (and still serve) as centres of major decision-making, as focuses of political, social, and cultural activities, and as keys to provincial and regional power structures. Thus urban histories that discuss and analyse urban society can serve as an important source of historical explanation. For society is not merely a picture of still life, a kind of background to the story which is being told, or a passive piece of scenery to be described. It is an active collaborator in the work of history. Historians must therefore conceive their story in terms of an underlying structure made up of many components, one of which is the city. In the attempt to arrive at a larger account of provincial, regional, or even national developments, therefore, scholarly and comparable studies of cities are a prime necessity.

Urban histories can also be useful in another area. Sociologists, economists, political scientists, geographers, and other social scientists are in need of historical perspective. Often the accuracy of the interpretation of current concepts used by these disciplines depends upon the delineation of the differences and similarities of the past. Whether or not the historian conceives new theories himself, he watches the other disciplines do so and sees them endlessly applying theses developed in one context in a series of others. He sees the tendency of sociologists to emphasize the aberrations of urban life and to overlook its normal routines, or that of geographers to isolate the purely geographical controls on town growth and to leave aside other dynamic factors. In the processes that combine in the urban unit the historian can make a positive contribution by placing in an historical context the large, complex, and often unintelligible forces that now beset the modern world. In order to clarify concepts long in use by other disciplines (concepts such as urbanization, assimilation, mobility, and so forth) links must be established between the concepts themselves and the experiences of the men and women who lived in the past. A prime function of historical research, informed by social science concerns, is precisely to edit, refine, and enrich theory by identifying and exploring important historical developments which cannot be neatly explained by existing theory. Finally, and perhaps most important for the future of history as a discipline, is the realization that in the study of the way in which an urban society has organized itself spatially and structurally and has developed such a variety of social systems and institutions, there exists an incomparable arena in which to bring together explicitly a number of disciplines.[8]

To write of the social aspects of urban growth the historian must, therefore, learn more about a city than the actions of its politicians and leading families. He must look beyond the patterns of politics or the ferment of ideas. Until recently this has often been the extent of our research, whether this approach concerned the life of one hundredth or one tenth of the population. There have been good reasons for this approach; most often that which was unique about a given area was the achievement of a small group of people and they were usually the only people who left detailed records. But there is a great need to learn more about greater numbers of people, a need to find out not only what was unique but what was commonplace. A good social historian must learn who made up the population and study its changing size, composition, and distribution; he must investigate the spatial and temporal dimensions of community life; he should deal with structural aspects such as the organization of the community and its parts; and, finally, he should concern himself with the influences of social groups upon attitudes, values, and actions.

These are all demanding approaches, full of pitfalls and frustration, and all do not offer the same possibilities from the standpoint of historical research. Nevertheless, in his search for evidence the use of statistical data can materially assist the historian. Through their use the historian can, to a certain extent, release himself from the domination of literary evidence. The statistical sketch, once obtained, can provide the historian with a general outline of the common life of the past as well as a number of useful reference points by which he can orient his study. Statistics must, of course, be used with care and understanding—they have no inherent magical qualities.[9] All census enumerations, for example, are subject to a variable degree of error: undercounts here, overcounts there, and occasional confusions of categories by the counters and counted everywhere. Hence the historian has to develop all the arts of the conjurer in manipulating even official census data to make his results consistent and comparable over time. Indeed, improper use of statistics often results in a blunting of the historian's perception by making him so aware of aberrations that he loses touch with reality. I have been aware of these qualifications in this study and have constantly tried to use statistical data only as an auxiliary tool.

One final note must be made about the use of a topical rather than a chronological chapter organization in this book. Since one of my major goals in this book was to deal with dimensions of past urban life that are most in need of study, I felt it was necessary to employ a topical organization that would facilitate systematic comparison and contrast. If, as a result, the various chapters seem to be a series of separate studies, I trust that this difficulty is outweighed by the advantages of comparability.

part one

the pre-urban era, 1863–74

[Winnipeg's location] was not thought to be suitable for a great city. It was said to be muddy and swampy and too far east from choice lands, and "unfortunate in its surroundings," but the finger of destiny and the energy and confidence of its citizens all pointed to its being the chosen city of the prairies.

George Bryce, *Illustrated History of Winnipeg,* 1905

1 / The Origins and Incorporation of Winnipeg

The unpromising beginnings of Winnipeg did not presage the remarkable development of that city in the years after 1874. Settlers and fur traders had inhabited the site of Winnipeg from as early as 1812.[1] Yet as late as 1849 the Red River Colony was still dominated by the stifling commercial monopoly and political control of the Hudson's Bay Company. The colony was dispersed over a wide area, dependent on subsistence agriculture and the buffalo hunt, and isolated from the settled regions of the continent. Only after 1849 did a series of developments begin to work major changes at Red River—changes which eventually were to give birth to the first truly urban community in the British Northwest.

In 1849 the Hudson's Bay Company post of Upper Fort Garry was the site of one of the most important trials in the history of the Northwest. A free trading Métis, P. G. Sayer, was charged with breaking the company's commercial monopoly by engaging in an illicit trade in furs with Indians. Sayer was found guilty but was not sentenced, and this event marked the beginning of the end of the old order in the Northwest. The company recognized its inability to enforce restrictions on trade within the colony, or between the colony and free traders outside. The subsequent establishment of free trade paved the way for the development of general commerce and the coming of the agricultural frontier and settlement.

This major event within the colony was matched by several external developments. The first was the advancement of the American agricultural frontier, marked by the formation of the Territory of Minnesota in 1849 and by the rapid growth of St. Paul as the centre of commerce for the upper Mississippi and Red River valleys. Trade between the colony and St. Paul grew steadily after 1849 and by the end of the 1850s free traders from the Red River Colony were spending well over $100,000 in that city every season.

This trade with St. Paul helped reduce the isolation of the Red River Colony. Ever since 1821 the colony's only connection with the outside world had been through Hudson Bay. And even this commercial outlet was limited to the commerce of the fur trade, carried in one or two ships annually. Compared to this arduous transportation route, the southern approach to the colony was much superior. This system consisted of a complicated interlocking of three means of transportation: railroads as far as the westward-moving head of steel; steamboats and keel boats wherever rivers would accommodate them; and beyond the river banks the Red River cart. The use of this southern route grew vigorously and by the 1860s Minnesota's ascendancy in meeting the commercial needs of the Red River Colony was unquestioned. Indeed, even the Hudson's Bay Company finally abandoned the Bay route and shipped in their supplies via St. Paul.

These southern influences were balanced by a resurgence of interest in Canada in the Red River region. A Select Committee of the House of Commons of Great Britain, set up in 1857 to report on the company's exclusive licence to trade in the Northwest, had recommended that Canada should eventually acquire the valleys of the Red and Saskatchewan. The committee hearing aroused considerable interest in the Northwest, especially when they were followed by the dispatch of two exploring expeditions instructed to gain geographic and climatic information.

Even more important than these events was the pervasive propaganda campaign conducted by George Brown in Canada West. In his influential newspaper the *Globe,* Brown eloquently called for the resumption of the old trade with the Northwest and the annexation to Canada of the entire region. His activities, combined with the other forces, resulted in a trickle of "Canadians" into the Red River Colony in the years after 1857. And, in 1859, a newspaper, *The Nor'Wester,* was established in the colony to advocate the annexation of the Northwest to Canada.

To this influx of Canadian settlers was added a steady flow of newcomers from the United States, most of whom were traders. The arrival of these groups indicated that the rule of the Hudson's Bay Company over the Northwest could not endure much longer; by 1860 the company's domination of the area was clearly at an end. Fortunately, the company and the British government realized that it was only a matter of time before the monopoly had to be legally ended and a new form of government established in the Northwest. The final decision came in 1870 with the entry of the Province of Manitoba into the Dominion of Canada, although throughout the decade this end result was by no means certain. The story of these years, however, properly belongs to a history of Manitoba, not Winnipeg. Suffice it to say that it was in this atmosphere of political uncertainty—but relative economic prosperity—that the village of Winnipeg sprang up.

The end of the old order in the Red River Colony was clearly indicated in 1859 when, for the first time, the Hudson's Bay Company found that the general trade of its store at Upper Fort Garry, close by the junction of the Red and Assiniboine rivers, had become more lucrative than the fur trade. Other business interests also discovered that with the increasing population of the area a demand had arisen for goods and services that could not be fully met by the company alone, and by 1862 there were over twelve business establishments surrounding the fort.[2] One of these was the Royal Hotel run by Henry McKenney. Born in Upper Canada of Irish parents, McKenney had operated a frontier trading store in the Minnesota Territory before coming to Red River in 1859. By the spring of 1862 he had prospered to such an extent that he decided to get out of the hotel trade and build a general store at a new location. His new establishment was to be the nucleus of the future city of Winnipeg.[3]

McKenney's store was built "just where the fur-runners' trail coming down the Assiniboine to Fort Garry crossed the trail running down the Red River," in present-day Winnipeg the corner of Portage Avenue and Main Street.[4] This choice of a site caused much amusement and even jeers from people at the fort and settlers at Point Douglas and points further down the Red. It was much too far from the river, they said, and in the spring the land was so low it was nothing but a swamp. But McKenney had caught his own glimpse of the future and was not to be laughed out of his plans. Before long his choice of a location was copied by others, and in a short ten years these few buildings would expand to swallow up both Point Douglas and Upper Fort Garry. McKenney had the last laugh, as it is reported that he sold his muddy corner for $15,000 in 1876.[5]

Despite confident predictions for future growth, the village of Winnipeg remained between 1863 and 1870 a quite unimportant part of the larger Red River Colony.[6] It was only in 1866 that the designation "Winnipeg" was first used to distinguish McKenney's store and the other buildings that were gradually built around it from the rest of the Red River Colony. The name Winnipeg was first used by the Nor'Wester on February 24, 1866. The previous issues of this paper had carried the designation "Red River Settlement, Assiniboia," on the masthead. The word has its origin in the Cree name given to the lake forty miles north, meaning *win*, muddy, *nippee*, water. This name gradually came into general use; by 1870 the town of Winnipeg was shown on maps of the area, even though the community was not then incorporated either as a village or town. But despite the gradual acceptance of the name Winnipeg within the Red River Colony, the new hamlet was for sometime known to the outside world as Fort Garry. It was not until May 1, 1876 that the post office had its name changed to Winnipeg.[7]

Winnipeg's modest development prior to 1870 is also revealed in a contemporary description of the place. As this visitor suggested, it took great foresight to imagine that from such crude beginnings an important city would grow.

> What a sorry sight was presented by that long-thought-of-town of Winnipeg on the day we entered it! What a mass of soft, black, slippery and sticky Red River mud was everywhere spread out before us! Streets with neither sidewalks nor crossings, with now and again a good sized pit of mire for the traveller to avoid or flounder through as best he could; a few small stores with poor goods and high prices; one little tavern where 'Dutch George' was "monarch of all his survey"; a few passable dwellings with no "rooms to let," nor space for boarders; neither church nor school in sight or in prospect; population about one hundred instead of one thousand as we expected—such was Winnipeg on July 4th, 1868.[8]

With the entry of Manitoba into the Dominion of Canada in 1870, however, Winnipeg's first boom began. "The North West had long been in need of advertisement and the Riel Rebellion had helped fill that need."[9] The results were recorded in Winnipeg's rapid population growth. From a population of only 100 in December 1870 the community grew to 215 in 1871, 1,467 in 1872, and 3,700 by 1874.[10] In those years the leading element in Winnipeg was a fusion of private free traders with newcomers, the latter, for the most part, Englishmen and Ontarians by origin. A careful enumeration of the population by the newly established *Manitoba Free Press* in November 1872 indicated that the population of 1,467 was made up of 1,019 males and only 448 females. This disparity, the paper noted on 9 November 1872, was commonly "noticeable in most Western towns, and is here explained by the fact that few immigrants are accompanied by their families, for whom they first secure a home, and then return or send for, as well as because so large a proportion is made up of young men, who left the crowded family homestead to take part in the vast lottery of this territory, where the great cities and Provinces of the future furnish the field for competition."

Why the unattractive village of Winnipeg and not Point Douglas or some other part of the Red River Colony should have attracted so many of the new arrivals after 1870 is explained chiefly by its geographical location. Winnipeg's proximity to the Hudson's Bay post of Upper Fort Garry was a key factor in the hamlet's early growth. Following the proclamation of the Manitoba Act in July 1870 the company establishment became the seat of government not only for the new province but for the Northwest Territories as well. And the government agencies, small though they were, greatly exceeded in volume and importance the petty business of the former District of Assiniboia. The first Dominion

Lands Office in the West, which handled the large and vexatious business of adjusting the titles of old inhabitants, administered the half-breed reserves, and registered the claims of new settlers, was also located there. In addition, the Canadian garrison was partially stationed at the Upper Fort until, in 1872, Fort Osborne barracks were built in Winnipeg. These troops naturally stimulated local economic development. Expenditures by the military on food, supplies, and entertainment greatly boosted local trade. Even more important in the long run was the fact that many soldiers elected to take their discharge on the spot in order to take up farms near the settlement of Winnipeg. And glowing reports sent home or carried home by those soldiers who returned were a powerful stimulus that induced waves of Ontario settlers to migrate west. In brief, Winnipeg's nearness to the old Hudson's Bay fort served to stimulate its growth; so much so that in a year or two after 1870 it was impossible to distinguish the two settlements. Significantly, it was Winnipeg that swallowed up the fort and not vice versa, for the city's rapid rise as a commercial centre transcended the old role the company had had in the Northwest.[11]

It is true, of course, that the old dependence on the fur trade was not completely replaced by other types of commerce. Indeed, the fur trade remained the chief business of Winnipeg until at least 1875, and along with the Hudson's Bay Company many private entrepreneurs maintained a vigorous business in furs. The point is that none of the firms confined themselves exclusively to fur. The opening up of the region after 1870 brought a greatly increased demand for merchandise, lumber, agricultural implements, and land. And Winnipeg's growth in the years 1870–74 was a result of that settlement's businessmen aggressively stepping forward to fill these needs.

The growth of Winnipeg as a commercial centre thus exceeded and overshadowed its growth as political capital of Manitoba. Increasingly after 1870 fur traders became retailers and wholesalers, as businessmen turned to supplying not only Winnipeg's needs but those of the merchants of the new settlements which rapidly sprang up across the province. The settlement of agricultural lands created a demand for a great variety of goods in a way the fur trade did not, and Winnipeg supplied them all.

Two examples of local business expansion may be taken as fairly typical.[12] A. G. B. Bannatyne had established himself in the Red River Colony in 1848. At first "his business house was confined to [meeting] the wants of the red man, but as civilization advanced the demands of the public changed and the class of goods carried also." By 1881 Bannatyne and Company were prominent among the wholesale and retail dealers of Winnipeg, dealing in fancy and staple groceries, provisions, wines, liquors, and cigars. His firm employed nine men and occupied "a fine brick building, 28 x 70 feet, three flats and a basement, with warehouse 30 x 90 feet connected, with 2 flats, at 292 Main Street." Even more successful was James H. Ashdown. He arrived in Winnipeg in 1868 and began business in a small way as a tinsmith and hardware merchant with his whole enterprise valued at $1,000. By 1875 Ashdown had begun to do some large contract work and his wholesale trade had so increased that he operated two separate establishments, one a retail and one a wholesale. By 1881 he was worth over $150,000 and had established branch stores at Portage la Prairie and Emerson. In his united manufacturing, retail, and wholesale business, both in Winnipeg and branches, Ashdown employed over seventy-five persons. The versatility of Bannatyne and Ashdown was characteristic of many other businessmen in Winnipeg. It was a quality that was appropriate to a period of transition from a fur to an agricultural economy and was to reach a climax when several firms further diversified by becoming the first grain-buyers in Winnipeg.[13]

Winnipeg's growth in the years after 1870 was also marked by a thriving business in real estate and finance. By 1880 there were no less than 59 separate financial and real estate interests in the city. These firms conducted a lively business in advertising the qualities of Manitoba land, in informing and directing land seekers, in arranging sales of land and scrip, and in buying on speculation both town lots and farm lands. Between 1871 and 1873 there was a mild boom—the first of many— in Winnipeg lots. Indeed, despite Winnipeg's growing importance as a commercial and agricultural centre, it was in real estate that the great fortunes of its leading citizens would be made.[14]

The growth and prosperity of Winnipeg during this period naturally expressed itself in a rapid physical expansion. Comprising only some thirty structures in the fall of 1870 Winnipeg had well over nine hundred by the end of 1873. "Twenty-seven of these were occupied by manufacturing industries, over one hundred by mercantile concerns, and the balance as offices, hotels, boarding houses, dwellings, and so forth."[15] It is important to note, however, that prior to incorporation Winnipeg's spatial growth was completely uncontrolled. The roads and streets of the village—if one can speak of streets at all—had mainly developed out of former fur-trading trails, or followed the survey lines of the early river lots. The individualistic, haphazard physical growth of Winnipeg in the years prior to incorporation was noted by a resident: "Now there is no such thing [as planning], and this individual or that one can plan a street on his property to answer his own individual purposes, irrespective of the community at large."[16] Only after incorporation was an orderly development of streets in Winnipeg attempted.

As Winnipeg grew and prospered there sprang up among the business and professional group that directed that growth, an unshakeable conviction of optimism that was perhaps the most significant development to emerge from these hectic years. The rapid expansion of Winnipeg during the tumultous months of 1871–73 should have left little time for the residents to concern themselves much with the future. But if there was one characteristic that was shared by nearly all Winnipeggers in these years, and for quite some time to come, it was the firm belief that the future of their community was boundless. A place where there had been no one but fur traders and Indians before, but which today numbered a thousand, might be expected to number tens or even hundreds of thousands tomorrow.

From the outset Winnipeggers were self-centred and aggressive, determined to protect their position against any town which appeared to challenge them. Whether Ontarian or Englishman, prosperous merchant or day labourer, young or old, Winnipeggers rapidly became and steadfastly remained avid city boosters.

Winnipeg was broad-viewed as well, however, for it was not looked on as just one more promising settlement in the West. Rather it was to be the region's central metropolis and chief spokesman, destined forever to play a role of unchallenged importance.[17] The rapid growth of large wholesale and real estate companies, for example, gave many Winnipeggers a regional, and at times even a national, outlook that often transcended local and provincial interests. Thus while Winnipeg was Manitoba's chief urban centre, it always thought of itself as more than that. Indeed, the metropolitan ambitions of Winnipeg were far more sophisticated than those of other western towns and cities. The large number of Ontario-born businessmen in Winnipeg were concerned with the progress of the whole dominion, not just Manitoba or the West. They realized their fortunes were closely connected with the economic growth and political stability of all provinces, not just their own.[18] In short, Winnipeg was a "Canadian" as well as a "Western" city, and this attitude is perhaps best shown by the nickname often used for Winnipeg—"Bull's Eye of the Dominion."

This broad outlook did not prevent the growth of a unique Winnipeg mentality. The city's businessmen, especially in the years after 1881, became conscious of their underprivileged position in such matters as transportation facilities and the Winnipeg Board of Trade led the fight against what it considered to be eastern exploitation.[19] But while Winnipeg could be accused of being very protective of its own position as the metropolis of the West, it could rarely be accused of being parochial.

Winnipeg's peculiar character and sense of destiny were noted by a number of observers. Since that spirit was to exert such a powerful influence on Winnipeg's history, some of those impressions deserve to be quoted at length. George H. Ham, a newspaper reporter, alderman, and long-time resident of Winnipeg, described the city as follows:

> Winnipeg is a live wire City. That does not have to be proven. Almost anyone of its progressive businessmen will admit that

... but it is doubtful if [in 1912] in its couple of hundred thousand or so of people it holds as many "live wires" as did the muddy, generally disreputable village that in, say, 1873, with a thousand or perhaps fifteen hundred people, straggled along Main Street from Portage Avenue to Brown's Bridge, near the present site of the City Hall, and sprawled between Main Street and the river.
It was without sidewalk or pavements; it had neither waterworks, sewage nor street lights. The nearest railroad was at Moorhead on the Red River, 222 miles away. Its connection with the outer world was one, or possibly two, steamers on the Red River in the summer and by weekly stage in winter. It boasted telegraph connections with the United States and Eastern Canada by way of St. Paul, during the intervals when the line was working. Although essentially Canadian it was practically cut off from direct connection with Canada. The Dawson Route to Port Arthur could be travelled with great labor, pains and cost; but did not admit of the transportation of supplies. All freight came by Northern Pacific to Moorhead; then by steamer, flat boat or freight team to Winnipeg.

But the Winnipeg of that day was recognized to be then, as it is now, the gateway to the Canadian Prairie West where lay the hope of Canada's future greatness. The transfer of governmental authority over Rupert's Land from the Hudson's Bay Company to Canada had taken place in 1869; Canadian authority had been established by the first Red River expedition of 1870; a transcontinental railway was to be built at an early date that would displace the primitive conditions then existing. The doors of vast opportunity lay wide open and Canada's adventurous sons flocked to Winnipeg to have a part in the great expansion—the building of a newer and greater Canadian West. They were big men, come together with big purposes. Their ideas were big, and they fought for the realization of them. They struggled for place and power and advantage, not with regard to the little isolated village which was the field of their activities and endeavors; but always with an eye to the City that now is and to the great plains as they now are.[20]

Winnipeg's characteristic optimism and, at times, even arrogance is perhaps best explained by the need of the city's new citizens (and that included nearly everyone in 1873) to justify the decision they had taken to establish themselves in Winnipeg. Having left their homes and invested their capital and energy in an as yet unstable commercial centre, they felt compelled to defend and justify their actions. They were undoubtedly also affected by the propaganda campaigns of Brown's *Globe* and its offshoot, the *Nor'Wester*, both of which stressed the great potential of the Northwest and the patriotic duty of adding a new frontier to Canada. But whatever the source, or combination of sources, optimism—unparalleled and unshakeable—was early established as an undeniable element in Winnipeg's development.

This optimism and arrogance were the most persistent and striking characteristics of Winnipeg during its early history. They were readily apparent in the city's attempt to extend its influence over the economic and political life of the hinterland, and in its struggle with Selkirk over the main line of the Canadian Pacific Railway. This struggle for primacy and power left a legacy of damage and achievement. Yet the damage was not immediately apparent; the achievement was. The fear of failure was a dynamic force, pushing Winnipeg's leaders into numerous projects and improvements, and furnishing an invaluable stimulus to commercial and industrial enterprise. And, as its best, urban "imperialism" bred a strong pride in community accomplishment.

There were, nevertheless, a few in Winnipeg during these early years who, while never speaking ill of Winnipeg's fortunes, urged caution and careful adherence to certain priorities to ensure that the city's future would indeed be great. These dissenters emphasized the need for long-range planning and stressed that the struggle for supremacy over the whole Northwest could be won only at great cost for future generations. Unfortunately, the dissenters were never able to convince anyone but themselves of the need for caution. Throughout, the boosterism of the many inhibited and overshadowed the caution of the few.

Nothing reflected the optimism of Winnipeg's citizens more than the popular, mass movement that arose early in 1872 to incorporate Winnipeg. As George Bryce, a prominent Winnipegger, who arrived in the city in 1871 to organize a church and college, remarked, "It showed a consciousness of its own importance when Winnipeg was incorporated that it became at once a city. It did not go through the chrysalis stage of village or town. . . ."[21] With the grand vision of quickly becoming the "Chicago of Canada" before them and with but two years of rapid growth behind them, Winnipeggers sought the clear and unambiguous title of "city"—a terminology, however divorced from reality, they no doubt felt would be more respected back east.

There were, of course, several other, more mundane reasons for the growth of an incorporation movement in Winnipeg in 1872 and 1873. Prior to incorporation municipal affairs in Winnipeg were administered under an arrangement established by the provincial government in 1871. Winnipeg was provided with an assessor, road surveyor and constables, but little else.[22] Residents of Winnipeg were thus forced to attempt a solution of their municipal problems on a private basis. In 1871, for example, it was immediately apparent that without a broad tax base and a set of recognized bylaws the burden of municipal services would be shared unequally and unfairly.

Early in January 1872 Alexander Begg, a local merchant, published the first number of the *Manitoba Trade Review* and in it he expressed the following sentiments:

> On the 16th of next month the Legislature will sit, and it is well for us to take into consideration the propriety of incorporating our town. If we let this chance slip, who knows but others more enterprising may get ahead of us, and thus change the whole aspect of the place in a few years. Our Province is bound to grow rapidly and we must not sleep, lest others, alive to the importance thereof, may incorporate a town just outside, or not very far from our present limits. There are many benefits to be derived from an Act of Incorporation. Why not, therefore, hold a meeting of the older heads to discuss the matter freely. . . .[23]

Subsequent articles by Begg stressed the benefits to be gained by such action. Corporate powers, he felt, would allow for fire protection, municipal works such as sidewalks and streets, and the preparation and enforcement of bylaws "to regulate matters generally, so as to answer to the public good and not the ideas of individual parties."

Begg's call for a public meeting was acted upon in February when at a mass gathering a series of resolutions were passed calling for incorporation. These were then forwarded to the legislature with every expectation that they would be acted upon promptly. To the citizens' dismay, however, the legislature adjourned with no mention of incorporation.

Whatever the reasons for the legislature's refusal to act immediately on behalf of Winnipeg's residents, the citizens quickly decided that it was because "certain interests" were opposed to incorporation.[24] These interests were the Hudson's Bay Company, who at the time owned approximately one-third of the taxable property in the proposed city limits, and four other property owners, who were said to own 25 per cent of the remainder. It was generally believed that the company delayed passage of the desired legislation in an attempt to avert paying taxes on its large holdings.[25] This belief was encouraged by a local newspaper, the *Manitoban*, which vigorously opposed incorporation. Since that paper was felt to be strongly influenced by the Hudson's Bay Company there was no doubt in most Winnipeggers' minds that the company was seeking to prevent incorporation.

Following this first rebuff indignation meetings were held throughout the summer and fall of 1872, culminating in a mass meeting in December. At this gathering unanimous support was expressed in favour of incorporation, and a citizens' committee was formed and entrusted with the responsibility of drafting a suitable bill to present to the legislature early in 1873.[26] A report on a draft bill was presented to the citizens at another meeting in February 1873. It called for a council of a mayor and eight aldermen, and a fixed, four-ward system; and it laid out a host of corporate powers including taxation. When the measure was quickly ratified by the citizens it was then sent to the legislature for approval.

Legislative action was taken this time but it was soon apparent that the citizens' bill was not to be left intact. Revisions proposed by the legislature were drastic. The possible rate of taxation on improved property was reduced by half while that on unimproved property was cut to one-twentieth of one per cent of the assessed value. The corporation was debarred from borrowing money, while fees collected for licences were to be turned over to the province. Finally, to add to the residents' consternation, the name Winnipeg was changed to Assiniboine.

The reaction to these revisions was predictable. At a meeting early in March the populace protested these emasculations, and appointed a committee which subsequently interviewed the Legislative Council and vigorously urged the restoration of the original bill. The council met Winnipeg's request by altering the clauses that had been "revised" by the lower body. In so doing, however, they tampered with a privilege wholly reserved to the lower body. Later their action was declared out of order by the Speaker, Dr. C. J. Bird.[27] In apparent retaliation for this latest rebuff, Speaker Bird was the object of a brutal tarring, a crime whose perpetrators were never detected.[28]

Ensuing attempts to organize under the general municipal statute were equally frustrated, with the major blame throughout being laid upon the Hudson's Bay Company and Winnipeg's representative, Donald A. Smith.[29] The latter was charged with compromising himself for private gain since he was known to have strong financial connections with the company. And, when Smith tried to answer the charges of obstruction made against him, he merely added fuel to the fire when he defended the company by stating that "I thought and still think that the Hudson's Bay Company, who are the owners of a very considerable portion of the land within the limits of the proposed city should in common fairness, have been consulted."[30] Furthermore, the fact that the sections of the bill most radically altered had pertained to property, confirmed in many peoples' minds the thinly disguised hand of the Hudson's Bay Company and its "agent," Donald Smith. The *Manitoba Free Press* explained: "The virtual non-taxation of unimproved lands means that the mechanic who buys a lot from the Hudson's Bay Company and builds a house on it, will pay the expenses of the corporation out of his hard earned money, while the Company, who owns the adjoining lots, does not pay. We cannot immediately effect the remedy but when D. A. Smith comes back for re-election the time will have arrived."[31]

In defence of Smith and the legislature, however, two points can be made. Smith argued that incorporation at so early a date, with its inauguration of taxation, would discourage entrepreneurs from locating in Winnipeg and persuade them that some other, as yet unincorporated, settlement in the vicinity offered a better position for their business. The legisature's action on licence fees can be partially explained by the fact that its income was so sparse that it felt it was only fair for Winnipeg to pay part of the fees to the province. Thus, while Winnipeggers were only interested in the establishment of an effective and financially sound civic government, many legislators were equally devoted to the same task at a provincial level.

Despite these two setbacks and all the arguments pro and con they brought forth, incorporation was finally attained at the 1873 fall session of the legislature. Several public meetings had preceded the sitting of the legislature and at these it had been decided to again use the draft bill prepared by the citizens' committee.[32] Apparently the vociferous protests of Winnipeggers and their threats of electoral retaliation had had their effect, for this time the bill received preferential treatment. Indeed, Premier Clark, in an interview with the citizens' committee, promised to sponsor the bill as a government measure. Clark himself guided the measure through the House and, in an attempt to further expedite enactment, printing of the French version was dispensed with. On 8 November 1873 royal assent was given and Winnipeg was incorporated as a city.[33]

One of the more noteworthy facts about the Act of Incorporation was that it was based on the Ontario system.[34] The provision for a ward system, property qualifications for aldermen and mayor, and the dates for nominations, elections, and meetings were all identical to Ontario statutes. The slate of elective and appointive officials and the powers of the mayor were also based on Ontario examples. Winnipeg, too, possessed all the bylaw-making powers of an Ontario city. In short, the remaking of Manitoba in the image of Ontario was begun most markedly in Winnipeg.[35]

The legislation incorporating Winnipeg as a city was quite elaborate and the act itself comprised some 128 sections and occupied over forty pages.[36] Corporate authority was vested in a council composed of a mayor and twelve aldermen, three for each ward. Council members, including the mayor, possessed judicial as well as administrative powers, although they could not impose penalities involving hard labour. Some of the numerous specific powers of the civic corporation included the passage of bylaws concerning nuisances, safety, sanitation, fire, police, and markets. And to administer their enactments council was empowered to appoint a clerk, assessors, collectors, city engineer, health officers, constables, and a host of other civic employees. Civic revenue was to be raised in a number of ways. Taxation could be imposed upon real and personal property, while various licence fees could be collected with only liquor levies having to be shared with the province. Enterprises such as auction rooms, liveries, and peddling were among those requiring licences.

Application of the new legislation was not long in coming, for Winnipeg's first civic election was held in January 1874. It was preceded by a lively campaign, the main issue being the extent of each candidate's connection with large property interests such as the Hudson's Bay Company. The winner of the mayoralty contest, F. E. Cornish, called the first meeting of Council on 19 January. Quite naturally Council's first activities involved the establishment of a framework in which they could operate. Accordingly, aldermen were selected to strike standing committees for the year. These included finance, assessment, local works, fire and water, and police and licencing. The mayor was an *ex-officio* member of each committee. City Council also adopted such parliamentary procedures as committee of the whole, notice of motion, three readings for bylaws, and adjournment through lack of a quorum, to facilitate their work. In February an assessor, chief of police, and city engineer were chosen, while previous appointments of city clerk and chamberlain were confirmed.

Financial activities served to bridge these purely structural efforts. Procedures, committees, and appointments only became purposeful when they achieved concrete results. Some of the first expenditures of Council were on sidewalks ($8,246), roads ($3,204), and bridges ($621).[37] During this first year all funds were provided from current income. Some conception of the Hudson's Bay Company's opposition to incorporation can be grasped when it is noted that their property, assessed at $595,312, provided a major portion of the property taxes collected in 1874. Liquor fees comprised the largest part of the licence revenue while fines, often as low as 25 cents, were a negligible factor.[38]

As could be expected in a new city such as Winnipeg was in 1874, there were many obvious and expensive local works that needed to be carried out. For this reason and also because of low current income City Council in 1875 gained popular approval of its first money bylaw. This measure called for the expenditure of $250,000 on such civic improvements as sewers, fire equipment, waterworks, civic buildings, and streets. Some interest was also shown in health matters when Council established a special committee to participate in the management of the Winnipeg General Hospital and granted a sum of $500 to that institution.[39] In short, many activities essential to the establishment of a "community" which had previously been ill-done or neglected were either attempted or projected. Winnipeg had begun to acquire the character and institutions of a city.

part two

"big men, come together with big purpose"

The doors of vast opportunity lay wide open and Canada's adventurous sons flocked to Winnipeg to have a part in the great expansion—the building of a newer and greater Canadian West. They were big men, come together with big purpose. Their ideas were big, and they fought for the realization of them. They struggled for place and power and advantage, not with regard to the little isolated village which was the field of their activities and endeavours; but always with an eye to the city that now is and to the great plains as they now are.

George H. Ham, *Reminiscences of a Raconteur*, 1921

2 / The Dominance of a Commercial Elite

The men who directed Winnipeg's growth in the years 1874–1914 held in common a certain set of values. Accepting the challenge of a vast, underdeveloped domain they saw themselves as agents of improvement. They were practical men, businessmen who were convinced of the desirability of material progress. Setting their sights from persuasive American examples—such as the rise of Chicago—they were optimistic, expansionist, and aggressive. Their interests lay in what has been called the "architectural aspects of society"—the broad lines of its material fabric.[1]

Measuring progress in material terms, Winnipeg's businessmen directed their efforts toward achieving rapid and sustained growth at the expense of any and all other considerations. Regarding Winnipeg as a community of private money-makers, they expressed little concern with the goal of creating a humane environment for all the city's citizens. Accordingly, habits of community life, an attention to the sharing of resources, and a willingness to care for all men, were not much in evidence in Winnipeg's struggle to become a "great" city. Rather, the most noteworthy aspect of Winnipeg's history in this period was the systematic, organized, and expensive promotion of economic enterprise by public and private groups within the city.

Private businessmen, and business organizations such as the Board of Trade, were continually successful in their attempts to persuade the municipal corporation to improve and expand the commercial environment of Winnipeg with public commitments and at public expense. Indeed, the common outlook of Winnipeg's businessmen that the expansion of economic enterprise should be the prime concern of the local government is a dominant theme throughout the period.

This reliance on the resources of the municipal corporation for the provision of the basic conditions necessary for continued and rapid economic growth arose out of the particular needs of Winnipeg's businessmen. One such need was dependence on transportation facilities. Settled communities in the East, such as Montreal or Toronto, needed railways to feed raw materials to their factories and to distribute finished products. But these urban centres could always fall back on water transportation for their commercial needs. Conversely, the Winnipeg businessman needed railways for his very lifeblood. For while Toronto or Montreal might grow or decline, prosper or languish, depending on its transportation facilities, there was no doubt that Winnipeg, without railways, would not be a city at all. Accordingly, when it was found that the transcontinental railway might by-pass Winnipeg, the city's businessmen conceived a variety of programs to attract railways. They soon found, however, that the expenses involved in their efforts—which included the building of an expensive railway bridge and outright cash grants—could be met only with the resources of the municipal corporation. Similar problems were faced in efforts to make Winnipeg a major manufacturing centre and in programs designed to attract immigrants.[2]

Table 1 / **Representation by Occupational Group, Mayor's Office, 1874–1914**

Occupation		Number	%
Merchants and businessmen		16	39
Real estate agents and financiers		15	37
Manufacturers and contractors		6	14
Professionals		4	10
Artisans and workingmen		–	–
	Total	41	100

Table 2 / **Representation by Occupational Group, Board of Control, 1907-14**

Occupation		Number	%
Merchants and businessmen		7	22
Real estate agents and financiers		21	66
Manufacturers and contractors		1	3
Professionals		3	9
Artisans and workingmen		–	–
	Total	32	100

As a result of this early recognition that so much was at stake in public decisions, Winnipeg's businessmen took an active role in civic politics, both to protect and to further their interests. Thus, when the various elective offices in Winnipeg's local government are analysed by occupational groups, several significant facts emerge. Most important, of course, is that the city's merchants and businessmen, real estate agents and financiers, contractors and manufacturers—in short, Winnipeg's commercial class—dominated every elective office throughout the period (Tables 1, 2, and 3).[3] In the case of the mayor's office, the commercial group had a representative in office for 37 of 41 years, or 90 per cent of the time. Their representation on the important Board of Control[4] is even higher, standing at 91 per cent. In the relatively less important positions on City Council their representation drops to 81 per cent, but it nevertheless remains impressively high.

Table 3 also reveals another noteworthy fact. It indicates that the commercial group's involvement in civic government was consistently high throughout the period, for when their representation on City Council is analysed decade by decade there is very little change. This suggests that the commercial group did not take an occasional interest in local politics. For although their early involvement in municipal affairs may have assured such things as effective transportation facilities, there was, they felt, a continuing necessity to control the municipal government. Attracted by the role the local government could play in promoting prosperity, in building the city, and in increasing the value of their property through improvements, the commercial group gave civic politics a great deal of attention.

The continuing and consistently high degree of involvement of Winnipeg's commercial class in municipal government is also noteworthy from another viewpoint. In many other North American cities businessmen gained control of the local government only by pushing aside an old and established social elite. Then, often in a short time, they were themselves pushed out of politics by other groups, the latter usually being "professional politicians" or men who depended on the ethnic vote for their political success.[5] Winnipeg's commercial class did not have to push anyone out because of the circumstances surrounding the city's foundation; Winnipeg was established by businessmen, for business purposes, and businessmen were its first and natural leaders. In fact, between 1874 and 1914, Winnipeg's commercial and social elites were indistinguishable; membership in one group was almost always accompanied by membership in the other group.

The second development—the businessmen themselves being pushed out—was forestalled at least until the post-1919 period; and even then the commercial elite retained a large degree of control over the running of the city. Indeed, it can be said that after 1919 they were forced only to share some of their power with others, for they were never entirely pushed out of office.[6] The reasons for the commercial group's continued success have to do largely with Winnipeg's restricted

Table 3 / **Representation by Occupational Group, City Council, 1874–1914**

Occupation	1874–85		1886–96		1897–1906		1907–14		1874–1914	
	Number	%	Number	%	Number	%	Number	%	Number	%
Merchants and businessmen	49	33	42	32	39	32	49	44	179	34
Real estate agents and financiers	70	47	45	34	40	33	36	32	191	37
Manufacturers and contractors	11	7	9	7	20	16	8	7	49	10
Professionals	14	10	29	22	17	15	11	10	71	14
Artisans and workingmen	3	2	7	5	3	2	8	7	21	4
Not classified	2	1	–	–	3	2	–	–	5	1
Totals	149	100	132	100	122	100	112	100	515	100

municipal franchise. This allowed the elite to control the municipal corporation from the outset, unhampered by opposition from any other group.

Occupational classification also reveals that Winnipeg's professional group succeeded in gaining an average of only 10 per cent of the various elective positions. But it should also be noted that their level of representation remained the same throughout the period. At no time were they driven out by the commercial group. Indeed, during this time there was never any serious conflict between the supposedly distinct professional, social, and commercial elite of Winnipeg.

Finally, the occupational classification of the holders of elective office at the municipal level reveal that Winnipeg's artisans and workingmen were grossly under-represented. They had no representatives whatever in the position of mayor or controller and out of a total of 515 aldermen elected only 21. Moreover, of these only a few can be considered as consciously representing the labour point of view. The first labour alderman, C. Hislop, was elected in 1896 and served only two terms. R. J. Shore was elected in 1910 and served four terms, and R. A. Rigg was an alderman in 1914.

All three of these men had firm connections with organized labour in Winnipeg. Hislop was nominated by the Trades and Labor Congress and ran as their candidate, as was the case with Shore. Rigg was not only a labour candidate but was also secretary of the Trades and Labor Congress and a prominent Winnipeg labour leader. From the evidence available, however, it would seem that these were the only labourers who consciously represented the workingman on City Council. And three representatives out of a total of 515 is not a very significant number.[7]

While classification of Winnipeg's civic leaders by occupation says much about who governed the city in this period, it does not tell the whole story. In fact, several other characteristics played an important part in determining a man's success in municipal politics. A glance at several of the men who held political office indicates that Winnipeg was governed by an elite group; for not only were workingmen excluded from office, so too were many businessmen. To illustrate this point six biographical sketches are offered here as examples of the leadership Winnipeg received during this period.

The men chosen for examination were those who occupied the mayor's office between 1901 and 1914. This position was the single most important office in Winnipeg's municipal government. The mayor chaired all Council meetings, sat as an *ex-officio* member of all committees, served (after 1907) as chairman of the Board of Control, and had the power of a limited veto over Council's actions. Even more important for purposes of this study, however, was the mayor's symbolic power. Since he was elected by city-wide elections rather than by the voters of a single ward, he represented and often came to personify the city. It was the mayor who received important visitors and the mayor who represented Winnipeg at outside functions. Accordingly, the electors of Winnipeg could be expected to take special care in their choice of a chief magistrate.

John Arbuthnot served as mayor of Winnipeg for three terms, from 1901 to 1903.[8] He was born in St. Catharines, Ontario, in 1861 and received his education there. He commenced his career in the lumber business in his home town but when he received a railroad contract to build part of the CPR west of Lake Superior he moved west, settling in Rat Portage (Kenora), Ontario, in 1888. Four years later he moved to Winnipeg and formed the John Arbuthnot Lumber Company, which soon had a number of outlets in the city and was a great financial success.

Shortly after his arrival in Winnipeg Arbuthnot became involved in the social and political affairs of the city. A conservative and a Protestant, Arbuthnot was as well a Mason and a member of the Independent Order of Good Fellows and the Union and Commercial clubs.[9] He served as alderman for two terms, 1897–98, and as chairman of Winnipeg's Parks Board for two terms during 1899 and 1900. He resided on Central Avenue in Armstrong's Point (Ward 3), one of the most exclusive residential areas of Winnipeg. Although Arbuthnot was the only man who was not a member of the Board of Trade to become mayor between 1901 and 1914, he was supported by three very important and wealthy Board members—D. J. Dyson, N. Bawlf, and R. J. Riley. The last, in fact, served as president of the Board of Trade in 1895. Furthermore, all three of these supporters had previously served on City Council.

Thomas Sharpe also served as mayor for three consecutive terms (1904, 1905, and 1906), one of these by acclamation. Sharpe was born in Ireland in 1866 and worked there for a time as a bank clerk before becoming an apprentice stonemason. In 1885, at the age of nineteen, he emigrated to Toronto where he worked as a stonemason and bricklayer. Six years later he moved to Winnipeg where he specialized in laying cement sidewalks. He was successful in obtaining several profitable civic contracts and he soon became one of the city's best known builders and contractors.

Like Arbuthnot, Sharpe took an active part in Winnipeg's social and political life. Prior to his becoming mayor he served as alderman for four years (1899–1903), three of which were spent as chairman of the Board of Works. During the years 1900–1903 he was a member of the Public Parks Board. He was also involved in provincial politics and in 1924 became president of the Winnipeg Conservative Association. He was a member of the Board of Trade, serving on several of that body's standing committees. Sharpe was a Presbyterian and belonged to numerous clubs and societies including the Masonic Order, the Carleton and Adanac clubs, and the Order of Foresters. He also served a term as the Grand Master of the Orange Lodge of Manitoba. Sharpe's rising social status can be measured by his changes of residence. When elected alderman in 1899 he lived in the predominantly middle and working-class Ward. 4. He then moved south to the wealthier Ward 2, and finally to Wellington Crescent in Ward 1. The latter was Winnipeg's most exclusive residential area.

James Henry Ashdown was mayor in 1907 and 1908, retaining the office by acclamation for his second term. Often described as a thoroughly self-made man and Winnipeg's "Merchant Prince," Ashdown was born in London, England, in 1844. He came to Canada with his parents in 1852 and at eighteen began a three-year apprenticeship with a tinsmith in Hespeler, Ontario. Once this was completed in 1865 he spent some time in Chicago, finally coming to Winnipeg in 1868. He purchased a small hardware store which over the years grew into a thriving wholesale and retail business. By 1910 Ashdown was a millionaire, being successful not only in business but in real estate speculation as well.

Ashdown was involved in the Red River Rebellion of 1870, as one of Schultz's "citizen guards." He was duly arrested and jailed by Riel. Following the entry of Manitoba into the Dominion of Canada he was given a commission as Justice of the Peace. In 1874 he became chairman of the citizens' committee which secured incorporation of Winnipeg from the province. He then served as alderman from 1874 to 1879. Ashdown was equally prominent in other activities. He was an original member of the Board of Trade (formed in 1879) and served as its president in 1887. By 1910 he was one of the most important businessmen in Western Canada. He was by then a director of the Bank of Montreal, the Northern Crown Bank, the Northern Trust Company, and the president of the Canadian Fire Insurance Company. In the social sphere he was a member of the Masonic fraternity, the Commercial Club, and the very exclusive Manitoba Club. He was a Liberal in politics and a Methodist in religion. In the latter connection he was one of the founders of Wesley College and later sat on its Board of Governors. He also took part in the meetings and discussions of the Historical and Scientific Society of Manitoba. Ashdown lived on the prestigious Wellington Crescent in Ward 1 when he was elected mayor.

Ashdown's return to active politics in 1907, after a long absence, came about when he was persuaded to run for mayor by "a citizen's committee composed of the best businessmen of Winnipeg."[10] His nomination papers included the signatures of most of the city's financial elite and he won an overwhelming victory. Significantly, his opponent was supported by organized labour.[11]

In brief, Ashdown was from the outset one of the leaders of the Winnipeg business community. In 1910 a local paper gave the following assessment of his career: "Few, indeed, are the enterprises of public moment that he has not been concerned in and in public affairs affecting the business and social progress of Winnipeg, he has been at times almost aggressively prominent since the City's beginning."[12]

William Sanford Evans also was mayor for more than one term, holding office from 1909 to 1911. Born in Spencerville, Ontario, in 1869 he attended public school in Hamilton, and went on to obtain a Bachelor of Arts degree at Victoria College in Cobourg, Ontario. Evans then did post-graduate work at Columbia University, receiving his Master of Arts degree in 1896.

Journalism was Evans' first area of interest and he joined the editorial staff of the Toronto *Mail and Empire* in 1897. In 1898 he made his first attempt to gain political office, running as a Conservative candidate for South Wentworth in the Ontario provincial elections. After being defeated Evans retired briefly from newspaper work and became treasurer of the National Cycle and Automobile Company of Toronto. In 1900 he married Mary Irene Gurney, the daughter of a former mayor of Toronto, and in 1901 they moved to Winnipeg. There Evans became editor of the *Winnipeg Telegram* and president of the Telegram Printing Company.

To this point Evans' education and career did not fit into the mold of Winnipeg's other mayors—that is, the successful businessman. But in 1905 Evans resigned as editor of the *Telegram* (he remained owner) and established the financial concern of W. Sanford Evans and Company. He was also instrumental in establishing a stock exchange in Winnipeg, and served as president of the Winnipeg Stock Exchange and president of the Royal Canadian Agencies, Canadian Industrial Securities Company, Estevan Coal and Brick Company, and Gurney Northwest Foundry Company. He was also vice-president of the Canadian Bond and Mortgage Corporation, a director of the Sovereign Life Assurance Company, and a member of the executive council of the Board of Trade.

It was this impressive business record that guaranteed Evans' success in municipal politics. In 1907, when Winnipeg was experiencing financial difficulties, he ran for the Board of Control and was successful. He served as controller until Ashdown declined to run for a third term, when he was then elected mayor.

As controller and mayor, Evans took a keen interest in municipal government. He served as vice-president (1909) and then president (1910) of the Union of Canadian Municipalities. In other organizations he served a term as president of the Winnipeg Canadian Club and one as the first president of the Associated Canadian Clubs of Canada. Indeed, Sanford Evans was a co-founder of the Canadian Club movement. He was also president of the Winnipeg Development and Industrial Bureau (1907–1908), chairman of the Town Planning Commission and a member of the Winnipeg Industrial Exhibition.

Mayor Evans was listed in the *Who's Who of Western Canada* as being a member of the Methodist Church "or any other [church] that makes for the highest good." Although he sat on the Board of Governors of Wesley College he was buried from the Anglican Church. His other activities included serving as a councillor of the University of Manitoba and as a member of the Masonic Order, and the Manitoba, Carleton, Adanac, Commercial and St. Charles clubs. Evans resided in Ward 2 and after his career in municipal politics sat as a Conservative member of the Manitoba legislature for fourteen years.

Richard Deans Waugh served as mayor in 1912 and again in 1915 and 1916. He was born in Melrose, Scotland, in 1868. He was a student in the Highfield Academy at Melrose and in 1883 came to Winnipeg, where he spent six years in the law office of Glass and Glass. In 1889 he turned his attention to the real estate field and to financial circles. By the time he was elected mayor, Waugh had come to be recognized as one of the prominent realtors in Winnipeg.

Waugh's involvement in the commercial life of Winnipeg was almost as deep as Evans. He, too, was one of the founders of the Winnipeg Real Estate Exchange and served a term as its president. He was also a founder of the Winnipeg Industrial Bureau, president of the Western Canadian Real Estate Association, president of the Red River and Hudson's Bay Navigation Association, vice-president of the National Association of Real Estate Exchanges, managing director of the Canadian European Mortgage Corporation, and director of several other financial institutions.

Prior to his election as mayor, Waugh had held several other public offices. In 1904 he became a member and chairman of the Winnipeg Public Parks Board and continued in that office until he resigned when elected as a member of the Board of Control in 1909. He also sat on the executive of the Union of Manitoba Municipalities, the Greater Winnipeg Water District, and the Cycle Paths Board.

Waugh was actively involved in athletic organizations in Winnipeg. He served as president of the Manitoba Curling Association and the Granite Curling Club, and as honorary president of the Winnipeg Cricket Association and the Winnipeg Swimming Club. He was also connected with many other organizations which promoted athletic activities.

Mayor Waugh was a Liberal and a Congregationalist and a member of the Traveller's Club. Although he lived in Ward 3 for a time, he was a resident of the more prestigious Ward I when elected mayor. Of some significance was the fact that Waugh was married to Harriet Lillie Logan in 1892. Miss Logan was the daughter of Alexander Logan, who was four times mayor of Winnipeg and one of the honoured pioneer settlers of the city.

Thomas Russ Deacon was mayor in 1913 and 1914. He was born and educated in Perth, Ontario, and later attended the University of Toronto, receiving an engineering degree in 1891. He then lived in Rat Portage for ten years and worked as city engineer. He also gained some experience in municipal politics in Rat Portage, serving as alderman and acting mayor.

In 1901 Deacon moved to Winnipeg and rapidly became one of the city's leading businessmen. As founder, president, and general manager of the Manitoba Bridge and Iron Works, he employed over four hundred men by 1903. In other business activities he was for a time vice-president of the Canadian Manufacturers' Association, sat on the executive council of the Board of Trade from 1906 to 1909, and was a director of the Winnipeg Industrial Bureau, the Winnipeg Builder's Exchange, the Western Canadian Accident and Guarantee Insurance Company, and the Canadian Enamel, Concrete, Brick and Tile Company.

Prior to his election in 1912, Deacon had never run for City Council, but he had served on the 1907 commission which investigated Winnipeg's water supply and was the forerunner to the Greater Winnipeg Waterworks Commission.[13] Accordingly, when Winnipeg was considering spending $13.5 million on a water aqueduct, Deacon was asked to run for mayor. His nomination papers included the names of several prominent Winnipeg businessmen, including J. H. Ashdown. An independent in politics and a Protestant, Deacon was a member of the Manitoba Club and lived in Ward 1 when elected mayor.

Drawing on these six biographical sketches and the information available on the entire membership of the Board of Control and City Council, it is possible to construct a fairly accurate group portrait of Winnipeg's civic leaders. It must be emphasized, however, that until historians undertake a thorough qualitative and quantitative study of all Winnipeg's civic politicians the collective portrait offered here must be considered as provisional in nature.

The most striking impression that one obtains from the above sketches is that success in business was an absolute necessity for political office. It has already been noted that the businessman dominated civic politics. But to this general impression must be added the significant distinction that it was wealthy businessmen—the richer the better —who were the most successful in gaining elective office. Indeed, wealth was the fundamental political resource; it conferred high social status (which can be measured by such things as place of residence and membership in exclusive clubs and associations), and the right to lead.

This connection between financial success, high social status, and political success is perhaps a distinguishing characteristic of any new urban centre. In older established cities such things as intellectual excellence and renown, or social prestige derived from something other than money, were often the basis of political power.[14] But in Winnipeg numerous men of humble origin and often little formal education were able to rise quickly to positions of prominence. The reward of political office went to the organizer, the projector, the risk-taker—in short, the man who had proved himself in the demanding business world. This alone brought the respect and support of the city's electors. Neither the specialized skills of the professional or the artisan, nor the acumen of the workingman, ensured the right to leadership. Only when the professional became a financier or a manufacturer, as did Evans and Deacon, was elective office obtainable. Between 1874 and 1914 money remained the key to political success.

It is also apparent that while financial success was a positive political asset, the city's financially successful took a participating role in municipal politics. Out of a total of nineteen Winnipeg millionaires (as of January 1910),[15] two had served as mayor, one as controller, and seven as aldermen. Moreover, numerous others, especially controllers and mayors, were wealthy enough to call themselves "gentlemen" and devote full-time attention to municipal politics.[16]

Next to financial success, participation in various business organizations was probably the most important political asset. The successful municipal politician did not limit his membership to only one organization. Most belonged to many such bodies and took active roles in them, often serving on the executive or on committees. These business organizations included the Winnipeg Board of Trade, the Real Estate Exchange, the Winnipeg Development and Industrial Bureau, the Builder's Exchange and so on. Equally significant, however, is the fact that many of the mayors, and a large number of the controllers and aldermen, were also members of regional and even national business organizations. These included the Canadian Manufacturers' Association, the Canadian Industrial Exhibition Association, the National Association of Real Estate Exchanges, the Western Canadian Real Estate Association, the Northwest Commercial Travellers' Association, the Western Canadian Immigration Association, and several others.[17] Membership in these organizations signifies that Winnipeg's commercial elite was something more than a parochial oligarchy. It also suggests one of the major reasons why Winnipeg rose to predominance in Western Canada at so early a date, and why it was able to retain its position for such an extended period.[18]

Membership in many non-business organizations was also a characteristic of Winnipeg's civic leaders. The city's commercial elite were usually members of the same social clubs. These ranged from the prestigious Manitoba Club to such clubs as the Carleton, Union, Adanac, St. Charles, Commercial, and others. Moreover, the successful politician and his family took part in an endless round of other social and cultural activities. Diversions from day-to-day affairs was found in amateur and professional theatricals and concerts, in quiet euchre parties, and formal balls. There was also a never-ending cycle of teas, weddings, and luncheons to attend.

The social life of Winnipeg's well-to-do included much more than these activities, however. The life style that is portrayed in the pages of *Town Topics*, Winnipeg's magazine of "Society, Music, and Drama," is one in which the elite often escaped from the city and travelled to Florida, California, Europe, and Eastern Canada. There were also frequent trips to resorts such as Grand and Victoria Beaches on the southern shores of Lake Winnipeg; to Minaki, "situated on a green clad promontory jutting out into the Winnipeg River"; and to Winnipeg and Lake of the Woods.[19] Significantly, these resorts remained preserves of the well-to-do throughout the period, since the families of working people, free to travel only on Sunday, were held in the city by a clause of the Lord's Day Act which prohibited the operation of special trains on Sunday.[20]

Within Winnipeg itself there was a wide range of cultural and sporting activities that the elite could enjoy. The Winnipeg Operatic and Dramatic Society, the Women's Musical Club, and the Women's Art Association were all active organizations. From the activities of the latter group during the period 1900–1912, for example, a considerable growth in art took place. The enthusiasm of the time resulted in the formation of numerous smaller groups—the Studio Club, the Arts and Craft Society, the Winnipeg Art League, to name but a few—which held exhibitions on their own, generally in the spring. The result was that in 1912 the Industrial Bureau, assisted by finances from individuals and City Council, erected a concrete addition as part of the Industrial Bureau Building, and an art gallery was formally opened in December 1912. Among those prominent in these developments were Mayor Waugh and ex-aldermen F. J. C. Cox and E. Cass.[21]

Other cultural pursuits of Winnipeg's elite included the establishment of the Historical and Scientific Society of Manitoba in 1879. The participation of Winnipeg's commercial elite in the Historical Society indicated that there was no sharp distinction between the city's professional, social, and commercial groups. From the outset, the society brought together all the city's elite to hear papers of a scientific and historical nature. Prominent among the participants and members were such notable civic figures as James Ashdown, Gilbert McMicken, Alexander McArthur, Alexander Macdonald, and W. G. Fonseca. Moreover, the strong influence of Winnipeg's commercial elite on the society is perhaps best shown by the energetic projects it undertook. The HSSM established a library in Winnipeg shortly after 1879, began to publish its transactions, and became an affiliate of the Royal Society of Canada. Furthermore, in later years, the society was to be responsible for the founding of Winnipeg's public library system.[22]

Several other non-business activities seemed essential if one was to be counted among Winnipeg's elite. One of these activities was participation in amateur athletic associations. Not only did Winnipeg's middle and upper class take part in such sports as sleighing, snowshoeing, skating, cycling, cricket, horse-racing, curling, canoeing, and rowing, they did so in an organized fashion. The first bonspiel was held in March 1889 and thereafter Winnipeg quickly became the greatest centre in North America for winter curling. Bonspiel Week, in February of each year, brought many rinks from all over Canada to Winnipeg. In 1903, for example, one hundred and twenty rinks, including nearly five thousand curling enthusiasts, gathered in Winnipeg to compete for the championship offered by the Manitoba branch of the Royal Caledonian Curling Association.[23] Curling was only one of the many organized sports, however. Others included the Winnipeg Rowing Club, the Winnipeg Swimming Club, the Winnipeg Cricket Association, the Winnipeg Canoe Club, the Lake of the Woods Yacht Club, the St. George's Snowshoe Club, the St. Charles Country Club, and so on.

Winnipeg's elite also took some interest in charitable organizations, although their efforts in this area did little to relieve Winnipeg's massive problem of coping with the tens of thousands of newcomers who arrived in Winnipeg in the space of a few years. Some of the more prominent organizations were the Children's Home, the Women's Hospital Aid Society, the Prisoner's Aid Association, the Aberdeen Association, the Margaret Scott Nursing Mission, All Peoples' Mission, the Winnipeg Lodging and Coffee House Association, and the Salvation Army. Of all the activities of the elite in Winnipeg, this was one of their less noteworthy pursuits, since support given to these valuable agencies by either City Council or private individuals was never adequate to meet the needs of the people the organizations served. Nevertheless, like their other non-business activities, participation in charitable organizations, token though it might be, served to make one known and respected among the electorate.[24]

Another characteristic of Winnipeg's commercial elite that deserves mention is their close association with provincial and federal politics. Almost all the city's successful civic politicians were members of the Conservative or Liberal parties. Moreover, a large number of Winnipeg's civic leaders went on to serve as MP's or MLA's. These include such people as Thomas Scott, R. W. Jameson, D. W. Bole, W. F. McCreary, F. E. Cornish, W. S. Evans, D. A. Ross, C. H. Campbell, T. W. Taylor, E. G. Conklin, and E. L. Drewry. The fact that members of the close-knit group that was the city's commercial elite often moved easily into provincial and federal politics was to help greatly in Winnipeg's rise to big-city status. Politics, at whatever level, remained throughout the period the preserve of the commercial elite.

Financial success and active participation in business, social, athletic, charitable, and political organizations—these characteristics go far to suggest the attributes necessary for political success in Winnipeg. But there were still other elements of almost equal importance to these: ethnic origin and religion. Winnipeg's civic leaders were, almost to a man, of Anglo-Saxon origin and Protestant religion. All the mayors or controllers throughout the entire period met this basic characteristic, while the number of aldermen who did not is so small that they can all be readily identified. Only two Jews (M. Finkelstein and A. Skaletar) and two Icelanders (A. Frederickson and A. Eggertson) served short terms on council. Despite the dramatic increase of persons of Ukrainian origin in Winnipeg after 1896 only one, T. Stefanik, served as alderman in 1912–13. It should be noted that four of these men were businessmen —some very successful—and one was a lawyer. And, lest it be thought that the various ethnic groups were unsuccessful in Winnipeg civic politics only because they took little interest in political matters, it can be noted that all three of the above-mentioned ethnic groups had active political organizations and ran their own candidates. The point is that despite their organization and numbers, these groups did not elect many representatives. Significantly, it was not until 1954 that Winnipeg elected its first non-Anglo-Saxon mayor, and even then it was a great shock to many Winnipeggers of Anglo-Saxon origin.[25]

The importance of each of the above characteristics for membership in Winnipeg's political elite is revealed when the thirteen unsuccessful candidates for mayor between 1901 and 1914 are examined. All lacked one or more of the basic qualifications. In terms of financial success none were as wealthy as their opponents, while few could match the prominence of the successful men in business, social, cultural, or even athletic organizations. In fact, two were workingmen and two were professionals with few outside interests. And while five of the six winners were members of the Board of Trade, only two of the thirteen losers were members. All thirteen were of Anglo-Saxon origin but one was a Catholic. Also, while all the successful candidates received open support and financial backing from prominent Winnipeggers (former mayors, controllers and millionaires), few of their opponents were as fortunate. Finally, as a further comment on social status, only six of the thirteen losers lived in the southern part of the city (wards 1, 2, and 3), the residence of all the successful candidates.[26]

It can thus be said that Winnipeg was governed between 1874 and 1914 by a very select group of men, a group that was at one and the same time a social, cultural, and, above all, commercial elite. The great majority of the elected members of the municipal government had in common a number of particular characteristics that distinguished them from all but a minority of their fellow Winnipeggers. All except five of well over five hundred elected officials were of Anglo-Saxon origin and most came to Winnipeg from Ontario or Britain. A large majority were of Protestant religion and members of the commercial class. Most were active members of several business, social and cultural organizations and had attained some degree of financial success in their own businesses. Few could boast of a very high degree of education and those that could were prominent in business as well. Many were men of humble origin who had proved themselves in the business world. And, finally, as the following chapters will show, all agreed that the basic task of the municipal corporation was to encourage rapid and sustained economic and population growth at the expense of any and all other considerations.

It might seem rather obvious that such characteristics were necessary for political success in Winnipeg. After all, as a newly established and rapidly growing urban centre Winnipeg required the skills the successful businessman could provide. And the linkage between wealth, high social status, and political power is certainly not surprising. There is, moreover, the simple fact that perhaps the majority of Winnipeggers agreed with the growth ethic of the commercial elite and voted for those most likely to implement growth-producing programs. Finally, Anglo-Saxons and Protestants were, in terms of sheer numbers, the largest group in Winnipeg.

This view of Winnipeg, however, must be balanced by other factors. First of all, non-Anglo-Saxons, especially after 1896, made up a significant proportion of Winnipeg's populace and thus should have been able to elect more representatives. This is particularly true of the aldermanic positions since these were ward-elected representatives and several of the city's wards contained non-Anglo-Saxon majorities from as early as 1901. Secondly, the group most likely to oppose the policies of the commercial elite, the city's workingmen and artisans, were early organized in Winnipeg. The city had a local of the Knights of Labor from 1884 and in 1886 a central Trades and Labor Council was formed. By 1895 an Independent Labor Party had been organized, the first in Canada. It must be emphasized, moreover, that these and other labour organizations were usually led by British-born men and hence cannot be dismissed easily as unimportant because of their "foreign" leadership.[27] It is apparent that the labour group in Winnipeg was organized to the extent that they should have been a major contender for municipal office.

It is true, of course, that Winnipeg's labour organizations quarrelled as much among themselves as with the "capitalist enemy," and a part of their failure to elect representatives stems from this basic fact. Compared to the stability, homogeneity, and singleness of purpose displayed by the commercial elite, organized labour remained throughout the period unstable, heterogeneous, and vacillating. There was continuous and often bitter infighting among various labour and socialist organizations and this caused a division of forces that labour could ill afford.[28]

There are, however, other important reasons for labour's lack of political success at the municipal level. For a variety of reasons the city's labour organizations directed their major political efforts at the provincial and federal spheres of government. That they did so was not because they felt municipal politics unimportant; it was rather a result of their assessment that they stood a better chance of electoral success at the senior levels.[29] There, at least, they did not have to overcome a series of election laws and practices that, at the municipal level, effectively disenfranchised labour and over-represented the commercial class. It was obvious, moreover, that if labour could have wielded sufficient political power at the provincial level they could have removed the impediments contained in the City Charter since the latter was granted by the province.

The means whereby Winnipeg's artisans and workingmen were effectively excluded from participation in civic politics are easily pinpointed. Beginning at incorporation and continuing throughout the period, all voters in municipal elections had to meet a series of qualifications that differed from those required in provincial or federal politics. Freeholders were required to be rated in the city's assessment role for at least $100, while leaseholders or tenants of real property required a rating of at least $200. The other three stipulations (male, over twenty-one years of age, and British citizenship) were the same at all three levels.[30]

Although this property qualification might not seem too high by today's standards it did disenfranchise thousands of Winnipeggers. In 1906, for example, when the population was over 100,000, there were only 7,784 registered voters.[31] Clearly the other 92,216 were not all females, under twenty-one, and of non-British citizenship.

An interesting and, at first sight, progressive measure was one introduced in 1895 that gave females the right to vote in municipal elections.[32] What this meant in operation was that those who held sufficient property would now have added influence. In other words, to the artisan or workingman who barely, if at all, met the property qualification for himself this move meant little in terms of giving his wife a vote. But for the affluent merchant or manufacturer, with property valued at several thousands of dollars, it now meant that both he and his wife could vote. It was thus the representation of property that was enlarged, not that of women. Significantly, women were not allowed to hold office until after 1916.

The aim of these qualifications was to represent property, not people. This was made abundantly clear in 1914 when City Council approached the provincial legislature with a request for an amendment to the Municipal Act that would have provided for any joint stock company owning property within the city the right to instruct its manager, a director, or an employee to vote on money bylaws and other questions of civic government. In defending the request Mayor Deacon and the city solicitor argued that:

> All collections of property were . . . the result of an expenditure of human energy. The heads of many business organizations in Winnipeg had worked up from poor boys, had established themselves in the confidence of their associates and built up a business. In his own case, [Mayor Deacon] had worked his way through university and when he came to Winnipeg did not have enough capital to establish the business that he wished. He had interested friends in his proposition and had formed a joint stock company. That company owned valuable property in Winnipeg, yet had no vote. On the other hand, the man owning a lot adjoining a lot made valuable through the efforts of the company did have a vote. A vote through a company was not a vote on bricks and mortar, but a vote on the energies of men. He could see no objection to instructed voting.[33]

Labour, of course, was vehemently opposed to the measure and attacked it as "a bad principle, vicious, and the worst piece of class legislation that the legislature had ever been asked to pass."[34] Fortunately for labour, the amendment never came out of committee, apparently because the Roblin government felt that the question was too controversial. By 1914 the labour movement in Winnipeg had matured somewhat and such a contentious issue would have cost the provincial government many votes in some sections of the city. At the same time it must also be stated that the provincial government, who through the Municipal Act controlled the question of electors' qualifications, did not feel compelled to reduce or, as labour requested, throw out all property qualifications.

The property qualifications discussed thus far referred to voting in municipal elections. Qualifications for voting on money bylaws and for candidates were even stricter. Prior to 1884 the qualifications necessary for money bylaws were the same as those for general elections, but from that date until 1891 one had to meet a $500 property qualification. The only other change that occurred throughout the period was in 1891 when the qualification was reduced to $400. For candidates, the Municipal Act stipulated even more severe property qualifications. From 1874 to 1895 candidates for mayor and alderman had to own $2,000 worth of property; this was reduced to $500 at the latter date but in 1906 it was again raised to its former level for mayor, remaining at $500 for aldermen. The $200 stipulation also applied to controllers after 1906.

The importance of property in municipal politics, moreover, did not end there. With the institution in 1890 of the plural vote the commercial elite effectively removed any possibility of sheer numbers carrying a municipal election. After 1890 a person could vote in every ward "in which he had been rated for the necessary property qualification." Until 1906 this meant that certain wealthy electors could possibly qualify in six wards, while after that date (when a new ward was added), seven wards. The importance of such a law is revealed by the fact that in 1910 it was estimated that the civic voters list had 6,000 repeaters.[35]

The changes to the Municipal Act that instituted the plural vote did, however, specify that this privilege extended only to votes for aldermen, controllers, and money bylaws; and that each voter could vote only once per ward. In mayoralty elections the elector was restricted to only one vote "at the polling subdivision in which he is a resident." But these limitations were only rarely acknowledged. Throughout this period the civic voters' list did not incorporate the qualifying provisions made in the act. In 1910, for example, when there were 72 polling subdivisions, "names of scores and hundred of citizens . . . appear on the printed [and official] voters' list as many as ten, fifteen, twenty, thirty times and upwards, even into the sixties. As instances, the name of ex-Mayor Andrews appears in no less than 66 subdivisions, and that of Mr. D. E. Sprague in over 60 subdivisions."[36] It was further noted that while the provincial list, based on full manhood suffrage, contained only 22,726 names, the civic list, restricted to tenants and owners, had 39,000 names. Given this situation, it is not surprising to learn that the defeated mayoralty candidate in the 1910 election called for an investigation. But the charge that "the real public opinion of Winnipeg could be defeated practically at any election" did not disturb the commercial elite.[37] Prior to 1914 no changes were made in the plural vote provisions of the Municipal Act, and many Winnipeggers continued to have inordinate electoral power.

Two other factors should be mentioned as bearing especially hard on labour. One was the provision that gave all property-owners the right to vote in civic elections, whether they were residents of the city or not. The absentee property-owner, however, did have to cast his vote in person and thus the measure probably had little effect on civic elections. Its existence in law nevertheless served to strengthen the argument that property, not people, was represented. More serious than this provision was the fact that elected officials at the municipal level received little remuneration for their work. In the early years when the job of alderman took little time perhaps this was to be expected. But as the task of running the city began to demand more and more time and effort and it became impossible to hold elective positions without giving up considerable time from one's job, the question of remuneration became especially important. For the average businessman or professional this meant little sacrifice, since his business could in most cases continue—for short periods at least—without his actual presence. But for the artisan and workingman, tied to a job that required his daily presence, it meant that unless the elected official received remuneration sufficient to support him and his family, he could not even consider running for office.[38] Until 1902 aldermen received no pay whatever, while from 1903 to 1909 they received the sum of $300 per year. This was increased to $500 in 1910. The mayor similarly received nothing until 1894 when a sum of $1,200 was set aside. This was increased to $2,500 in 1907; to $4,000 in 1908; and finally to $5,000 in 1911. Controllers—a full-time job from the outset—received only $625 in 1907. However, this was increased to $2,500 in 1908 and in 1910 it rose to $3,600. Finally, in 1911 the salary was increased to $4,000.

These property qualifications and other restrictions that worked against the workingman and artisan were also effective in minimizing the participation of Winnipeg's various ethnic groups. Most of the city's "foreign" immigrants were unskilled and poorly paid workers, and they thus had even less opportunity to involve themselves in municipal politics than did their Anglo-Saxon neighbours. The newly arrived Slav, Jew, German, and Icelander had also to overcome a language barrier and meet a citizenship qualification. The combined effect of all these restrictions was to allow a commercial elite to govern Winnipeg with but little regard for either the labour or ethnic vote.

It should be emphasized, however, that it was the property qualifications and the plural vote more than anything else that determined the nature and course of municipal politics in Winnipeg. For if the latter is compared with the provincial sphere it is obvious that such limitations as citizenship and poor salaries were in effect there as well. Yet provincial politicians went to great lengths to curry the favour of labour and ethnic voters of Winnipeg. Throughout the period under study the provincial government's "political machinery was based on city saloons," where a workingman's vote could be bought for a drink.[39] And between 1900 and 1915 Premier Roblin and his Conservative government was also careful to woo the support of the non-Anglo-Saxon, especially the foreign voter of Winnipeg's North End. Indeed, a good deal of Roblin's manoeuvring on such issues as temperance and the Manitoba schools question was a result of his recognition of the power of the ethnic vote.[40] Thus, even though the workingman and the foreigner might have been bribed or even cheated into voting for a particular provincial political party, they were at least given that much respect. In Winnipeg civic politics, the dominant commercial elite rarely considered them at all.

The exclusion of labour and ethnic groups from civic politics, whatever the cause, had serious consequences for Winnipeg. Since the majority of the city's people were not involved in the political process the commercial elite who occupied positions in the municipal government did not have to bother about strong public backing. They could pursue their growth ethic at public expense and with a minimum of argument; they were, in fact, permitted full rein in their ambitious plans for garnering the wealth of the city and its hinterland. Indeed, if anything was out of the ordinary in this period of Winnipeg's history it was the extremely rare reluctance of the municipal corporation to come quickly to the assistance of those who desired to further the city's welfare by making themselves—and only themselves—rich.

This is not to say that all the publicly supported schemes advocated by the commercial elite were somehow of no benefit to anyone else. A few, in fact, were of great public advantage.[41] Rather, the sterility of municipal politics meant that such schemes were the exception and not the rule. Caring little for the city as a whole, the commercial elite avoided dealing with such crucial issues as social welfare and comprehensive city planning and in so doing left to their successors problems of enormous magnitude.

The course of civic politics in this period also left unresolved questions of class and race. With no clash of values within the political structure, with no influential minority able to threaten replacement or destruction of the system which the commercial elite had created for itself and which nurtured it, there was no need to seek a broad and more genuine community consensus in order to forestall the minority. There was, in essence, no need for the very cornerstone of meaningful political process—compromise. Significantly, when some broadening of the consensus proved necessary in the years after the Winnipeg general strike of 1919, the accompanying clash of values resulted in Winnipeg enjoying much more effective civic government in the 1920s and 1930s than it had prior to 1914.[42]

3 / Civic Politics: The Search for Business Efficiency in Municipal Affairs

The commercial elite that dominated Winnipeg society and politics throughout the period agreed on the fundamental role the municipal corporation should play in advancing their fortunes. They sought an administration that would attend to the finances and day-to-day processes of municipal government in a businesslike manner and, when called upon, would use public funds to promote the growth the businessmen desired. In general, Winnipeg's businessmen had little trouble achieving the latter goal, but in their desire to have day-to-day municipal affairs run in a businesslike manner they were not so successful. Indeed, one of the most noteworthy observations that can be made about Winnipeg civic politics between 1874 and 1914 is that there was an almost continuous debate over the manner in which the affairs of the city were conducted.

Winnipeg's civic leaders, like their counterparts in other North American cities, felt the governmental structure of the city should be modelled on the efficient business enterprise.[1] They consistently criticized the simple mayor and council system established at incorporation with the argument that "no business could conduct its affairs that way and remain in business." Their main objections were that the council system, based on ward representation and the ideas and practices of representative government, involved too wide a latitude for the expression of "popular" interests. Since political power was equally shared by many aldermen elected from various wards there was a tendency for local interests to dominate. Often, it was agreed, aldermen spoke for their particular wards to the detriment of the city as a whole. Another criticism was that there was no separation of executive and legislative functions. In such a situation aldermen "were so loaded up that each had to spend a vast amount of time and labour in the discharge of duties that are badly done, and which no committee of a fluctuating chamber elected by popular vote can ever do well."[2] A favourite proposal to remedy these problems was the establishment of a full-time, salaried executive committee. In such a structure the role of Council would be reduced to the formulation of general policy, while the executive committee would actually run the city.

During the period between 1874 and 1914 Winnipeg's commercial elite complained of many other problems caused by the simple council system and offered a countless variety and number of alternatives. It is impossible in a brief survey to deal with all the variations, but by concentrating on three specific reform movements—1881–84, 1897, and 1904–7—the most important episodes in the elite's search for business efficiency in municipal affairs can be observed and analysed.

Winnipeg's commercial elite was first made aware of the shortcomings of decentralized council system in the months following the collapse of the "boom" of 1881–82. The real estate boom of these years began primarily as a result of the optimistic predictions that accompanied the location of the western shops and yards of the CPR in Winnipeg. Prior to that time municipal affairs in the city had been routine and progress in civic projects had matched the slow population growth of Winnipeg.[3] But almost overnight this slow pace had changed. Describing the state of municipal politics between 1881 and 1884 the *Winnipeg Times* noted:

> For four years Winnipeg had been governed on the high pressure principle. . . . When the council showed a disposition to lag in the race for fame it was promptly spurred on by the citizens, who sent in a petition for this and got up a mass meeting for that and the other. There was no rest, no cessation. Other cities had sewers, and paved streets, and expensive public buildings, and a few were talking of the electric light. As Winnipeg was the greatest city on earth, it would never do to be eclipsed by such slow growing places as Toronto or Montreal, and all these things had to be provided at once. Expense was no object. Get the money anyway it could be raised, and go on. So little concerned were the citizens about expenditure that a by-law to raise three-quarters of a million of dollars attracted no attention—what cared Winnipeg for such a trifle as that? We rushed forward with a full head of steam on. Extravagance was in the air. We swaggered, and boasted, and puffed until we were busting with happiness. Nothing was too good for us, and the more it cost the better.[4]

The extravagance complained of by the editor was based on two developments. Winnipeg's population had more than doubled during the boom, rising from slightly over six thousand in 1881 to almost fourteen thousand in 1882. And accompanying the sharply rising population figures was an equally astounding rise in Winnipeg's land and building assessments. At incorporation this figure had stood at $2.5 million and rose but slowly to a figure of $4 million in 1880. In 1881 it was estimated to stand at $9 million, while in 1882 the optimistic City Council calculated the assessment at $30 million. At least part of this vast increase was due to the addition of Fort Rouge to the city in 1882, but later accounts would show that the greatest proportion was simply the result of the vastly inflated land values that accompanied the boom. Four years later, in 1886, the assessment stood at only $22 million.[5]

Inflated or not, it was on the basis of these figures that the City Councils of 1881, 1882, and 1883 set about to improve Winnipeg. Prior to 1882 Council had issued three sets of bonds for civic improvements. In 1874 a $250,000 bond was issued for the construction of a city hall and a wooden sewer system. In 1880 a $300,000 bond was used for the construction of the Louise Bridge across the Red River. And in 1881 another bond issue of $200,000 was handed over to the CPR Syndicate as a bonus for establishing their workshops in Winnipeg.[6] Thus at the outset of the boom in 1881 the total bonded indebtedness of Winnipeg stood at $650,000. The Council for 1882, however, quickly responded to the boom by passing a bylaw to raise $1,250,000 for "permanent improvements to the City." Requiring submission to the electors, this bylaw passed by a vote of 39-1 in December of 1882.[7]

Over the next year this money was quickly spent on a variety of projects, including a new city hall, a new sewer system, a police station, a fire hall, street and bridge improvements, and a host of other items. In fact, the money was used up so quickly that Council found it necessary in November 1883 to submit a bylaw calling for the issuance of another $500,000 worth of bonds to cover expenditures already made.[8] But by this time the city's commercial elite felt that things had got out of control.

The first signs that something was amiss in municipal affairs were noted by the Winnipeg Times as early as April 1883 when it called attention to the soaring costs of the new city hall, "the dreadful condition of the streets," and the "culpable negligence and incompetence that mark the administration of the city's affairs"; a condition, the editor was sure, "that no businessman would tolerate in the management of his business or estate."[9] At first the only response these criticisms elicited were protests from Winnipeg businessmen and aldermen that "such items are calculated to hurt the country" and "that recent criticisms of the City Council are injudicious because likely to hurt the city."[10] A prominent Board of Trade member and ex-alderman, William Bathgate, even complained when the Winnipeg Times reported the collapse of the new City Hall.[11] But the businessmen of Winnipeg soon regained their senses and, led by the Winnipeg Board of Trade, began a thorough investigation of civic affairs.

At least part of the elite's concern with the conduct of civic affairs was a reaction to the collapse of the real estate boom. Although the end of the boom was apparent in April 1882, many had optimistically clung to the hope that the check was only temporary and that the boom would be renewed. But by the spring of 1883 it had become painfully clear to all that the inflated property valuations and brisk activity of the boom years would not soon be restored.[12] And it was with this gloomy outlook as a background that Winnipeg's businessmen turned to a close examination of the municipal corporation. Indeed, it is important to note that numbered among the originators of the move to investigate civic affairs were at least five individuals who were to make themselves millionaires, primarily through successful land speculation. These men were J. H. Ashdown, Alexander Macdonald, J. A. M. Aitkens, D. McMillan, Alexander Logan, and W. F. Alloway. Also included in this concerned group were W. G. Fonseca, G. F. Carruthers, and H. T. Champion. All these men also made fortunes in real estate transactions.[13]

The first action taken by the business community was to call a "citizens' meeting" in May 1883.[14] Mr. C. J. Brydges, president of the Board of Trade, was elected chairman and the gathering set out to discuss the civic situation and to outline a future course of action. Reviewing the activities of the councils for the past few years, Brydges pointed out that in May 1883, calculating the total bonded indebtedness at $1,900,000, the interest the city had to pay, "without reference to the sinking fund," was $114,000 a year. "Now, $114,000 a year means 38 per cent of the total taxes of the city. The assessment last year was something over thirty millions, and the rate was one per cent, making the amount of taxes receivable $302,000. . . ." And, as if the problem caused by the falling assessment was not problem enough, Brydges pointed out that up to 31 December 1882, "out of $302,000, only $168,968 of taxes had been paid, leaving arrears of $133,032." Moreover, after all the money that had been expended, "nothing of a permanent character had been done to the roads; and anyone who is acquainted with the condition of the roads during last spring must know that it was a most serious injury to the trade of the city." There were also problems connected with drainage, sewage, and waterworks that needed immediate attention. Brydges predicted that "in order for Winnipeg to keep her position . . . the city must either increase its debt, obtain an additional loan, or increase the rate of taxation, which many of the citizens think extremely high [already]."[15]

The president of the Board of Trade then pointed out that the only solution to these problems was for "the property owners and ratepayers of Winnipeg to place civic affairs on such a basis as will ensure the economical and advantageous expenditure of the money." He continued:

> In submitting a plan for this purpose there is no desire to make an attack upon any individual or anybody. Some people may think City Council has not done all that it could, but we do not suggest that questions of this sort be entered into. What we feel is that the MODE OF GOVERNMENT hitherto adopted has not proved successful and it is desirable . . . to devise some remedy.

The first step taken in this direction was the formation of a "Property Owners' Association" whose object would be:

To protect the citizens from unnecessary or wasteful outlay in civic matters; to consider carefully all proposals for the creation of loans to be raised upon the security of the property of the citizens; to watch the expenditure of the proceeds of the loans; to consider the proceedings of City Council, and prevent as far as possible all unwise or wasteful proceedings on their part, and generally to ensure the honest, careful and judicious management of the affairs of the city.[16]

After this resolution was unanimously passed a committee was formed and given instructions to draft a plan that would satisfy these aims.[17] Accordingly on 29 May the committee presented fifteen proposed amendments to the City Charter.[18] After recommending that the number of aldermen be reduced to twelve from eighteen and that they be elected for a two-year term instead of one, the committee turned to the question of dividing municipal affairs into legislative and executive functions. Council would be the legislative body while a mayor, a treasurer, and a commissioner of works would carry out executive duties. It was also proposed that the latter men be elected on the following franchise: every holder of property to the value of not less than $500 shall be entitled to one vote; from $2,000 to $10,000, two votes; $10,000 to $25,000, three votes; $25,000 to $50,000, four votes; $50,000 to $100,000, five votes; more than $100,000, six votes. The plan went on to outline in detail the duties of the three executive officers and the Council, with a special emphasis on financial matters.

The Property Owners' Association's plan for reforming Winnipeg's governmental structure contained at least two noteworthy recommendations. The first was a heightened recognition of the property principle. Indeed, the proposals contained in clause four of their proposed amendments to the City Charter went far beyond restricting the franchise to those who owned a certain amount of property. It tied the number of votes one was entitled to cast to specified property values. In short, the municipal corporation was to become a joint stock company with only those contributing a certain amount of capital being allowed to share in the direction of its affairs. Even more significant, however, was the recommendation to strip Council of most of its powers by the establishment of an executive committee. For even though Council still had to approve the committee's actions and pass estimates, they could not "increase any item or insert any not included in the scheme brought before them." In effect, the city was to be governed by three men, the executive committee, elected on a very restricted franchise.

During the remainder of 1883 the proposed plan was discussed at several meetings, although the major proposals were not implemented prior to the civic elections of 1883. The POA, however, did undertake to make some immediate changes. They succeeded in persuading City Council, as an economy measure, to reduce the size of council to twelve members, two for each of the city's six wards.[19] The association then turned its attention to defeating a proposed $500,000 civic works bylaw. It was argued that only by this course of action, "expressing a want of confidence in the present council," could new candidates for 1884 be dealt with intelligently.[20] The POA's efforts in this regard were also successful, for when the bylaw came to a vote in November, it was soundly defeated by a vote of 441-40. [21]

The key activity of the association, however, was their support of a slate of candidates for civic office for 1884. Heading the list was Alexander Logan, a long-time resident of both the Red River Colony and Winnipeg. He was a respected businessman and had served as alderman from 1874 to 1878 and as mayor in 1879, 1880, and 1882. Also, as a result of his dealings in real estate in the 1870s, Logan was a very wealthy man and could presumably be counted on to sort out the city's financial problems. Most important of all, however, was Logan's "modest, unassuming and unostentatious" character since his opponent, the incumbent Alexander McMicken, had been accused of getting the city into its current difficulties by his desire to show off and be "feted in such places as New York." With the backing of the POA and the Board of Trade, Logan easily defeated his opponent. His majority was 514 votes out of a total of 1,492 cast.[22]

Despite these notable successes in 1883, the POA's plan to institute a new era in the conduct of municipal affairs soon ran into difficulty. Although they received co-operation from the newly elected Council, they did not succeed in having their proposals for a new mode of government enacted into law by the province. Early in January Council had agreed to the appointment of special auditors to look into the financial condition of the city.[23] And while waiting for this report Council had met with the POA and had approved the latter's scheme for governmental reform. Council also agreed to submit the plan to the provincial government where, it was hoped, it would become law.[24] But once it had reached this stage the proposals died.

Although there is little evidence to indicate the reasons for the province's refusal to comply with Winnipeg's request, one local newspaper does provide some clues. The *Winnipeg Times*, a strong supporter of the POA, discussed the problem the association was out to solve and offered an explanation for the legislature's negative response:

> Our municipal system of government is based on the principle that all men are equal. But when, after having been born equal, one man accumulates more property than another, it is certainly not reasonable that their equality, in regard at least to controlling municipal taxation, should further continue. The Council of a municipality bears the same relation to the rate-payers as a director of a bank to its shareholders. Bad management in either case is

disastrous, the larger shareholders and the larger taxpayers losing more than the smaller. But while in the election of bank directors the votes cast by each shareholder are as the number of his shares —those who have much at stake having a more potent voice than those who have less—in municipal elections no such discrimination is made. The man who is assessed for five hundred dollars of property . . . has just as much influence in determining the election of aldermen as the ratepayer who stands to lose a hundred times as much if the Council turns out . . . incapable. This is an anomaly which in the case of urban municipalities, where property is more unequally divided than in rural districts, is gradually corrupting and breaking down the whole system.

Turning to the reception that attempts to remedy this anomaly received in the legislature, the paper stated:

The members from the towns contended that the measure was "a blow at the poor man," while the representatives of rural constituencies, not having experienced the evils [the Property Owners' Association] sought to remove, were easily persuaded that they did not exist. This poor-man cry has lead to the defeat [of the measure]. . . . But in this as in most matters, the wirepuller is not the poor man's true friend. For while at first sight it does appear that the poorer ratepayer has less to lose through the operations of an incapable Council or the ravages of a scalawag board and its parasites, it must not be forgotten that when the . . . merchant is over-assessed or unduly taxed, he compels the poor man to bear a portion of his loss by raising the price of goods, increasing rents, or cutting down wages. In short while the large taxpayer is robbed of a dollar in the first instance and the poor man escapes with the loss of ten cents, the latter in the long run suffers . . . more. . . .[25]

Faced with the legislature's refusal to enact the desired amendments, the POA turned their attention to other means of improving the processes of municipal government. It was hoped that the long-awaited Auditors' Report would be a first step toward a solution of Winnipeg's financial problems in that it was expected that the auditors would be able to sort out the malaise of inefficient practices and point the way to "sane financial policies." But the POA's hopes soon suffered another setback when the report, presented to Council in June 1884, was not immediately made public. Only two months later, in August, were the POA and the press able to obtain copies of the report and even then the City Council appeared to be hiding something.[26] Of the two hundred copies of the report printed only twenty were distributed and the conclusion reached by the POA was that the Council "did not want the report in the hands of the electors."[27]

The reluctance of Council to make the report public stemmed from the fact that the auditors were critical not only of previous Councils but of the incumbent one as well. The gist of the report was contained in the statement that the auditors found "an utter lack of system" for keeping accounts. Moreover, the auditors reported that "there has been no effort on the part of city officials to place the accounts before us in proper shape for auditing."[28]

For the members of the POA the report was most alarming, especially since it emphasized that there had been little improvement in methods since the beginning of 1884. According to the association, ". . . the end has now been reached. The present deplorable state of our public affairs renders a new departure in their management so unmistakeably necessary that further neglect can only indicate that the mad recklessness of despair has taken hold of the people."[29] In this atmosphere there was no time for changes in the structure of government. Something had to be done—and done quickly—to satisfy the business instincts of the dominant commercial group. And, quite naturally, it was the Board of Trade that took the lead.

Late in October the Board issued invitations to a large number of "representative" citizens to a convention to be held "for the nomination of fit and proper persons" to constitute the Council for 1885. The meeting, which came to be called the "Citizen's Convention," was held on October 22nd and it was quickly decided that civic affairs could be straightened out only by electing a slate of candidates "with proven business ability." It is important to note, however, that at this and subsequent meetings it was pointed out that the "Citizens' Committee" censure of the 1884 Council did not include "all the members of the present Council. Some of the members of that Council have done the best they could, and have endeavored to administer the affairs of the city honestly and faithfully."[30] Moreover, there were no charges of dishonesty or corruption laid at the feet of the previous councils; rather, it was a question of capability. As the *Manitoba Free Press* stated: "We must place in charge of our affairs men who are not only honest but capable—men who having ascertained exactly the position in which the city now stands will proceed unhesitatingly and in the right way to lead us back once more to firm ground."[31] Following these expressions of intention a slate of candidates was nominated by the convention and put forward under the banner of the "Citizen's Ticket." The platform on which they ran included "a thorough investigation of civic affairs in order to reduce the expenditure to the lowest point consistent with progress and efficiency."[32]

The Citizen's Ticket was headed by Charles E. Hamilton and included such prominent realtors and businessmen as G. F. Carruthers, George H. Campbell and T. Ryan, all members of the Board of Trade. The incumbent, Mayor Alexander Logan, was rejected by the convention because "although he is admitted to be a good intending upright man . . . he lacks discernment and decision [and] has an unwarranted trust in others." The new "citizen's" candidate, Charles Hamilton, was a lawyer in the firm of millionaire and prominent Winnipegger, J. A. M. Aitkins. Hamilton was considered tough enough to solve Winnipeg's problems and received the enthusiastic backing of the Board of Trade.[33]

It was the expressed intention of the Citizens' Committee that the slate of candidates they put forward should be elected by acclamation, a step that would restore confidence in the city. But while this would be the case the following year in most wards, the civic election of 1884 turned into one of the most intensely fought campaigns in Winnipeg's history. Both sides came out for "reform" of one sort or another and the election really turned on a personal basis. The result was an acrimonious contest, both sides indulging in personalities which left considerable bitterness afterwards.

It was clear from the outset that the Citizen's Ticket was immensely popular but the former aldermen "quite naturally made up their mind not to stand calmly by and hear themselves denounced as boodlers."[34] And the incumbents received support from the civic officials who were apprehensive that the reform advocated by the Citizen's Ticket would mean "either that their salaries will be reduced to something in keeping with the stringency of the times and that they will be expected to earn that by doing the work now performed by numberless assistants, or that their services will be disposed with entirely and they be thrown upon the world to earn their livelihood in the same manner as the ordinary citizen."[35]

The elections of 8 December left no doubt that the electorate agreed with the position of the Board of Trade. With the exception of two aldermen, the entire slate offered by the Citizen's Ticket was elected, including their mayoralty candidate, Charles E. Hamilton. The two "opposition" candidates, moreover, were elected by majorities of only seven and fifty votes respectively.[36]

The overwhelming success of the Citizen's Ticket in the 1884 elections removed for a time any overriding concern with the form of municipal government. Indeed, between 1885 and 1892 there were no further attempts to reform Winnipeg's governmental structure, since the conduct of municipal affairs during these years offered little reason for concern. Despite the slow growth of Winnipeg, the city's debt was steadily reduced and "a better class were prevailed upon to enter city council."[37]

It was not until 1892 that a desire for changes in Winnipeg's form of government again became a matter of public discussion. During the reform movement of 1892–97 the arguments put forward by Winnipeg's businessmen in support of a new mode of government remained consistent. The guiding principle throughout was that the work of conducting the city's affairs was business, not government. The framing of bylaws and the other strictly legislative functions of City Council were, it was observed, matters of secondary importance. The municipal corporation was conceived of as "first and foremost a guardian of public order and private property; a builder of streets, sewers, parks, and other agencies of public convenience; a purveyor of water and light and a regulator of transportation."[38] All these activities involved problems of business, not of government, and could best be managed in accordance with the laws of everyday business practices.

During these years many criticisms were made of the council system and all began with the observation that this form of government was the very antithesis of an efficient business organization. Since the city was a contractor and a seller of public services it seemed ridiculous that

> ... it had to undertake its work with as many millstones placed around its neck as those which encumber a municipal department. What would be thought of a private concern that undertook to service the public efficiently while managed by a committee, this committee subject to control by ... a council, and this council, in turn, subject to the day-by-day pressure of popular criticism? How long would a concern under such management remain out of liquidation?
>
> The twentieth-century city ... is trying to do business with an organization created for the making of laws. It has reproduced in miniature the complicated machinery of a national government ... with all the paraphernalia of a sovereign lawmaking authority. Hence it is exceedingly well fitted to do work which it gets little chance to do, and just as eminently unfitted to perform the ordinary business functions which it is called upon to undertake everyday in the year.[39]

In an attempt to solve these shortcomings three plans for the reform of Winnipeg's municipal government were put forward between 1892 and 1897.[40] Although the three proposals varied in certain details all made the basic recommendation that the civic corporation should be run by a full-time, salaried executive committee. It was felt that such a body could "fill the place which the board of directors occupies in the organization of a private business concern." And, continuing the analogy to private business, the city council would be "relegated to the position of a board of stockholders to whom ... the board [of directors would] submit its acts for confirmation or rejection."[41]

Explaining the need for a strong and full-time executive the *Winnipeg Tribune* made the following observations in 1892:

> Mayor Macdonald and the members of the Council (and we have the best mayor and council we ever had) ... find that the present system is not a success, that in fact it is largely a failure. They

find that the council is pretty much in the hands of the officials and that the latter, if they chose, could easily block legislation. They find that there is no head and no permanency to the present system. It is almost useless to try and work any partial reform. If anything satisfactory is to be done the entire system must be changed. At present there is no head, no one to give general direction, no one in fact, to manage the city. It is not that the officials are not good men, for most of them are; it is that there is no responsible head, and as a new council comes in every year the officials are not concerned to please and the result is that there is an entire lack of harmony and an entire absence of community effort and as a result the city suffers. What the city needs at present, and what it must have if it is to be successfully run, is a general manager. As the mayor well said the other day, even the CPR with all its boasted financial strength would be in the hands of a sheriff in a year if it was run on the same basis as Winnipeg. . . . It is the system that is wrong, and it is high time that a change were made.[42]

Similar arguments were constantly put forward by the press and at various mass meetings. In the face of this almost unanimous agreement among Winnipeg's civic leaders that the city's governmental structure needed changing, it is difficult to explain why none of the proposals put forward between 1892 and 1897 were enacted into law. Unlike 1884, the proposed amendments to the city's charter were never even presented to the provincial legislature for consideration and the lack of action cannot be blamed on that body. The major reason why no proposals reached the legislature seems to be that there were no pressing problems facing the municipal corporation in the 1890s. All the arguments put forward during these years were general ones; unlike a decade earlier, there was no financial crisis to be solved. In such an atmosphere the various proposals—similar in principle but different in detail—became associated with particular individuals and people took a stand on personalities rather than issues.

This characteristic makes any discussion of the day-to-day controversies of these years of little value. But to illustrate the type of discussion that took place a glance at a typical meeting may be useful.[43] A meeting of the Citizens' Committee on Government Reform was held in November 1895 in order to discuss changes proposed by their subcommittee. The entire meeting, chaired by J. H. Ashdown and attended by only fifteen businessmen, was taken up with a discussion of clause one of the proposed plan which called for the appointment by Council "of one chief officer who would have charge or general supervision of the general management of civic affairs." When this clause was moved for adoption a series of amendments were proposed. These included the election of the general superintendent rather than his appointment; the replacement of the one man by a committee of three men elected by a city-wide vote; the appointment by Council of four of their own number to serve as an executive committee; and so on. Each proposal was discussed at length with particular attention being paid to "matters of economy." The original general superintendent proposal of the subcommittee was defended since the alternative, a three- or four-man executive committee, would involve the payment of large sums in salaries. But before agreement on any of these matters could be reached it was moved that the meeting be adjourned until January 1896 "as it would be a most unfortunate thing to subordinate civic reform to the municipal elections" of December. And, after a lengthy discussion on the virtues of delay, it was decided to continue the discussion at another meeting. Thus an entire evening was spent on one clause with agreement on only two points—that some change was needed, and that another meeting would be held.

The lack of any specific moving cause seems to have been the main reason for an inability to agree on the details of any plan. A local newspaper, the *Nor'Wester*, made the following comment on 17 October 1895:

> The desire for civic reform [in Winnipeg is not] animated by the same causes that have affected other cities. Incompetency and corruption in municipal affairs have largely contributed in many cities to increase the force of this desire. Accordingly arguments which might be delivered with telling effect in communities where corruption is rampant would fall flat in Winnipeg. For no one has dared to breathe a word against the honorable character of the present mayor and council. Whatever criticism has been offered regarding the proceedings of council has been of "faults that leaned to virtue's side" [such] as a too minute treatment of details and a too great fondness for lengthy discussion. . . . It seems strange then in the face of this admission that our civic government is honestly carried on that this should be the time when civic reform should be instituted. But still it may be that many look at it in the light that the present system has had . . . a fair trial and is found wanting, . . . and they deem that the present is the most appropriate time to advocate a change in municipal government. . . .

With reasons as general as these it is not surprising that proposals for civic reform resulted in little but talk. It is, nevertheless, important to note that all the proposals did agree on one major point: all called for a greater degree of centralization, to be brought about by a full-time executive. It is thus reasonable to assume that had the commercial elite been forced to act in order to deal with some specific problem, agreement could have been quickly reached. Such was to be the case in 1905.

Although there was some interest expressed in new forms of municipal government in the years after 1897, it was not until 1905 that serious proposals were once again put forward. This time there was rapid agreement on a new mode of government, for in June 1906 Winnipeg instituted a Board of Control and at last achieved the long-sought-goal of a strong executive committee operating on a full-time basis.

There are several factors that must be considered in explaining why a new structure of municipal government was instituted in 1906 when all previous efforts had failed. The first is the fact that the new flurry of activity that got underway in 1905 did so in an atmosphere very different from that of 1892–97. By this time the Progressive Movement was well underway in the United States and the institution of such things as commission government were a familiar happening. And since Winnipeg's businessmen took great pride in boasting of their city's progress, it was natural that they should look to a restructuring of their municipal corporation if only to have "the most modern form of government known."[44] Moreover, such civic leaders as Mayor Sharpe and Alderman Latimer attended conferences of the American Municipal League in 1905 and often expressed their admiration for the advances being made in American cities under varying forms of commission government.

A renewed interest in municipal matters in the years after 1900 was also a result of Canadian developments. A Union of Canadian Municipalities had been formed in August 1901. The aim of the Union was to provide a forum where ideas of municipal advancements and innovations could be discussed. Winnipeg's civic politicians had quickly become active members of the Union and from the outset at least one, and often more, were members of the executive.[45] Winnipeg's interest in the organization was also revealed by its acting as host to the conference of the Union of Canadian Municipalities in July 1905. The influence of the Union was further increased in that same year by the publication of a monthly journal, the *Canadian Municipal Journal*, which contained numerous articles on municipal reform.

But, important as these outside influences were, it was internal developments that caused the first constructive steps toward municipal reform to be taken. The resurgence of interest in reform of Winnipeg's government structure coincided with the election of Mayor Thomas Sharpe in 1904. Sharpe, one of Winnipeg's most popular mayors, was a very successful contractor prior to being elected to Council in 1900. He served as alderman from that year until 1904, when he was elected mayor. While an alderman he was chairman of the Board of Public

Works and this experience, coupled with his own work as a private contractor, explain his deep concern over the lack of business efficiency in Winnipeg's government.

The general reform atmosphere and the leadership of Mayor Sharpe, however, do not fully account for the quick institution of a Board of Control system in 1906. During 1905 and 1906 Winnipeg faced a series of major problems that the commercial elite felt could be handled only by a strong executive body. A typhoid epidemic in 1905, a proposal to construct a municipal power plant, and a growing concern over an inadequate water supply all combined to produce a sense of urgency in matters of municipal government.[46] Indeed, given the experiences of 1892–97, it is doubtful if any of the proposals put forward by Mayor Sharpe in 1905–1906 would have come to fruition were it not for these pressing problems.

After visits to Montreal and Toronto in 1904, to Toledo in 1905, and following the convention of the Union of Canadian Municipalities in July 1905, Sharpe's ideas had crystallized enough for him to take the first steps toward a new system.[47] In September 1905 Sharpe announced that he was about to investigate the advisability of the addition of a Board of Control to Winnipeg's municipal government.[48] He indicated that he was already partially convinced that the Board would be a good thing in Winnipeg, but before pressing strongly for it he had decided to write Toronto officials "to know definitely how and with what success the controller system had been operated."[49] He also stated that he "had been influenced in [his] consideration of the controller system by the fact that much of Winnipeg's civic business drags along . . . for the lack of men to go into detail and present matters to council in such a shape that no great delay is necessary." With the addition of four full-time controllers, any question could be put "before council in a business-like manner and the matter could be disposed of in short order."[50]

Accordingly the mayor, in close cooperation with the Board of Trade, called a meeting of various Winnipeg business organizations to draft a new form of civic government. On 8 November 1905 the following motion was passed unanimously:

> That in the opinion of this meeting, the present method of civic government has been found unsatisfactory and entirely inadequate to grapple with the many municipal problems that present themselves, in connection with the rapid and unprecedented growth of the city. Therefore, be it resolved that it is expedient to formulate some improved system for the management of the city's affairs.[51]

Following this initial meeting, an additional meeting was held the following week when it decided "that it is desirable to adopt the system in vogue in Toronto, viz., that of a government by a Board of Control."

After the municipal elections of December, the new Council continued to move quickly toward the institution of a Board of Control. Alderman Cox, chairman of the Legislative Committee, reported to Council on 8 January 1906, recommending that the city solicitor be instructed to prepare legislation to provide for a Board of Control. This was quickly done and on 16 March the required amendments to the city charter received royal assent.[52] The only remaining step to be taken was to submit the question to the electors for their approval and the date for this was set for 28 June. It is important to note that the vote on the Board of Control was to take place on the same day as that on the municipal power question,[53] for in most of the arguments in favour of the new system the Board of Control and the municipal ownership referendum were grouped together; the success of the latter depended, it was argued, on the implementation of the former.

As June 28 approached considerable interest was created by the proposed changes and all the newspapers carried editorials supporting the implementation of the new system.[54] The result of the balloting was a foregone conclusion; the Board of Control measure passed by a vote of 3,517 to 852.[55] The vote revealed that the conservatism of the business community was shared by nearly all the property owners in the city. Indeed, the overwhelming support the commercial elite, headed by the Board of Trade, received for its new form of government, designed to "restrain any financial rashness of the City Council in guiding the growth of the booming city," clearly reveals their dominant position in the community.[56]

The Board of Control system served the needs of Winnipeg's commercial elite well over the next seven years. The population of the city grew at an unprecedented rate, as did opportunities in real estate speculation, wholesale and retail trade, and business in general. And, while the city's leaders were not prepared to assign the reasons for this phenomenal growth and prosperity to any one cause, they nevertheless felt a large part of it was due to the combination of efficient machinery and the "right people in office."[57]

Three significant observations can be made about the various attempts to reform Winnipeg's system of government in the years from 1884 to 1906. First, the source of reform was not the general public but rather the city's businessmen. Indeed, the vast majority of Winnipeggers—including organized labour—were effectively barred from taking an active part in governing the city and either ignored civic politics or turned their attention to provincial and federal politics. Secondly, the target of attack was never particular individuals but rather Winnipeg's mode of government. The commercial elite went to considerable effort to point out that even the best-intentioned and most honest alderman was prevented from doing a good job because of the cumbersome council system. In other words, the purpose of reform was not to remove a corrupt or dishonest group from political power and replace it with another, more acceptable group. There was never any doubt as to who would control the government; the question was how best to enable the holders of public office achieve the goal of "business efficiency in municipal affairs."

Finally, and perhaps most important for an understanding of Winnipeg during this period, the various reform proposals and achievements reveal that the commercial elite were not out to expand popular participation in the government process, but rather to lessen its importance in the running of the city. By the institution of a strong, full-time and salaried executive committee, elected by the entire city rather than by wards, the commercial elite effectively centralized the system of municipal government. The institution of the Board of Control placed the continuous, day-to-day processes of government fully in the hands of a very small group of individuals. In theory, City Council, as the legislative body, could still reject the Board's recommendations. But in practice this never happened, for few aldermen had either the time or resources to challenge the powerful and prestigious Board. A restricted franchise, plural voting, and a centralized form of government assured Winnipeg's businessmen that their conception of desirable public policy would prevail.

part three

the growth ethic in action

The two great wants of this country are railroads and settlers. The former is necessary to secure the latter.
Manitoba Free Press, 1873

I can conceive of no way in which the city can with more certainty and profit enhance its growth, permanent revenues from taxation, and general prosperity than by promoting, directly or indirectly, hydro-power development.
J. T. Fanning, *Report on Water-Power,* 1889

Reduced to its ultimate analysis, the essential and paramount need of the West is, Population. This assured, all other things shall be added in due season; with this withheld, permanent progress toward the realization of our manifest destiny is impossible. . . . This fact . . . permits of no argument. It is an axiomatic truth.
Manitoba Free Press, 1904

4 / Winnipeg's Legacy: Geography, Railroads, and a Triumphant Growth Ethic

The most serious question faced by the youthful city of Winnipeg throughout the 1870s and early 1880s was the problem of transportation. It was not a new problem. Ever since 1812 the community at the confluence of the Red and Assiniboine rivers had been forced to rely on the inadequate and arduous routes used by the fur traders for connections with the outside world.[1] And the plain facts of geography— one thousand miles of rock, muskeg, and tangled waterways—which separated the settlement from the Canadas had not yielded easily, even to the rough and experienced men of the fur trade. Nor had the gruelling overland route to the Bay, used by the Hudson's Bay Company, proven any less difficult. As a result, development at the Forks had been "obscure and prosaic" and in 1870 "the whole country was still a Great Lone Land treked by Indians and Traders."[2]

The entry of Manitoba into Confederation did not solve these transportation problems. It was apparent to all concerned that despite political unity there remained a gross geographical discrepancy that had to be overcome if union was to be meaningful. Early efforts were concentrated on constructing a wagon road from Fort William according to the suggestions made by S. J. Dawson in 1859. But progress on this project was painfully slow; by 1870 only twenty-nine miles had been opened for carriage travel.[3] It was only with the outbreak of the Riel Rebellion at Fort Garry in 1869 that sufficient stimulus was given to the construction of the Dawson Road, which was opened in 1871.

From the outset, however, this means of transportation proved far from adequate for the needs of Winnipeg. The military expedition under Colonel Wolseley that travelled over the route in 1870 experienced hardships and delays that few settlers would be prepared to endure. By 1873 the Dawson route had become the subject of much criticism by the people of Winnipeg. According to the local press "quite a number of immigrants have already arrived by the amphibious route which bears the name of Mr. Dawson . . . and [the travellers] are loud in their denunciations of the whole concern."[4] Attempts were made by Ottawa to improve the route when a contract was signed with W. H. Carpenter and Company whereby the government gave a bonus to the company to keep open a line of transportation for passengers and freight. Passenger stages and freight wagons were to be run at least three times a week, the passengers to be conveyed in ten to twelve days and freight in fifteen to twenty days. Low rates were scheduled to encourage traffic.

These efforts were hardly successful. A group of one hundred and fifty recent passengers over the route met in Winnipeg in 1874 and sent a memorial to the Minister of Public Works citing a long list of grievances.

> We . . . consider it our duty to make known to you . . . the state of affairs and the way passengers are used by the Company on this route. . . . Parties were detained from two to five days after arriving at Prince Arthur's landing and . . . some passengers have been twenty-three days completing the journey. The accommodation afforded at different stations is wholly inadequate. The buildings are too small and in a very filthy condition. The arrangements are wholly unfit for women and children [and] many of the passengers had to content themselves by sleeping outdoors. Generally speaking meals could not be had and those supplied were of a verry [sic] inferior quality. As we advanced on the road we found that at many of the stations no provisions could be had. . . . Fancy large families of young children sent forward by Carpenter and Company without any provisions. . . . Is this the way to treat people most of them who have left comfortable Canadian homes and are now seeking to better their condition in the new country towards which they are travelling. The people travelling over the road were lead to believe they would be provided with comfortable means of conveyance both by land and water but what are the facts. The passengers have to work their own way through. . . . They have to carry their own luggage off and on wagons and boats [and] women and children have to walk over portages. . . . Many of the men employed on the road are rough swearing characters who have not the civility to restrain themselves from giving expressions to the most unseemly oaths even in the presence of women and children. . . . A number of the boats used for conveying passengers and luggage are very leaky and unsafe [and] much property has been injured in this way.

In concluding their statement the immigrants stated their regret that they had not travelled to Winnipeg by the American route. By this means "they could easily have reached Fort Garry . . . in five days and at no greater expense than by [the Dawson route], leaving out the consideration of time they would have saved."[5]

Although shorter and easier than the Dawson route, the American route was not without its disadvantages.[6] It consisted of a trip by rail to Chicago and St. Paul, or by water to Duluth, then by boat or stage to

Winnipeg. The last segment of the journey was particularly difficult, for from St. Paul to Winnipeg the transportation network had been designed for commerce and not passenger travel.[7] But what was most disconcerting to Winnipeggers was that those who travelled through the United States were wooed by American immigration agents commissioned to procure settlers for the still vacant lands of the American Midwest. In the decade 1870–80 over forty-seven thousand Canadian-born immigrants moved to the American Midwest while Manitoba and the Canadian Northwest received only half that number.[8]

In view of the obvious inadequacies of these routes it was not surprising that an insistent demand arose in Manitoba for railway connections with Canada. Winnipeggers were convinced that the most important feature in the economic life of a community was its commercial connections with the rest of the world. No city, they reasoned, could enjoy any considerable prosperity or make notable social progress without a flourishing commerce with other communities. Indeed, Winnipeg's business leaders were so sure of the truth of this argument that they were prepared to do almost anything to attract railways to their city. Railways were the key to growth, the one essential without which all the commercial elite's plans for Winnipeg would fall. The *Manitoba Free Press* stated the issue bluntly: "The two great wants of this country are railroads and settlers. The former is necessary to secure the latter."[9]

These hopes for an early railway link with the East appeared guaranteed when the federal government in 1871 committed itself to a transcontinental railway by an agreement with the newly created province of British Columbia. From this first announcement of plans for a Pacific Railway, Winnipeggers were but little concerned with any aspects of the undertaking other than the choice of a route and the time required to connect Winnipeg with the East. And of these two considerations the former was by far the most important. The selection of a route would affect the direction and the speculative element in settlement. Lands on or near the main line would obviously be of greater value than those more distant. Indeed, a community's very future depended on its proximity to the railway. As long as location of the railway through Winnipeg was assured, temporary delays in construction could be endured. For, secure in the knowledge that it would be on the main line, Winnipeg would not have to fear that some other Manitoba community would prosper at its expense. On the other hand, if the route did not pass through the city, Winnipeg's demise as a commercial centre seemed inevitable.

Aware of the key role of the transcontinental railway, Winnipeggers watched developments closely. Even before definite surveys were completed they assured themselves that Winnipeg would be on the main line.[10] This assumption was based on four points. First of all, the Dawson Road terminated in Winnipeg and it seemed reasonable that the railway would follow this same route. The city was, as well, the largest community in the Northwest and it again seemed reasonable to assume that it would receive special consideration. More important, however, was a map published in 1872 as a result of exploration surveys made in 1871. It clearly laid down the CPR main line as running south of Lake Manitoba, in the vicinity of Winnipeg.[11] Finally, the wording of the Act to Incorporate the Canadian Pacific Railway Company passed in June 1872 seemed to indicate Winnipeg would be on the main line. Section 3 of that act, giving Hugh Allan and Associates authority to construct branch lines from the main line, stipulated that such a line could be built "from Fort Garry or Winnipeg to Pembina." This wording was quickly interpreted as indicating that Winnipeg would be on the main line. In fact, as time passed, this interpretation became so widely accepted in Winnipeg that many felt Winnipeg had been explicitly promised the main line. Unfortunately, Winnipeggers could never produce concrete evidence to this effect.

In any case, it was on this somewhat nebulous evidence that Winnipeggers assumed their city's rise to its destiny as the dynamic commercial capital of the Northwest was assured. And with an over-zealous optimism that was to characterize it through the years, City Council, meeting for the first time in January 1874, planned a vigorous program of public works. By December, however, the city's optimism had been shattered, at least temporarily. By that time it appeared as if Winnipeg would not be on the main line, and all the inherent advantages would be lost to some other Manitoba community. For over six years the question of the route of the Pacific Railway overshadowed all other matters in Winnipeg.

The assumption of office by the federal Liberal party in November 1873 did not, at first, cause much alarm in Winnipeg. The city, of course, protested Prime Minister Mackenzie's "pay-as-you-go" program for the transcontinental railway but assumed he was committed to a route that included Winnipeg on the main line; that is, the route Winnipeggers felt had been outlined in the 1872 act.[12] The Liberal government, however, soon made it clear that it had decided on a route that crossed the Red River at Selkirk rather than at Winnipeg.

This decision was announced in December 1874 and was based on the report of Sandford Fleming, engineer-in-chief of the transcontinental project.[13] Fleming proposed that west of Lake Superior the railway be built from Fort William to Selkirk, there cross the Red River, go on to cross Lake Manitoba at the Narrows, and proceed northwesterly towards Edmonton (see Map 1 on page 66). This route was not only shorter than the one through Winnipeg, it had obvious engineering and economic advantages. A railway bridge at Selkirk would have the benefit of more stable banks than existed further upstream and, even more important, both bridge and railway would be safe against flooding. The site of Winnipeg, it was known, had been flooded seven times since 1812, while Selkirk, situated on a high ridge of land, had never been flooded.[14] Finally, Fleming pointed out that the selection of the northwesterly route toward Edmonton was dictated by Palliser's report of 1857 which had stated that the central prairie region—Palliser's Triangle—was too arid for settlement. If the railway were to open up land for agricultural use, it would have to be built through the Park Belt which lay to the north of the flat, dry plains.[15]

Winnipeggers reacted immediately to news of the route change. A Citizens' Railway Committee was formed on 18 December and a petition protesting the change was drawn up. A delegation that included the mayor and a prominent businessman was then sent off to Ottawa to plead Winnipeg's case.[16]

Winnipeg's delegates reached Ottawa in March 1875 and arranged a meeting with Prime Minister Mackenzie. They then proceeded to present a series of arguments designed to convince Mackenzie that the route must pass through Winnipeg. "The chief settlements of the Province," they asserted, "lie to the South of Lake Manitoba, and the capital City of the Province, viz: Winnipeg . . . in the centre of the above-mentioned settled districts, is the natural key of the fertile country. . . ." They agreed that although the southern route may be somewhat longer, this "route would at once receive a traffic of freight and passengers which would more than repay the cost of any slight deflection south of a possible more direct line." Also, "the route to the north would entail greater expense on the Dominion Government than the route south of the Lake in consequence of the necessity which would still exist for the completion of branch lines and extentions to different parts of Manitoba." The key to their argument, however, lay in the statement that the present government would be breaking faith with the settlers who ". . . have selected their homesteads and invested their means on the strength of the statements and pledges of the Dominion Government," and had settled in anticipation of a route through Winnipeg and west to Portage la Prairie.[17]

Mackenzie was not impressed. He informed the delegation that the information with which he had been furnished differed materially from that of the delegation. He noted that the northern route would pass through land equal to that of southern Manitoba for settlement purposes; that the cost of procuring ties was "sensibly lessened by taking the route from Rat Portage to the Narrows; and that as the CPR was a Dominion enterprise he should not feel himself justified in adding thirty miles to the main line when such an alteration would not only be an additional capital expenditure, but a permanent drawback to through travel and traffic, and that with every desire to serve the Province of Manitoba . . . he could hold out no hope that any departure from the so-called Northern route would be made."[18]

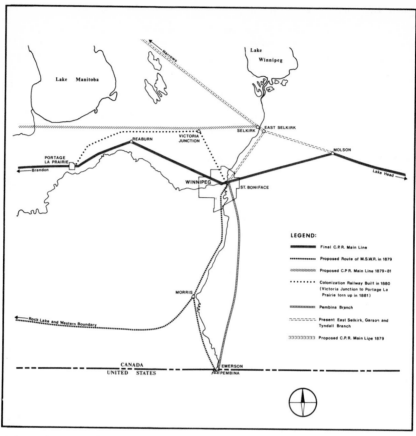

Map 1/Proposed and Actual Location of Railways in Vicinity of Winnipeg

Finding that there was no probability of inducing the prime minister to change the route of the main line, the delegation sought to gain government support for the rapid completion of the Pembina branch. This railway was to follow the cart trail to St. Paul and give interim railway connection with eastern Canada by utilizing American railways while the difficult Canadian route was being completed. Winnipeg hoped it could persuade the government to have this line cross the Red River at Winnipeg and join the main line at a point west of the city. The prime minister agreed only to look into the matter and stipulated that he would aid Winnipeg in building a bridge across the Red River only if this did not add materially to the distance of the Pembina branch.[19] The Winnipeg delegation also sought federal support for a colonization railway south of Lake Manitoba and westward through the province, but the prime minister pointed out that the Dominion government could not assist a line competing with the CPR.

Surveys by the federal government on the Pembina branch took place during the summer of 1875 and construction of the line was started in the spring of 1876. During this time Winnipeggers continued their attempts to have the railway pass through the city and join the main line of the Pacific Railway west of the Red River. City Council even went so far as to offer to build the bridge at Winnipeg at civic expense.[20] But Mackenzie's only concession was to have the Pembina branch "deflect so as to come to the bank of the river opposite the city."[21]

Despite these repeated failures, Winnipeg's commercial elite continued their efforts to secure adequate railway connections. In January 1877 a mass meeting was called and a new approach to the railway question was outlined. It was observed that "the surest way to build a bridge across the Red River was to branch out boldly in a railroad westerly . . . [for once] such a road was built, a bridge would follow. If a bridge were built at Winnipeg and not at Selkirk, it would settle the question of our railway future forever. . . . A second bridge would not be built, and the Dominion Government would not run a road parallel with this one, a few miles north, through a barren country. . . ." For this road to the west, Winnipeg, "as the richest place, . . . should take the initiative." A resolution was thus passed calling upon the civic corporation to pay a cash subsidy of $200,000 to any company that built a railway from Winnipeg to the western boundary of the province. The resolution included the demands that the federal government furnish an appropriate land grant to such a railway, and that the provincial government "enact laws facilitating the establishment of municipal institutions" throughout the province so that they could also vote grants of money to aid the proposed railway.[22]

With this mandate the executive of the Citizens' Railway Committee met on 17 February and organized the Manitoba Southwestern Railway Company. As originally proposed, this railway was to run southwest from Winnipeg through Morris. It was, furthermore, to have connections with the Pembina branch and the CPR main line by means of a bridge at Winnipeg. A line would also be built to Victoria Junction and then westward to Portage la Prairie. Once these routes had been agreed upon, the executive conducted meetings throughout the province and received promises of aid from several municipalities.[23] And finally, the executive wrote their federal representatives and asked them to press the matter of railway connections in Parliament. Accordingly, these members of Parliament urged Mackenzie to change the proposed route of the CPR or, if refusing to do that, to be prepared to give a generous financial grant to the MSWR. In once again urging a change in the route of the main line they argued that any talk of Winnipeg's only connection with the east being the Pembina branch would be disastrous. "It is important in the highest degree that immigrants from other Provinces and from Europe should have access to the North West without being subjected to the cajolments, the bullying, and the swindling too often practiced upon them on their way hither through the United States."[24]

When Mackenzie refused to make any changes in the main route, the Manitoba MPs turned their attention to the Pembina branch and the matter of a land grant for the MSWR. They urged an early completion of the former and a generous bonus for the latter. But they succeeded only in eliciting a promise from the government to send surveyors to Manitoba to look into the question of land grants. In the meantime the Railway Committee pressed the urgency of the matter of land grants on David Mills, Minister of the Interior.[25]

Subsequently, in March 1878, a bill was introduced by Mills in the House of Commons entitled "An Act for facilitating the colonization of Dominion Lands by the formation of railway companies and aiding the construction of such railways traversing such lands." Winnipeggers were happy with this step, for they felt the government was finally "disposed to do something in way of compensating the people who settled between Lake Manitoba and the Assiniboine River upon reasonable faith that the Pacific Railway would pass through that district."[26] The optimism that followed the passing of the act by the House of Commons was soon dispelled, however, for late in May the bill was defeated in the Senate, where the Conservatives held a majority, on the grounds that it was a bill to kill the Pacific Railway. Moreover, the annual report of the Minister of Public Works for 1878 was "accepted as conclusive evidence that the main line will not pass south of Lake Manitoba . . . despite Winnipeg's offer of the inducement to cover the full cost of a bridge at Winnipeg." Thus, after four years of effort the community's struggle to make Winnipeg the "Gateway to the West" appeared fruitless.[27]

The closing months of 1878 were, nevertheless, brightened by the completion of the Pembina branch and the inauguration of direct rail service between St. Paul, Minnesota, and Winnipeg. The city at last had an effective outlet for the wheat crops of its surrounding hinterland and good times once more seemed in store for the young community. This prediction appeared all the more reasonable since in September Macdonald and the Conservative party were returned to office. During the campaign they had broadly hinted that, if elected, they would pass the transcontinental line through Winnipeg. Winnipeg had thus voted heavily for the Conservative candidate in the election.[28] And the Citizens' Railway Committee and City Council had grasped at this last hope. While it was true that the railway had entered Manitoba, it was still on the other side of the river. Hoping to persuade Macdonald to change the main line route by quick and determined action, they hurriedly called a mass meeting for November 8. A memorial was drawn up, sponsored by the Board of Trade and endorsed by City Council, that indicated the injustice under which Winnipeg felt it suffered. The most important aspect of this memorial, however, was the offer of a bonus of $300,000 to aid in the construction of a bridge at Winnipeg.[29]

The memorial was sent to Ottawa and a bylaw was drawn up that provided for the raising of $300,000 by the city. Prime Minister Macdonald acknowledged the offer in December, but it was not until April 1879 that Winnipeg received the good news. The Conservative government announced that the prairie section of the Pacific Railway would be built along a more southerly route than that projected by the previous government and, furthermore, that in so far as possible the road would be built through existing centres of population.[30] To the great consternation of Winnipeggers, however, the federal Minister of Public Works, Charles Tupper, made it clear that although his government had decided to build the main line south of Lake Manitoba, it would not pass through Winnipeg.[31]

Following this clarification of the government's position yet another meeting was held in Winnipeg, another petition drawn up, and a new delegation dispatched to Ottawa. The Winnipeg delegates argued "that a colonization line should be built, under the control of the government and forming part of the Pembina Branch, across the Red at Winnipeg and running northwesterly to intersect the proposed main line north and west of the city."[32] Tupper promised the delegates that if the city built a bridge across the Red River his government would build the desired colonization line, and that this railway would be built before the main line west from Selkirk.

In light of the city's many setbacks, Tupper's promise was greeted with considerable enthusiasm in Winnipeg. It meant that the city was assured immediate railway connections with the east by means of the Pembina branch that would cross the Red River at Winnipeg. Even more important was the fact that a colonization railway would be built from the city to connect with the main line of the Pacific Railway north and west of Winnipeg. Although this was not nearly so acceptable as having the main line passing directly through Winnipeg it at least gave the city an indirect connection with that "life-line."

In the months following Tupper's pronouncements there was considerable activity in Winnipeg. City Council passed the bylaw to raise $300,000 to finance the construction of the railway bridge, with the stipulation that it would serve both the MSWR and the colonization railway to be built by the government.[33] By September the federal government had called for tenders for the construction of one hundred miles of track west of Winnipeg and the contract stipulated that it was to be completed within twelve months. The first twenty miles of the road, referred to as the "Colonization Railway" to distinguish it from the main line of the CPR, was to proceed in a northwesterly direction from

Winnipeg to Victoria Junction, where it would connect with the main line running from Selkirk. The remaining eighty miles was to proceed due west from Victoria Junction and become part of the main line (see Map 1).

During this latter part of 1879 considerable confusion prevailed in Winnipeg regarding the Colonization Railway. Tupper had clearly stated it would be only a branch line of the CPR. But his action in having it constructed before the main line from Selkirk to Victoria Junction was built caused many Winnipeggers to hope that this line would eventually be the main line. But in either case the changes in the route meant that major alterations were necessary in the MSWR charter, for this road, as originally planned, covered part of the new colonization route. It was agreed by the company's directors to withdraw that part of the bill coinciding with the Colonization Railway and confine themselves to an exclusive, southwestern route. This would commence at Winnipeg, where it would have connections with the Pembina branch, and follow a line southwesterly to Morris and then to Rock Lake, near the western boundary of the province.[34]

The most important element, in both the MSWR and the Colonization Railway projects, as far as Winnipeg was concerned, was the crossing of the Red River at Point Douglas. Although the municipal corporation was to pay for the cost of the Louise Bridge, it was not anxious to take on the added responsibility of superintending its construction. But after both the MSWR and the federal government refused to do so, City Council accepted the task and let tenders in January 1880.[35]

Meanwhile, the Conservative government continued attempts to persuade private capitalists to undertake the construction and operation of the transcontinental railway. Prime Minister Macdonald led a cabinet mission to Britain in the fall of 1879 in an effort to interest British capital, but was unsuccessful; British capitalists still remembered the misfortune of the Grand Trunk Railway and, in any case, regarded the project of a Canadian transcontinental railway as grandiose and premature. Shortly after this failure, active negotiations were begun with a group of Canadian capitalists headed by Donald A. Smith and represented by D. J. McIntyre and George Stephen, the same group that had resurrected the St. Paul and Pacific Railway and had completed the first American rail connection to the Manitoba boundary. An agreement with this group was reached by September of 1880, the contract signed in October, and on December 10 was brought down to Parliament for approval.

The new agreement caused considerable speculation in Winnipeg. The city remembered that the change of government in 1878 had meant one alteration in the route of the main line; perhaps the private syndicate could be convinced that Winnipeg should be incorporated into the main line of the transcontinental railway since they, unlike the federal government, would be more concerned with immediate profits than with long-term goals. The Winnipeg Board of Trade, at a meeting in October, suggested that when Tupper visited the city in November "the Winnipeg case should be pressed . . . and the advantages of Winnipeg for all the workshops of the CPR be pressed . . . and, if necessary, some inducements be offered in the shape of taxation exemptions."[36] City Council promptly agreed to this suggestion.

When Tupper arrived in Winnipeg in November 1880 he was presented with a memorial expressing appreciation for changes already made in the main route, but also urging more. The city was prepared, the memorial read, "to exempt . . . from civic taxation for an extended number of years" all the railway buildings and grounds of the CPR syndicate "should [they] decide to build [their] work shops and depots in Winnipeg." The response of the Minister of Railways was encouraging:

> He was satisfied that the Government has pursued a wise course in diverting the railway south of Lake Manitoba [and they] would have failed in their duty had [they not extended] a branch line to Winnipeg, and he was more satisfied than ever of the wisdom of the Government in making the change. He had no doubt this change would have been followed by the location of the workshops at this point if the work of construction had remained in the hands of the Government. They had carefully considered and discussed the matter, and had come to the conclusion that they would be consulting the best interest of the railway by locating the workshops in this large centre. As soon as parliament ratified the agreement, he had no doubt the syndicate would look at the matter in the same light. He would certainly have felt it to be his duty to report the matter to his colleagues, as it was in the best interest of the road, and he had no doubt the syndicate would hold the same view.[37]

Winnipeg seemed, at last, to be in a position to acquire the main line and the workshops without any more commitments on its part and this fact should have encouraged a reassessment of the situation. Tupper's remarks indicated that Winnipeg had his influential support. Also, the economic advantage of being the largest centre in the Northwest (with a population of about five thousand) was bound to be considered by the syndicate. But perhaps most important was the well-known fact that Donald A. Smith, head of the CPR syndicate, was a long-time employee (and by 1880 a majority stockholder) of the Hudson's Bay Company which stood to make large gains if Winnipeg was chosen as the site for the workshops and western headquarters of the CPR. For although the company had surrendered its claim to the North West

Territories in 1869, the Dominion government had allowed it to retain blocks of land in the vicinity of its trading posts. One of these blocks amounted to 1,750 acres of land in and around Winnipeg.[38] In the boom that would surely follow the passing of the CPR through Winnipeg, this property could be sold at high prices. Another factor that Winnipeggers should have considered at this juncture was that the civic corporation was already committed to the construction of the bridge at Winnipeg and had pledged a $200,000 bonus to the MSWR. Any further commitment would seriously burden the already tenuous finances of the young city.

Unfortunately for Winnipeg's future, neither Council nor the Board of Trade were in a cautious mood, and a delegation made up of members of both these bodies was hastily sent off to St. Paul to interview members of the syndicate. They proposed that in return for locating the main shops of the CPR in Winnipeg "the city will furnish land to the extent of 30 acres free of cost within the limits of the city, . . . and further that the city will exempt the Company from all city and school taxes for twenty years."[39] The syndicate, of course, agreed to consider the offer but by May 1881 had still not reached a decision. Council, meeting with the Board of Trade, decided to encourage the syndicate by extending the taxation exemption to perpetuity. Finally, on June 16, the syndicate formerly offered to locate its workshops in the city and, by implication, run the main line through Winnipeg. But the offer also included plans "for the construction of a branch of its railway from a point on the main line in this vicinity [i.e. Winnipeg] in a southwesterly direction through the Province of Manitoba."[40]

This latter proposal added a new dimension to the negotiations for it meant, in effect, the end of the MSWR scheme and the establishment of a railway monopoly in the province. Winnipeg, however, was under a moral obligation to this company by virtue of earlier agreements and had, only a few days earlier, passed Bylaw 145 giving the MSWR its bonus. Also, in view of the concern expressed over monopoly at the time of the passing of the CPR bill by the House of Commons in December of 1880, it was logical that City Council would have wanted another company to build in southwestern Manitoba.[41] But if the city paid the bonus to the MSWR, the Canadian Pacific syndicate threatened to locate its workshops at Lower Fort Garry, between Selkirk and Winnipeg. If it did not pay the bonus to the MSWR, however, that company would be practically doomed, as would be the prospects of competitive rates.

It was obvious to some in Winnipeg that the syndicate sought more than the $200,000 bonus they would receive for building a southwestern line. Reviewing the entire railway situation, the *Winnipeg Times* declared on 20 July 1881:

Instead of beseeching railway companies to come to us, the reverse seems to be the case. From being a suitor, Winnipeg has become the sought. Satisfactory as this may appear, however, our position is still a perplexing one. We now have two companies asking consideration at our hands—the Canadian Pacific Co. and the Manitoba South-Western. Each seeks a bonus of $200,000 for a southwestern line—the former with some little extras—and in return Winnipeg is promised the workshops of the roads. . . . It is to be regretted that these complications which have arisen should even give cause for apprehensions of the City being drawn into and made the loser by the quarrel. There is no reason why it should. We have dealt liberally with both. . . . We have constructed a $200,000 bridge over the Red River. . . . We have donated a valuable site for a station, and offered exemption from taxation, and another site for the workshops to the CPR Co. And the Manitoba South-Western solemnly bound itself to locate its workshops here, in consideration of the bridge being handed over to it. We have done our part of the bargain. . . . In the struggle between the rival roads, Winnipeg should not be placed in a false position. She desires all the rail facilities that can be afforded; but, if in this contest she is to be an offending victim, it may perhaps be better for her to stand entirely aloof, and, devoting her energies and her capital to other means of retaining her commanding position not even attempt the useless task of seeking to conciliate the bitterly rival organizations with peace offerings in the shape of bonus By-Laws.

Winnipeg City Council refused to stay out of the rivalry and, ignoring the advice of the *Times*, dropped the MSWR bonus bylaw and drew up a new one giving the $200,000 bonus to the CPR. It also exempted "the property now owned or hereafter to be owned by the said railway company for railway purposes within the City of Winnipeg from taxation forever," and "conveyed to the said company lands sufficient and suitable for a passenger station."[42] Finally, it gave the company free use of the bridge over the Red River which the city had constructed. In return, the CPR at once commenced the construction of workshops, a freight shed, and a passenger station in Winnipeg.

The location of the transcontinental railway through Winnipeg promised that the city, strategically located at the entry to the western plains, was destined to become the entrepôt of a great agricultural and commercial economy which would come into being in the Northwest.[43] The prospect implied that the land upon which the city stood would have great value, as businessmen vied for commercial locations in the developing metropolitan centre, and home builders for residential sites. Out of such anticipation the Winnipeg boom of 1881–1882 developed.[44] During the boom Winnipeg experienced the wildest sixteen months of its existence. The boom began with speculation in Winnipeg lots and in other Manitoba townsites and continued with a mounting delirium until lots in Edmonton, Prince Albert, and even Port Moody, which was represented as having been chosen as the Pacific terminus of the projected CPR, were bought and sold in Winnipeg in a turmoil of gambling excitement. The hotels, some of which had only canvas roofs, were crowded. The many bars which sprang up overnight were jammed and noisy, early and late. All the frontier gambling devices were in operation and the merchants did a roaring trade. Stories of great fortunes picked up in this new Eldorado flew about, and the more exaggerated they were the more readily they were believed by all the hopeful souls in a community where almost everybody was dreaming of wealth from land gambling, and a substantial number were finding their dreams come true.

Such frantic activity could not last, of course, and the boom collapsed in the spring of 1882. But during the boom the physical structure of Winnipeg trebled and although growth slowed down in the years after 1882, it by no means stopped. Indeed, an immense volume of construction activity continued in Winnipeg and the West, especially in the years after 1896, and this supported a local building materials industry of major proportions. Moreover, financial firms from eastern Canada and Great Britain erected imposing western headquarters in Winnipeg, while a continuing accumulation of substantial fortunes by Winnipeg's commercial elite supported the organization of locally owned financial institutions.[45] In short, Winnipeg assumed the role of the great metropolitan centre of western Canada, housing the leading educational, administrative, economic, and entertainment institutions of the region. It even served as the chief labour reservoir for the West, furnishing the labour requirements of farming, railway construction, and commercial building.

Thus, if economic growth and the rise to metropolitan status were the primary goals in attracting the Canadian Pacific through Winnipeg, the taxation privileges, land grants, $200,000 bonus, and $300,000 bridge granted the company were justified.[46] Yet the high cost of obtaining the CPR involved much more than these inducements. The upsurge in Winnipeg's fortunes that followed the coming of the CPR re-affirmed in the minds of the commercial elite the conviction that railways were the key to rapid and sustained growth. Thereafter City Council did everything to encourage railway development and nothing at all to control it. This attitude had serious long-range consequences for the city's physical appearance and social fabric.

The commercial elite's lack of foresight revealed itself over and over again as new railways entered the city; the municipal corporation simply did not have a comprehensive plan to ensure a humane environment through planned land use. Railways thus turned Winnipeg's streets into a "nightmare."[47] The *City Planning Commission Report* of 1913 summed up the problem:

> The steam railways entering the city at present are the Canadian Pacific Railway, the Canadian Northern Railway, the Grand Trunk Pacific Railway and the Midland Railway. Each of these railways with their numerous branches, yards and shops, cuts off the city into many different sections. It does not seem that the entrance of these steam railways has been considered on any road scheme which would be convenient and beneficial to either the city or to the Railways themselves, but, that the entry has simply followed the line of least resistance.[48]

The major difficulty caused by the entrance of these different railways into Winnipeg, each at different points, was the great number of level crossings that resulted. Some of these problems were eventually solved by the building of subways or overhead bridges, but from 1900 to 1914 the effects of Winnipeg's railway policy were a matter of continued controversy. In 1900, for example, when the Canadian Pacific asked for permission to extend its freight and marshalling yards, City Council promptly acceded to the request. The *Winnipeg Telegram* agreed with the decision "from a business point of view" but the *Winnipeg Tribune* was opposed for the following reasons:

> The subway agreement allows the CPR to extend its freight yard tracks eastward across [several streets]. It practically gives free a large amount of real estate to the CPR for this purpose, and an additional large amount it actually and explicitly agrees to deed to the CPR. That is a cheap way for the CPR to get additional yard room. The railway company could, of course, get any amount of land for extending its yards on the west side, but it might have to pay for it.
>
> The present arrangement is not cheap, for the city . . . will be involved in a loss resulting up to hundreds of thousands of dollars to say nothing of the very serious injury to the value of all property north of the track. . . . A partial remedy will also have to be found for the condition that will be created on streets between the station and the river, where the increase of the CPR traffic will soon make the crossings as bad or worse than that on Main Street now. A new crossing or a new overhead bridge will be required, then we will have thru crossing to the North of the tracks, just as we now have thru crossings to the West of the river. But not even all this costly work will undo the injury to the north end caused by its separation from the rest of the city and the inconvenience of access to it.
>
> If there is any valid objection, either from the point of view of the CPR or from the point of view of the city, to having the rail-

way come into the city from the northwest, clearing Main Street and all steets east of any CPR traffic during the day, and making the city one continuous compact whole none has been offered.[49]

Despite this sound advice, the compartmentalization of Winnipeg continued, most notably with the closing of East Broadway for the Grand Trunk Pacific in 1904, and with the entrance of the Midland Railway in 1911.

The tragedy of the commercial elite's short-sighted railway policy was that it was not necessary. It is highly probable that the syndicate would have passed the railway through Winnipeg and located their shops and western headquarters there without the inducements granted by City Council. Once the decision to locate in the city had been made the municipal corporation had nothing to lose by controlling the entry and location of the CPR. Furthermore, after the CPR had established, itself in Winnipeg and the city became the "Gateway to the West," other railways had to pass through as a matter of good business. In other words, in the years after 1881 Winnipeg had the upper hand and could have controlled the entry of subsequent railways with no fear of forfeiting the commercial advantages railroads brought with them. Instead of taking this long-term approach, one that took into consideration the harmful as well as the beneficial effects of railway development, the commercial elite gave the companies a free hand to enter and leave Winnipeg at their convenience. They thus left to future generations of Winnipeggers a poor legacy, for geography, railroads, and a blind commitment to growth combined to turn Winnipeg's environment into an uncoordinated and socially disruptive series of self-contained ghettos.

5 / Winnipeg: Port of the Northwest

Not all Winnipeg's efforts in the field of transportation development were centred on railways. Even while the city's future as a railway centre was being decided, Winnipeg's leaders were taking steps to make the prairie capital the "port" of a great inland navigation system they felt could be developed in the Northwest. An account of Winnipeg's efforts in the area is notable not only because it represents another dimension of the elite's concern for growth-encouraging schemes, but also because it illustrates that water transport—so important in the early history of the West—continued in the railway age to be considered a worthwhile means of moving both men and goods.

The idea of placing steamboats on the Red River came from St. Paul merchants. Their interest in the Red River settlement had been quickened in 1858 when the Hudson's Bay Company had sent off a trial shipment of trade goods from Great Britain, via St. Paul, to Fort Garry. The company's action—taken in an effort to circumvent the gruelling and slow overland route from Hudson Bay—was pronounced a great success. And it made St. Paul merchants aware of the possibilities of their city serving as the hub of a new transportation system for the continental Northwest. They reasoned that if Hudson's Bay Company goods could be moved profitably between St. Paul and the Red River settlement by means of a stage line, they could be transported even more profitably if the Red River was used. Accordingly, in the fall of 1858 a group of American businessmen conducted a survey of the Red River between St. Paul and Fort Garry and pronounced it fully navigable.[1] Indeed, one enthusiastic person, James W. Taylor, read a paper to the St. Paul Chamber of Commerce that proved, to his audience at least, that a steamer on the Red could follow the river and lake system of the British Northwest all the way to the Rockies.[2]

The result of all this activity was the offer of $1,000 by the Chamber to Anson Northup if he could successfully navigate the Red to Fort Garry during the coming summer. Northup constructed a tiny, shallow-draughted ship that winter, and then, performing a near miracle, manoeuvred the *Anson Northup* into Fort Garry on 11 June

1859. It was cordially welcomed, and signalled the beginning of the end for the old cart brigades to St. Paul. Even though her life was short, the *Anson Northup* was the first of a succession of steamboats that navigated the Red River from St. Paul.

Between 1862 and 1864 two steamers, the *Freighter* and the *International*, plied the Red River below Fort Garry under the control of H. C. Burbank and Company. In the latter year, the interest in this trade was sold to N. W. Kittson, who carried it on until 1871 when he joined with Hill, Griggs and Company to form the Red River Transportation Company which controlled the trade to 1874. Then, in an effort to lower rates, an opposition line was formed by a group of Winnipeg and St. Paul citizens called the Merchants International; it operated two boats, the *Manitoba* and the *Minnesota*. At first it seemed successful but by 1876 it, too, was taken over by Kittson, who again reigned unopposed. Traffic continued to increase, and although rail connection between Winnipeg and St. Paul was established in 1878, Red River shipping prospered. It was not until 1909 that the last steamer ran from the United States to Winnipeg.[3]

The significant point about the successful development of Red River shipping between Winnipeg and St. Paul was that it awakened Winnipeg businessmen to the possibilities of utilizing the river and lake system that existed north of the city. Since this region was sparsely settled, development of the Red River between Winnipeg and Lake Winnipeg naturally evolved more slowly than did the southern route. But the major impediment to navigation on this stretch of the Red River were the rapids at St. Andrew's. This obstruction, some sixteen miles from Winnipeg, was the only obstacle on the forty-mile stretch of water that existed between the city and Lake Winnipeg. Once the lake had been reached, Winnipeggers insisted, navigation was possible all the way north to Hudson Bay and west as far as Edmonton and even the Yukon. St. Andrew's Rapids, however, so impeded navigation that passage was possible only with very light loads during high-water levels. During normal periods transshipment was necessary, and besides the cost of that operation it was essential to have capital laid out for two sets of vessels, one for the lake and the other for river navigation. With the exception of such compact cargoes as fish and oil, no article of commercial value could bear these added costs.[4] For the river and lake system north of Winnipeg to be of any value to the city's businessmen, therefore, cargoes had to be able to arrive there in bulk, and this could not be done without a continuous low-water channel of at least six to eight feet.

The improvement of the Red River, and particularly the removal of the obstruction at St. Andrew's Rapids, would have been of considerable value to Winnipeg. Over the years the Winnipeg Board of Trade, together with City Council, compiled an impressive number of arguments to prove this point to the federal government. The prime advantage of the work, they argued, would be to open up direct and unimpeded communication between Winnipeg and Lake Winnipeg. This lake was over three hundred miles in length and had some three thousand miles of well-timbered shoreline. Spruce, tamarack, cedar, jack-pine, and white poplar abounded on the shoreline, as well as on islands in the lake and on the banks of rivers that entered the lake. Tamarack was especially valuable since it was used for railway ties both in Canada and the United States. Since ties required replacement every seven years, the market was steady.[5] The other woods were also in demand, whether for shingles, paper, or fuel.

The quantity of lumber available for fuel was particularly important to Winnipeg. It had been hoped, prior to the coming of the Canadian Pacific in 1885, that once the city had railroad connections there would be plenty of cheap fuel. It was soon apparent, however, that with its monopoly on transportation facilities, the CPR had little inclination to offer low rates.[6] Since their cars were more profitably employed in other business, the fuel supply was always precarious and insufficient and did not meet the needs of the rapidly growing city. Cordwood, when available, commanded from $9 to $12 a cord. The Board of Trade pointed out numerous times that if a canal was made at St. Andrew's Rapids, lake vessels could bring up four to five hundred cords in a trip, and one vessel owner insisted that under such circumstances he could supply wood at $3.50 per cord. A difference of even $3 per cord in 1892, when consumption was about two hundred thousand cords a year, would have meant a saving of $600,000. It was also argued that lower fuel costs would encourage the development of manufacturing in the city.[7]

Improvements in river communication might also lead to a vigorous fishing industry on Lake Winnipeg. In addition, the brick, limestone, and sand near the lake could be used for building and street construction in the city. Finally, it was claimed that the shores of Lake Winnipeg had a substantial iron ore body of forty-five million tons. The potential value of this ore was illustrated in 1893 when the McCormick Harvesting Company turned down an offer to locate in Winnipeg "because of the lack of raw materials needed in the construction of their machines." The mayor and Council felt this rejection was directly attributable to the obstruction at St. Andrew's Rapids which prevented the utilization of the iron deposits of the lake.[8]

The arguments used in the campaign for improving the Red River navigation system went far beyond the potential of Lake Winnipeg, however. Considerable effort was spent in extolling the benefits of continuous water communication to Edmonton and beyond—a chain of navigable rivers and lakes some two thousand miles in length. The country that could be reached by this cheap transportation route included the settlements of Prince Albert, Battleford, Edmonton, and others.[9]

Navigation was also considered feasible to Hudson Bay, opening "the most direct and natural route for transporting the grain of the west to the markets of the old country." It was argued that the route would be so economically viable it could attract American farmers and with this trade, that of Manitoba, and all the region drained by the Saskatchewan River system, the Hudson Bay route could carry on a booming business.[10]

The enormous potential of such a scheme caught the imagination of at least one Winnipegger. G. T. Orton, in urging City Council and the Board of Trade to take action and obtain funds to carry out a preliminary survey of the route, spelled out for the public the supposedly inevitable benefits that could be derived from such a waterway:

> The annual profits of agriculture would increase 25%. Products travelling by this channel would find a route and market in Britain and Europe for our unrivalled white fish as well as other fine species of the finny tribe found in almost all the innumerable inland lakes of our country. The great problem of freight rates would be solved, nor would our national highway, the CPR, suffer. Increased passenger traffic would be created and all her force would be more than needed (it is true, at lower rates) to move the increased productions of our immense territory; her lands, with all the other in the country, would soon be trebled in value. The horrible nightmare which has taken hold of our people that we are doomed to be the slaves of a huge corporation, and to receive for our labor only a living, unless competition is obtained will be removed. Hope, buoyancy and energetic action will replace the present stagnation. Population and capital will be attracted from abroad. . . . An immense trade would flow down the Red River from the bordering States. Winnipeg [would be] converted into an inland seaport like Manchester. The great Saskatchewan will begin to pour down its latent wealth from the very Rockies. Wheat, cattle, coal and oil, with the precious minerals will blend together and soon make that noble stream a busy line of industries. Surely all will unite, both Manitoba and the Northwest, in carrying out this great achievement—a waterway direct to Liverpool.[11]

Besides a desire for improvements at St. Andrew's, it was also hoped that the federal government could be persuaded to undertake work on the Assiniboine River. In its six-hundred-mile course through Manitoba and the Territories this river touched a vast area of wheat-raising land, and the farmers of the region "would find in the new waterway a sincere friend with regard to the movement of their crops." The work required to make this all possible, it was pointed out, would be "the cutting of a canal through the narrow height of land which separates the head waters of the Saskatchewan and Assiniboine Rivers."[12] The water supply of the Saskatchewan could thus be partially diverted into the Assiniboine. Still another plan was proposed when it was pointed out that a canal cut from Lake Manitoba to the Assiniboine River would open a waterway from the city to that lake as well as Lake Winnipegosis, "thus taking in another immense area of country which is rich beyond the power of words to describe in natural products of every kind."[13]

These last two plans received less attention than did the one designed to open up the river route to Lake Winnipeg by improvements at St. Andrew's Rapids. It was felt that the latter was the key to "the chain of water routes connecting with almost every important centre in the west" and until it was completed no progress could be expected elsewhere.

The campaign to have the federal government build locks at St. Andrew's got underway in earnest in 1880 and between that date and 1893 the city's commercial elite did not let up in its efforts. Petitions, memorials, delegations, letters of support from local MPs, businessmen, and engineers all regularly stated Winnipeg's case.[14] In 1892, for example, a joint committee of City Council and the Winnipeg Board of Trade sent a memorial off to Ottawa which included not only their own signatures, but those of the Boards of Trade from Dufferin, Morden, and Portage la Prairie; the councils of St. Boniface, Emerson, and Portage la Prairie; and the rural municipalities of Morris, Springfield, and St. Andrew's. The joint committee also asked for, and received, endorsations from the members of Parliament for Winnipeg, Selkirk, Marquette, and Provencher, all of whom were Conservatives. The provincial government also signed the memorial. Finally, the federal member for Winnipeg, Hugh John Macdonald, wrote directly to the Minister of Public Works on the matter. "The people of Winnipeg are red hot on this subject," he stated, "and I should be obliged to you if by prompt action you would show that the government is anxious to meet their wishes as far as the public interest will permit."[15]

This impressive display of support for the St. Andrew's project, like others before it, failed to convince the federal authorities. The chief objections were the cost—variously estimated at between $400,000 and $1,000,000—and the fact that the work was considered to be of a local nature. Ottawa argued that the territory that would benefit from the project was of a very limited area, "Winnipeg being the one locality which would derive the greatest, if not all the advantages which would result."[16]

Winnipeg's businessmen responded to both arguments by charging that the government was sacrificing the interests of western Canada to those of the east. It was argued that "since there is no instance where improvement could produce better results for the money spent, or results more needed" the only conclusion was that since "they are sure of a servile support from this constituency they can direct their expenditures not so much according to where it is needed for the benefit of the country as according to where it is needed to corrupt the electorate. Citizens, and the Board of Trade especially, have seen to it that at least the Government cannot plead ignorance of the need and value of the improvements." The fact that the government could ignore a "province which, unlike every other province, is deprived of Crown property as a source of revenue, which is further tolled by heavy freight rates and a robbing tariff" in a way that would not be attempted with "some unimportant district in Quebec," made the city especially angry.[17] Predictably, when Hugh John Macdonald resigned his seat in the House of Commons in May 1893, a Liberal was elected in his place in a by-election the following November.

The indignation and frustration of Winnipeg's businessmen was compounded when they learned of a dubious expenditure of over $500,-000 in the constituency of the Minister of Railways and Canals, J. G. Haggart. Apparently a canal had been constructed in his constituency connecting the Rideau Canal to Haggart's home town of Perth, Ontario, and this "ditch" had earned a grand total of $135 in revenue in 1893. The crowning irritation, however, was the reputed statement of Haggart that the rationale behind the work was that he had become "disgusted at the amount of public money expended all over Canada and thought his constituents ought to get a slice also."[18]

As convinced as they were of the righteousness of their cause, City Council in January 1894 opened a serious breach in their wall of arguments. Up to that point they had insisted that, since the federal government had undisputed authority over all rivers, it was their responsibility to improve them, "especially, as in this case, when the work would be a benefit to the whole country." But Winnipeg's governing commercial elite were so taken up with the need for growth that they ignored their own reasoning. City Council, acting upon a suggestion made by the Board of Trade, requested power from the provincial legislature "to grant a bonus of $100,000 to the Federal Government towards the cost of the desired improvements on the Red River."[19] When this proposal was being discussed one of the influential members of Council and the Board of Trade, Alderman G. F. Carruthers, urged that "time not be lost by submitting the question to a vote" of the electors of the city. City Council, after some argument, decided the matter had to be submitted but agreed they would ask for power "to submit the bylaw to the people for their assent, . . . such bylaw to be considered as having received such assent when at most 20% of all resident electors who are entitled to vote have actually voted on said bylaw and at most 3/5 of those so voting have voted in favour of the bylaw."[20]

The dubious nature of this "democratic" procedure did not receive the near unanimous support in the provincial legislature that it had received in Council. It was opposed by members on at least three grounds. The first was the fact that "as the work was one of importance to the whole province it should be undertaken wholly by the Dominion Government. If the city were given the power [asked for] it would afford the Government a loop hole to get out of its obligation." The proposed amendments to the Municipal Act were also opposed on the opposite ground:

> The advantages to be derived from the works would not be at all commensurate with the cost. For instance, the lumber on the shores of the lake have proved to be no better, in any case, than a poor third class quality. The slight reduction that river communication would make would not cause any more of this article to be sold. [The member] thought that fuel was as cheaply sold in Winnipeg as it would be when boats could come up to Winnipeg. Against rail rates there would have to be placed the extra water haul, the lock tolls and the extra cost of unloading from boats over that of unloading from cars. He did not think ... industry would be increased by the change. The memorial placed on the tables of members of the house said shipping had quadrupled, while the rates were only one-fourth what they were before the river was dredged. As a matter of his own experience he could say that shipping was not so great as ten years ago. He believed the power to grant a bonus should not be given to the city.[21]

Finally, one member was most concerned with "allowing a very fractional quantity to represent a large number of landowners."

Despite these objections, the legislature passed the amendments requested by the city in March, the majority of the members apparently agreeing with the argument that "since a large number of prominent citizens had requested the [legislature] to let the city vote on the matter, that desire should be granted." It can be noted, however, that the provincial government changed the legislation so that 40 per cent of the voters had to turn out and three-quarters of these had to consent to the measure.[22]

Shortly after City Council received the authority to submit the bonus bylaw to the electors, developments in Ottawa caused the aldermen to discard the plan. In the House of Commons the Liberal member for Winnipeg, Joseph Martin, had attacked the Conservative government on the grounds that it was neglecting Manitoba in the matter of public works and he had cited the St. Andrew's Rapids project as an example.[23] Mr. Ouimet, the Minister of Public Works, in reply stated that the works would cost a million dollars and he did not think it reasonable for him to recommend the expenditure of such a sum, even with a $100,000 bonus from the city of Winnipeg. Furthermore, "he did not think the people of Selkirk wanted the work anyway."[24] When Martin objected on the grounds that he was sure they were in favour of the undertaking, he was informed by A. W. Ross, the member representing the town of Selkirk, that:

> The majority of my people are against the improvement of St. Andrew's Rapids; and with regard to the rest of the [surrounding] country, some are against and some are for the project. . . . I have run three elections in this country and the question has never been discussed once on the platform. The improvement of St. Andrew's Rapids was never a question at issue. It never once came out at a single meeting. I know there is considerable feeling in Winnipeg, but so far as [the federal riding of] Lisgar is concerned, there is very little feeling whatever on the subject.[25]

Ross's statement was only partially true. There was a strong feeling in Selkirk—against any improvements. A memorial was later sent to the Dominion government from that town protesting against the expenditure of any public money on the St. Andrew's Rapids on the gounds "that Winnipeg alone and not the province generally would reap an advantage, and that at the expense of [this] community."[26] In other words, Selkirk itself desired to remain as the "head of the inland navigation system of the North West." Having lost the main line of the Canadian Pacific to Winnipeg, Selkirk was not prepared to come out second best again. Conversely, Winnipeg's businessmen were aware of Selkirk's advantageous position *vis à vis* water transportation and undoubtedly part of their efforts to make Winnipeg the port of the Northwest were inspired by this knowledge.

The final blow to Winnipeg's case came at a public meeting in September 1895. Both Prime Minister Bowell and Minister of Interior Daly were present. In the course of the evening it was pointed out by a Winnipeg spokesman that "if the government gave half a million dollars toward the work" the city itself would construct the dam and locks. This was a far cry from the city's earlier position that the Dominion government should bear the whole, or at least the vast proportion of the cost of the works, and the change was not lost on the ministers. In the major speech of the evening the prime minister suggested that if the works were so important and the benefits to be derived so great the city, or a private company, should undertake the work themselves, with no assistance from the federal authorities. On the other hand, if the works would not be beneficial enough to warrant independent action, the city of Winnipeg would just have to wait until his government had studied the matter further. [27]

Here the matter stood until after the federal election of 1896, which resulted in the election of a Liberal government. Despite the change of government and the election of a Liberal member for Winnipeg in a by-election in 1897, negotiations with Ottawa had not met with any success by the end of 1899.[28] Considering their many setbacks, the determination shown on the part of Winnipeg City Council and the Board of Trade is noteworthy, for rather than being discouraged they continued to send the usual heavy barrage of memorials and delegations to the federal authorities. Early in 1900, an election year, their efforts finally paid off when the Liberal government made a firm commitment to undertake the construction of locks at St. Andrew's.[29] Following the election of June the government, returned with an increased majority, conceived a number of excuses for delay. But Winnipeg's businessmen refused to relent in their efforts and they continually and vigorously protested the delays and lack of funds set aside for the project.[30] Finally, in July 1910, at a ceremony presided over by Prime Minister Laurier, the St. Andrew's locks were opened for business. Winnipeg had achieved her goal; the locks had been built by the federal government as a public work and it was now up to Winnipeg's commercial community to prove that the project was all they had made it out to be.

Even before the locks at St. Andrew's had been completed the *Manitoba Free Press* had urged City Council to "devote immediate attention to the securing of the full advantage that should accrue to the city as a result of the practicable waterway to Lake Winnipeg and the territory adjacent to the shores of the Lake."[31] The immediate problem was one of securing a proper landing place for river and lake craft at Winnipeg. It was not until April 1911, however, that Council took its first halting steps towards solving this problem. A special committee was appointed "to take up and report in conjunction with representatives of the Board of Trade on the subject of wharfage and dockage."[32] By this time, however, the problem had already become serious. In a letter to the Board of Trade a coal and wood dealer complained that he had brought a barge load of lumber from the lake but due to a lack of dockage facilities he had been unable to unload his cargo. In desperation, he was finally forced to take the cargo back to Selkirk where it was loaded on railway cars and sent back to the city.[33] It was not until July 1912 that the city set up a harbour commission and appointed three unpaid commissioners to oversee the development of Winnipeg harbour. But the commission achieved little and confined its efforts to appealing to Ottawa for "necessary funds."[34]

The developments necessary to ensure full commercial use of the Red River went beyond wharfage and dockage facilities. In a detailed memorandum submitted to the Board of Trade in November 1911, the Lake Winnipeg Shipping Company outlined what it felt were the necessary improvements. It complained of a lack of any published chart or survey of the river for the guidance of masters of craft; a complete absence of the necessary range lights, targets, and other aids to navigation required to mark the river's channel; absence of lights at the docks themselves; insufficient crib work above and below the docks; and a host of other problems. The company was particularly perturbed about the lack of planning:

> Some $2,000,000 have been spent upon the construction of St. Andrew's Locks, and a further sum upon blasting and dredging the Red River and its approaches, with a view to improving navigation, but the whole of this expenditure is practically useless to shippers owing to several important defects and omissions and to the lack of any well defined plan for finishing the work. . . . Most of the defects which at present make the Locks useless to the Port of Winnipeg could and should have been attended to before completing the Locks.
>
> Until the Red River is made safe for navigation and insurance rates have thereby been reduced, it is useless to expect that anyone will go into business of building large craft as this Company has done to develop trade in the natural resources of the country north of Winnipeg. . . .[35]

In view of all these difficulties it is surprising that the completion of the locks added to the use of the river. The tonnage of commodities passing through the locks in 1910 was recorded at 8,238 tons and for two years this increased significantly; in 1911 it rose to 47,135 tons, while in 1912 it stood at 95,549 tons. By 1913, however, this had dropped to 81,295 tons and by 1914 to the low level of 42,013 tons.[36] For an investment of well over two million dollars and almost forty years of effort this hardly seems a reasonable return.

A further reason for the failure of any sustained trade to develop was that by 1910 Canada's transportation needs were more than being filled by the railroads. In the days of the Canadian Pacific monopoly there was perhaps justification for the idea of developing an inland navigation system that would have connected Winnipeg with Edmonton and the towns, cities, and natural resources in between. But with the advent of two new transcontinental railway systems after 1900, the Grand Trunk Pacific and the Canadian Northern, the idea behind river navigation simply lost its validity. By 1914 Winnipeg had been assured competitive rates, and if anything, western Canada had an excess of transportation facilities. Under these circumstances an inland navigation system that was, at best, inefficient had little chance of survival. When ignored, as it was by the Winnipeg business community, it was doomed. Winnipeg by 1914 had become a railway city and its rivers, the sole natural adornment of the prairie city, were left in slattern neglect. The earlier enthusiasm for a great inland navigation system was completely lost by 1914.

Despite this failure of water transport to develop into a thriving and sustained venture, it is significant that Winnipeg's efforts were not considered a poor investment. Most of the arguments advanced for improving the Red River were based on the conviction that major economic advantages would be achieved. Though rarely mentioned, another important consideration was at the root of all Winnipeg's efforts in this area. This was the fear that Selkirk would challenge Winnipeg's position as the commercial centre of Manitoba and the Northwest. Until the obstruction at St. Andrew's was removed Selkirk was the head of the inland navigation system. But with the construction of navigation facilities at St. Andrew's in 1910, Winnipeg removed any possibility of Selkirk benefiting from water transport at its expense. Secure in this knowledge, Winnipeg was able to ignore the river and allow the once bustling waterfront to become the forgotten backyard of a too-busy city.

6 / The Search for Cheap Power: Private Enterprise, Monopoly, and Municipal Ownership

In 1912 Winnipeg boasted that it led all other Canadian municipalities in the ownership of public utilities. As evidence for this contention, it was pointed out that Winnipeg owned the waterworks system, hydroelectric system, stone quarries, gravel pits, and asphalting plant. The only two public services not under the control of the civic authorities were gas and street railways.[1] Despite this impressive record, Winnipeg's many ventures into "municipal socialism" had not come about because of any firm belief in the principle of municipal ownership. The commercial elite's interest in public ownership had a pragmatic cast; its rationale was economic rather than social. In the case of the city's hydroelectric system, for example, the decision to embark on this experiment in municipal socialism had come about only after all attempts to persuade private capital to undertake hydro power development had failed, and after the sole private supplier of power in the city—the Winnipeg Electric Railway Company—had refused to sell its power at reasonable rates. Convinced that this lack of cheap power was hindering the city's commercial development, Winnipeg's business leaders reluctantly established a public power utility. The story of Winnipeg's search for cheap power thus involves not only an account of the formation of Winnipeg Hydro, but also a discussion of the role private enterprise, and especially the WERC, played in the decision to establish a public system.

During the feverish speculation of the boom of 1882 city boosters prophesied a great future for the prairie capital. Many predicted that Winnipeg would have a population approaching half a million by 1900. But with the sudden collapse of the boom estimates of the future were considerably less optimistic as the city's commercial group came to realize that "population cannot grow on nothing."[2] Assured of adequate rail connections with the east and south, and hopeful about the St. Andrew's Rapids development, Winnipeggers were confident that the city would become the leading commercial centre of the entire Northwest. Great benefits were also expected from the fact that Winnipeg was the seat of the provincial government and university.[3] But a critical component in the city's growth was always held to be the development of a vigorous manufacturing industry.

For such enterprises to develop Winnipeg's business leaders felt there were two prerequisites: a market, and an abundance of cheap motive power. As regards the first, it was frequently observed "that there is no country in the world today which offers a better market for manufacturing than the country tributary to Winnipeg."[4] The city's lack of cheap power, however, presented a formidable problem. In the early 1880s power was supplied by steam plants. At this time Winnipeg drew its fuel supply from the Pennsylvania coalfields. After the coal was delivered at Lake Erie ports it had to be transported to Port Arthur by ship, and then hauled over four hundred miles by rail. The resulting high costs meant that Winnipeg looked helplessly on when would-be manufacturers came to the city, looked over the situation, and promptly left. According to City Council and the Board of Trade, all had the same reason: given the exorbitant power costs it was much more feasible to manufacture in the east and ship west, even while paying high freight rates.

In an effort to overcome this lack of cheap power Winnipeg turned its attention to the latent hydro power of the rivers that flowed through the city. One of the first schemes discussed was a plant to build an aqueduct from a point on the Assiniboine River west of Winnipeg through the city to Point Douglas, and utilize the fall thus obtained for the purpose of supplying power. But it was not until 1887 that such speculation was turned into a pragmatic plan when H. N. Ruttan, the city engineer, presented to City Council the first of many reports dealing with the possibilities of harnessing the water-power of the Assiniboine River.

Besides detailing the technical aspects of the scheme, Ruttan's widely publicized report set out the many advantages that would accrue to the city as a result of the development of the water-power of the Assiniboine River. He stated that the steam power used in Winnipeg at that time was equal to only 1,000 h.p. and cost 35 cents per h.p. per day. "The proposed water-power would be equal to about 10,000 h.p. and could be readily let at 10 cents per day." The expenditure in building mills and other manufacturing complexes to use the 10,000 h.p. would "probably be $5,000,000. The cost of private dwellings and the increase in the value of real estate in the vicinity would be at least as much, making a direct increase in assessable property of $10,000,000— this is not taking into account the indirect benefits to trade by the increase of population and manufactured articles and consumption of raw materials."[5]

Ruttan's preliminary report was well received by Winnipeggers. The Board of Trade was particularly impressed and sent a delegation to City Council in February 1888 urging that preliminary surveys be carried out at once.[6] City Council promptly agreed to the request and voted $2,000 to the city engineer to carry out the required work. The following July Ruttan presented a detailed report that confirmed his earlier study and urged immediate action.[7] With uncommon caution, Council decided to have an outsider make surveys as well and commissioned J. T. Fanning, a noted Minneapolis engineer, to study Ruttan's report and conduct his own examination. Fanning's report, presented in June 1889, was equally optimistic. His concluding statement was especially well received.

> The inducements for Winnipeg to make itself a manufacturing center seem very great, and an exceptionally favorable opportunity is presented through the development of its great water power. I can conceive of no way in which the city can with more certainty and profit enhance its growth, permanent revenues from taxation, and general prosperity than by promoting, directly or indirectly, this Assiniboine water-power project, until its ten thousand horse power shall be loaded with busy machinery.[8]

Since the Assiniboine was a navigable river, the first step required before any works could be constructed was to obtain permission from the federal government. This authority was quickly granted, although Ottawa did stipulate that Winnipeg could not proceed until it had submitted plans of the works that included provisions "for securing the free navigation of the river."

Once this necessary authority was given, Council moved quickly to have work started on the project and in July 1889 read Bylaw 452 for the first time. This bylaw was to raise $450,000 by debentures for the construction of the proposed water-power development as a public work. But the bylaw was never to pass second reading; the press, the Board of Trade, and even many of the aldermen raised loud objections to the city getting directly involved in such a project. The major objection to the city constructing the hydro-power dam and navigation facilities was "first and foremost the general principle that civic corporation should not engage in enterprises that should properly be controlled by private parties."[9] In any case, "the civic authorities could not be depended upon to carry out the enterprise with thorough business efficiency and economy and afterwards administer it in the best interests of the public."[10] Objections were also raised by the business community on the grounds that "the financial obligation that would be imposed upon the City is greater than it can bear."[11] The Board of Trade, for example, felt it "would be injurious on the part of the city at the present time to incur the liability necessary to complete the works in view of the already large indebtedness of the city."[12] It was one thing for City Council to give financial assistance for such things as railway development or to a Vacant Lands Committee; it was quite another to step into an area completely and take over from private enterprise.

The opposition of many influential businessmen to the city building and operating the works prompted City Council to enter into negotiations with private companies. Between 1889 and 1900 numerous groups of capitalists were approached, but all refused to undertake the works.[13] The major stumbling block was the federal stipulation that provision had to be made for navigation facilities. All the private companies consulted objected to this clause on the grounds that it would so increase the cost of the project as to make the whole scheme economically impractical. In response to this frequent objection City Council made a concerted effort to have the clause removed, but their memorials, petitions, and delegations were not enough to have the federal government change its ruling.[14]

The failure of all efforts to have a private company undertake water-power development in no way reduced the attractiveness of cheap motive power, and it is thus difficult to explain the continued reluctance of City Council to construct the works as a municipal project. Their own city engineer had shown it would mean a substantial saving, and could even produce a profit by the sale of surplus power. Perhaps even more important were the economic returns the city would reap if it became a manufacturing centre: cheaper prices for manufactured goods, increased employment opportunities, real estate sales as a result of population growth, and so on. Besides these convincing and frequently voiced arguments there was the fact that by 1900 the idea of public ownership had been accepted for Winnipeg's waterworks, stone quarries, gravel pits, and asphalting plant. It had often been stated, as well, that Council would not hesitate to build the works itself if no agreement could be reached with a private company.[15]

In spite of all these potential advantages and precedents, City Council continually refused to advance in the matter of public ownership. The *Winnipeg Telegram* summed up the reluctance of the city's elite to get into the power business in an editorial on 15 December 1898:

Too many schemes of municipal socialism on Council at one time will not only add enormously to the work of the Aldermen but is bound to throw the affairs of the city into such a muddle that the reputation of the most conscientious of Aldermen is likely to be destroyed. There is little doubt that the internal economy of civic administration will have to be materially readjusted in order to enable the city to successfully manage the semi-commercial enterprises which, it is evident, public sentiment is in favor of the city undertaking. To crowd these enterprises upon the city before the city has not only not effected this reorganization, but has not even considered how the reorganization may best be effected, is simply to invite failure in respect of all the enterprises concerned. .... The city has not even decided how it will manage the new waterworks system. Yet, with this unsolved and serious problem on its hand, some people are ill-advised enough to urge the citizens to throw upon the Council the additional responsibility of organizing and operating a hydro-electric power plant. It is to be remembered the results achieved by the city will have to bear comparison with the results of competing private concerns, which have, by long experience, brought their system of management to the maximum of efficiency and the minimum of cost; perhaps the most material factors in cheap production.

These, and similar objections, were to keep Winnipeg from considering public ownership for several more years until, by 1906, it was realized that all the power resources in the city were controlled by one huge firm. It was this monopoly situation that served as the catalyst for a publicly owned hydro power system.

With the rapid growth of Winnipeg that commenced after 1896 the supply of power became more and more inadequate and the cost exorbitant. By 1900 the situation had become so intolerable that it became a civic election issue and the Council for that year was returned only after it pledged to bring new life into the old scheme to develop the power of the Assiniboine River. The city's efforts to have the navigation clause removed, however, proved no more successful than in previous years and the scheme was soon dropped.

While the city thus continued to focus its attention on the potential of the Assiniboine River, private companies were forging ahead in different areas. In 1901 the Ogilvie Milling Company and the Winnipeg Electric Railway Company organized the Manitoba Water Power Electric Company to develop hydroelectric power on the Pinawa Channel of the Winnipeg River.[16] This venture into an entirely new area—one with far greater potential than the Assiniboine—caught the imagination of many businessmen. A great rush developed to secure suitable sites in the region, for there was no navigation clause problem here, and it was correctly reasoned that a successful developer could realize substantial profits by selling power to the city and to prospective manufacturers. City Council was content to let private enterprise take its course and made it known that it would accept competitive offers for the supply of power from companies prepared to develop the potential of the Winnipeg River.

While City Council's calm attitude toward the water-power question was the result of two factors. First of all, regulations imposed by the federal Minister of the Interior seemed to assure favourable rates being charged for Winnipeg River power. Shortly after the Manitoba Water Power Electric Company had announced its intention to develop water-power on the river the government moved to group the lands it held in such a way that each purchaser would have only one water-power site. The lands leased would also be subject to the condition that within a certain period the water-power had to be developed or the land would revert to the crown.[17] Winnipeg was in a favourable position by virtue of the fact that it would be the major customer of any company at the outset. Other than such large concerns as the Ogilvie Milling Company and the Winnipeg Electric Railway—both of which consumed large quantities of power in their own operations—there were few enterprises in the city that could use enough power to enable the developer of a water-power project to realize a profit on his investment. Indeed, without the city's promise to use such power and also to help bring manufacturers to Winnipeg in the future, no developer seemed willing to proceed.

By March 1903 City Council had received no less than seven offers from companies to supply it with power. In order to deal with the numerous proposals a special committee was appointed to consider the various schemes and report back to Council. Their report, presented in September, was not optimistic.[18] All the proposals had been rejected for various reasons. In nearly every case the company was not prepared to develop enough power, or it insisted on charging what the city felt were prohibitive rates. It must be emphasized that in all cases Council was not merely concerned with the price the city would be charged. They still believed that the chief value of securing cheap motive power was that it would attract manufacturers to Winnipeg. But while the private companies were willing to charge the city what the latter considered a reasonable price, they were not so generous when it came to other prospective customers and all refused to be bound to a strict rate schedule.[19]

These endless and frustrating attempts to reach a satisfactory agreement with private companies might, by themselves, have eventually caused City Council to undertake water-power development as a public work. Between 1900 and 1905 the local press and the Board of Trade continued to point to the many advantages to be derived from water-power development. The local press even carried reports that several large manufacturing firms had virtually promised to set up plants in Winnipeg if adequate power and low power rates were available.[20] Considering the growth ethic of the governing commercial group it was not likely that such arguments and hopes would be long ignored.

All such arguments notwithstanding, a majority of Winnipeg's business leaders consistently opposed the development of a publicly owned and operated power project, until they were finally forced to act. Paradoxically, it was the very success of a private company that ultimately persuaded them of the necessity of a municipal scheme.

The private firm that brought about the change was the Winnipeg Electric Railway Company. Incorporated in 1892 with a capital of $100,000, the WERC had grown quickly. At first it had been involved only in operating a street railway system, but by 1905 its interests were much more diverse. It had acquired control of the single other street railway company in Winnipeg, as well as two other firms that were involved in selling power for lighting and other uses. And by 1904, when it acquired complete control of still another power company that had been established to develop a water-power source on the Winnipeg River, the WERC found itself with a virtual monopoly in the areas of power supply, lighting, and street railways. Its capital stock in 1906 amounted to over $4 million and it was backed by the powerful team of Ross, Mackenzie, and Mann. The company had first paid dividends of $15,000 in 1900, but by 1904 these had risen to over $120,000. In fact, the various enterprises of the WERC were by this time proving so successful that it planned to develop still another water-power source on the Winnipeg River to supply Winnipeg's growing power demands.[21]

The problem created by this success story as far as City Council was concerned was that the WERC's monopoly position meant that power rates remained very high. Without competition the company seemed little inclined to lower its rates in any sort of relation to its growing profits.[22] In the final analysis it was this awesome power of the WERC that finally led to a publicly owned water-power development.[23]

City Council took the first step toward a municipality owned power project in January 1905 when it appointed a committee to confer with the city engineer and "report on the best method of procuring power for manufacturing purposes. . . ."[24] The real impetus for quick action, however, came not from Council but from the business community. At a general meeting of the Board of Trade in May 1905 the following resolution was passed:

> Resolved, that this Board appoint a committee of three to co-operate with representatives of other business organizations in Winnipeg in petitioning the City Council to procure and bring, or cause to be brought in, as a municipal enterprise, an electric power for manufacturing, as well as for municipal and other purposes.[25]

Subsequently a meeting of the Winnipeg Builders' Exchange, the Employers' Association, the Printers' Board of Trade, and the Trades and Labor Council took place on 26 May 1905. After hearing from two private companies who offered to supply power but would not divulge their rates, the meeting turned to a general discussion of municipal ownership. It was pointed out by the advocates of private enterprise that a private company could furnish rates at the lowest possible figure. But, while these arguments would have been accepted at face value five or six years before, they were now open to vigorous opposition. It was argued that the WERC, even though it enjoyed a monopoly in its streetcar system and lighting and power plants, had never reduced its rates. "In fact, its rates were extortionate. The only relief is municipal ownership."

It was further argued that if a company could carry out such an enterprise at a profit, a municipality should be able to do so. The benefits from such a scheme would be great.

> In favoring municipal ownership of power, speakers pointed out that Medicine Hat, Rat Portage and many other towns offered greater facilities than Winnipeg, and manufacturers on this account have often passed over Winnipeg and helped to develop other places. It was essential to the progress and stability of the city that inducements be offered to manufacturers. If power at a reasonable basis of taxation be provided, the city would develop at a great rate, and would rapidly take its due position among the cities of the continent.

Not unexpectedly some businessmen urged caution, pointing out that such a program would add considerably to the municipal debt. But the majority at the meeting dismissed this argument:

> The credit of the city, so far from being lessened by previous undertakings such as waterworks had been strengthened and that the resulting advantage of the incoming of manufacturers and the consequent development of the city would more than counterbalance the interest on the debt. The public was strongly in favor of it and too much time had been lost already. The question should be gone into thoroughly, exhaustively and immediately. . . .

The meeting closed with widespread support for a resolution urging City Council to take immediate steps "to secure cheap power for manufacturing and other purposes."[26]

In June over sixty delegates representing various organizations in the city and calling themselves the "Power Committee" met with Council and presented their resolution. Council responded by granting $1,000 to the power committee to enable it to make inspections and surveys of the power sites on the Winnipeg River. It was also allowed to engage the services of Cecil Smith, consulting engineer for Ontario's public power development. In the months that followed the power committee was able to acquire an "excellent" site at Point du Bois, fifty-five miles northeast of Winnipeg.[27]

The securing of a site, however, did not solve all the city's problems. Further advance was hindered by the stipulation—inserted in the city's charter by the Roblin government on request of the WERC— that the city must buy out existing power plants (i.e., the WERC plant) before it could sell any power.[28] To circumvent this clause a "Power Association" was formed and included among its directors most of Winnipeg's leading businessmen—J. H. Ashdown, John Arbuthnot, A. Macdonald, D. W. Bole, R. J. Riley, E. L. Drewry, and others— "names that will be freely accepted by the public as a guarantee of the method employed to overcome the limitations of the city's power in regard to power development." This method called for the association to act, for the city, as the *de jure* company developing the water power at Point du Bois. The city and the association entered into an agreement whereby the city would guarantee the company against loss while "the company agreed, when called upon by the city, to assign all their rights and interests to the city when it is enabled by legislation to assume them."[29]

This legislation was not long in coming. Apparently impressed by the drastic steps to which the city was prepared to go to overcome the restrictions of provincial legislation, and aware of the political liability of continued attacks on it by the elite of Winnipeg, the Roblin government gave the city the right to develop and sell power in 1906. It did, however, still require Winnipeg to buy out the WERC's plant in the city before the power developed could be sold for lighting purposes. The city was, of course, unhappy with this action but displayed some optimism since the new legislation at least gave them the right to develop power for manufacturing purposes. Moreover, many were confident that the government's stand would be changed so as to give the city the power to sell electricity for any purpose whatever. In any case, the legislation removed the necessity of acting through the Power Association and this body was quickly disbanded.

Having overcome two of the major practical difficulties that lay in the way of a successful public power scheme, the city's power committee received an unexpected moral boost in 1906. Adam Beck, in a widely publicized address to the Toronto Board of Trade, spoke of the great opportunities inherent in hydroelectric development not only in Ontario but in the whole country. He paid particular attention to Winnipeg and the prosperity it would enjoy following "the harnessing of the powers at her door." Beck's address carried considerable weight among the Winnipeg business community since he was not only an Ontario cabinet minister but president of the Municipal Power Commission appointed by the Whitney government. This commission had just reported that it favoured government-developed electric energy at Niagara Falls. Beck was particularly critical of the private companies that had developed power up to that time and charged that "the price you are asked to pay is not what power costs, but what those companies can get from you."[30]

Shortly after this address the power committee of City Council received a final report from H. N. Ruttan, city engineer, and Cecil Smith, consulting engineer. The report included plans, estimates, and explanations of a very detailed nature. Although the initial development would produce only 17,000 h.p., it was stressed that capacity could be increased to 60,000 h.p. without any major additional construction. The report further stressed that the engineers considered the power site at Point du Bois to be one of the most desirable in Canada, and certainly the best on the Winnipeg River.[31]

When the report was presented to Council the majority of aldermen were not only pleased but were in favour of immediate action being taken. They quickly drew up and passed a power bylaw and scheduled its submission to the electors on June 28. By the terms of the bylaw Council was authorized to create a debt of $3,250,000 for "the purpose of securing cheaper power for the city."[32]

Following the announcement of plans to submit the bylaw to the electors there was a flurry of activity among council members, the Board of Trade, and the various business and labour organizations in the city. They were all afraid that the opponents of the scheme would somehow be able to defeat the measure at the polls. One committee of "citizens of Winnipeg" wrote Council expressing their fears and urged the carrying out of various measures to ensure the passage of the bylaw: "a series of public meetings [should] be called in various parts of the city . . ., effective and attractive advertising [should] be made use of to the fullest extent, and a strong prospectus [should] be issued to every voter, setting forth in exhaustive detail the merits of the bylaw and of rival projects."[33] This advice was followed almost to the letter. During the three weeks preceding the vote meetings were held in favour of the project nearly every night. Mayor Sharpe, Alderman Cockburn, and City Engineer Ruttan were especially busy in this area and received encouragement from two of the Winnipeg daily newspapers; the Conservative *Winnipeg Telegram* alone opposed the bylaw. Moreover, the labour newspaper, *The Voice*, vigorously urged its readers to vote for the bylaw.[34] Both the Canadian Club and the Board of Trade came out strongly in its favour. The latter even felt it necessary to call a special meeting to endorse the measure; the vote recorded was 43-18 in favour of the power project.

But the major effort taken to secure passage of the bylaw was the power prospectus issued by Council on June 11 and distributed to every elector in the city. It stressed the importance of cheap power as an inducement to manufacturing activity and listed several areas where the power could be used: "flour milling, wood pulp manufacture, woollen manufacture, commercial and city lighting, general manufacturing, and heating." The prospectus also stressed that a public project was the only means whereby the city could be assured of cheap power:

> The only means by which power can be supplied at bare cost is by the construction of the necessary works by the people as a whole—and not by a private company—which could not be expected to sell at cost.
>
> The people as a whole will benefit by the increase in values and the greatly enlarged field for business and employment.
>
> The people as a whole can borrow money on more favorable terms than a company, can construct the works as cheaply, and do not require a surplus revenue to pay dividends.

All proposals received by the city from Companies require a contract or guarantee from the city to furnish sufficient revenue to enable them to float bonds.

Why should the city not use its credit for its own benefit?[35]

The prospectus emphasized that the rates of the WERC were at present $35 per h.p., while the city's estimated price would be less than half that amount. Considerable space was devoted to arguments of this nature since this was one of the major points being raised by the opponents of a public system. Moreover, early in June, when the WERC plant on the Winnipeg River was completed, the company had announced a cut of one-third to one-half the rate they had previously charged. They also promised further reductions.[36] To meet this situation the prospectus included a detailed rate schedule (Table 4). The advocates of a public system naturally used these figures relentlessly in their public meetings and in newspaper reports.

Table 4 / "Power Prospectus" Rate Schedule, 1906

| | Winnipeg Electric Railway Company rates | | | | City proposed rates | |
| | Old | | New | | | |
Service	Per kw hour (cents)	Per hp year (dollars)	Per kw hour (cents)	Per hp year (dollars)	Per kw hour (cents)	Per hp year (dollars)
Elevators	20	1,307	6	390	2	130
Motors	12.5	817	–	–	–	–
" to 50 hp	–	–	6	390	1.5	98
" to 100 hp	–	–	4	260	1	65.33
" over 100 hp	–	–	3	195	.75	49
" 500 to 1,000 hp	–	–	–	–	.5	32.66
" over 1,000 hp	–	–	–	–	.25	16.33
Lighting	20	1,307	10	650	3	195

Source: "Power Prospectus," p. 5.

Another major criticism that had to be met was based on the argument that the governmental structure of the city was so inefficient that any public venture was bound either to fail completely or produce rates much higher than those presently offered by the WERC.[37] Of all the criticisms levelled at the power scheme this was perhaps the most potent. It had, after all, been used successfully many times in the past. In 1906, however, it was met head on with the reply that the inefficient system of municipal government would soon end, since a bylaw to provide for a Board of Control was to be submitted on the very same day. It is most significant that organizations like the Board of Trade were strong supporters of the Board of Control system and stressed that the power project could only be successful if coupled with this "improved form of Municipal Government."[38] The business community had arrived at the decision to support a public scheme only when they were positive that private enterprise could not supply the cheap power the city needed. Once having decided on the public project they meant to overcome the dangers they felt were inherent in such projects. This they did by instituting the Board of Control and by stressing the need for the electorate to elect only "business-minded" candidates to the new council.

The most notable element of the municipal power campaign, however, was not the arguments themselves but the high and sustained pitch with which they were put forward. Although it was argued then, and since, that there was a concerted effort on the part of the opponents of the scheme to have the bylaw defeated, there is hardly any concrete evidence to support this assertion.[39] Quite naturally the WERC opposed the scheme, but the only significant support it received was from the *Winnipeg Telegram*, and even this was not very strong. Only one alderman on the Council in 1906 openly opposed the measure, while several former council members and mayors were strong supporters. The final story is told by the vote itself: 2,382 supported municipal power and only 382 were opposed.[40]

Perhaps the only explanation for the notion that there was significant opposition comes from the fact that in 1907 and 1908 considerable controversy did develop within the groups that formerly supported the measure.[41] These divisions resulted when the power project had to be postponed for over two years because of the city's poor financial condition. Those who supported the postponement were led by Mayor Ashdown and argued that they were not opposed to the scheme, but rather that the project had to wait until "suitable conditions" for its financing were arranged. The proponents of immediate construction, on the other hand, expressed fear that Ashdown's delay resulted from outside interference (that is, the WERC) and continually urged that the scheme move rapidly ahead. Ashdown was true to his word, however, for in January 1909 the contract for the power plant was let and Winnipeg's experiment in municipal power was under way. The plant was officially opened on October 16, 1911.[42]

The immediate success of the venture was analysed by the *Manitoba Free Press* in 1913:

Immediately prior to the establishment and operation of the plant, the rate for lighting in the city was nine cents per kilowatt. This has been reduced to three cents per kilowatt which in light and power is calculated to have saved the people of Winnipeg $6,000,000 in the first year of operation.

That it is the logical answer to the reason for the extraordinarily rapid growth of the city during the last two years, and the reason why the growth will continue at perhaps even a greater ratio, is shown by the number of industries which, through the work of the Industrial Bureau, have located in the city, cheap power being one of the principal inducements offered. In 1911, the year in which power was turned on, 41 new manufacturers established plants here, and the number is steadily growing. The annual value of the output of the factories of the city is now in excess of $40,000,000 and there are more than 20,000 people employed here.[43]

On the fiftieth anniversary of Winnipeg Hydro in 1961 this favourable impression of the public utility was unchanged.

The most noteworthy aspect of the municipal power project, other than its long-term success, was that Winnipeg's business community seemed to have accepted the principle of municipal ownership as a useful tool in the development of their city. They offered a lead in a public project that resulted in Winnipeg having the lowest power rates on the continent, a situation from which every citizen in the city derived some benefit. Thus at first glance the story of Winnipeg's power development appears to be a time of victory for the community as a whole, and a defeat for the principle of privatism in which the first duty of the businessman is the private search for wealth with no concern for others.

A closer look at the project, however, reveals that this division into victory and defeat is not a clearcut one. The decision to back a public scheme was made only after all other approaches had been exhausted and was not made solely on the merits of municipal ownership. Only after the civic and business leaders realized that a powerful monopoly existed in their midst, and that this monopoly threatened to keep all the profits to itself, did they move in another direction. Thus, paradoxically, it was the very success of private enterprise that led to municipal ownership. The profits and power of the WERC caused resentment and fear, and in an attempt to remedy this situation Winnipeg's business community looked to the power and financial backing of the civic corporation.

Perhaps the best indication that Winnipeg's business community did not measure the value of the municipal power project in public terms is provided by the following statement: "[Public] power is the force which has carried real estate values upwards in phenomenal bounds, and which has created many fortunes for the holders of property."[44] It was as if the city's elite were saying that it was wrong for the

WERC alone to make a fortune, but it was satisfactory if they, too, could share in the economic returns. Significantly, no mention was made of the fact that the project benefited all citizens, not just those who had large real estate holdings. It was beyond the capacity of Winnipeg's governing commercial elite to think of the city in terms of a public environment and care for all men, not just successful men. Their first duty remained the private search for wealth, and public ownership merely served in this one instance as the best means of achieving that goal. Public good was simply a dividend; it was not the operating principle.

7 / The Campaign for Immigrants and Industry

Despite efforts to secure adequate transportation facilities and cheap power, Winnipeg's civic leaders were convinced that continued progress was dependent primarily upon a large and growing population. A Winnipeg newspaper explained:

> Reduced to its ultimate analysis, the essential and paramount need of the West is—Population. This assured all other things shall be added in due season; with this withheld, permanent progress toward the realization of our manifest destiny is impossible. This fact has been asserted by every politician, and has been reiterated by every newspaper, for the past quarter of a century. It is an article of faith with every man possessed of the most elementary knowledge of the conditions and needs of the west. It permits of no argument. It is an axiomatic truth.[1]

Given this truth, another equally self-evident proposition followed—"to secure population there must be publicity." Publicity was necessary, it was asserted, because "of what avail is it that there are in Western Canada millions of acres of the finest land that lays open to the sunshine, awaiting only settlement and development to give its cultivators comfort and competence, unless the advantages they offer to the homeseeker are made known to the people their possession would benefit? Publicity is the secret of success. . . ."[2]

It is noteworthy that in stressing the need for population growth and publicity, Winnipeggers spoke of the West and not just the city itself. Since Winnipeg was thought of as the commercial centre of the entire Canadian Northwest, its growth and prosperity was directly related to "the settlement and advancement of the great territory of which it is the entrepôt." But besides expecting to profit through increased trading activities with the hinterland, there was another reason why Winnipeg's business leaders supported immigration propaganda that promoted the farm lands of Manitoba and the Northwest and not just the city itself. Many Winnipeg businessmen were speculators in the farm lands of the West. Significantly, the many leading Winnipeggers who had such real estate interests enjoyed so commanding a position in the community that they were able to convince a majority of citizens that the expenditure of civic funds for the purpose of attracting newcomers (who were, of course, prospective buyers of land) was a worthwhile project.[3]

The lead given by Winnipeg's elite was not accepted by everyone, however. Labour spokesmen were continuously and vehemently opposed to the expenditure of public funds for what they considered were private goals. Labour's objections stemmed from the simple matter of self-interest. Immigrants were looked upon merely as cheap labour and their recruitment as a plot by the "plutocracy" to reduce wages. The views of the Winnipeg Trades and Labor Council were explained by *The Voice*:

> [It] does not raise the slightest objection to the fullest welcome to suitable immigrants who come of their own accord; but it does most emphatically object to the taxation of labour in order to flood the labour market against the wage earner. . . . The glowing and highly colored statements and reports sent from this country give an entirely misleading, not to say mendacious, account of the prospects for immigrants, and mostly emanate from interested sources. The steamship and railway companies naturally desire passengers; the business classes hope to profit by the influx of people; the employers seek to intensify competition in the labour market, while the Government itself is not above suspicion, as it is entirely representative of those various interests. There is thus a gigantic conspiracy to promote and welcome the tide of immigration that has set in toward this country. . . .[4]

But labour had little power or influence in municipal, provincial, or federal politics in this era and their objections received no consideration in the various schemes brought forward by Winnipeg's leaders. In fact, the only significant stumbling block encountered by the governing commercial elite was the apathy of city electors. Notwithstanding this apathy, numerous costly promotional schemes were undertaken prior to 1914.

Prior to 1880 Winnipeg's civic and business leaders directed considerable effort and resources toward securing immigrants. Although the major landowner in Manitoba at this time was the Dominion government, Winnipeggers were not satisfied with its program for advertising and settling the West.[5] They were especially concerned about the government's choice of European immigration agents. The *Manitoba Free Press* explained:

> . . . since the Dominion owns all the lands that are open to settlement, it is plainly her duty to make such an appointment and bear

the expenses therewith. . . . Manitoba has a heavier claim upon the Federal Government in this respect than either of the other provinces, seeing that in this province alone she retains the administration of public lands. Up to the present time of all the immigration agents sent to Europe no one has had more than a theoretical knowledge of Manitoba. . . . Nothing more, surely, need be urged than to make a good demand upon Canada to select at least one resident of Manitoba to represent our case in Europe. . . .[6]

Despite such protestations, the results of the federal program for the West were meagre. In 1877, for example, the Winnipeg Immigration Agent reported only 1,505 arrivals in the city.[7] To say the least, Winnipeg's leaders were dissatisfied with such returns and their dissatisfaction went beyond mere editorial comment, for in 1877 they became directly involved in the search for immigrants. In February a resident of Winnipeg, Alexander Begg, approached City Council and requested financial aid for the publication of his work entitled *A Practical Handbook and Guide to Manitoba and the Northwest*. Council was so impressed with the pamphlet that they promptly recommended the purchase of ten thousand copies for public distribution. Following this initial subscription City Council acceded to several other requests for aid during the next few years. These included such items as the purchase of a special article on Winnipeg that appeared in the *Chicago Commercial Advertiser*, subscriptions to two thousand copies of Thomas Spence's *Prairie Lands of Canada*, and two hundred copies of *Ten Years in Winnipeg*, by Alexander Begg and Walter R. Nursey.

After this material was received it was distributed widely. Copies were mailed directly to persons who had requested such information,[8] and material was also sent "to each of the 768 Public Libraries in Great Britain and to each of the 251 Public Libraries and mechanics institutes in Eastern Canada."[9] A substantial amount of the advertising material was also given to the provincial government for distribution.

City Council took other measures to advertise Winnipeg and the Northwest prior to 1885. In cooperation with the provincial Department of Agriculture and Statistics they sent a display to the Ontario Provincial Exhibition in Kingston in 1882. In the same year they provided a lunch and a tour of the city for both an excursion of Ontario press agents and of railway conductors. Considerable effort and expense was also put forward for the visit of the British Association in 1884. A special souvenir pamphlet was written for the British scientists and each member was presented with a copy. Copies were also forwarded to England to be distributed there to members who could not make the trip.[10]

Despite these efforts, it was evident that after 1880 the city's hopes for the future lay not with their own exertions but with the settlement policies of the Canadian Pacific syndicate and the activities of the Dominion government. The CPR was especially active in its efforts to gain passenger traffic and exploit its extensive land grants. It lost little time in launching an advertising campaign in Great Britain and eastern Canada. Much to the satisfaction of Winnipeggers, Alexander Begg was appointed General Emigration Agent for the CPR, thus assuring that Winnipeg would receive favourable mention. Moreover, by the autumn of 1881, an attractive publication, *The Great Prairie Province of Manitoba and the Northwest Territories,* had been issued in England, setting forth in interesting form the advantages offered to settlers in the Canadian West. By 1884 folder maps and pamphlets prepared in the London office of the CPR had been published in English, German, French, Gaelic, Welsh, Swedish, Norwegian, Finnish, Danish, and Dutch, and were being distributed through thousands of agencies in Great Britain and over two hundred centres in northern Europe. And while the office staff answered the thousands of enquiries concerning Manitoba and the Northwest which the propaganda elicited, agents carried the good word to the countryside. Other techniques were also used to attract immigrants. The CPR offered free transportation and other facilities for examining the country to individual journalists, groups of farmers, and others. It also sent exhibition vans to travel the highways and country roads in Europe, eastern Canada, and in the Dakotas and Minnesota.[11]

Naturally the efforts of the CPR had an effect in Winnipeg and over the years city newspapers expressed their appreciation in the form of editorials.[12] But the overall result of the efforts of both the CPR and the Dominion government fell far short of Winnipeg's expectations. By 1885 the city had a population of only twenty thousand, a figure that hardly fulfilled the commercial elite's hope that Winnipeg would rapidly become the "Chicago of the North." Accordingly, in the years after 1885 civic authorities and business leaders took some drastic steps to promote Winnipeg's growth.

A major stumbling block in the campaign for immigrants involved the so-called "vacant lands question." This problem had originated with the entry of Manitoba into the Dominion of Canada in 1870. As a reward to the members of the Wolseley expedition the federal government had given to each soldier a free grant of 160 acres of land. Practically all this land was taken up along the Red River in the vicinity of Winnipeg for the simple reason that the rest of the western country was virtually unknown. But most of the soldiers eventually disposed of their land certificates and returned to eastern Canada. The purchasers of these certificates—usually speculators—had little success in disposing of their property, since new settlers could have all the land they wished by fulfilling the requirements of the Homestead Act of 1872.

An even more difficult situation arose from the attempts of the federal government to settle the Halfbreed Claims. In this case 1,400,000 acres of Manitoba land were set aside for the Métis. But with the mass exodus of these people to the Saskatchewan plains in the years after 1870 their right to the land—"script" as it was called—was bought up by speculators and applied to the land in the vicinity of Winnipeg, mainly in the parishes of St. Boniface, St. Norbert, and St. Vital. The result was that there was virtually no free land available in that area.[13]

To make matters still worse there were other reserves in the vicinity of Winnipeg: Hudson's Bay Company Reserves, Railway Reserves, land reserved for "hay privileges" and "staked claims."[14] The *Manitoba Free Press* found the overall result intolerable:

> The unwisdom upon the part of any government locking up tracts of the most fertile and attractive lands in the world is painfully apparent in Manitoba which may be said to be painfully reserved to death by Acts of Parliament. . . . It is really painful and exasperating to see the newly-arrived immigrant, with a large family and liberally supplied with all necessary implements of agriculture, in his struggle to obtain an eligible location by purchase, or otherwise. Pleased with the City of Winnipeg and astonished at its growth and business activity he gains a position where he can obtain a birds-eye view of it. . . . His eyes rest upon an illimitable carpet of glorious green. . . . He wonders and enquires and is told "the magnificient land, bursting with fertility and stretching in every direction is mostly reserved and you cannot be permitted to cultivate *that*." Despairing of obtaining a homestead within a reasonable walk from the city, he takes a team and drives over miles of vacant land until he is surely out of the region of reservations. . . . Having located his family and already commenced agricultural operations he takes the first opportunity of visiting the land office in Winnipeg where he is bluntly told he is on 1,400,000 acres of land reserved for halfbreeds.
> He makes another move. . . .[15]

This initial bypassing of lands surrounding Winnipeg caused still another problem. Prospective settlers coming to the province assumed that the "vacant lands were not settled because they were not desirable." In time it became almost impossible to persuade a settler to locate around Winnipeg.

The predicament the city found itself in was not helped by the two great immigration agencies of the country, the Dominion government and the CPR. The major potential source of immigrants in this period was eastern Canada, and since the national government could hardly encourage the movement of people from Ontario or the Maritime provinces to the prairies, this work devolved almost entirely on the Canadian Pacific. Although the company ultimately realized that it was bad policy to move settlers from one part of the country to another, it was restrained by no such feeling in these early years. The CPR's major goal in the 1880s and 1890s was to create settlements in the West which would provide traffic and the rudiments of a settled society around which increasing numbers of farmers might gather. In such circumstances where the settlers came from was not important. Winnipeg, of course, was anxious to secure these migrants. What concerned the city's leaders was that the CPR seemed determined to have these people by-pass Winnipeg in favour of points farther west, "thereby getting the greatest amount of fare from them in the first place, and making the haul of goods and whatever they have to ship out the longest possible."[16] This same tendency operated in connection with foreign immigrants. Moreover, while the federal government may not have encouraged easterners to move West, they did encourage overseas immigrants to do so. The problem here was that they, too, seemed anxious to have settlers by-pass Winnipeg and Manitoba. The reasons for such a policy were explained by the *Free Press*: the foreign immigrant's "presence will go far to settle the Indian question; and, besides, the lands [in the territories] are largely in their hands; while [in Manitoba] they have passed to others."[17]

The first step taken by civic and business leaders to overcome these difficulties was to urge action from the provincial government. They hoped that if the Province would carry out an extensive program of land drainage and road building, while at the same time setting up an "active and progressive" immigration bureau, the problem would be well on its way toward solution. The city even offered the provincial authorities, free of charge, the facilities of its immigration sheds to aid the program. When these initiatives failed, it was decided to take action at the municipal level.

The Board of Trade was especially active. Many board members owned vacant lands and at their request a committee was established to study the question in depth. This move was soon followed by the appointment of a similar committee by City Council to act in conjunction with the Board. By April 1887 the Joint Committee on Vacant Lands had finished its study. After a careful analysis of the entire matter the committee recommended that immediate steps be taken to issue

> ... in a concise form a statement of facts regarding our vacant lands which might ... take the form of a report presented by a Joint Committee of the City Council and the Board of Trade. ... This report issued by authority and coming from such a source would be relieved of the many disadvantages of an emigration publication. ... The special facts in connection with our lands could be set forth in terse language clearly showing that a settler would have a better market, a higher price and more ready sale for all

description of farm produce; that he could build cheaper, purchase his supplies at lower figures than within the same distance of any of the small towns or villages west or southwest of this point.[18]

It was not until February 1888, however, that substantial and practical steps were taken. Twelve thousand copies of a pamphlet showing the land available for sale were distributed in Ontario,[19] and "two good practical men, thoroughly acquainted with the City and its surrounding . . ." were appointed to act as immigration agents and sent to Ontario and Quebec. Other men were hired to take charge of the Vacant Lands Committee's office in Winnipeg, to supervise the city immigration shed, and to help immigrants on their arrival in Winnipeg. A special bonus system was also developed to encourage agents and settlers. For every family that located near Winnipeg the agent received $25; if a family arrived without the intervention of agents, it received a bonus of $40.

All of these activities, of course, cost money and City Council's original allocation of $3,000 was meant to cover only the first few months of operation. Attempts were made to gain financial support from the federal government, but the city's presentations failed to impress Ottawa. Council was therefore forced to raise the $15,000 needed for the activities of the Vacant Lands Committee by civic bylaw.

Considering that City Council was already spending large sums of public monies on the vacant lands program it is noteworthy that it took from April to November before the bylaw was actually submitted to the voters. To the great consternation of the Vacant Lands Committee the "Colonization Bylaw," as it came to be called, was defeated by a vote of 279 to 154. Apparently the defeat was a result of the activities of the Winnipeg Knights of Labor. The local branch of this organization, founded in 1884, had opposed the money bylaw on several grounds, but particularly because the funds for the committee had been spent before Council had had any legal authority to make such an appropriation. A more reasonable explanation for the bylaw's defeat, however, is that so few voters turned out. Three thousand were eligible to vote and undoubtedly the measure would have passed had even half this number voted, since the labour movement in Winnipeg was hardly powerful.[20] Many of their members could not even vote because of the fact that only those who owned property valued at $500 or more could cast a ballot on money bylaws. In short, the apathy of the majority of the populace, so often spoken of by the civic and business leaders, had curtailed their plans. After this defeat the city's elite were to take more care in their preparations of plans for submitting money bylaws.

Despite the fact that City Council had no legal authority to do so, they appropriated $12,000 for the purposes of the Vacant Lands Committee prior to the defeat of the bylaw in November. This sum enabled the city's immigration agents to do a good deal of work during the spring and summer of 1888. The two agents assigned to Ontario stated in their report to the joint committee that sixty-seven names of settlers had been recorded as having settled on the lands around Winnipeg. One of the agent's reports also detailed his method of operation in the total of forty-five cities, towns, and villages visited:

> The course adopted by me in each Town visited is to make myself known to some of the citizens who from their official position or occupation are likely to know of such farmers as may be talking of migrating with the view to interview the latter and place before them the facilities for settlement on land near Winnipeg. . . . Visits were planned on Market Days or occasions which may bring farmers together and thus have an opportunity of drawing attention to my work by conversation and distribution of advertising matter.

The reports also mentioned the reception the agents received and the numerous erroneous impressions they were able to correct concerning Manitoba lands. Both concluded with a note of optimism: "I am persuaded that, whatever may be the results of the efforts of this committee this season, the work done in Ontario will exert a beneficial effect for years to come."[21]

The report of the agent at Winnipeg also revealed a considerable amount of activity. Since 18 March he had met over one hundred and eighty trains and had "interviewed almost every passenger and supplied them with all necessary information, answered all enquiries about the lands, talked up the benefits and advantages offered to the settlers on the vacant lands, distributed pamphlets and cards." He summed up simply by saying that "good results have been the outcome [as] several of them purchased farms within the twenty mile limit."[22]

Although the lack of public financial support curtailed the immigration activities of City Council and the Board of Trade in the years after 1888, their subsequent efforts reveal that these civic leaders retained their commanding position in the community. In 1889, for example, the Board of Trade drew the attention of City Council to an alarming situation that existed at the CPR station in Winnipeg. Apparently many of the towns and villages of the province had employed agents to represent them at the station and the Board argued that unless Winnipeg did the same the city might be in danger of losing its predominance. Without any legal authority Council promptly appointed two paid immigration agents. Thus, during 1888 and 1889 City Council spent over $13,000 without ever having such an appropriation made legal under the terms of the Provincial Municipal Act. Only in the area of "growth producing schemes" could such a flagrant disregard of law be so openly practised and condoned.

Between 1890 and 1895 Council took little action in the matter of securing immigrants. The Board of Trade, however, was instrumental in the formation of the Winnipeg District Colonization Company in 1893. There remains little or no record of the successes or failures of this company but it can be noted that as each year passed the problem of vacant lands received less and less attention in the newspapers. Most probably these lands were gradually filling up although the problem still appears to have existed as late as 1898.[23] In any case, Council's hesitancy after 1890 to become financially involved in the immigration business was most likely a result of the fact that the city was suffering from financial difficulties. The comfortable prosperity and steady growth which Winnipeg had experienced after 1880 came to a temporary halt in the early 1890s. With the low price of wheat, the shortage of capital, decline in the CPR's traffic, and a slump in the real estate market, retrenchment became the watchword.

This setback in the economic fortunes of Winnipeg proved to be only temporary and in the years following 1896 confidence quickly returned. Indeed, both for the Canadian West and for Winnipeg itself, 1896 marked the termination of one era and the beginning of another. Prairie settlement, previously uncertain and hesitant, was now transformed as thousands of immigrants poured into the West and the depression of the nineties gave way to a period of unparalleled prosperity and expansion. Political changes played a part as the long period of Conservative domination in Canada was ended and the Liberals took office. With this change the federal government began to assume an increasingly vigorous and aggressive role in the problem of filling up the open spaces on the prairies. Without question the creation of a new society in the three prairie provinces was the outstanding feature of Canadian development in the years between 1896 and 1914.[24]

In the years after 1896 a variety of factors contributed to the successful settlement of western Canada. The first was a railway or, more specifically, a "favorable ratio between the price of wheat and the cost of transportation."[25] Although the Canadian Pacific was completed in 1885, it was not until the late nineties that the advance in the price of wheat and the decline in the cost of transportation produced this favourable ratio.[26] The second factor was the discovery of a variety of wheat adapted to the short growing season in the West, thereby avoiding damage from frost which had brought discouragement to the settlers in the eighties. By 1896 the planting of Red Fife Wheat on the prairie was general. Finally, there was the introduction of farming methods suitable to the prairie environment with its light rainfall. By the close of the century the dry farming technique, developed in the Great Plains area of the United States, had crossed the border to Canada.

Fortunately these developments within Canada coincided with a worldwide economic expansion. Late in 1896 the depression which for several years had gripped the world began to lift. There came an upturn in the price of wheat; new discoveries of gold in South Africa and in the Klondike, combined with the cyanide process for extracting gold from low grade ores, brought a sharp increase in the world's gold supply; and as prices advanced, business confidence was restored.[27]

Economic recovery and expansion, combined with rapid technological change, resulted in far-reaching dislocations among the industrial and agricultural workers of Europe. Better transportation facilities gave to these classes a new mobility and western Canada beckoned to them. Although the United States continued to be the chief beneficiary of this exodus from Europe, Canada attracted increasing numbers of the land-hungry folk of the old world. But the movement was not merely one between hemispheres; within the new world itself the migratory tendency was accentuated. People from the Maritime provinces and from Ontario poured into the West of Canada in increasing numbers. Emigration from the American middle western states, hitherto a mere stream, broadened into a flood.[28]

There were special reasons for the exodus of the mid-westerner to the prairies of Canada. The motives which impelled this migration were principally economic. The rise in the cost of the land and in rents in the United States; the mechanization of agriculture which reduced the need for labour and made possible the profitable cultivation of vast areas of western Canada; and the decline of older soils, resulting in increases in the costs of production—all were forces behind the movement. But political and psychological incentives also played a part in American emigration to western Canada, as did the appeal of Canada to certain racial and religious groups.[29] Together, these four factors led thousands of American farmers to the "last, best West."

With this happy conjunction of auspicious circumstances, agencies advertising western Canada could now hope for success where before they had largely failed. And there was no dearth of media for advertising to the world the opportunities of the Canadian West. Land companies, the Canadian Pacific, and the Dominion government were quick to seize the chance which awaited them. In eastern Canada the Canadian Pacific made known the possibilities of the West. In Great Britain and continental Europe both the railway and the Dominion government carried on a vigorous advertising campaign. In the United States, Canadian government and railway officials enjoyed the cooperation of a multitude of land companies which were then exploiting large tracts of fertile Canadian land. And, finally, the business leaders of Winnipeg engaged in a new and vigorous program of immigration propaganda to ensure that the city received its share of the incoming settlers.

Winnipeg's renewed interest in the immigration question began late in 1895 when the city was invited by the Commercial Club of St. Paul, Minnesota, to attend an Immigration Convention to be held in

November. Accepting the invitation, a delegation consisting of the mayor, four aldermen and members of the Board of Trade attended the gathering. The purpose of the convention was to urge each of the nine northwestern states and Manitoba to establish a bureau of information so that publicity issued about the region would bear the "stamp of authority." This would overcome, it was hoped, exaggerations and misstatements. To achieve this desired goal the meeting proposed setting up an organization to be called the Northwest Immigration Association. Annual meetings would be held and activities coordinated.[30]

The most significant aspect of the gathering for Winnipeg and Manitoba was the presence of Hon. Thomas Mayne Daly, federal Minister of the Interior and MP for Selkirk. He was convinced that such an immigration organization needed to be established in Canada and that such a body could work in conjunction with the federal government. Accordingly, plans were made shortly after the meeting to hold a convention in Winnipeg in 1896. This time, however, no Americans would be present in an official capacity and the meeting would deal exclusively with the problems faced by the Canadian West. In view of the criticism levelled at the Winnipeg delegation at St. Paul for cooperating with their rivals, this move was generally applauded in Winnipeg. As the *Manitoba Free Press* explained on 26 November, 1895:

> There can be no objection to the visit of those Canadian delegates, but notwithstanding all that has been said it is a question if immigration to the Canadian Northwest is to be promoted via St. Paul. It will be safer and in the end more advantageous if we depend on our own efforts and our own agencies. The *Free Press* will confess to itself that it has no confidence in immigration schemes devised by rivals who outnumber us in proportion to 50-1. Union is unnatural. It has been pointed out that even U.S. States are rivals. But it is nonsense nevertheless. They are all under the one flag, and immigrants have no hesitation in passing from one to the other as necessity or advantage may suggest. They will not pass from those States to the Canadian side until crowded out, and we can scarcely afford to wait until that condition shall arise. We want settlers in the meantime, and there is little doubt we shall have more success in getting them if we depend on ourselves and leave St. Paul alone.

Initiatives on the part of the city were necessary, it was explained, because "government methods, if they are to be judged by the results, are sorely in need of being supplemented." It was pointed out that even if the proposed meeting in Winnipeg did nothing more than stir up the federal government to greater efforts it would be a success. It was hoped, however, that the meeting would do more than talk about immigration, since "we have had enough talk to float a million shiploads of immigrants; what is required now is action, and the Convention is expected to present a plan on the likes of which something practical and effective can be accomplished."[31]

During January and February of 1896 a committee of Winnipeg civic and business leaders, calling themselves the Western Canadian Immigration Association (WCIA), organized a brief convention.[32] It ran for two days, was well attended by delegates from all points in western Canada, and received wide publicity.[33] But aside from the passage of several resolutions it was clear to all present that little actual advertising for immigrants could be done without funds. It was thus decided to send a delegation to Ottawa to ask for financial assistance. In the meantime, the initial expenses of the Western Canadian Immigration Association were met by a grant of $500 from Winnipeg City Council.

The defeat of the Conservative government in the June elections of 1896 cut short the negotiations between the Government and the WCIA, and the new organization succeeded in obtaining a mere $1,000 grant. Subsequent appeals to the new Liberal government were even less successful, for the new Minister of the Interior, Clifford Sifton, refused to give any money to the WCIA. But before the short-lived immigration association was disbanded in December 1897, it did manage to undertake one fruitful project. Using grants from Winnipeg City Council and the former Conservative government, it communicated with some five thousand farmers who had achieved a reasonable success on the prairie, sending to each a list of questions to answer. This effort elicited about two thousand replies, giving information which served as a basis for the pamphlet, "A Few Facts." Sifton was sufficiently interested in the pamphlet to give the work both his endorsement and financial assistance, and during 1897 thirty thousand copies were distributed. The idea for this questionnaire was neither new nor original. Alexander Begg had used the same method in Britain for the Canadian Pacific in the eighties. The refinement which the Department of the Interior and the Winnipeg-based WCIA gave to it was the use of the facsimile of the settler's letter in order to impart a more realistic touch to the procedure.[34]

Beyond this significant publication the impact of the WCIA was slight, and the organization was quickly forgotten in the outburst of activity that followed the appointment of the new Minister of the Interior. Undoubtedly the work of the Immigration Association would have continued beyond 1897 had either the federal government or the organization's members contributed to it financially. But no funds were forthcoming and the City of Winnipeg was content to leave the immigration question in the hands of the government, the Canadian Pacific, and private land companies.[35]

It was not until 1904 that Winnipeg once again found itself involved in the immigration business. The reason for its efforts at this time, after a lapse of nearly six years, was the fear that the migration of Americans northward, hitherto constant and substantial, was being threatened. Between 1897 and 1904 the federal government and the Canadian Pacific had carried out a large-scale publicity campaign in the United States designed to direct the American immigrants to the Canadian Northwest. These two agencies were aided in their task by land and colonization companies formed around the turn of the century to exploit railway and Dominion land in the western territories.[36]

Winnipeggers looked on all this activity with understandable contentment, for it resulted in the movement of hundreds of thousands of Americans into Canada. But, paradoxically, it was the very success of the campaign that forced Winnipeg to act. For the awareness of the dimensions of this exodus resulted in a series of organized countermoves on the part of concerned Americans.[37] Meeting in St. Paul in March 1904, a group of American businessmen organized the American Immigration Association of the Northwest "for the purpose of keeping moving Americans away from Canada." Coupled with this effort was the work of the National Irrigation Association which by 1904 had "about 20,000 members and a well-filled treasury and was preaching everywhere the advantages of irrigated lands."[38] The United States was flooded with its literature and it had sufficient lobbying power in Washington to obtain a pledge of $30 million from the American federal government for work on several great irrigation projects. The goal of these projects was to eventually make "room in the west for 75,000,000 people." Finally, other organizations in the South, Southwest, and on the Pacific Slope sprang up designed to press their various claims on intending American settlers.[39]

Against this combination of forces it was apparent to those owning land in western Canada that more had to be done to keep the attractions of the Canadian Northwest before the American people. Early in 1904 a meeting of those owning Canadian lands, as well as others interested in the region, was held, somewhat ironically, in St. Paul, Minnesota. The initiative for this gathering seems to have come from American businessmen who owned Canadian lands, but the meeting was well attended by official delegations from Winnipeg City Council, the Board of Trade, and the Real Estate Exchange, as well as private businessmen. Indeed, at this initial meeting such men as aldermen J. Russell and J. G. Latimer, ex-aldermen G. F. Carruthers and D. W. Bole, and prominent businessmen such as W. S. Evans and W. Georgeson were much in evidence and were subsequently to become members of the executive and standing committees of the new organization. In fact, the executive committee of ten members was made up of no less than seven Winnipeggers.

At the first session of the convention the name of Western Canadian Immigration Association was chosen for the new organization. It differed from the old organization of the same name, however, in that the new body was concerned only with American immigrants and not with overseas migrants. Once the name had been decided upon, discussion quickly turned to the methods that could be employed in promoting American immigration to western Canada. It was decided that best results could be obtained by the use of editorial notices, the general dissemination of news regarding western Canada, and the correction of false reports and impressions about that region. A second objective would be securing lower railway rates and other transportation concessions to facilitate the movement of settlers to western Canada. The association also decided that $50,000 would be required during its first two years of operation. The meeting broke up after it was resolved to leave the working out of details with the executive committee which had full authority to act.[40]

When the Winnipeg delegates returned home they immediately began the task of raising their share of the $50,000. At the organizational meeting it had been pointed out that the proper method would be to get a very large amount of private subscriptions before approaching either the federal or local governments of Canada. Accordingly, a meeting of Winnipeg businessmen was held 24 February 1904 and the delegates optimistically explained the organization and purposes of the WCIA to them. They then turned to the question of finances. The three Board of Trade delegates, D. W. Bole, W. S. Evans, and D. E. Sprague, explained that "the commercial interests of Winnipeg and the West depend largely upon the continued growth of population—the more people the more trade. A well defined policy of emigration, under the auspices of the Association just formed, must therefore commend itself to the businessmen of Western Canada and is entitled to their support."[41] When some of those present at the meeting suggested that the businessmen of the city "should not be canvassed too rigidly for subscriptions," but rather that the federal, provincial, and local governments should be the main contributors, it was pointed out that it would be unfair to have the workingmen of the city contribute through their taxes. The onus, it was pointed out, "lay wholly on the land men, the bankers, the merchants, the wholesale houses, the hotel men, and others of the business community. If they could not care . . . they had better quit."[42] In the ensuing weeks of canvassing, however, subscriptions from the Winnipeg business community were slow in coming and the major portion of the funds collected or pledged came from the federal government ($10,000), and various large grants from Canadian railway companies. Only when these pledges were made did the Winnipeg business community come forward with pledges amounting to $6,000. Indeed, throughout the life of the WCIA, its major financial support was to come from governmental bodies and railway companies rather than from the Winnipeg businessmen and real estate agents who stood to reap immediate benefits from an influx of American settlers.

During the four years of its existence (the wcia was disbanded in March 1908), the association's activities were largely directed from Winnipeg. Throughout, Winnipeg's business and civic leaders were in the forefront of the work, serving in all capacities within the organization itself as well as acting as effective lobbyists in Winnipeg City Council and in Ottawa.[43] The annual meetings in 1905, 1906, 1907, and 1908 were held at Winnipeg, and each year the mayor welcomed the delegates and expressed, on behalf of the city, his appreciation for what the organization "had to do with the prosperity of the city."[44] Winnipeg's domination of the association, however, caused problems during the four years. One of the major weaknesses was the absence of support from the different cities, towns, and rural municipalities of the West. Apparently these localities felt they could carry on publicity campaigns for their own areas better than could an organization centred in Winnipeg.[45] The wcia was more successful in getting financial assistance from the provinces of Alberta and Saskatchewan, as both gave grants of $2,500 to the association.

The wcia utilized a wide variety of techniques to spread its message. A full-time secretary published numerous articles in American newspapers and agricultural journals. He also encouraged newspapers to direct their attention to western Canada. The most effective tool of the wcia, however, was the organization of free tours for American correspondents through the West. A description of one such tour is given in the association's report for 1906 and, because of the popularity of this method of securing publicity, deserves to be quoted at length:

> The second Washington correspondents' tour occupied twenty-seven days, from July 12th to August 8th [1906], during which time twelve known newspaper writers, no one of whom had ever visited Canada before, travelled twice across the Dominion and up and down the wheat fields, the tour comprising many thousand miles. Leaving Washington on July 12th the party rode in a standard Pullman car from Washington to Buffalo, where the chartered car was picked up. . . . Entering Canada on the Grand Trunk they traveled over this line to Toronto and Montreal. Leaving Montreal . . . on the Canadian Pacific, the party visited Ottawa, Fort William, Port Arthur and Winnipeg, where the car was switched to the Canadian Northern tracks and the trip through the wheat fields began. Among the places visited before reaching Banff were Warman, Saskatoon, Prince Albert, Rosthern, Edmonton, and Calgary. . . . On the return trip Lethbridge, Raymond, Cardston, Magrath, Medicine Hat, Moose Jaw, Regina, and

Indian Head were visited. The party stayed in Winnipeg on the return trip.

. . . The newspaper men and the papers which they represented were, Irving C. Norwood, the *Washington Star*; Angus McSeveen, the *Philadelphia North American*; William E. Moore, *Chicago Inter-Ocean*; Thomas J. Pence, *Raleigh News and Observer*; Edward G. Lowry, the *New York Evening Post*; Richard H. Lindsay, *Kansas City Star*; D. Hastings McAdam, the *St. Louis Republic*; William G. Miller, the Scripps-McRea Press Association; Jesse L. Carmichael, *Detroit Free Press*; William S. Couch, *Cleveland Plaindealer*; Maurice Splain, the *Pittsburg Post*; Jackson Elliot, the Associated Press. [46]

The result of this particular trip, as reported by the secretary, was "one hundred and eighty-two columns of matter on Canada. . . . The space occupied by the articles would make a book of more than 270,000 words." After several tours of this type had been completed, the WCIA gathered together the views of the newspapermen and published a pamphlet entitled "What Famous Correspondents Say About Western Canada," which was widely distributed throughout the United States.[47]

Among the many other methods of securing publicity employed by the WCIA only two more need be mentioned.[48] Late in 1906 it was decided to have the association publish its own magazine and after several false starts the first issue of *The Canada-West* was published in October 1906. Every enquirer writing to the association received a year's subscription; by January 1907 over 1,468 American farmers and investors were receiving the magazine. During 1907 the circulation increased rapidly and the project was considered one of the most successful operations of the association. The other technique employed was the setting up of a general information bureau in 1906. Prior to this time the WCIA had merely sent to interested enquirers a complete list of members—that is, lists of the various land agencies selling land in the West. But at the 1906 general meeting it was decided to send out more material than this standard form of follow-up letter. Thereafter, included with the list of members was a copy of *The Canada-West*, copies of regular Dominion government literature, information about freight and passenger rates from the Canadian Pacific and Canadian Northern Railways, and from the provincial governments and various boards of trade in the West general information, crop reports, and so on. Thus, from fifteen to twenty-five pieces of literature went to each enquirer.

It is, of course, impossible to measure the success of the association in relation to the efforts of either the Dominion government or the CPR. The task of determining the effectiveness of the association's efforts, moreover, is made all the more difficult by conflicting reports regarding its work. According to D. W. Bole, one of the original organizers of the

WCIA and its president for 1905, "a very large portion of the immigration from the Western and Southwestern States has been due to the efforts of the secretary [of the WCIA] during the past year."[49] This view was shared by the *Manitoba Free Press* which stated in an editorial in February 1906 that:

> The work done by the WCIA since its formation two years ago has been of invaluable benefit to this country. . . . [Its work] has been carried out with results so far exceeding even the most sanguine anticipation that its continuance has been decided upon with enthusiastic unanimity. No more convincing proof of the success of the Association's work and of the value of the service it is rendering could be afforded than is given by the action of the CPR in doubling its subscription to the Association's fund. . . . In every way the work by the Association is ably planned and successfully carried out. . . .

In direct contradiction with these evaluations were the opinions of the federal government immigration agents working in the United States. In a memorandum to the Superintendent of Immigration at Ottawa, the Inspector of U.S. Agencies, W. J. Whyte, expressed the following view: "Personally I do not think the Western Canadian Immigration Association, or its Secretary, were the means of bringing six additional people to Canada during the last year. On the other hand this Association interferes in many ways with the general work of the Department." In an expansion of his views a year later, Mr. Whyte reported similar opinions:

> You asked me if the WCIA is of any assistance to our work in the United States. Unhesitatingly I say it is of no value whatever. Before this Association was organized we had succeeded in arousing the greatest interest in all parts of the United States where we were likely to secure settlers and especially in the farming communities. No attempt was made to arouse interest in the Cities as it was felt that it would only be increasing the price of land to the settler and this is one of the things we wish to avoid. We were covering this work entirely and did not require any assistance. The work of the WCIA, as nearly as I can make out, is in the matter of publicity, amongst magazines which circulate in cities and amongst businessmen and speculators. In this way speculators may be induced by the glowing accounts written of the country to invest in lands and I know for a fact that many of these speculators are holding the lands for even higher prices than at present prevail. Magazine advertising is not in the interest of our work if our work means the settlement of the country. On the other hand it will be retarded as it raises the price of land to a figure higher than the settler may be able to pay.

This is the view I take of the Association—that it is of no service to us as a means of securing settlers.[50]

The Commissioner of Immigration at Winnipeg agreed wholeheartedly with this assessment. When asked his views by the Superintendent of Immigration he replied that the WCIA "is nothing less than a big real estate concern, and they are using the public money for the purpose of assisting real estate men to sell their lands at a profit." He went on to recommend that in the future no public funds be put at the disposal of the association.[51]

In view of these adverse comments, the Superintendent of Immigration undertook to obtain the views of all the agents working in the United States. The response was unanimous; all stated that the work of the WCIA had in no way aided their efforts and many agents reported they had not even heard of the body.[52] In the light of this evidence it is surprising to learn that in 1907 the federal government granted the WCIA $6,200. One can only conclude that the association's members were effective lobbyers in Ottawa.

But whatever the view of the work of the WCIA, the organization thrived until it was decided at an executive meeting in January 1908 that the work of the organization was complete. The final meeting of the association was held at the CPR's Royal Alexandra Hotel in Winnipeg on March 31, 1908. Perhaps the best conclusion that can be reached regarding the activity of the WCIA is that it supplemented the work of the Dominion government and the CPR. With the publicity it created the American exodus to the Canadian West was perhaps heightened, but without it the exodus would have taken place regardless. For, as a noted authority has remarked, "propaganda . . . was not the basic cause of the migration across the line."[53]

As W. L. Morton has noted, "1912 was the climax of the great boom in Manitoba."[54] The end of the great western boom had been foreshadowed by rising freight rates and falling farm and land prices, and was ultimately followed by the collapse of the real estate market. By 1912 the real estate agents and the land speculators had found it difficult to dispose of farm lands and impossible to interest buyers in suburban developments. Scores of urban subdivisions and dozens of attractively named suburbs died on agents' prospectuses and on drafting boards. Winnipeg once more found itself surrounded with a belt of land held for speculation. Seeking the cause of this recession the people of Manitoba noted that while immigration into the West continued at a high level, the census of 1911 had revealed that in population Manitoba was falling behind Saskatchewan and Alberta. They responded in typical fashion in an effort to continue the golden years of prosperous growth.

Winnipeg's attention was first officially drawn to the problem by a resolution it received from Louise Municipality in May 1911. Calling for a general meeting of all Boards of Trade and Municipal Councils of the province, the resolution outlined the problem:

> . . . large numbers of settlers are daily coming into Western Canada from Ontario, the British Isles, and the United States, practically all of whom are passing through the Province of Manitoba and taking up land and homes for themselves in the Provinces to the west of Manitoba;
> . . . we have in Manitoba lands open for homesteading purposes the equal of the homestead lands in any other province in the Dominion of Canada;
> . . . we have in Manitoba improved and unimproved lands of unsurpassed quality which can be purchased as cheaply as similar lands in the other western provinces;
> . . . the Province of Manitoba has great and lasting advantages to offer the new settler. . . .[55]

The outcome of this resolution, and similar ones all over the province, was a meeting called in January in Winnipeg to outline a "gigantic plan to increase immigration into Manitoba."[56] The meeting was presided over by Mayor Waugh of Winnipeg and it was quickly decided to organize a "Million-For-Manitoba League." After speeches outlining the problem Manitoba faced, it was decided to take the following course of action:

> It is proposed to divide the province into five districts of which Winnipeg would be one. In each division a separate organization will take charge of the work. One means of raising funds will be by the sale of attractive buttons. A nominal fee for league membership will be fixed and a definite campaign will be undertaken to secure larger contributions from businessmen, hotelmen, and the public-spirited residents of the province generally. Boards of Trade, real estate exchanges, the lodges of various orders and even the school children will be drawn into the work.[57]

Following this initial meeting the campaign for funds got under way and by July over $3,000 had been spent on advertising in Great Britain and the United States. But by this time the league was encountering serious financial difficulties, as few of the towns or municipalities of the province came forward with expected grants. The league struggled on into 1913 but by the end of that year had been disbanded. The fact was that by 1913 Winnipeg and the province was entering a depression; credit stringency was manifest throughout the region and no amount of "booming" could bring a return of good times. Winnipeg was on the threshold of a new era and would soon be forced to face one of the consequences of the boom—the unresolved questions of race and class relationships.

The promotional energies of Winnipeg's businessmen during the period of the great boom were also directed toward attracting industry. Early in 1906, in anticipation of the passing of the Hydro-Power bylaw, two Winnipeg newspapers set out the urgent need of a publicity bureau in Winnipeg. Pointing out that Toronto, Fort William, Regina, and many other cities already had such organizations, they warned that unless similar steps were taken by Winnipeg the city would be in danger of losing its position as a manufacturing centre, "to which she is justly entitled." As outlined by the *Manitoba Free Press* such a bureau could be charged with the following functions: inducing new industries to establish themselves in Winnipeg; "extending a helping hand to meritorious, but struggling industries already started"; securing financial co-operation for a new industry or additional capital for a weak industry already started; and acting as a means of bringing conventions and public gatherings to the city.[58]

Acting on these suggestions the Winnipeg Board of Trade appointed a committee to interview the City Council and the Trade and Commerce Committee of that body "to urge the necessity of having some proper descriptive literature issued for the purpose of affording information regarding the opportunities presented in Winnipeg to industrial enterprises." The major advantage the Board wished to have publicized was the lower rates to be derived from the hydro-power development. This initiative on the part of the Board met with almost instant agreement, for at a meeting held in May 1906 and attended by all the major business organizations of the city, it was decided to organize an association under the name of the Winnipeg Development and Industrial Bureau. This meeting defined its objects in the following motion:

> That this meeting announces the object of this association to be the attraction of industries of Winnipeg and the development of the commercial interests of the city; and recommends the appointment of an Industrial Commissioner to take executive charge of the work under an Advisory Board.[59]

A committee was appointed to prepare a constitution and bylaw and by July the WDIB was fully organized and operating.

The speed and apparent unanimity with which the WDIB was organized serves to confirm the observations made elsewhere that the growth ethos of Winnipeg's civic and business leaders was shared by nearly the whole of the populace. But it is significant to point out that one newspaper, *The Winnipeg Tribune*, was absolutely opposed to this latest venture. In a long editorial it brought forward several objections that were never to be met throughout the life of the bureau.

> It is claimed that Winnipeg should set aside at least $25,000 a year to be spent in "promoting the city's interests."

If there were any sound reason to believe that the spending of this money would really result in "promoting the city's interests," there would be no opposition to the plan. But how would the money be spent, and what would be the effect of establishing the "bureau" for the purpose of spending it?

It is suggested that advertising literature should be on hand in large quantities, and that every inquiry concerning Winnipeg should precipitate upon the head of the unfortunate inquirer an avalanche of this stuff.

The effect of such action by the "publicity bureau" can readily be imagined. Any responsible man who might have some idea of locating here would conclude that the city must be a boom town, on the hunt for easy marks, or it would not employ boom town methods. Such a man would probably give such a place a wide berth.

It is also suggested that assistance should be given to new firms that might locate here as well as to struggling industries that are already established.

There is not a dead or dying horse in town that would not loudly applaud this feature of the proposed departure from well-established methods. How the successful competitors of these "struggling industries" and of these new-comers would receive such a suggestion is that "a considerable portion of the money at the command of the organization should be used in entertaining possible investors."

What a glorious opportunity for wholesale and retail graft! Why, there would not be a traveller who would pass through the city without announcing in unmistakable terms that he could be "induced" to invest in Winnipeg.

Let Winnipeg once become known as a city that is running after investors and offering them "inducements" and every industry that locates here will demand a bonus exemption from taxation and a score of other special privileges.

There is just one legitimate way in which the growth of Winnipeg can be hastened—that is not by coaxing or paying people to come here but by creating advantageous conditions that their business sense will not permit them to ignore.

Continue to make the city healthy, beautiful, pleasant; establish a first class water supply and sewage system; make cheap light and power realities by establishing municipal gas and electric power plants with all possible haste—and Winnipeg will have all the FREE publicity that most patriotic citizens could desire. . . .[60]

Such strictures would no doubt have been harsher had the *Tribune* foreseen the large expenditure of public funds the wdib precipitated.

The founders of the bureau had pledged that any grant from City Council would be matched or even surpassed by the Winnipeg business community. Yet up to the end of 1914 City Council had given $112,000 to the bureau while subscriptions from the business community totalled only $65,000. In light of the grave social problems Winnipeg was experiencing from its rapid growth before and during this period, such a large expenditure for the purpose of accelerating the growth rate was questionable, to say the least.

During the first seven years of existence the WDIB was very active in almost every phase of civic life. Under the direction of a special committee it carried out a fantastic amount of advertising. Reporting on these activities for the period 1907–10 the commissioner of the bureau reported that he had handled 58,000 enquiries for information and had in that time sent out as many letters in reply. He went on to say that "we have distributed over 2,000,000 pieces of printed matter including every size from a four page leaflet up to a hundred page, highly illustrated, booklet. In our Press service department we have supplied over 1,000,000 lines of news matter about Winnipeg to magazines, newspapers and other publications in the British Isles, Eastern Canada and the United States and with these we have furnished over 2,000 photographs for illustrations."[61]

The commissioner claimed that as a result of the bureau's efforts 267 manufacturing plants were attracted to Winnipeg. He was quick to point out, moreover, that the lists he compiled did not include industrial establishments of a wholesale character, "nor does the list take into account any of the big extensions of railway shops and local manufacturers who have added largely to their manufacturing equipment in this time."[62] Although it was undoubtedly an exaggeration for the bureau to take credit for attracting all of the new firms, the fact remains that Winnipeg had developed into a considerable industrial centre by 1914. Table 5 illustrates the substantial growth in Winnipeg's manufacturing employment and output.[63]

Table 5 / Manufacturing in City of Winnipeg, 1881–1915

Year	Population	Capital	Employees	Salaries & wages	Net value of products
		($)		($)	($)
1881	7,985	691,655	950	410,744	1,700,320
1891	25,639	3,124,367	2,359	1,176,861	5,611,240
1901	42,340	4,673,214	3,155	1,810,845	8,616,248
1911	136,035	25,820,430	11,565	7,506,148	35,502,380
1915	150,000	73,320,176	15,295	11,117,093	47,686,070

The bureau was also active in other areas. One of its proudest achievements was the building of a permanent "Exposition Building" in 1912. The idea behind the project was to have a centre where businessmen who visited the city could come "to be informed of the industrial conditions and circumstances of our capital, and . . . definitely plan out the founding of new enterprises in our midst." The building had on display all the products manufactured in the city, and the commissioner of the bureau was always on hand to answer questions.[64]

In 1911 the bureau also began to program "for assisting worthy British workmen to bring their families to Winnipeg." The objects of the Imperial Home Reunion Movement were described by the bureau as follows: "Apart from promoting better conditions and surrounding men with family life, the plan works out to be the betterment of the business community as a whole in-as-much as it gives the workmen a greater degree of stability and contentment; it brings no inconsiderable number of new people to our city as residents and as consumers, where otherwise money for their support was largely sent out of the city." Although the work of this branch of the bureau was curtailed by the outbreak of war in 1914, the Imperial Home Reunion Association pointed out with pride that up until the end of 1913 they had brought out a total of 2,427 wives and children.

Other work carried out by the bureau included the opening of the first civic art gallery in Canada in Winnipeg in December 1912; preparation of illustrated lecture material for use in England, Eastern Canada and the United States; "investigation of the utilization of Canadian flaxstraw, wire grasses and other natural resources"; the production of moving pictures; the promotion of an "Annual Business Men's Tour of the West to promote closer business relations with Winnipeg"; and the setting up of a Civic Improvement Committee to work in conjunction with the City Planning Commission.

The significance of these various campaigns for immigrants and industry should not be measured only by the number of newcomers that were encouraged to come to Winnipeg and Manitoba, or the rate of the city's economic growth. Rather, they are important for what they reveal about society in the period. In the case of advertising for immigrants, the fact that the commercial elite could spend public monies on programs designed to benefit private speculators indicates a great deal about the distribution of influence and power in this era. Indeed, many of the people active in the Vacant Lands Program and the wcia, were themselves large landholders and made substantial profits as a result of the city's efforts. This does not mean there was any explicit corruption involved. The point is that such a connection between private fortunes and municipal government was considered natural. Furthermore, when such expenditures of public funds are seen in relation to the social conditions of the mass of the Winnipeg populace at this time, an even grimmer picture emerges. Taken in the light of Winnipeg's shortage of housing, inadequate educational and recreational facilities, lack of proper water and sewage disposal resources, and a host of other problems, programs designed to encourage population growth and thus cause even more acute problems, are something of a paradox. It was rather like trying to repair, maintain, and fuel a car while pressing the accelerator to the floor boards. And viewed from this perspective, the advertising campaign stands as a monument to the failure of Winnipeg's leaders to develop a mature social conscience.

The creation of the WDIB is also questionable on these same grounds; it, too, says much about Winnipeg's civic and business leaders, for it clearly displayed their concern with rapid and sustained growth. It is true, of course, that many of the activities of the bureau were worthwhile and added much-needed facilities to the community. But it is also true that Winnipeg had many social problems that should have taken priority over economic growth. The folly of the elite's overriding concern with population and economic growth made itself apparent in the social strife Winnipeg was to endure in 1919 and after.

part four

the urban community: people and neighbourhoods

Winnipeg holds a place by itself among Canadian cities. Less than half its people are Canadians, while one-third are either foreign born or the children of foreign parents. . . . The rapid influx of immigration during the past fifteen years has been the cause.

G. F. Chapman, "Winnipeg: The Melting Pot," 1909

Even without the tendency of newcomers to live with their own kind, Winnipeg, by the very nature of its geographic setting, was pre-ordained to develop into a sprawling, gap-toothed collection of ghettos.

James Gray, *The Boy from Winnipeg*, 1970

8 / Population Growth and Change

Like their counterparts in most North American cities, Winnipeggers were fascinated with the growth of their community. The city's politicians, businessmen, and newspapers were constantly measuring their community's progress in quantitative terms—miles of streets and sewers, value of manufacturing output, dollars of assessment, numbers of buildings, and so on. But the one index that stood out from all others was that of population growth. The number of residents the city had at any particular time was considered to be of paramount importance, especially in comparing Winnipeg's advancement with that of other cities.[1] Almost as important in a community whose ruling elite were exclusively Anglo-Saxon and Protestant was the ethnic and religious composition of the city. For although Winnipeggers were firm believers in the virtues of immigration, most did not easily reconcile themselves to the resultant polygot population. The pride that came with the sharp rise in population was diminished by the knowledge that much of this growth was caused by "foreign" elements.[2]

The population growth of Winnipeg is detailed in Table 6.[3] A close examination of these figures reveals that the two columns do not agree; up to and including 1891 the federal returns are consistently higher while after that date the reverse is true. In the earlier period it is next to impossible to account for the discrepancy, especially in view of Winnipeg's habit of boasting about its rapid progress. In the later period, when the city's returns are consistently and substantially higher, an explanation is much easier. At least some of the difference can be accounted for by the city's tendency to include "floating population" in its count. This classification of persons was made up almost entirely of single males who had come west to obtain work. In most years after 1890 eastern harvest excursionists streamed into Winnipeg in large numbers. During 1912, for example, the number was estimated at twenty-five thousand.[4] In addition, the city served as the main recruiting centre for railway and bush contractors and thus attracted men in search of positions in these areas.[5]

All these jobs were seasonal and in the fall the men would be

Table 6 / **Population Growth by Years: City of Winnipeg, 1871–1916**

Year	Federal census figures	City Assessment Office figures
1871	241	700
72		1,467
73		
74		1,869
75		2,061
76		
77		2,722
78		3,180
79		4,113
1880		6,178
81	7,985	6,245
82		13,856
83		
84		16,694
85		19,574
86	20,238	19,525
87		21,257
88		22,098
89		21,328
1890		23,000
91	25,639	24,068
92		29,182
93		32,119
94		34,954
95		37,124
96	31,649	37,983
97		38,733
98		39,384
99		40,112
1900		42,534
01	42,340	44,778
02		48,411
03		56,741
04		67,262
05		79,975
06	90,153	101,057
07		111,729
08		118,252
09		122,390

1910		132,720
11	136,035	151,958
12		185,000
13		201,000
14		203,255
15		212,889
1916	163,000	201,981

released from their summer occupations and would trek to Winnipeg, seeking winter employment. A few of these received positions in bush camps through the efforts of private employment agencies. This work began in the winter following the first heavy snowfall when logs and supplies could be easily hauled over the snow. But such job opportunities during the cold winter months were very limited. Some of the slack was taken up by casual work, whether stoking furnaces, splitting wood, or shovelling snow. Others left the city for a milder climate where construction activity might be carried on and work available. Yet this still left a large number who stayed in Winnipeg, encouraged to remain by the metropolitan facilities of the city—its theatres, bars, pool rooms, cheap cafés, rooming houses, and brothels. Europeans were particularly eager to spend the time in a familiar cultural milieu.[6]

Aside from the unsettling effects this ebb and flow of transient workers had upon Winnipeg's social life, it served to inflate population figures. After 1891 city officials included in their population count all those who "from night to night sleep in the city"; that is, they included all the population of the city at the time the census was taken. The federal census, on the other hand, would include only permanent residents.

Even using the inflated City Assessment Office figures contained in Table 6 it is significant that the population growth of Winnipeg fell far short of the expectations of some of its boosters. The fact that Winnipeg did not grow as rapidly as the commercial elite would have liked helps explain why such a large proportion of the elite's talent and energy, as well as the municipal corporation's resources, were channelled into programs designed to accelerate the city's growth rate. This drain of public funds into growth-producing schemes left little for the program so desperately needed by the poorer groups in Winnipeg.

But while Winnipeg's rate of growth did not satisfy the expectations of the commercial elite, it was still impressive when compared with national or provincial growth rates. Viewed from a national perspective, Winnipeg's rise to one of the ranking cities of Canada demonstrates that its growth rate exceeded that of nearly all other Canadian cities during the period 1871–1921. As Table 7 reveals,[7] the village of Winnipeg in 1871 with its 241 residents ranked sixty-second among all

Table 7 / Population of Canadian Cities and Rank by Size, 1871–1921

City	1871 Population	Rank	1881 Population	Rank	1891 Population	Rank	1901 Population	Rank	1911 Population	Rank	1921 Population	Rank
Montreal	115,000	1	155,238	1	219,616	1	328,172	1	490,504	1	618,506	1
Toronto	59,000	3	96,916	2	181,215	2	209,892	2	381,833	2	521,893	2
WINNIPEG	241	62	7,985	17	25,639	8	42,340	6	136,035	3	179,087	3
Vancouver	–	–	–	–	13,709	11	27,010	9	100,401	4	117,217	4
Hamilton	26,880	5	36,661	4	48,959	4	52,634	5	81,969	6	114,151	5
Ottawa	24,141	7	31,307	7	44,154	5	59,928	4	87,062	5	107,843	6
Quebec	59,699	2	62,446	3	63,090	3	68,840	3	78,710	7	95,193	7
Calgary	–	–	–	–	3,876	55	4,392	66	43,704	10	63,305	8
London	18,000	8	26,266	8	31,977	8	37,976	9	46,300	9	60,959	9
Edmonton	–	–	–	–	–	–	–	–	31,064	72	58,821	10

urban centres in the country. But by 1891 it had risen dramatically to eighth place and by 1911 to third. By the latter date Winnipeg was undoubtedly a major Canadian city, both the "Gem of the Prairies" and the "Chicago of the North."

Analysis of the growth rate of Winnipeg by decades also reveals several important features of its growth. Table 8[8] indicates that while the average decennial growth rate for the period 1881–1921 was over 135 per cent for Winnipeg, it was only 81 per cent for Manitoba and 20 per cent for Canada. These figures show that the city attracted far more newcomers than did either the rest of the province or the country as a whole. A close examination of the table, however, also discloses that the rate of increase for Winnipeg has been subject to major variations coinciding with successive waves of immigration to Canada. Indeed, it is apparent that Winnipeg's population growth, while always substantial, was concentrated in two decades: namely, 1881–91 and 1901–11. During the latter decade, when the city's population increased by almost 100,000, Winnipeg residents witnessed the most spectacular increase their community had ever undergone, or would ever undergo.

Although the size and rate of Winnipeg's population growth delighted most city boosters, it also presented an almost countless series of problems. The establishment and maintenance of social order and the protection of public welfare required endless attention. The difficulties of maintaining a truly representative form of government, enforcing laws, safeguarding public health, providing municipal services, and securing consensus on social values were all magnified as the city's population increased. The problems connected with population size, moreover, were greatly compounded by Winnipeg's rate of growth. For not only did the problems have to be solved, they had to be solved in a very short period of time. And it is clear from such occurrences as a severe typhoid epidemic in 1904–5 that the city's rapid growth had disastrous effects. It can in fact be said that Winnipeg grew so fast that consciousness of community lagged far behind the erection of the urban physical structure, and community services accordingly rested on no solid basis of collective sentiment.

Winnipeg—and, indeed, all cities—achieved population growth through three main channels: the arrival of immigrants, natural increase, and annexation of new sections. These three sources, however, are by no means equal in importance. Of least significance in Winnipeg's case was the extension of boundaries. As Map 2 demonstrates, there have been several large additions to the territory of the city.[9] The boundaries as determined by the charter of the newly incorporated City of Winnipeg in 1873 were then considered to be fairly large. But the rapid advance of the city during the next few years, and especially during the boom years of 1881–82, caused these early attitudes to be quickly

Table 8 / Population Growth by Decades: City of Winnipeg, Province of Manitoba, and Canada, 1871–1921

| Area | Population in 1871 | 1871–1881 | | Population in 1881 | 1881–1891 | |
		Numerical Increase	Per Cent Increase		Numerical Increase	Per Cent Increase
City of Winnipeg	241	7,744	3,624.1	7,985	17,654	221.1
Province of Manitoba	25,228	37,032	146.8	62,260	90,246	144.9
Canada	3,689,257	635,553	17.2	4,324,810	508,429	11.8

| Area | Population in 1891 | 1891–1901 | | Population in 1901 | 1901–1911 | | Population in 1911 | 1911–1921 | |
		Numerical Increase	Per Cent Increase		Numerical Increase	Per Cent Increase		Numerical Increase	Per Cent Increase
City of Winnipeg	25,639	16,701	65.1	42,340	93,695	221.2	136,035	45,052	31.7
Province of Manitoba	152,506	102,705	67.3	255,211	206,183	80.8	461,394	148,725	32.2
Canada	4,833,239	538,076	11.1	5,371,315	1,835,328	34.2	7,206,643	1,581,306	21.9

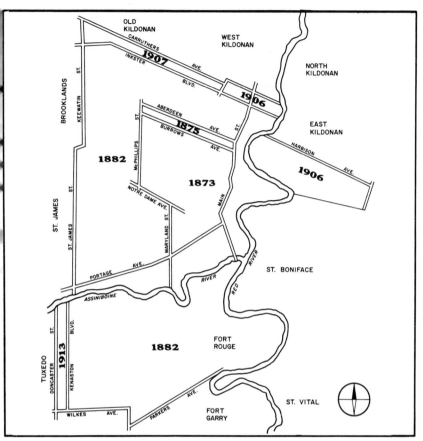

Map 2/Winnipeg Boundary Extensions 1873–1914

replaced by more grandiose ones. Between 1873 and 1882 the boundaries were extended several times, particularly in the northern and western sections of the city. Yet it was not until the latter date that all the changes were formally enacted by the issuance of a new charter. The result was that the limits were extended on all sides except the east where the Red River acted as a natural boundary.

These extensions were large and practically brought the city of Winnipeg up to its present-day size. It is important to emphasize, however, that the new additions which were added to the city by the charter of 1881 did not contain many residents, but rather reflected the great optimism prevailing as a result of the boom. Detailed and accurate figures for all the areas are not available but for the section known as Fort Rouge (it became Ward 1 when a new ward system was established in Winnipeg that year) the population was only about 150.[10] In the case of the areas to the north and west, the land was largely unoccupied and consequently added very little in terms of population.

Following this major addition it was twenty-four years before any other annexation of new territory was made. In 1906 part of the municipality of Kildonan was brought into the city limits. This newly added land was considered to be sufficiently large to form a new ward and thus Ward 7 was added to the city. In this instance the new area contained approximately 2,700 residents. It was in the same year that another addition was made to the city. Lots three and four of Kildonan were annexed and formed part of Ward 6. These areas in the Elmwood district added another 620 residents. One final extension of Winnipeg's boundaries occurred before 1914. Tuxedo Park, situated in the western district of the city, was annexed in 1913, but once again the extension did not represent any significant addition to the population.

It should also be mentioned that in the decade leading up to 1914 attempts were made by Winnipeg City Council to annex three other large areas. But the adjacent communities of St. James, St. Vital, and St. Boniface resisted these overtures, arguing that since Winnipeg was already having difficulty supplying such local improvements as water and sewer services to its residents, there was little to be gained by joining the city. These arguments, used by all three municipalities, were bolstered in the case of St. Boniface by ethnic considerations. As one St. Boniface alderman pointed out, the addition of a predominately French-speaking area to an English city such as Winnipeg would only lead to conflict. Moreover, St. Vital officials argued that if any changes were to be made that area would be more interested in joining St. Boniface than Winnipeg. In any case, the significant fact was that these three districts kept an independent status and Winnipeg was denied the contribution these areas would have made to her population growth.[11]

The large additions to Winnipeg's area, then, did not substantially increase Winnipeg's population. The various annexations to Winnipeg's territory between 1874 and 1914 probably added only about 3,500 persons. It is thus apparent that the reasons for Winnipeg's rapid rate must be found in other causes.

Table 9 delineates the role natural increase played in the population growth of Winnipeg.[12] The lack of early statistics made the task of including figures for the period prior to 1890 impossible. Also, it must be emphasized that even after this date the birth and death statistics are probably inflated, since throughout the period some of the statistics are by "place of occurrence" rather than by "place of residence."[13] Winnipeg health officials often used this argument in an attempt to play down the city's death rate, but the process of people entering city institutions to have babies or to die probably balanced out. But even with these qualifications there can be no doubt that natural increase played an important, if varied, part in the population growth of Winnipeg.

Table　9 / Natural Increase as a Factor in the Population Growth of Winnipeg, 1890–1914

Years	Total pop'n increase	Births	Deaths	Natural increase	N.I. as % of tot. pop. incr.
1890–1895	14,124	5,467	3,035	2,432	17.2
1895–1900	5,410	6,035	3,185	2,850	52.6
1900–1905	37,441	8,696	6,138	2,558	6.8
1905–1910	52,745	18,234	9,177	9,057	17.2
1910–1914	70,535	21,081	8,483	12,598	17.8

It was, however, from the third source of population growth—the arrival of new immigrants—that Winnipeg received the bulk of its new residents. Of the total population growth of 180,255 in the period 1890–1914, natural increase accounted for 29,495, or about 16 per cent. Accordingly, migration accounted for about 84 per cent of the city's growth. The importance of migration is further revealed by a glance at the figures contained in Tables 10[14] and 11.[15] They demonstrate that for the period of 1881–1916 almost 80 per cent of the city's population was born outside the province of Manitoba. But to restate the well-known fact that migration was the most significant factor in Winnipeg's population growth prior to 1921 is not enough, for this observation raises more questions than it answers. Chief among them is the question of where the immigrants came from; was it primarily an interprovincial movement or did many of the settlers come directly from other countries? Some general answers to these questions have been dealt with in various migration studies, but little has been done on specific urban communities.[16] The following section attempts to pinpoint the areas that contributed to Winnipeg's population growth.

Having established immigration as the chief source of Winnipeg's population growth, it is now possible to look at another dimension of Winnipeg's demography and analyse the populace according to birthplace, origin, religion, age, and sex. It must be emphasized, however, that the following analysis does not suggest that these are the only important factors in Winnipeg's social make-up. All urban communities have an immense variety of possible groupings. Cities contain families and households, and a large number of business establishments engaged in the production of goods and services. Beyond that, an urban community supports a large complement of specialized units of public or quasi-public nature: governmental bodies and agencies, schools, hospitals, and so on. Besides these numerous operating units there are substantial numbers of formal and informal associations. These draw upon the resident families and other units for their membership and

Table 10 / Birthplace of Winnipeg's Native-Born Population, 1881–1916

Birthplace	1881		1891		1901		1911		1916	
	No.	%	No.	%	No.	%	No.	%	No.	%
Prince Ed. Island	42	.5	83	.3	139	.3	471	.4	463	.3
Nova Scotia	206	2.6	371	1.4	446	1.1	1,505	1.1	1,587	1.0
New Brunswick	126	1.3	279	1.1	303	.7	799	.6	847	.5
Quebec	567	7.1	1,146	4.4	1,365	3.2	2,799	2.1	2,758	1.7
Ontario	3,395	42.5	7,242	28.3	10,419	24.6	20,564	15.1	21,062	12.9
MANITOBA	1,032	12.9	5,510	21.5	13,322	31.5	31,849	23.4	49,648	30.5
Saskatchewan	–	–	–	–	–	–	587	.4	1,083	.7
Alberta	–	–	–	–	–	–	221	.2	279	.1
British Columbia	8	.1	25	.1	32	.1	175	.1	307	.2
Yukon and Territories	31	.4	57	.2	325	.8	52	.1	16	.1
Not stated	–	–	–	–	–	–	945	.7	439	.2
Total Canadian-born	5,387	67.5	14,713	57.3	26,351	62.2	59,967	44.1	78,489	48.2
Total population	7,985	100	25,639	100	42,340	100	136,035	100	163,000	100

they may be loosely or tightly linked to each other in still other associations. This bewildering array of units constitutes the social organization of a community.[17]

In this study it is the birth, origin, and religious groupings that will be emphasized. Throughout most of the period Winnipeg was a frontier community with few established traditions of its own. Thus the racial and religious characteristics of the immigrant population served as a provisional base for society until a new order (with its own traditions and culture) could be developed.[18] The various ethnic groups, with their unique backgrounds, culture, and living standards, each had their own reaction to the Winnipeg environment and in time helped shape that environment.

It must be stressed that these observations are valid only in a community where migration is a continuing and important factor in population growth. As soon as the immigration stream slows down and ethnic groups no longer receive fresh recruits from the mother country, the strength and vitality of most of these groups will wane and eventually become submerged in the culture of the new community.

Table 11 / Birthplace of Winnipeg's Foreign-Born Population, 1881–1916

Birthplace	1881 No.	%	1891 No.	%	1901 No.	%	1911 No.	%	1916 No.	%
England & Wales	879	11.0	4,436	17.4	5,299	12.5	24,260	17.8	27,854	17.1
Scotland	453	5.7	1,563	6.1	1,671	3.9	10,949	8.1	13,182	8.1
Ireland	359	4.5	1,225	4.8	1,218	2.9	4,655	3.4	5,584	3.4
Other British	6	.1	19	.1	115	.3	308	.2	641	.4
Total British	1,697	21.3	7,243	28.4	8,303	19.6	40,172	29.5	47,261	29.0
United States	365	4.6	877	3.3	1,405	3.3	5,798	4.3	6,608	4.2
Scandin-avia & Iceland	32	.4	1,193	4.7	2,199	5.2	3,669	2.7	3,137	1.9
Germany	37	.5	399	1.3	699	1.7	1,866	1.3	713	.3
Austria-Hungary	–	–	–	–	1,343	3.2	9,449	6.9	4,788	2.9
Russia & Poland	6	.1	500	1.9	1,398	3.3	8,577	6.3	11,470	7.2
Galicia & Bukowina	–	–	–	–	–	–	647	.5	6,891	4.3
France	18	.2	40	.2	87	.2	323	.2	293	.2
Belgium	–	–	–	–	50	.1	155	.1	181	.1
Italy	10	.1	13	.1	99	.2	517	.4	704	.3
Asia	–	–	16	.1	164	.4	757	.6	780	.3
Others	433	5.4	705	2.7	424	.6	4,138	3.1	1,685	1.1
Total Foreign-born	2,598	32.5	10,926	42.7	15,989	37.8	76,068	55.9	84,511	51.8
Total population	7,985	100	25,639	100	42,340	100	136,035	100	163,000	100

The offspring of migrants will learn the language and the social mores of the host community and in time participate in its economic, political, and social life without encountering prejudice. In a general sense this is what slowly took place in Winnipeg in the period after 1914. The important point in terms of this study is that prior to the First World War Winnipeg was still receiving large numbers of migrants and a man's birthplace, ethnic origin, and religion told a good deal about his position in the community.

Tables 10 and 11 classify Winnipeg's population according to place of birth. It is immediately apparent from Table 10 that one major source of Winnipeg's native-born population was Ontario. Up to 1891 persons born in Ontario made up the largest single group within the city. After that date Manitoba-born persons became the dominant group, although Ontarians remained very significant right up to 1916. The only other province that made a significant contribution to Winnipeg's population was Quebec, and even then the number of Quebeckers was relatively small. In 1881 7 per cent of the city's populace was made up of Quebeckers, but by 1916 this had declined to less than 2 per cent. This preponderance of Ontarians, coupled with the relative lack of Quebeckers, was to have a distinct influence on many factors of Winnipeg's social life.[19]

The statistical sketch contained in Table 10 reveals one other noteworthy aspect. This is the declining proportion of native-born migrants in Winnipeg's total population make-up. In 1881 over 67 per cent of the city's residents had been born in Canada. By 1916 Canadian-born persons accounted for less than half (48 per cent) of the city's population. This meant, of course, that the proportion of foreign-born immigrants underwent a corresponding increase. In 1881 32 per cent of Winnipeg's residents could be classified as foreign-born while by 1916 this had risen to 52 per cent.

Table 11 reveals that among the foreign-born the British group far outweighs any other. For each time period this group constituted well over one-half of the total foreign-born within the city. And, within this category, it was those born in England that constituted the largest group, those from Scotland second, and those born in Ireland third.

There are several other important trends that can be located in Table 11. In 1881 Americans made up the only other significant foreign-born group but they never became nearly as important as the British-born. In contrast to the West's other major cities, Winnipeg's American-born residents were small in number and percentage.[20] By 1891 several other groups were beginning to make a noteworthy impression. The most important of these was the Scandinavian-Icelandic group, which rose from less than 1 per cent to almost 5 per cent of the total foreign-born. The German-born were also beginning to make a relatively strong showing. Significantly, both these latter groups outnumbered the American-born in 1891. It was not until 1911 that Americans once again outnumbered the "Northern European." The last group of consequence in 1891 was those born in Russia and Poland. And, if this classification is grouped together with those born in Austria-Hungary and Galicia and Bukowina under the broad category of "Slavs," it is apparent that they accounted for the most dramatic increase between 1891 and 1916. At the former date the Slavs made up only 2 per cent of the total population, but they grew steadily in the following decades, reaching a peak of 14.4 per cent in 1916.

These statistical sketches reveal several important characteristics about Winnipeg's population. Of primary significance was the fact that the overwhelming majority of the city's residents were of British-Ontarian stock. Since Americans and Quebeckers were relatively unimportant, it meant that the traditions and culture of the British-Ontarian group would be predominant in the city. Winnipeg's only other important ethnic groups were Northern Europeans (Germans and Scandinavians) and Slavs (Russians, Poles and Ukrainians). Both of these groups grew rapidly during the period and this had profound repercussions on the social fabric of Winnipeg. From the standpoint of the dominant group there was little doubt about its ability to absorb the American or even the Northern European immigrant.[21] But the Slavs were a different matter and a variety of severe strains developed, whether over educational matters, housing, or job opportunities. Since the dominant English-speaking majority clearly regarded the Slavs as second-class citizens, their only hope for improvement was complete assimilation.

Although place of birth data provide some insight into the nature of a city's population, they do have several limitations. Chief among these is the fact that the ethnic origins of immigrants do not always correspond with their countries of birth. Thus the ethnic origins of those born in the United States remain hidden, and those of Jewish origin born in any country are unidentifiable. Moreover, in a new country like Canada, with large numbers of immigrants arriving throughout the period under study, the native-born figures also hide ethnic origins. For example, a child born in Ontario to recent German immigrants would be officially classified as native-born, but would probably consider his origin to be German rather than Canadian. For these reasons and in order to obtain a more complete picture of the contribution of the foreign-born to the total ethnic structure, ethnic origin data must also be examined.

Table 12 contains data relating to the origins of the city's population.[22] The major differences between this table and Table 11 are the allocation of those born in the United States by ethnic origin and the separation of those of Jewish origin from the various countries of birth. Also, the native-born are distributed here into ethnic groups. Significantly, the trends observable in the three tables are quite similar, for the major conclusion to be drawn from Table 12 is the overwhelming importance of those of British origin. They averaged almost 75 per cent of Winnipeg's population throughout the period. This figure roughly equals the proportions of British-born, Ontario-born, and American-born contained in Tables 10 and 11. These gross similarities are confirmed if the ethnic origins of the native-born and the Americans are analysed. In 1916, for example, almost 75 per cent of the native-born gave their origin as British while 66 per cent of the American-born did so. Moreover, the numbers of those born in Quebec and France coincide

Table 12 / Origins of Winnipeg's Population, 1881–1916

Origins	1881		1886		1901		1911		1916	
	No.	%	No.	%	No.	%	No.	%	No.	%
English	2,332	29.2	6,946	34.3	14,559	34.5	42,408	31.2	57,190	35.1
Scotch	2,470	30.9	5,380	26.6	9,190	21.7	25,789	19.0	31,392	19.3
Irish	1,864	23.4	4,391	21.7	7,324	17.3	15,432	11.4	19,466	11.9
Other British	13	.2	78	.4	157	.4	923	.7	1,190	.7
Total British	6,679	83.6	16,795	83.0	31,230	73.9	84,552	62.3	109,238	67.0
Scandinavian & Icelandic	409	5.1	1,350	6.7	3,322	7.9	4,956	3.6	5,921	3.6
German	186	2.3	545	2.7	2,283	5.4	8,912	6.6	5,632	3.5
Austro-Hungarian	–	–	–	–	1,147	2.7	6,072	4.5	4,022	2.5
Russian & Polish	6	.1	293	1.4	624	1.5	6,301	4.6	8,606	5.3
Ukrainian	–	–	–	–	–	–	900	.7	8,621	5.3
French	450	5.6	610	3.0	1,379	3.3	2,695	2.0	3,115	1.9
Dutch	5	.1	50	.2	92	.2	535	.4	795	.5
Italian	26	.3	59	.3	147	.3	769	.6	1,276	.8
Asian	2	.1	16	.1	121	.3	586	.4	660	.3
Jewish	4	.1	61	.3	1,156	2.7	9,023	6.6	13,473	8.2
Indian-Métis	9	.1	331	1.6	142	.3	30	.1	32	.1
Negro	4	.1	19	.1	44	.1	165	.1	224	.1
Others	205	2.6	109	.6	653	1.5	10,539	7.6	1,385	.8
Totals	7,985	100	20,238	100	42,340	100	136,035	100	163,000	100

almost exactly with the numbers giving their origin as French in Table 12.[23] Unfortunately data do not exist to allow similar comparisons for all the groups contained in Table 12, but the evidence for the British and French groups clearly indicates that this statistical sketch represents a fairly accurate picture of Winnipeg's ethnic composition.

While Table 12 reveals the large and continuing importance of those of British origin, it also indicates that this group's proportion of the population steadily declined between 1881 and 1911. Correspondingly, the Northern European, Slavic, and Jewish groups increased substantially. Indeed, by 1911, those of Jewish origin formed one of the most important ethnic groups in Winnipeg.

The net effect of changes in the ethnic composition of Winnipeg's population may be seen in Figure 1.[24] The employment of the broad grouping utilized here renders the analysis somewhat less useful than Table 12 because of a loss of information about specific ethnic groups. On the other hand, it does allow for a quick comprehension of the trends that were noted in the three previous sketches.

Table 13, on religious affiliation, provides additional insight into the social composition of Winnipeg's population.[25] Religious affiliation plays an important role in the social make-up of any community, for it reinforces cultural and language differences, reduces the possibility for intermarriage, encourages segregation, and even helps to create differences in educational opportunity. Similarly, emphasis placed on ethnic loyalties enhances religious groupings.[26]

There is no doubt that Winnipeg was a predominantly Protestant community. Religions such as Anglican, Methodist, and Presbyterian

Table 13/Religious Affiliations of Winnipeg's Population, 1881–1916

Religious denomination	1881 No.	%	1891 No.	%	1901 No.	%	1911 No.	%	1916 No.	%
Anglican	2,373	29.7	6,854	26.7	10,175	24.0	31,338	23.0	39,391	24.3
Baptist	349	4.4	1,046	4.2	2,055	4.9	5,062	3.7	4,766	2.9
Congregationalist	111	1.4	1,050	4.2	1,300	3.1	2,086	1.5	2,110	1.3
Methodist	1,380	17.3	4,310	16.8	6,741	15.9	15,387	11.3	17,488	10.6
Presbyterian	2,365	29.6	5,952	23.2	10,172	24.0	30,367	22.3	38,905	24.0
Lutheran	292	3.7	2,291	8.9	4,253	10.1	11,151	8.2	10,370	6.6
Protestant	–	–	15	.1	117	.3	3,158	2.3	1,862	1.2
Roman Catholic	1,020	12.7	2,470	9.6	5,143	12.1	19,729	14.5	24,013	14.1
Greek Church	–	–	–	–	230	.5	3,411	2.5	6,254	3.9
Jewish	21	.3	645	2.5	1,145	2.7	8,934	6.6	13,443	8.4
Salvation Army	–	–	99	.3	196	.5	500	.4	648	.4
Non-Christian	–	–	–	–	–	–	152	.1	235	.1
No religion	–	–	–	–	6	.1	1,163	.9	386	.2
Various sects	15	.2	234	1.0	524	1.2	1,883	1.4	2,589	1.6
Unspecified	59	.7	673	2.6	283	.7	1,714	1.3	540	.3
Totals	7,985	100	25,639	100	42,240	100	136,035	100	163,000	100

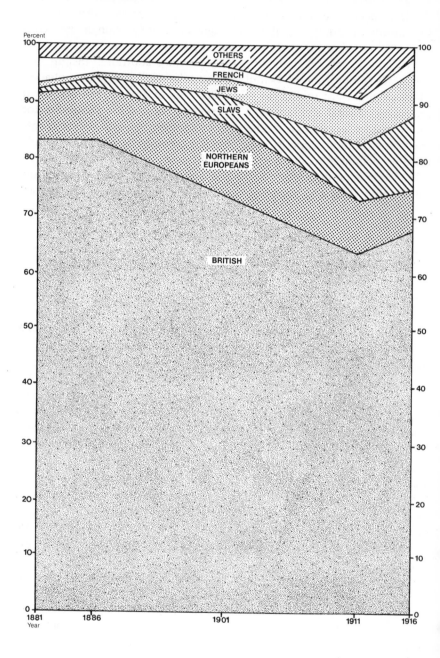

Figure 1. Percentage Distribution of Winnipeg's
Population by Ethnic Origin, 1881–1916

account for well over one-half of the city's religious make-up. The German influence is seen in the strength of the Lutherans, and the Slavic in the Roman Catholic and Greek Church categories. By 1911 there was as well a significant number of those of Jewish faith.

While the racial and religious background of the population are undoubtedly important in determining the social development of a young city, there are other factors which should be taken into consideration. The age and sex distribution of the population are significant for several reasons. First of all, they have a direct effect on a city's growth rate. A particular age-sex distribution determines fertility and mortality rates, and by extension the growth or decline of a city. For example, a city with a substantial share of its population over forty will have a lower rate of natural increase than a city of young adults. Similarly, a city with an extreme imbalance of the sexes would not be expected to have the same birth rate as a city with a more even distribution. For the social historian, however, the age-sex characteristics of a population are also important from another standpoint. Such information is valuable in explaining a host of urban demands and characteristics. The number of taverns and brothels, the degree of interest in city beautification plans, the nature of the labour force, or the particular composition of municipal services—all reflect to some degree whether the population is predominantly male or female, young or old.

Table 14 gives the age distribution of Winnipeg's population in 1891 and 1916 and compares it with that of Manitoba and Canada.[27] It is significant that Winnipeg had its highest percentage of population in the 20-40 age category while Manitoba and Canada had their highest percentages in the 0-19 age group. It should also be noted that for those 45 and older Manitoba and Canada both have higher percentages than does Winnipeg. In other words, Winnipeg had a relatively young population.

The reasons for the high percentage of people in Winnipeg in the active and productive age groups (20-44) are easily located. It is a well-known fact that cities are attractive places for persons of productive age, and that such persons tend to migrate to urban centres in large numbers.[28] Winnipeg was no exception, as Table 15 demonstrates.[29] The large number of active, foreign-born in Winnipeg clearly indicates that the city's particular age distribution was the product of immigration. But it can be noted that in this period Manitoba also had a young population and clearly appealed to migrants.

It has been stated that in a young urban community such as Winnipeg, where growth is primarily a function of migration, there is a considerable attraction for young adults. Table 16 reveals that in such areas there are also more males than females.[30] This indicates that more males migrate than do females, since the sex-ratio at birth is almost

Table 14 / Age Distribution of the Population: City of Winnipeg, Province of Manitoba, and Canada, 1891 and 1916

1891

Age groups	City of Winnipeg		Province of Manitoba		Canada	
	No.	%	No.	%	No.	%
0–19	11,023	43.0	71,349	46.4	2,251,508	46.7
20–44	12,013	47.0	59,317	39.0	1,682,382	34.9
45–64	2,252	8.8	13,723	9.0	617,443	12.7
65 and over	305	1.1	2,621	1.7	218,790	4.2
Unknown	46	.1	5,496	3.9	63,116	1.5
Totals	25,639	100	152,506	100	4,833,239	100

1916

Age groups	City of Winnipeg		Province of Manitoba		Canada	
	No.	%	No.	%	No.	%
0–19	64,473	39.6	249,127	44.9	3,070,030	42.6
20–44	76,192	46.7	221,081	39.9	2,788,971	38.7
45–64	18,934	11.6	67,961	12.3	1,008,930	14.0
65 and over	2,988	1.8	14,062	2.6	338,712	4.7
Unknown	413	.2	1,629	.3	–	–
Totals	163,000	100	553,860	100	7,206,643	100

constant.[31] Accordingly, Winnipeg and Manitoba—as recipients of large numbers of migrants—contain significantly more males than females. A close analysis of Table 16, however, reveals another important fact. The city of Winnipeg, while constantly having a majority of males in the population, had more females proportionately than did Manitoba as a whole. There is an important economic reason for this rural-urban sex-differential. Cities provide more economic opportunities for females than do primary economic activities such as agriculture. And with the advancing industrialization of Winnipeg during this period more and more job openings were available for females in service industries and light manufacturing. In fact, the proportion of females in the population

Table 15 / Age Distribution of the Native and Foreign-Born Population: City of Winnipeg and Province of Manitoba, 1916

	City of Winnipeg				Province of Manitoba			
	Native-born		Foreign-born		Native-born		Foreign-born	
Age groups	No.	%	No.	%	No.	%	No.	%
0–19	46,498	59.3	17,975	21.3	204,023	61.5	45,104	20.4
20–44	24,322	31.0	51,870	61.3	92,196	27.7	128,885	58.1
45–64	6,318	8.0	12,616	15.0	28,910	8.7	39,051	17.6
65+	1,107	1.4	1,881	2.2	6,104	1.8	7,959	3.6
Unknown	244	.3	169	.2	913	.3	787	.3

Table 16 / Sex Distribution of the Population: City of Winnipeg and Province of Manitoba, 1891–1916

	City of Winnipeg				Province of Manitoba			
Year	Male		Female		Male		Female	
	No.	%	No.	%	No.	%	No.	%
1891	13,406	52.2	12,233	47.7	84,342	55.3	68,164	44.7
1901	21,940	51.9	20,400	48.1	138,504	54.3	116,707	45.7
1906	50,461	56.0	39,692	44.0	295,183	56.1	160,505	43.9
1911	74,404	54.7	61,631	45.3	252,954	54.8	208,440	45.2
1916	82,227	50.4	80,773	49.6	294,609	53.2	259,251	46.8

of Winnipeg probably would have been much greater were it not for the waves of predominantly male migrants in the period 1901 to 1911.

One important aspect of Winnipeg's age-sex distribution was its relation to the commercial elite's economic programs. Any young male would be deeply concerned with obtaining and holding a job and it is not unrealistic to assume that a city of predominantly young men would look kindly on programs designed to create employment opportunities. Only as Winnipeg's population became older and more evenly balanced in terms of sex would programs (such as city beautification) that measured social, as opposed to strictly economic, returns grow in popularity.

9 / The Urban Environment

At any given time the arrangement of streets, buildings, and neighbourhoods in a large city represents a compromise among many diverse and often conflicting elements. Winnipeg was no exception. Its heritage of river-lot farming and fur-trade routes determined to a large degree the city's street patterns. Winnipeg's rapid rate of growth and large foreign-born population played important roles in shaping the city's distinctive neighbourhoods. The Red and Assiniboine rivers and the lack of effective intra-urban transportation for a time prevented the spread of the urban area beyond the distance a man might walk in a short time. Only when new modes of transportation, such as the bicycle and street railway, came into general use could Winnipeg's real growth continue unhindered into the surrounding countryside. Winnipeg's role as the railway centre of the West also affected the city's physical appearance. Together these factors combined to turn Winnipeg into a series of self-contained enclaves; "a sprawling, gap-toothed collection of ghettos."[1]

One of the first issues that confronted City Council after incorporation in 1873 was the layout of Winnipeg's streets. Main Street was already well established as the most important street in the city. This former trail along the Red River, which had been a main route between the early Selkirk settlement and the Hudson's Bay Company's post of Upper Fort Garry, was never straightened, however, and its crookedness was to cause City Council many headaches over the years. But the adoption of a 132-foot right-of-way for Main Street and for Portage Avenue partially compensated for these streets' irregular course. The width of Portage Avenue and Main Street was not dictated by visions of eight-lane traffic but was based on the mode of travel of the early Red River carts. The carts tended to move in a rough echelon pattern which took up a great deal of space. There were reasons for this: a long single file of carts would have been vulnerable to ambush, and by travelling in a random fashion they avoided the deep, muddy ruts made by the vehicles ahead.[2] In any case, the heritage of the rivers and the fur-trade routes that followed them were clearly apparent in Portage Avenue and Main Street.

The familiar and historic pattern of long, narrow strips of land fronting on the river provided the basis for new street plans.[3] Thus all the streets north of Notre Dame, which ran west from the Red River and crossed Main Street, closely followed the boundary lines of the early lots. Similarly, in the area between Notre Dame and the Assiniboine River, the streets ran north from the latter, meeting Notre Dame at a sharp angle.

In these early years Notre Dame Avenue was intended to become, after Main Street, the most important street in Winnipeg. It acted somewhat like an axis, for streets leading northwest from the Assiniboine River swung east at Notre Dame and then ran out at right angles across those running west from the Red River. Significantly, in these early plans Portage Avenue (then called Queen) and the area south of it were unplanned and undeveloped.

Given this real and planned importance of Main Street and Notre Dame Avenue it is not surprising that the residential sections of the city tended to group around them. In the area between Main Street and the Red River were located most of the residences built before 1874. Point Douglas, surrounded by the river on three sides, was, prior to the coming of the railroad, one of the most desirable locations in the young community. Many of the founders of Winnipeg had homes there, including James H. Ashdown, W. G. Fonseca, Robert and Stewart Mulvey, Dr. Schultz, and others.[4] Close to Main Street was also the desired location of a large number of boarding houses which were a prominent feature of the growing city. The lack of sufficient space in hotels and the shortage of housing for the large floating population[5] had led many homeowners to provide accommodation to meet the great demand. The streets leading to the waterfront and wharves were also dominated by boarding houses. Finally, it was in the area west of Main Street, and particularly along the streets running parallel to and adjoining Notre Dame Avenue, that most of the post-incorporation residences were situated.

Prior to 1877, then, the built-up portion of the newly incorporated city comprised only a small fraction of its political extent: probably about one-fifth of the administrative area of Winnipeg. This concentration was largely the result of the speculative manipulations of the Hudson's Bay Company. The company had opposed incorporation since it would have had to pay large amounts of taxes on the 450 acres of land that it owned within the proposed city's boundaries. Following incorporation the company at first sold only a very limited number of lots in its "reserve" in the area bounded by Notre Dame Avenue, Main Street, and the Assiniboine River. Consequently, up to 1877 Winnipeg tended to spread north of Notre Dame, leaving this southern section almost untouched. After 1877 the company sold a large number of lots and by 1883 had apparently reaped profits of over $2 million. This area quickly developed and became the most desirable residential district in the city. Soon Hudson's Bay officials, government officials, and successful businessmen either located or relocated (moving from Point Douglas) here, giving the district a certain eminence. The land values were higher, the lots larger, and the houses bigger than in other parts of the city.[6]

With this rapid development between 1877 and 1884 of a "desirable" residential location on the Hudson's Bay Company reserve it became possible to distinguish somewhat between the different areas of the city. In very general terms, most of the middle-class residences were situated on streets north of Notre Dame or east of Main Street where the lots were smaller and the houses simpler. In the reserve area the normal lot size at this time was 50 by 120 feet with a 20-foot lane. Indeed, the company, in an effort to keep land values high, stipulated that lots could not be any smaller. Conversely, lots north of Notre Dame were sold in a size 66 by 99 feet, without lanes. And many of the lots in this area were subsequently subdivided into 33 by 99-foot lots.[7] In addition to the advantages created by regulation, the land in the reserve afforded some natural advantages; for example, it was at a somewhat higher level than land to the north of Notre Dame and was less liable to flooding. It must be emphasized, however, that at this time there was no pronounced lower-class residential district anywhere in Winnipeg. This development did not take place until the appearance of more industry and the routing of the main line of the Canadian Pacific through Point Douglas.

In this early period there was little residential segregation of ethnic groups. The preponderance of the British and Ontarians precluded any significant cultural conflicts that might have been manifested in residential segregation. At incorporation Winnipeg had been divided into four wards—North, South, East, and West[8]—but these divisions generally served only as convenient electoral and administrative boundaries and none of them acquired the distinctive characteristics that would mark the different wards of the city in a later period.

The commercial and industrial development of Winnipeg tended to follow the spatial patterns established by residential building. The part of Main Street between "Portage Road" and Point Douglas had most of the commercial establishments located on it, and even as early as 1875 the corner of Portage and Main was the centre of most commercial activity. The southern part of Main Street was dominated by Upper Fort Garry, the walls of which cut across the southern end of the street. This was the chief reason why there were only a few com-

Map 4/
City of
Winnipeg
1907

mercial buildings here. By 1881, however, Fort Garry had lost much of its reputation as the major component in the commercial life of "the Forks" and during the boom of 1882 all the fort except for one gate was torn down to make way for more profitable land use.

The industries of the city during this period consisted mainly of saw and grist mills which were located on the waterfront of the Red River. Two breweries occupied sites at a considerable distance from the built-up area, and a distillery and a soda-water factory were located in the centre of Winnipeg. To complete the industrial picture mention need be made only of several carriage and wagon factories and two foundries.[9]

At the beginning of 1881 Winnipeg was a thriving yet relatively small settlement with very tenuous connections with its hinterland and the eastern provinces. All this changed with the routing of the Canadian Pacific Railway through the city. The real estate boom and the great influx of newcomers after 1881 had marked effects on the urban landscape of Winnipeg. One of the most obvious changes that occurred was the expansion of the city's boundaries and the adoption of a new ward system. Winnipeg was divided into six wards in 1882 (a seventh was added in 1906).[10]

In the years following the real estate boom of 1881–82, there developed in Winnipeg a series of distinctive environments. The clustering of economic activities, the segregation of classes and ethnic groups, the unequal distribution of municipal services, and different types of residential construction—all created a considerable variety of specialized and unique districts within the city. Indeed, the presence of neighbourhoods of distinctive character—the business district, the foreign quarter, the "sylvan suburb," and so on—distinguished the large city of Winnipeg from its more jumbled predecessor, the small, almost rural community of 1874–84.[11]

It is impossible in a brief canvas to survey all the variations of neighbourhood which existed in Winnipeg in the years 1884–1914, but by dividing the city into three large districts, and by discussing suburban growth separately, the most important variations can be observed and analysed. In general, wards 2 and 4 became the central core; wards 5, 6 and 7 became the North End; and wards 1 and 3 formed the South and West Ends, respectively. By 1910 a few areas in Winnipeg had been fully built up and some residents and industries were moving out. In the years after 1910 Winnipeg was fast spilling over into the new suburbs beyond the municipal boundaries. These districts and suburbs, radiating as they did from Portage and Main, reflected the general directions of growth that Winnipeg took in this period.

The Central Core

By 1885 the intersection of Portage and Main had become the core of Winnipeg's commercial district. Commercial land use spread along Main Street and on streets east and west of this major thoroughfare. Buildings in residential use prior to 1885 eventually gave way to this growing commercial district.[12] In the central portion of the city real estate prices were relatively high, and in the years after 1885 only business enterprises could afford to purchase lots here. In general, lots on Main Street were priced about twenty times higher than those on the fringe of the central business district. As an example, a lot twenty-eight feet wide on Main Street was assessed at $19,600 in 1885 while one on the eastern fringe of Ward 3 was assessed at only $1,000.[13]

Besides a large number of retail stores and service-orientated establishments (such as real estate agencies), Winnipeg's central core was dominated by the institutions connected with the grain and wholesale trade. With the construction of a Grain Exchange Building near City Hall in 1882, Winnipeg became firmly established as the headquarters of the western grain trade. This new function in the economic structure of the city resulted in the establishment of grain companies, facilities for handling the grain, and new and larger financial institutions. By the early nineties there were the beginnings of a concentrated financial section in the vicinity of City Hall. By 1901 no less than twenty-six companies and brokers dealing in grain had their offices in the Grain Exchange Building, and three banks opened branch offices in the neighbourhood. As a complement to the grain trade a marked concentration of dealers in agricultural implements appeared in the vicinity of the Grain Exchange Building. In 1901 there were eleven such dealers, including the Massey-Harris Company and the McCormick Harvesting Machinery Company.[14]

In 1906 a new Grain Exchange Building was built close to the corner of Portage and Main and this move resulted in a similar step being taken by banks, stockbrokers, and grain merchants. By 1914 more than twenty-five buildings used exclusively for banking and stockbroking were concentrated on Main Street, just north of Portage Avenue.[15] This district was the headquarters for the financial and grain-marketing operations of the Canadian West and over the years it gained international recognition.[16]

With the emergence of retail stores in the new agricultural communities along the railway lines, Winnipeg merchants began to profit from an extensive wholesale trade. Within a short time after 1885 this trade assumed a dominating position in Winnipeg's economic structure; in 1890, for example, there were over eighty wholesale firms in the city doing an aggregate turnover of $15 million annually.[17] And the establishments of the wholesale dealers were almost entirely located in the central core, in the area just west of City Hall.

In the choice of a location for their premises the wholesale companies tended to avoid main thoroughfares such as Main Street and Portage Avenue. The loading and unloading of goods required space which could hardly be obtained in suitable amounts and at a reasonable cost on these streets. Yet a central location was still required, preferably close to the local concentration of retail stores and not too far from the railroad. Consequently the streets branching off Main Street were considered the most suitable. Big buildings were erected here, especially adapted to the wholesale trade. As the city and province grew, this wholesale district expanded so greatly that structures previously in residential use were torn down and replaced by warehouses.[18]

This particular concentration of the wholesale trade in the core was encouraged by two developments occurring in 1904 and 1912. In 1904 the Canadian Pacific built a spur from their main line into the heart of the district to serve the many wholesale traders located there. And between 1910 and 1912 the Midland Railway was also constructed to serve this district. Its right-of-way ran almost the whole length of Ward 4 and warehouses were built astride the tracks. Thus even the western portions of Ward 4 became marked by extensive development of the wholesale trade.[19]

In terms of industrial development the central core did not dominate the city as it did in retail and wholesale establishments. Most of Winnipeg's heavy and medium industry was located in other districts. Light industries (such as the garment industry, printing, cigar manufacturing, saddleries) were, however, spread throughout the central area of the city. Unlike heavy and medium industry, which needed both extensive space and close proximity to transportation facilities, the only requirement of light industry was that it be near the central business district and the wholesale and retail companies that it served. Thus such businesses frequently took up a few rooms in an office building or warehouse, or made use of buildings on the fringe of the business district. A particular concentration of these light industries occurred just west of City Hall, in the heart of the wholesale district. In 1914, for example, there were seven clothing manufacturers established here.[20]

It was in the central core as well that the great majority of Winnipeg's other non-residential structures were located. Ward 2 had within its boundaries the Legislative Buildings, Fort Osborne Barracks, the University of Manitoba, the Court House, Provincial Gaol, Post Office and numerous other administrative structures. Here, too, were many of the city's leading hotels and clubs, including Hotel Fort Garry and the prestigious Manitoba Club. Similarly, Ward 4 contained a large number of administrative structures, hotels, theatres, and so on. These included City Hall, the Winnipeg General Hospital, and the Winnipeg, Orpheum, Pantages, and Walker theatres.

It was the hotels of the area, however, that had the greatest impact on the character of the central core. The area between the CNR and CPR stations was Winnipeg's "hotel row," since along this portion of Main Street were upwards of sixty hotels. In this pre-prohibition era hotels were first and foremost places to drink. The bars of the hotels were all well-stocked with whiskey, while the decor included a brass rail, paintings of nudes, spittoons, and other period paraphernalia. And because of this high concentration of bars, "pedestrians were never beyond the range of the aroma of booze that wafted through the windows and doors of the hotels." The hotels also often had poolrooms attached while in between the hotels were "wholesale boozeries" and "Free Admission Parlours." In the latter customers could choose between flicking card movies, slot machines, target practice, and a prostitute in the back room.[21] It was this area of pickpockets, pool sharks, prostitutes, confidence men, and booze that inspired one writer to suggest that the city deserved to be called "Winnipeg the Wicked."[22]

This concentration of such a large amount of Winnipeg's nonresidential structures in the central core tended increasingly after 1890 to give this area a distinct commercial character. This development was a mixed blessing in terms of the core as a residential area. On the one hand it was certainly an advantage in the early years of the "walking city" for citizens to live close to the central business district where, of course, a good deal of the residents worked. On the other hand, the rapid growth of this district as the entertainment, commercial and administrative heart of the city had its disadvantages, for it brought with it noise, dirt, crime, and overcrowding, all of which tended to reduce its appeal as a prime residential area.

Encroachment of the residential areas of the central core by railways was perhaps the most notable development after 1900. Besides the CPR spur track and the Midland Railway in Ward 4, the Canadian Northern Railway yards and station took up a good deal of desirable waterfront land in Ward 2. In 1904 this development resulted in the closing of one of the ward's major streets and thereafter the upper-class residents who remained in the ward tended to live close to the Assiniboine rather than the Red River.[23] This development is an important one for it hastened the growth of a north-south split in Winnipeg, with desirable residential locations concentrating around the Assiniboine River.

While railway development thus affected the eastern areas of Ward 2, general expansion of the business district encroached on the area between Notre Dame and Broadway. Expansion westward along Portage Avenue had been sparked by the building of a huge retail store by the T. Eaton Company in 1905. With this development other commercial establishments, particularly retail stores, began to fill in the space between the store and Main Street. By 1914 retail trade had extended along Portage Avenue well into the West End and soon land values here exceeded the land values along Main Street. Portage Avenue, with its newer stores and office buildings, became more attractive than the central part of Main Street, where the commercial establishments were older and often too small for the increasing number of customers.

The decline of the central core as a residential area was also a result of the city's rapid population growth. While it is true that the proportion of the city's population residing in this district declined after 1890, it was only a relative decline. In 1885 the core contained only 12,000 residents. By 1912 this had increased to 63,000. This much larger number of persons in the same geographical space meant that the residential areas of this district took on a new appearance. In 1887, for example, a local newspaper carried a series of articles on the homes situated on the Hudson's Bay Company reserve. In every case the large size of the lots and the generally spacious appearance of the area was stressed.[24] But as more and more people came to Winnipeg and the demand for homes increased, earlier limitations on lot size were disregarded and vacant lots were occupied. Individual real estate agents had not the long-term interest in keeping land values high by lot restrictions; concern for quick profits was met with subdivision of lots until by 1914 a large majority of the lots in the area were less than fifty feet wide.

This process of subdivision was not confined to land, for many of the reserve's handsome structures were themselves divided and their rooms rented. A survey of one area of Ward 2 revealed that of 416 homes inspected, 122 were improperly occupied as tenements by from two to eight families.[25]

Table 17 / **Population Distribution by Districts, 1885–1912** *

Years	Central Core		North End		South and West Ends	
	No.	%	No.	%	No.	%
1885	11,793	59.7	6,880	34.9	1,063	5.4
1890	13,778	60.0	7,819	33.9	1,403	6.1
1895	16,211	47.5	12,164	35.6	5,749	16.9
1900	18,160	46.1	14,592	36.8	6,782	17.1
1906	32,252	31.9	43,527	43.1	25,278	25.0
1912	63,009	34.1	62,503	33.8	59,218	32.1

* The data for this table are taken from local newspapers. There are no official figures available.

Ward 4 also suffered from this subdivision of land and houses in the years after 1885, although the process was not so marked. Since Ward 4 had never reached a high point as the "most desirable residential district" of the city, residential blight was never so apparent as in Ward 2.[26] Even before the pressures of an expanding business district and a rapidly growing population began to affect Ward 4, lots were of a smaller size than in Ward 2—usually thirty-three feet wide. This in itself prevented further division and this area fared much better in terms of overcrowding than did the previously more prestigious Ward 2.[27]

The gradual deterioration of the residential areas of the central core was not caused only by business encroachment and population pressure. It is highly likely that the upper class of Ward 2 and the middle class of Ward 4 would not have moved out were it not for the development of other accessible and desirable residential locations. "Accessible" was the key word, for it was not until Winnipeg's rivers had been bridged and the bicycle and street railway came into general use that the South and West Ends—both far removed from the central business district—developed significantly.

Finally, if Winnipeg had not enjoyed boom times throughout most of the period, it is possible that the original residents of the core would have been held to their old neighbourhoods. In other words, the long period of economic prosperity enjoyed by Winnipeg promoted rapid class turnover in the old central city housing and large-scale migration to the new upper-class and middle-class wards and suburbs.

To refer to "old central city housing" in a city as young as was Winnipeg in 1914 is not, of course, perfectly accurate. Naturally some of the homes built in the seventies and eighties had deteriorated by that date; but a large number of the original homes, built as they often were for quite well-to-do persons, remained fine, useful structures which

Table 18 / **New Residential Construction by Districts, 1900–1912**

District	Modern brick dwellings		Modern frame dwellings		Non-modern frame dwellings	
	No.	%	No.	%	No.	%
Central core	86	20.6	264	8.4	145	8.8
North End	63	15.4	861	27.7	1,067	62.8
South and West Ends	266	64.0	1,992	63.9	483	28.4
Totals	415	100	3,117	100	1,695	100

continued to command substantial rents and prices. Thus, as original inhabitants moved out, their places were not quickly filled by the lower class for whom the rents and prices remained too steep. Rather, the residential areas of the central core declined only very gradually. The result was that Winnipeg escaped a core of poverty simply because of its newness as a settled community. The growing working class and the large numbers of disadvantaged immigrants tended to gravitate to the North End, where land was cheap and a large number of working-class homes were constructed in the years after 1895. In general, then, Winnipeg's spatial growth was marked by a core of middle and working-class elements, surrounded on the south by the middle class, and on the north by the working and lower class.

These general trends show up in the type of residential construction that went on in the various districts.[28] The central core had fewer middle and lower-class homes being built after 1900 than did either of the other districts, but it still accounted for a significant percentage of the new upper-class structures. In most cases these brick homes were located in the southern part of Ward 2, close by the Assiniboine River. Excluding brick dwellings, the central core was the slowest growing area of the city by 1900 in terms of residential construction. The fact that its population was still increasing indicates that many of the dwellings in the core were being put into multiple family use, or converted into rooming houses.

The central core in 1886 had a somewhat diverse ethnic mixture (Table 19).[29] Like all districts in the city at this time it was dominated by those of British-Ontarian stock, but in addition it had substantial numbers of Scandinavians and Germans and a smattering of Slavs and Jews. In the years between 1886 and 1916 the British remained the

Table 19 / Specified Ethnic Groups in Winnipeg's Central Core, 1886–1916

Ethnic Group	No.	1886 % of total group pop'n	% of district pop'n	No.	1901 % of total group pop'n	% of district pop'n	No.	1916 % of total group pop'n	% of district pop'n
British	10,109	60.2	85.6	14,814	47.4	78.5	54,538	45.4	81.3
Slavic	53	18.0	.5	280	15.8	1.5	2,448	11.2	3.6
Jewish	58	95.1	.5	125	10.8	.6	1,191	8.8	1.8
Scandinavian	648	48.0	5.5	1,446	43.5	7.7	1,315	22.9	2.0
German	282	51.8	2.4	766	33.5	4.1	3,924	61.4	5.9
Others	643	53.9	5.5	1,426	55.3	7.6	3,622	43.2	5.4

core's dominant group. And while all the other ethnic groups except the Scandinavians increased their percentage of the district's population, the core's general ethnic mix was substantially retained. Thus, without attempting to account for all the variations that occurred in this thirty-year period, it can be noted that in terms of ethnic composition the central core was the "middle" district of Winnipeg. For while it contained fairly large numbers of all city's the ethnic groups, none except the Germans had a majority of their group located in this district. The great majority of the Slavs, Jews, and Scandinavians were situated in the North End, and it was the South and West Ends that had the greatest percentage of British by 1901. In the trend to ethnic segregation in Winnipeg the central core was the city's most unremarkable and stable district.

The North End, "Foreign Quarter"

Wards 5, 6 and 7 comprised what came to be called by contemporaries the North End; a label that then and since has carried with it a good deal more than geographic meaning.[30] The North End was a synonym for the "Foreign Quarter," "New Jerusalem," and "CPR Town." Perhaps the best example of the images conjured up in the minds of Winnipeggers when the North End was mentioned exists in a novel written about that area. The central character, an East European immigrant, lives amid the "mean and dirty clutter" of the North End; "a howling chaos, . . . an endless grey expanse of mouldering ruin, a heap seething with unwashed children, sick men in grey underwear, vast sweating women in vaster petticoats."[31] Another Winnipegger remembered that "the so-called foreigners occupied one gigantic melting pot north of the CPR tracks."[32]

The image of the North End as an undesirable residential location for prosperous Anglo-Saxons was not, of course, formed overnight. Indeed, in the years before the coming of the railroad and the great influx of immigrants, Point Douglas in Ward 5 was the most prestigious residential location in Winnipeg. But this designation did not survive the routing of the CPR main line through the district. By 1895 the North End had in fact become dominated by the working class and by large groups of foreign immigrants. Moreover in 1906, at the peak of immigration into Winnipeg, the North End, which comprised less than one-third of the city's geographical area contained 43 per cent of the population. In short, population pressure also contributed to the North End's deterioration, accompanied as it was by considerable overcrowding.

The development of railway facilities in the North End went through two stages. Between 1882 and 1884 the CPR built its yards, shops and roundhouse in Ward 5. These original facilities did not last beyond 1903. In that year the railway, in response to the growth of Winnipeg as commercial and grain centre of the Canadian West, began a vast expansion program that brought their facilities to the size shown on Map 4. This "most remarkable advance" in the fortunes of Winnipeg as a railway city was hailed as a great boost to the city's economy, as indeed it was. The actual expansion project was a great windfall for the city's construction and building supplies industry. But the intrusion of "the longest railway yards in the world" into what was the geographical centre of Winnipeg had profound effects on the North End as a residential area.[33]

The role of the Canadian Pacific in changing the character of the North End was apparent in four general areas. The construction of a large station, locomotive shops, stores and office building, foundry, freight-car shops, powerhouse, scrap yard, and immense marshalling yards (120 miles of tracks and space for 10,000 cars) represented a considerable industrial development in their own right. The huge CPR facilities were, in short, the dominant physical feature of the North End. No one could enter that portion of the city without being vividly aware of a maze of buildings and tracks, noise, dirt, and smell. In contrast to the central core and the South End, which also had considerable railway facilities located within their boundaries, the CPR yards were in the heart of the North End and not on the extremities.

The continuing development of Winnipeg as a major railroad centre also meant that the railways, and particularly the CPR, employed thousands of Winnipeggers. Indeed, by 1911 over thirty-five hundred persons were employed by the CPR, "more than in any other institution in the West." And these working-class elements located themselves in the vicinity of their place of work, on either side of the tracks in wards 5 and 6. Thus the designation "CPR Town." The growth of the North End as a working-class area was also a result of the role the railway played in attracting heavy and medium industry. Easy access to the railroad, as the predominant means of transport, was of vital importance for most of these industries. This factor became so important that old-established companies left their sites on the Red River and moved west to locations astride the railway tracks. In 1901, for example, north Point Douglas was the location for the Oglivie Flour Mills, Vulcan Iron and Engineering Works, and several saw mills. And by 1914 the location or relocation of medium and heavy industry on both sides of the tracks from Point Douglas to the western boundary of the city was most apparent. Medium industries, such as the manufacturing of carriages and wagons, farm implements, electrical appliances, and malt liquors occurred in the vicinity of Higgins and Jarvis avenues. Heavy industries, such as bridge and iron works, machine shops, and concrete companies also located on both sides of the tracks, particularly in the western areas of the North End. Although harmful and unsuited to the residential districts around them, these industries, and particularly those in the Point Douglas area, remained in their locations long after it was obvious that more suitable sites were available on the outskirts of the city. The large capital investment and high expenses involved in moving prevented any relocation.

Finally, the running of the CPR main line across Ward 5, followed by growth of that company's facilities and the attraction of other industries, effectively cut off the North End from the rest of the city. The result of this large area of industrial development was described in 1912:

> For many years the north-end . . . was practically a district apart from the city. . . . The true cause of this isolation was the level railroad crossing intersecting Main Street. The traffic grew immensely; there were many passenger trains constantly going in and out of the station just east of Main Street, and in addition hundreds of freight trains choked the tracks to such an extent that traffic on Main Street was often blocked for hours. The street cars did not cross the tracks and passengers for the north-end had to transfer at crossings, often waiting many minutes in all kinds of weather. Naturally, with such conditions, . . . those who located north of the tracks were not of a desirable class.[34]

This major impediment to a free movement of residents in and out of the North End was overcome only slowly. By 1914 only two overhead bridges and two subways provided access to the North End, and it was not until after 1908 that the city's street railway had more than one crossing of the CPR tracks. In general, then, the extensive development of the street railway system in the North End encouraged spatial growth there but discouraged social contact between that area and the rest of the city.

This partial isolation of Winnipeg's residents meant that the image of the North End held by those living in the rest of the city was rarely disturbed by reality. In such a circumstance exaggerated tales of "bestial orgies" and "un-Christian activities" thrived.[35] The North Enders, moreover, rarely travelled to the other districts. A thriving retail and service trade grew up along North Main and Selkirk Avenue and with this and the proximity of their places of work, North Enders had little reason to leave. Unfortunately, such isolation was not conducive to the assimilation process and Winnipeg in 1914 was a severely divided city, both geographically and socially.

The general character of the North End as the home for the working class and immigrant was encouraged by Winnipeg's developers and real estate agents. Since Winnipeg had no large stock of old housing to accommodate the thousands who entered Winnipeg in the years after 1896, a great demand arose for new and cheap dwellings. To meet this demand, large tracts of land in the North End were purchased, developed, and sold to the newcomers. But, in order to make large profits, the developers pinched on land. Thus, when a vast construction boom got underway after 1896, too much structure was set on a disastrous land plan; the average lot in the North End was only twenty-five or thirty-two feet wide. Not one of the rules of good design were followed: the grid street pattern was dull and monotonous; the narrow lots presented a terribly cramped appearance, since houses were built to the very edge of the property; the façade of the dwellings showed little diversity of building styles; and parks and playgrounds were conspicuously absent since land was meant to be used, not "wasted." In later years streets could be widened, sewers laid, new schools constructed, and stores and offices moved into the area only with the greatest difficulty and expense. Because the land was so crowded with structures, modernization could only be achieved by the enormously cumbersome, disruptive, and expensive process of urban renewal.[36] The irony of this private building process was that at the very moment the building was going on developers knew how to build better, and Winnipeg had a plentiful supply of land and a dynamic street railway company to permit more spacious development. But, as in other instances, the growth ethic did not allow commonsense or long-range goals to interfere with the immediate need for growth and profit.

The working-class nature of the North End is apparent in the type of residential dwellings built in the district. It was here in the years after 1900 that the vast majority of the city's non-modern frame dwellings (63 per cent), and a sizable number of modern frame dwellings (28 per cent), were constructed. The North End was noticeably lacking in the construction of the more affluent brick homes (9 per cent, Table 18). The large number of labourers in the North End is accounted for by the presence of the shops and yards of the CPR and the large concentration of heavy and medium industry. As was true throughout much of the city, employees tended to live near their place of employment.

The validity of the image of the North End as Winnipeg's "Foreign Quarter" cannot be questioned (Table 20). In the early years foreign immigrants tended to concentrate in the vicinity of Point Douglas where, because of this area's relative age, some old and cheap housing was available. Their early example was followed by others and by 1916 the North End was unquestionably cosmopolitan. Here were located over 80 per cent of the city's Jews and Slavs, 67 per cent of the Scandinavians, and 22 per cent of the Germans.

The economic factors already mentioned—the lack of a sufficient quantity of old cheap housing in the central core, the rapid development of a supply of cheap homes and boarding houses in the North End, and proximity to places of work—played the largest role in attracting the

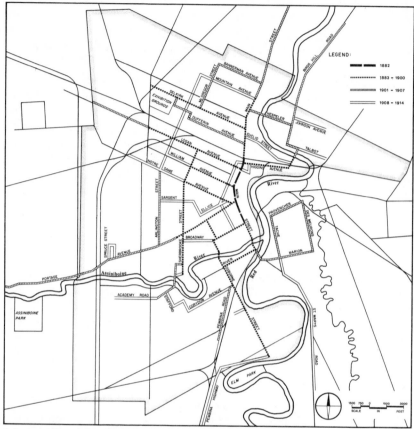

May 5/Growth of Street Railway Trackage in Winnipeg and Suburbs 1882–1914

foreign immigrant to this area. But in time, as churches and lay institutions were located in the North End to serve the foreigner, these became by themselves one of the factors attracting the newcomer. The presence of Jewish stores in the North End, for instance, at the moment when Polish, Russian, and Ukrainian immigrants started to arrive in masses, was among the factors that resulted in the area becoming inhabited by these groups. The owners of the stores, natives of Eastern European countries, could speak, or at least understand, the immigrant language. Moreover, "they used to sell commodities on credit in the way and under arrangements practised in the small towns" and villages of Eastern Europe. "The Jewish merchant knew the likes and dislikes of the Slav immigrant and tried to meet them."[37]

Still another factor which contributed to the foreign make-up of the North End's population was the desire of the immigrant to enjoy

Table 20 / Specified Ethnic Groups in Winnipeg's North End, 1886–1916

Ethnic group	No.	1886 % of total group pop'n	% of district pop'n	No.	1901 % of total group pop'n	% of district pop'n	No.	1916 % of total group pop'n	% of district pop'n
British	5,965	35.5	80.8	1,023	32.6	64.3	23,624	19.6	38.9
Slavic	240	82.0	3.2	1,422	80.4	9.8	18,280	83.3	30.2
Jewish	3	4.9	–	832	88.5	6.5	11,746	86.7	19.4
Scandinavian	579	42.9	7.9	10,174	25.1	5.3	3,864	66.6	6.4
German	242	44.4	3.2	1,360	59.6	9.3	1,411	22.1	2.3
	353	29.5	4.9	771	29.9	4.8	1,691	20.2	2.8

a lively social life. Since ignorance of the English language separated the immigrants from social intercourse with the native community, they preferred to settle down in areas where they could interact with fellow immigrants. Moreover, slowly and gradually the concentration of foreigners in the North End was strengthened by the development of distinctive business and professional establishments operated by the city's Jews and Slavs. These institutions, together with the establishment of churches, synagogues, clubs, and other communal institutions, gave the North End a distinctive character.

In 1912, for example, the *Manitoba Free Press*, in a series of articles entitled "Cosmopolitan Winnipeg," described the extensive social, cultural, and educational activities of the city's foreign immigrants. It is impossible to discuss the nature and extent of these activities for all the city's ethnic groups, but the institutions of Winnipeg's Ukrainians and Jews may be taken as typical. The Ukrainians of Winnipeg had an active press and published at least five newspapers; "*The Ukrainian Voice*, the national paper; *The Canadian Farmer*, the organ of the Ruthenian Liberals in politics; *The Working People*, the mouthpiece of the Socialists; *The Canadian Ruthenian*, under the Greek Catholic dominance; and *Ronok*, the organ of the Independent Ruthenian church." Social life as indicated by clubs and societies was also very active. There were two musical and dramatic societies, the Boyan and the Zankowecka, and several educational societies, including the Zaporoska Sicz and the Socialist Club. The Ruthenian National Society had also been formed by 1912 and was collecting funds for a Ruthenian National Home in Winnipeg. In education, the two Greek Catholic churches and the one Greek Orthodox Russian Church all had parochial schools such as the ten-room St. Nicholas School on Flora Avenue in Ward 5.[38]

The institutions of the Winnipeg Jewish community were even more numerous than those of the Ukrainian. According to the *Manitoba Free Press* there were twelve synagogues in the North End by 1912 and "at least three full time rabbis." Attached to some of these synagogues were Hebrew Free Schools which were intended as supplements to the public school system. The purpose of these schools was "to teach the

Hebrew language, the Bible, and those matters peculiar to the Jewish religious and national life." Indeed, one of these schools, the Winnipeg Hebrew School (Talmud Torah), located in the northern part of Ward 5, was the heart of the Winnipeg Jewish community. The school was a spacious two-storey building with classrooms, two meeting halls, a boardroom, and a library on the first floor. On the second floor was a large auditorium which was used as a meeting place for numerous Jewish activities—conferences, weddings, festivals, meetings, lectures, concerts, and fund-raising campaigns.

Other Jewish communal institutions were the United Hebrew Charities, the North End Relief Association, the Workman's Circle, the Zionist Society, and several loan and immigrant agencies designed to aid the newly arrived immigrant. There was also a Jewish newspaper, *The Canadian Israelite (Der Kanader Yid)*, a chapter of the B'nai B'rith order, and a Yiddish theatre on Selkirk Avenue.[39]

This "foreign invasion" of the North End by disfavoured ethnic groups had a decided effect on the Anglo-Saxon residents of the area. As one contemporary noted, "The newcomers not only filled the empty spaces but in time displaced the original inhabitants of the district, most of whom moved to other parts of the city. . . ."[40] The author of this statement, a school principal, offered the following statistics to back up his claim:

Table 21 / **Enrollment by Ethnic Group in Two Elementary Schools in Winnipeg's North End, 1905 and 1915**

Ethnic group	Aberdeen School—Ward 5				Strathcona School—Ward 6			
	1905		1915		1905		1915	
	No.	%	No.	%	No.	%	No.	%
British	473	98	221	17	411	95	100	8
Jewish	–	–	833	67	–	–	526	42
Slavic	–	–	124	10	–	–	250	20
German	–	–	50	4	–	–	276	22
Others	10	2	25	2	22	5	100	8
Totals	483	100	1,243	100	433	100	1,252	100

Despite the fact that the percentage of British in the North End steadily declined, this group remained throughout the period the largest ethnic group in the district. This, of course, reflects their predominance in the city as a whole. In terms of residential segregation, however, the important point is that only 20 per cent of the British population of Winnipeg were located in the North End by 1916. Furthermore, a large number of these were located in specific parts of the district, places that were as much ghettos as were areas where foreigners congregated. One of these concentrations was in the western portion of Ward 5, close to the CPR shops on Logan Avenue where railway employees lived. A more prestigious area—"a desirable location with refined associations"—was that east of Main Street in the vicinity of St. John's Park in Ward 6. Here an "exclusive well-to-do class with a yearning after the refined suburban life" was located "in the delightful sylvan district on the borders of the Red River."[41] Most probably it was here that the majority of the brick homes built in the North End after 1900 were located.

In spite of Winnipeg's high incidence of ethnic residential segregation, it is significant that large numbers of the city's non-British citizens settled outside the foreign ghettos. These people accomplished their Canadianization without the immediate benefit or hinderance of a neighbourhood crowded with their fellow countrymen. Both the Germans and Scandinavians were proud of this fact, and could point to their dispersal throughout the city. The differential that existed between these two groups and the Slavs and Jews suggests that Germans and Scandinavians not only had more cultural affinities with the charter group, but also that they had the financial resources and work skills to advance their economic status.[42] Unfortunately, the important question of whether or not these "outsiders" returned to the ghetto for special foods, entertainment, or the ethnic Church cannot be answered here.

Despite the inclusion of Anglo-Saxons in the North End and the dispersal of some foreigners to other parts of the city, this district's character was determined by its large foreign element. The poverty and illiteracy of the foreign immigrants and their ignorance of the local language and customs had a detrimental influence upon the appearance of the district. Overcrowded houses and tenements, lack of sanitary installations, dirty back-yards, muddy, foul-smelling streets, and poor lighting conditions made up the atmosphere in which the population of North Winnipeg had to live in the years prior to 1914. The entire responsibility for this state of affairs could hardly lie with the foreigner, since the civic authorities and the commercial elite neglected this area. There were never a sufficient number of schools for the immigrant child; there were few day-nurseries, kindergartens, dispensaries, or parks; drunkenness was widespread and gambling places and brothels were wide open. Indeed, it was not for many years after 1914 that the city administration and general public opinion became interested in introducing improvements in the North End.

South and West Winnipeg

The South End ("home of the economic upper-crust") and the West End (the district of the prosperous middle class) were the last areas of Winnipeg to fill up. The greatest periods of growth in the West End were 1890–95 and 1900–1912. In the South End it was only in the latter period that large numbers of persons moved into Fort Rouge. In terms of population density both districts, but especially South Winnipeg, remained throughout the period the least built upon.

There are many factors that explain the relatively late development of South and West Winnipeg. Prior to 1895 there was sufficient room in the central core for a good deal of expansion and it was only in the years after that date that population pressure began to force residents of the core, and newcomers, to look for new areas in which to live. Coupled with this "push" factor was the development of new means of intra-urban transportation. An article in the *Manitoba Free Press* in March 1899 noted: "No more remarkable development has been witnessed in our day that the growth in the use of the bicycle. It has furnished a new means of locomotion, has solved for a great many people the old problem of rapid transit in the cities."

More important than the growth of the use of the bicycle, however, was the aggressive expansion of Winnipeg's street railway system in the years after the turn of the century. During this time lines were not only considerably lengthened, but service was frequently increased and improved. Thus in 1900 less than 3.5 million passengers were carried, in 1904 the paid fares had reached 9.5 millions, in 1908 20 millions, and in 1913 almost 60 millions. These substantial increases were also reflected in the gross earnings of the Winnipeg Electric Railway Company, for these jumped from $28,000 in 1900 to over $4 million in 1913.[43] This continuous expansion of surface transportation had a cumulative effect on Winnipeg's spatial growth. The pace of centrifugation and suburbanization, at first slow, went forward with increasing acceleration, until by 1910 it attained the proportions of a mass movement. In the period 1900–1912, for instance, South and West Winnipeg gained more new residents than did any of the other districts of Winnipeg.

The construction of bridges across the Assiniboine River also facilitated the growth of South Winnipeg. The Osborne Street Bridge was built in 1883, the Maryland in 1894, and the Main Street in 1897, the latter replacing a private toll bridge. Only two of these, however, were crossed by street railway lines before 1900 (see Map 5).[44]

Two other factors deserve consideration in the development of the South and West Ends. Unlike the other districts, these areas had relatively little commercial or industrial development. Although the Canadian Northern Railway yards and the retail and service establishments along Portage, Ellice, and Sargent avenues employed some residents, these districts were inhabited primarily by commuters who travelled long distances to their places of work. Only with the development of intra-urban transportation and the willingness to use it could these areas grow. The second restraining factor on the development of these districts was that developers, in contrast to the North End, clearly thought of these areas as desirable residential locations. With wider streets, larger lots, and frequent building restrictions, only the more affluent of Winnipeg's residents could move to these areas.

The conscious desire to develop exclusive districts in West and South Winnipeg is apparent in the following advertisements placed in local newspapers. Referring to Armstrong's Point in the West End, one advertisement read:

> This most desirable resident portion of the city is now controlled by a syndicate who have authorized us to offer a limited number of Lots for Sale, with building restrictions, ensuring the construction of handsome residences. The improvements now being made by the city and those contemplated by the syndicate with the serpentine drive. . . will make the Point not only the finest locality for artistic and stately homes, but it will become . . . "The Faubourg St. Germain" of Winnipeg, the most fashionable drive in the city.

A similar description was given of Crescentwood in the South End:

> Within and around the graceful crescent on the Assiniboine appears to be the spot which is destined to contain the most attractive residences of Winnipeg. . . . The Maryland Street bridge, three hundred feet from the electric cars, touches about the centre of this property. . . . A large portion of Crescentwood is beautifully wooded with native elms, ash, oak, and balsams. It is well drained and is the highest part of the city. . . . Wellington Crescent . . . is now being widened to a hundred feet. For its whole distance of about two miles this Avenue will be lined on one side by river lots having a depth of 300 feet or more, and on the other side by large lots having a depth of from 200 to 300 feet, which will be sold only with building conditions. By the terms of the deeds, the houses will have to be set well back on lots and will be limited as to minimum of cost. With these advantages possessed by no other street, Wellington Crescent should soon become the best residential street in the city.[45]

The restrictions, the advertisers explained, were that lots three hundred feet deep were only for houses costing over $10,000; all houses on the Crescent must cost at least $6,000, and no house in the entire area could cost less than $3,500.

Besides generous lot sizes, building restrictions, "magnificent trees," and proximity to the river, both these areas had other attractive features that would have appealed to Winnipeg's upper-crust. The peninsular configuration of Armstrong's Point, for example, kept rapid traffic from the streets and tended to give the area a sense of identity. Indeed, the Point's isolation from the city, and the privacy this afforded, was apparent in the fact that many Winnipeggers did not know the Point existed. And yet this privacy and isolation was coupled with easy access to the city and adjacent neighbourhoods.[46]

The combined effect of all these restrictions and natural advantages were described by one Winnipegger: "There were no houses in [Armstrong's Point]. There were only castles, huge castles three full stories in height, some with leaded glass windows, and all, certainly, with dozens of rooms. They were built in an assortment of architectural styles and peopled by names from Winnipeg's commercial and industrial Who's Who. I was awe-stricken by the sheer size of the house."[47]

Similar reactions were recorded by North Enders when they crossed the Assiniboine into Crescentwood and passed along Wellington Crescent. The following description caught both the tangible and intangible atmosphere of this area:

> It was as though he had walked into a picture in one of his childhood books, past the painted margin to a land that lay smiling under a friendly spell, where the sun always shone, and the clean-washed tint of sky and child and garden would never fade; where one could walk, but on tip-toe, and look and look but never touch, and never speak to break the enchanted hush. . . . In a daze he moved down the street. The boulevards ran wide and spacious to the very doors of the houses. And these houses were like palaces, great and stately, surrounded by their own private parks and gardens. On every side there was something to wonder at.[48]

The substantial number of brick dwellings built in South and West Ends confirms these districts as the home of Winnipeg's upper class (see Table 18). But building statistics also reveal that both areas had a large number of more modest structures as well. Indeed, the exclusive and upper-crust nature of South and West Winnipeg must not be exaggerated. In the area between Notre Dame and Portage Avenue, for example, a great deal of development occurred that differed but little from that carried out in the North End. The area between Portage Avenue and the Assiniboine River, of course, yielded higher land prices because of closeness to the river, and a distinctly middle-class development occurred here. Thus a reporter in 1909 observed that homes north of Portage ranged from "scores of shacks which have cost $150 to $200" to "new cottages and houses averaging $3,000 a piece," while in the area south of Portage homes "usually cost from $3,000 to $5,000." And, to complete this cost comparison, it was further reported that in the "middle-class areas of central and southern Fort Rouge" homes ranged in cost "from $2,000 to $15,000."[49]

Another dimension of the distinctive character of South and West Winnipeg is their ethnic make-up (Table 22). All of the South End and most of the West End was overwhelmingly inhabited by those of British

Table 22 / Specified Ethnic Groups in West and South Winnipeg, 1886–1916

Ethnic group	1886 No.	% of total group pop'n	% of district pop'n	1901 No.	% of total group pop'n	% of district pop'n	1916 No.	% of total group pop'n	% of district pop'n
British	721	4.3	67.8	6,242	20.4	79.0	42,024	35.0	86.5
Slavic	–	–	–	69	3.8	.9	1,213	5.5	2.5
Jewish	–	–	–	8	.7	.1	618	4.5	1.3
Scandinavian	123	9.1	11.6	1,044	31.4	13.2	593	10.2	1.2
German	21	3.8	2.0	157	6.9	2.0	1,056	16.5	2.2
Others	198	16.6	18.6	381	14.8	4.8	3,072	36.6	6.3

origin. It was only in the northern portion of the West End, particularly along Ellice and Sargent avenues, that significant concentrations of Germans and Scandinavians occurred. It was, moreover, usually only the more successful of these groups who lived in these areas, those who by education or economic success had "graduated from Point Douglas to the West End."[50]

With the development of South and West Winnipeg as the domain of Winnipeg's largely British upper and middle class, the city's spatial and social patterns were firmly established. In 1914 there was a distinct north-south dichotomy in Winnipeg which, despite the passage of more than fifty years, has changed but little. Indeed, the ethnic and class segregation of Winnipeg has survived almost intact into the 1970s.[51]

Suburban Growth

Except for St. Boniface, it was not until after 1901 that the first traces of suburban growth appeared in Winnipeg. This development was dependent on numerous factors. It was only with the increased popularity of the bicycle and the extension of street railway lines that settlement of these outlying areas was possible.[52] Also, as long as there was a sufficient amount and variety of building sites within the city of Winnipeg there was little reason to settle in areas that were far from places of employment and shopping and entertainment facilities. But in the years after 1901 the transportation problem was solved and the city, or at least many sections of it, were completely built up.

St. Boniface was organized as a municipality in 1880 and then successively became incorporated as a town and a city in 1883 and 1908.

The first signs of an urban pattern appeared in St. Boniface in 1883 when some of Winnipeg's residents and businessmen took advantage of the drastic differences in land values and tax rates between that town and Winnipeg, and built their homes or industrial plants there. But prior to 1901 only a small area of St. Boniface, close to the Red River, was built up. Great strides were made after the turn of the century, however, in both residential and industrial building. It was during these years that the St. Boniface landscape became marked with flour mills and abattoirs, and the city established itself as a noted meat-packing centre.

The development and growth of St. Boniface was not, however, entirely dependent on differences in land values and the growth of industry. For it was also the cultural centre of French Canadians in western Canada. Here were to be found the important buildings of the Roman Catholic Church—its cathedral, hospital, college, schools, and so forth. Thus in 1916 its population of 11,021 was made up of 4,530 persons of French origin. Moreover, the French were the largest single group in St. Boniface at that time, outnumbering even those of British origin.[53]

St. James was the suburb second in importance and size. Situated on the western outskirts of Winnipeg's West End, St. James served primarily as a residential area for the city. It was reached directly from the business centre of Winnipeg by way of Portage Avenue. This single major access route tended to cause the development of St. James to cling closer to the southern part, near the Assiniboine River, than it might otherwise have done had there been another major thoroughfare to provide a connection from St. James to Winnipeg.

Table 23 / **Population of Winnipeg and Suburbs, 1901–1916**

Suburbs	1901		1911		1916	
	No.	%	No.	%	No.	%
Assiniboia	357	.8	681	.4	900	.8
Charleswood	450	.9	701	.5	766	.4
East Kildonan	563	1.2	1,488	.9	4,828	2.4
Fort Garry	730	1.6	1,333	.9	1,768	.9
St. Boniface	2,019	4.2	7,483	4.8	11,021	5.4
St. James	257	.5	4,535	2.9	9,545	4.7
St. Vital	585	1.2	1,540	1.0	2,101	1.0
Transcona	–	–	–	–	3,356	1.7
Tuxedo	–	–	–	–	192	.1
West Kildonan	668	1.3	1,767	1.1	3,676	1.8
WINNIPEG	42,340	88.3	136,035	87.5	163,000	81.1
Totals	47,969	100.0	155,563	100.0	201,153	100.0

St. James offered an excellent area for residential purposes. No drainage problems, a reduced flood danger, low municipal taxes, and large lots favourably competed with residential areas in Winnipeg.[54] The development of an independent street railway system in St. James, along with street lighting, cement sidewalks, and asphalted roads were also attractive features. All gave St. James distinct advantages over the eastern and northern suburbs of the city.[55]

St. Vital was incorporated as a municipality in 1903. It was made up of parts of the old municipality of St. Boniface and was situated east of the Red River, immediately south of the urban area of the town of St. Boniface. By 1914 a residential community came into existence in the northern sections of St. Vital. St. Mary's Road and some streets branching off to the east were developed by this time but the greater part of St. Vital remained in agricultural use.

The only other concentrated development in Winnipeg's suburbs took place in Kildonan and Transcona. The former was an area in which many of the Selkirk settlers had established themselves and the area had grown sufficiently by 1914 to cause the area to be divided into two municipalities, West Kildonan and East Kildonan, on respective sides of the Red River. Winnipeg's Main Street extended into West Kildonan and it was here that the first northern suburban growth took place in the years after 1901. A similar, but smaller, suburban development took place in East Kildonan, mainly along Bird's Hill Road (now called Henderson Highway). The town of Transcona was incorporated in 1912 and it developed as a residential community for those working in the Grand Trunk Pacific yards and shops which had been established there.

The remaining suburbs of Winnipeg—Assiniboia (incorporated 1880), Fort Garry (1912), Tuxedo (1913), and Charleswood (1913)—remained prior to 1914 largely rural in nature, with few people, and hardly warrant attention as extensions of Winnipeg.

In general the growth of Winnipeg's suburbs was just getting underway when war broke out in 1914. Yet even at this early date a distinct pattern emerged; one that was to be followed for several decades.[56] The areas of greatest growth were those to the west (St. James), south (St. Vital and Fort Rouge), and east (St. Boniface). The northern expansion of Winnipeg's urban area, while significant, was never of the same proportions as any of these other areas. The most probable explanation for this was that Winnipeggers who thought of moving out of the central portions of the city naturally tended to avoid the North End. Not only did they have to cross an area of marked deterioration in the vicinity of the Canadian Pacific tracks, but the physical obstruction caused by the railway was itself an obstacle. Moreover, the same ethnic and class divisions that occurred in the city of Winnipeg itself tended to be followed in suburban development. The

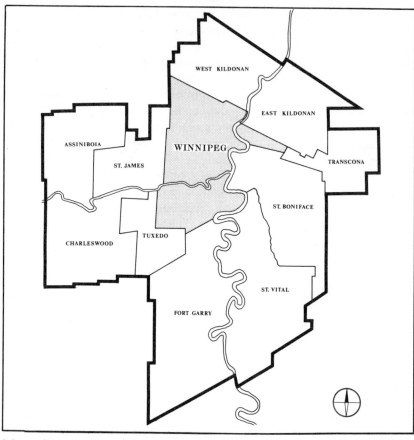

Map 6/Winnipeg and Suburbs 1914

northern suburbs were for the most part settled by working class—and usually foreign—persons while the others, particularly in the south and west, were dominated by the more affluent—and usually British—persons. The exception, of course, is St. Boniface which retained its French character.[57]

There were few, if any, cities in Canada in 1914 that could match the dynamic changes that had taken place in Winnipeg. In only forty years Winnipeg grew from a small fur-trading post with less than two thousand inhabitants to a sprawling metropolis one hundred times that size. The physical expansion that accompanied this growth in population was equally great. When incorporated in 1874, over 3.1 square miles were included within the boundaries of the city of Winnipeg, an area which then bore no relation whatever to the built-up extent of the city. Yet by 1914 the city's boundaries had not only grown to include 23.6

square miles, but most of this area was in either residential or commercial use. Indeed, by 1914 Winnipeg's population and industry were spilling over into surrounding municipalities.

The rapid growth of Winnipeg brought numerous other major changes. It was transformed from a city of pedestrians and horses to one of bicycles, streetcars, and even a few automobiles. The old residential area of 1874 had become by 1914 the principal zone of work—the industrial, commercial, financial, and communications centre of the Canadian West. At the same time the older dwellings of the central area that were not torn down for industrial expansion were on their way to becoming the homes of the lower-income half of the population. Beyond the central core three distinct areas of new houses had sprung up. To the south the more affluent and chiefly Anglo-Saxon elements of the population resided; to the west was a large middle-class area of somewhat more mixed ethnic composition; and to the north was the working-class and foreign ghetto.

Winnipeg in 1914 was very much a city divided; divided into areas of work and residence, rich and poor, Anglo-Saxon and foreigner. By this time, too, many of the familiar modern problems of urban life were beginning to emerge: the sudden withdrawal of whole segments of an old neighbourhood's population; the rapid decay of entire sections of the city; the spread of the metropolis beyond its political boundaries; and, above all, the discipline of the lives of Winnipeg's residents into specialized transportation paths, specialized occupations, specialized home environments and specialized community relationships.

The establishment of such patterns of growth had serious consequences for Winnipeg. In the short run, of course, residential segregation had a pacifying effect. Income and ethnic segregation held conflicting groups apart. The upper class of the South End, the middle class and prosperous working class of the West End and central core were separated from the lower class and foreigners of the North End. Each district had a neighbourhood homogeneity that gave a sense of place and community. But the social consequences of such patterns in the long run were equally obvious. Many Winnipeggers never lived in mixed neighbourhoods and thus failed to develop the tolerance which must exist in such areas. In seeking the freedom of living informally among equals in certain districts of the city, many residents escaped the demands of respect for different goals and values. And, if any one characteristic stands out in such events as the Winnipeg general strike of 1919, it is this lack of any willingness to understand the point of view of others.[58] From this one example it is apparent that decisions made by city officials, businessmen, and home builders in one era had a profound effect on future events. Indeed, many of the ideas, values, and residential patterns that emerged in Winnipeg between 1874 and 1914 have never disappeared.

part five

the challenges of urban growth

If we are to make this a great city we must improve the homes of these foreigners. The boys must be educated, the girls must be educated, and the adults must be educated. We must do what we can for the present generation and see to it that the next generation is well brought-up. The girls must be taught to become good housekeepers and good mothers. This is what counts most of all.
Ex-Mayor Ashdown, 1909

Winnipeg has great problems to face and solve. The future success and prosperity of the city depends upon their proper solution.
Winnipeg Telegram, 1910

10 / The Immigrant Problem: Accommodation, Disease, and Economic Adjustment

Winnipeg was a city of immigrants. Immigration accounted for nearly 80 per cent of the city's population increase during the prewar period and without this vast influx of people from all over the world Winnipeg's growth would have been slow indeed. Moreover, besides those immigrants who arrived in the city with the intention of settling there, Winnipeg was the gateway through which all western-bound immigrants passed, no matter what their final destination. To the businessmen who viewed population growth as "the essential and paramount need of the West," the arrival of tens of thousands of immigrants meant prosperity for their real estate and commercial concerns. For Winnipeg was not only the "Gateway to the West," as its boosters advertised, it was also the tollgate of the West. "Nothing—neither people, nor goods, nor chattels—moved into or out of prairie Canada save through Winnipeg [and] the tolls levied by Winnipeg business, industry, commerce, and labour sparked the Winnipeg boom" and the city's rise to the position of the "Bull's Eye of the Dominion."[1]

Yet for all the advantages of Winnipeg's position it was found that the immigrant was a mixed blessing. For while he may have been the keystone to economic prosperity he was often an economic and even a social liability. It is true, of course, that some immigrants—particularly Ontarians, Englishmen, and Americans—arrived in Winnipeg with adequate capital or with assured employment, and were quickly absorbed into the mainstream of Winnipeg society. But many others were not so well prepared. The Slavs and Jews, for example, usually came to Winnipeg with meagre or even no capital, and with the added handicap of a foreign language and culture. From the moment of their arrival in Winnipeg these newcomers had to be housed, fed, found employment, and assimilated into the life of the community. Also, since many of the overseas immigrants arrived in Winnipeg infected with contagious diseases, the municipal corporation had to take precautionary measures that often taxed the city's medical facilities to the full. Many immigrants needed help to see them through the transitional period that lay between the status of immigrant and taxpaying citizens. Thus, while the arrival of tens of thousands of immigrants in

Winnipeg may have satisfied the growth ethic of the dominant commercial elite, it also presented this governing group with some of its most serious problems.[2]

There was another side to this immigrant influx, however, and this was the formidable adjustment problem faced by the immigrants themselves. From their perspective everything and everyone seemed different; the city was strange and the townspeople strangers. And notwithstanding their best intentions, entry into the mainstream of Winnipeg's economic, social, cultural, and political life was bound to be difficult.

Generally, the problems faced by the newcomer fell into three distinct but related categories. The most pressing concern, of course, was to obtain employment. For those whose background had equipped them with a specific skill or trade there was little difficulty in adjusting to the economic conditions of their new surroundings. Many, however, were poverty-stricken peasants with neither training nor capital, and for them the adjustment was bound to be a good deal more severe. The second major area of adjustment was a broader and more complicated one and it was not so easily achieved as was economic security. This was the matter of assimilation, a process that could be considered complete when the immigrant learned the language and social usages of the city well enough to participate in its economic, political, and social life without encountering prejudice. The emphasis here was on external indices, such as ability to speak English, and adoption of the dress, the manners, and the social ritual of the dominant group with whom the newcomer came in contact. Finally, and most difficult of all, was the matter of acculturation, a process of inter-penetration and fusion in which the immigrant acquires the memories, sentiments, and attitudes of the city's dominant group and, by sharing their experience and history, becomes incorporated with them in a broad and all-embracing cultural life.

In Winnipeg during the years 1874–1914 only the first two phases of the adjustment process were achieved to any extent. This is not surprising for acculturation is a very gradual process, usually requiring two or three generations. It is also the part of the adjustment process that is most difficult to observe, for it is only in the daily experiences of the immigrants that one may find clues to the ways in which people reared in an old world environment gradually accommodate themselves to the new world and become part of a new society and culture. It is in the mind of the immigrants that the confusions, tensions, and emotional conflicts develop as they strive to reconcile the ideas, values, and attitudes they discover in their new world with the social heritage they acquired in their homeland. From time to time they define their situation in a new way and make decisions as to their course of action in the future. These may find outward expression in such activities as learning a new skill, renewing efforts to become proficient with a new language, moving to another part of the city, or putting savings aside for a definite purpose. The significant fact, however, is that a sustained effort over a period of years is usually required to reach such goals.[3]

The most immediate problem created by the influx of immigrants into Winnipeg was one of accommodation. In some cases this meant providing food and shelter for the newcomers only for a day or two until they moved on or found employment and became self-sufficient. In other cases, and particularly in those years plagued by economic recession, the immigrants were forced to rely on federal and civic agencies for months at a time. But regardless of whether they had to be accommodated for only days or for months, the very size of the influx meant that the problem was one of vast proportions. In the period between 1886 and 1896, for example, the federal government accommodated an average of 4,382 immigrants per year. And this was not one of the most notable decades for immigration to Canada.[4]

The bulk of the responsibility for accommodating the immigrants in Winnipeg throughout the period fell upon the federal government. The city had a federal immigration agent even before incorporation in 1873 and this person was charged with aiding the immigrant on his arrival.[5] As early as 1872 the federal government had immigration sheds in Winnipeg and each immigrant was entitled to free shelter for a period not exceeding seven days. After that time they were allowed to stay on for an indefinite period at no cost depending on how great the demand.

Between 1872 and 1914 the immigration sheds in Winnipeg went through a series of changes in size and location, although it was not until 1905 that a satisfactory building was constructed near the CPR station.[6] Prior to that date the premises were frequently overcrowded and in a state of disrepair. A description of the sheds in 1883 indicated that the buildings were run like army barracks with "lights out" and the doors locked at ten o'clock. Printed rules were posted throughout the simple structure in several languages and "any disorderly character who is not controllable by ordinary means is handed over to the police."[7] But despite these regulations the buildings were unpleasant accommodation at best because of their inability to meet the great demand.

An even grimmer picture of the buildings that served as immigrant shelter was presented by the federal immigration agent in 1892. The building had not been provided with a foundation or "weeping drains" and as a consequence was frequently flooded up to the main floor level. The baths had been placed in a room in the basement "and for a long time were unprovided with hot water." And since the bathrooms themselves were unheated they were useless during the cold months. Turning to the question of ventilation the Winnipeg agent stated flatly that there was none whatsoever. Also, "in summer a latrine in one corner of the grounds is used by the men and constitutes a danger and a nuisance to the establishment and neighbourhood generally." The agent went on to recommend major renovations and alterations, as well as an additional building. And, he added,

> I have no hesitation in stating that I consider it urgent and of the greatest necessity that more ample provision should be made here for the reception and temporary accommodation of immigrants. It has never been sufficient. During the last year the constantly crowded state of the sheds has caused much inconvenience and hardship and no doubt illness, and in view of a probable increase in the stream of immigration from this time forward the present available space, even with the completion of the present building by the addition I have insisted upon, will be found to be totally inadequate.[8]

In an attempt to provide accommodation for the overflow of immigrants who could not be housed in the government buildings various schemes were devised. At times the Fort Osborne army barracks were utilized to provide accommodation for 250 newcomers. But as the yearly influx continued to increase even this measure proved inadequate and the Winnipeg immigration agent was authorized to buy and erect large tents to provide at least temporary shelter. Vacant warehouses and hotels were rented by the government at various times and "temporary buildings," often with canvas roofs, were also used.

In these efforts to provide accommodation the federal agents frequently turned to the civic authorities for aid. In 1903, for instance, they requested the use of several of the city's exhibition buildings for shelters but the request was turned down. Cooperation from the city was also not forthcoming in another instance where the immigration agent asked for help. The great demand for accommodation by the immigrants resulted in the growth of a black market in housing for many years. The report of the agent in 1855, for example, complained of the "numerous and closely packed, badly ventilated shanties that are huddled together in close proximity to this agency." He noted that these buildings lacked privies and drains and that the landlords did nothing "for the health and comfort of their tenants." Yet, despite his repeated complaints to City Council, nothing was done to clean up the area.[9]

City Council's view of the whole problem of immigrant accommodation was perhaps best summed up in a report of the Special Committee on Emigrant Accommodation made in 1877. Stating that it was best to leave the problem in the hands of the Dominion government, the report went on to express the opinion that "it is not advisable to do anything that would diminish the energy or self-reliance of the new settlers which would inevitably happen if they were too comfortable." Council's only positive action at this time was to urge that all those who had rooms to let should furnish their names to the immigration agent.[10]

Notwithstanding this statement of philosophy the city of Winnipeg did go into the business of providing immigrant accommodation for a two-year period between 1882 and 1884. During the feverish optimism of the great boom it was decided to erect a city immigrant shed. By the end of March 1882 a building with sixty rooms on two floors and a large room with thirty bunks was opened and a caretaker hired. Significantly—in contrast to the free federal government accommodation—the city charged 50 cents a day for the rooms and 15 cents a day for the use of the bunks. During its short period of operation the building did a thriving business; in 1882, for example, it made a net profit of $2,000.[11] But with the advent of a sharp recession in April 1882 the expenditure of public funds on this project came under attack and the sheds were finally closed after the 1884 season and were eventually disposed of by the city.[12]

Other than this brief experiment in the matter of immigrant accommodation, the city's efforts over the years consisted largely of making frequent and vigorous complaints to Ottawa that the federal authorities were not doing enough. On several occasions letters of protest and petitions were sent to the responsible minister and in 1889 a delegation travelled to Ottawa to support their contention that the city needed larger facilities. In view of the city's lack of cooperation, fully documented in the annual reports of the federal government's immigration agents, these representations were not received with great enthusiasm and it took until 1905 for the government to construct the spacious new quarters.

These attempts to shift responsibility for the shelter and care of the immigrant between the two levels of government frequently prevented either from solving the serious problems that daily faced thousands of newcomers. That some difficulty should have arisen in this area was perhaps natural. After all, neither the federal nor the civic authorities had any experience with a problem of such great proportions. But since both governments were continually predicting that great numbers of immigrants would come West and were also spending vast sums to attract them, it is not unfair to suggest that a great deal more effort could have been extended in preparation for the immigrants when they did finally arrive. For, as one Winnipegger shrewdly pointed out, if City Council had properly cared for the newcomer and had concentrated on making the city "healthy, beautiful, and pleasant," with an adequate water and sewage system, Winnipeg would have had "all the FREE publicity" it could have desired in the form of a contented citizenry.[13] In other words, if the city's elite had spent some of the money used on advertising and boosterism on caring for the immigrant, it would have had both population growth and a stable and healthy community. Instead, in their callous approach toward the immigrant and to social questions in general, Winnipeg City Council caused great hardships to be endured by many new arrivals.

While the lack of adequate accommodation for the immigrant at Winnipeg caused hardship only for the new arrival and thus was not of immediate concern to established Winnipeggers, the same was not true of the matter of infectious diseases. The federal government's lax attitude to immigrant inspection for disease posed a problem that was of direct and immediate concern to all Winnipeg's citizens. The city was first made aware of this danger in September 1876 when a smallpox epidemic broke out among newly arrived Icelandic immigrants at their settlement of Gimli, north of Winnipeg.[14] This outbreak was attributed to "overcrowding on the Duluth steamers" that had carried the settlers into Winnipeg that summer and it was immediately apparent that the city had only narrowly missed being subjected to the dreaded disease. In their apprehension that the disease might spread beyond the borders of "New Iceland" the settlement was put under strict quarantine, causing a great deal of hardship to that infant community. But the important lesson that should have been learned as a result of this unfortunate experience—that all incoming immigrants should be forced to undergo some sort of medical examination before entering the province—was lost on both the provincial and civic authorities.

The city's and province's ad hoc approach to this problem, and the hardship it caused by necessitating widespread quarantines instead of just dealing with the few infected persons at an early stage, was one that brought on them a considerable amount of criticism. In a report to the Council's Health Committee in 1882, the city's medical health officer pointed out the dangers to which Winnipeg was being exposed by the influx of large numbers of immigrants. In his report Dr. J. Kerr urged that representations be made to both the federal and provincial governments asking for proper inspection facilities to be established at ports of entry. He suggested that one of those governments should appoint a "duly qualified Quarantine Officer" whose duty it would be to inspect all immigrants "with the object of detecting contagious diseases and if necessary removing such cases for proper treatment and isolation." Dr. Kerr further recommended that the federal government be asked to provide a suitable building for the isolation and treatment of such diseases.[15] Another local physician agreed with this view, noting that "with a population coming from all quarters of the globe, including the floating population of Great Britain, the United States, and other countries it need not be expected that this city will ever continue free from smallpox for any length of time. Hence it is important that there be municipal and governmental action not only in Winnipeg, but all along the line of travel. Organization is needed."[16] Winnipeg's Board of Trade also added its considerable prestige to these recommendations early in 1883, but despite repeated outbreaks of typhoid and smallpox during 1882 and 1883—albeit none of epidemic proportions—there is no evidence that City Council took any positive course of action.

The problem took on added potential danger in 1885 with the opening of rail connections with the East. Winnipeg's health officer, Dr. W. Neilson, was quick to stress the need for concerted action. As he explained in a report in October, 1885:

> In view of the more intimate relations that will exist between Montreal and Winnipeg upon the opening of CPR traffic [and] the possibility of the introduction of the contagion of smallpox into our city from Montreal [where an epidemic was at this time raging], it becomes us to adopt such precautionary measures as circumstances will admit of. It is the intention of the Provincial Government to place a physician on each incoming train to make an examination of all persons travelling west from Port Arthur, to allow no person to proceed without evidence of vaccination and to detain anyone suspected of having the disease. But as smallpox may be present in the system 10-15 days without any outward appearance of its existence, a diseased person may be examined several times without giving rise to any suspicion of his true condition, and as the contagion may be introduced into the city in different ways we must take precautions. . . . The most effective measures in limiting an outbreak are disinfection, isolation, and vaccination.[17]

The city's only response to this warning was a crude attempt at vaccination of city residents in 1885 (those vaccinated were charged a fee and thus this precaution was anything but universal) and it was not until 1889 that Council got to the root of the problem.

In a memorial to the federal Minister of Agriculture in December 1889 City Council asked that the federal government take three steps to protect Winnipeg. They urged that the government must first of all provide adequate medical inspection facilities at Quebec City and Halifax to deal with the immigrants as soon as they disembarked from the steamships. Secondly, the federal immigration sheds in Winnipeg needed expansion and improvement, especially in regard to sanitary facilities. And, finally, in case diseased immigrants did arrive in the city there had to be suitable quarantine stations built, at federal expense, to deal with such cases. It should also be noted that in respect to the latter two recommendations the government's immigration agents were also urging improved facilities in Winnipeg.

Despite all these warnings nothing was done by either federal or civic authorities prior to 1893 and it was only a matter of time before Winnipeg was confronted with a potentially explosive situation. In this whole problem it must be emphasized that it was at least theoretically up to the federal government to deal with the immigrant, and in view of their knowledge of the conditions existing in Winnipeg there can be little excuse for their refusal to take adequate steps. On the other hand, City Council was responsible for protecting their citizens: yet, other than a memorial to Ottawa, they did nothing. In light of their encouragement of immigration and their expenditure of large sums on immigration propaganda they could reasonably have been expected to provide some facilities for the immigrant once he arrived. Or, barring this kind of direct and expensive involvement, they might have urged action on the part of the federal authorities in a more aggressive and convincing manner. Interestingly, Council did find the energy and funds to pressure Ottawa for such things as river improvements, railway facilities, and other such projects. That they did not in this case is only another indication of their lack of concern for social, as opposed to economic, matters.

As a result of this lack of activity by the two levels of government and following an alarming number of deaths in the immigration sheds during the summer of 1892 (thirteen in forty days), a committee made up of local physicians and Board of Trade members decided to act on their own. This joint committee was convinced that the deaths that summer had been a combined result of inadequate medical inspection of immigrants and overcrowded and unsanitary accommodations at the immigrant sheds. They thus sent a memorial to Ottawa urging that steps be taken to remedy this state of affairs. But the committee also felt that the city should take steps to protect itself and they therefore advocated the passage of a provincial Public Health Act which would provide for the establishment of district health boards to oversee all matters affecting public health in the province. These district boards would be directly responsible to a provincial board and would thus not depend on local initiative to function. The committee did, however, approach Winnipeg City Council with the view of having that body send an official city delegation to the premier to support their cause. But when Council treated the committee "as a set of kicking taxpayers" they decided to act on their own.[18]

The fact that these representations were successful (a Public Health Act was passed in April 1893) was not only a result of their convincing arguments but also because Premier Greenway, who also served as Minister of Agriculture, Statistics, and Health, had been investigating the situation on his own. A report commissioned by him in August 1892 had stated that as a result of the poor facilities for immigrants in Winnipeg the city "was not only menaced with, but actually had in its midst, a source of serious danger not only to the City of Winnipeg but to the Province." The report had further urged that the province take some measures to remedy the situation.[19] But even before the new district health officers could be appointed and given time to deal with the immigrant problem, Winnipeg was forced to deal with an outbreak of smallpox using only its own inadequate and ill-prepared health staff.

In April 1893 a case of smallpox was discovered at the CPR station and after a hasty meeting between the federal immigration agent, the general superintendent of the CPR, the mayor, and the city's health officer, it was decided to establish a quarantine for some 302 passengers who were on the train that had carried the infected immigrant. Having no quarantine facilities in the city, the main bulk of the passengers were confined in a vacant federal building while facilities were quickly set up. The remainder were placed in two railway cars and taken out of town under the charge of special constables. Shortly thereafter the city erected "more suitable quarters some distance out upon the prairie, in an isolated position," to which all the suspected persons were removed and placed in quarantine. The latter lasted until the end of June when the camp was finally broken up. Apparently these actions proved sufficient, from the city's point of view at least, for although there were several fatal cases among the immigrants the disease did not spread to the city at large.

Throughout the period of the quarantine the city of Winnipeg took full charge of and financial responsibility for the matter and the final bill came to around $13,000. From the outset, however, the civic authorities fully expected to be reimbursed for the total amount. Indeed, they had what they felt was a firm agreement to this effect from the federal authorities. When the smallpox was first discovered in April the mayor had notified Ottawa to the effect that although he felt it was a federal responsibility Winnipeg City Council would take charge of the situation for the simple reason that at the time there was no alternative. The federal government, however, agreed to pay only $5,000 of the expenses.[20]

During the ensuing four years the civic and federal authorities kept up an extensive correspondence over financial responsibility for the 1893 quarantine, with Ottawa finally agreeing to pay half of the costs. The importance of this controversy over so paltry a sum lies in the fact that while it raged nothing was being done to prevent the same thing from recurring. Thus the same ad hoc approach prevailed in 1896, 1897, and 1898 when new cases of infectious disease were discovered among immigrants arriving in Winnipeg, necessitating quarantine measures similar to those undertaken in 1893.[21] Each of these was similarly followed by prolonged and often heated arguments over financial responsibility. It was apparently lost on both sides of the dispute that there were lessons to be learned from the 1893 outbreak.

While the civic authorities thus continued to be obsessed about the financial aspects of the immigrant question and failed to deal with the more important matter of securing long-term protection for Winnipeg, other groups set out to convince the federal government of the need for improved facilities both in Winnipeg and at ports of entry. The provincial Board of Health and the Board of Trade united in their efforts to impress upon Ottawa the danger to which Winnipeg was constantly exposed. Dr. Patterson of the Health Board travelled to Ottawa in 1898 and personally presented the city's case to the Minister of Agriculture. After dealing with the normal recommendations that quarantine and inspection facilities at Halifax be improved and that the city's immigrant sheds be enlarged, Dr. Patterson further urged "that the City of Winnipeg, being the terminal point of what might be called the trunk line of their journey; either temporary or permanent accommodation should be secured a short distance East of the city, where all would be first landed, inspected, cleaned up, and sorted out, before distribution on branch lines to all parts of this Province and the Northwest." Although this presentation produced a promise of "consideration," the two bodies followed it up by sending a memorial to the federal government, again impressing upon them "the propriety and the necessity" of more stringent precautionary measures.[22]

It is impossible to ascertain whether these pressures were the cause of new measures undertaken by Ottawa in 1899 or whether the Laurier government would have acted anyway. Certainly the delegation and the carefully reasoned memorial did not hurt. In any case, the Board of Trade and the provincial Board of Health were assured, early in 1899, that improvements had been undertaken at Halifax and, even more important, that a check quarantine would be established east of the city. Furthermore, the Board of Trade was assured in a letter from the Deputy Minister of the Interior that in future "such measures will be taken as will prevent your Board having any further cause for complaint."[23] And, during the ensuing years of massive immigration into Winnipeg and the West, this proved to be the case.

As far as accepting the final responsibility for dealing with the problem of infectious diseases among immigrants, however, the question was never really resolved. After 1898 a more proficiently operated Interior Department with Clifford Sifton at its head, coupled with the experience of dealing with the question for several decades, resulted in cases of diseased immigrants arriving in Winnipeg only rarely. But when they did, as in the summer of 1901, the controversy over reimbursement arose again. Winnipeg City Council repeatedly argued that it was the government's duty to ensure that all immigrants arriving in Winnipeg were of sound mind and body and in those cases when this did not happen they could not be held responsible. Yet even when Ottawa did fulfill this obligation, Council refused to accept anything more than a token role in aiding the immigrant. This is clearly revealed in a consideration of the city's part in providing relief and assistance for destitute, but healthy, newcomers.

Once the problems of immediate accommodation and infectious disease had been overcome, the immigrants turned to the question of economic adjustment. In this process they were fortunate in that Winnipeg enjoyed economic prosperity throughout the decade.[24] With the exception of a few severe but short-lived recessions, such as in 1907–1908, employment opportunities were plentiful.[25] But finding employment did not necessarily mean that the newcomer achieved economic security. A study conducted by J. S. Woodsworth in 1913 indicated that "a normal standard of living" in Winnipeg required an income of at least $1,200 per year.[26] Yet, Woodsworth continued, "it is difficult to find an actual workingman's family budget which maintains a normal standard. . . . Large numbers of workmen are receiving under $600 per year, many under $500, half of what is necessary. . . ." The result of these economic realities was that many immigrants were forced to resort to drastic measures in their struggle for survival. Often families were broken up as mothers and even children went to work to supplement the incomes of their husbands and fathers. These practices, according to the report, were the "source of much truancy and juvenile crime," and overwork on the part of women and children "complicates and aggravates" disease. Attempts to make up the difference between income and the normal standard by saving on food and rent were equally harmful. For while the former led to "under-nourished women and children," the latter caused overcrowding, "which means insanitary conditions and often immoral conditions." And while the health and moral well-being of many newcomers were thus affected, strains upon family organization were also severe. Already tested by the new conditions of life in Winnipeg, the demoralizing effects of low wages greatly compounded the problem.

The fact that thousands of families had an inadequate standard of living in an apparently prosperous city was brought to the attention of City Council many, many times, particularly after 1900. Private charities, individual investigators, the Trades and Labor Council, and even agencies of the municipal corporation reported on the manifestations of the maldistribution of income and called for improved health and building bylaws, municipal housing, fair wage schedules, public works programming, and a host of other progressive measures.[27] For the most part these pleas were ignored. Although the city had a relief committee as early as 1874, its work never extended beyond aiding those in particularly desperate straits and in the period 1900 to 1913, for example, it spent on the average only $6,200 a year on relief.[28]

The best indication of the civic authorities' attitude toward the economically distressed is illustrated by an examination of a report by the Associated Charities Bureau made in 1912. This body had been formed in 1908 "to prevent overlapping of relief by conducting a Joint Registration Bureau of all cases assisted by other societies in the city; ... its purpose was to prevent fraud and overlapping." The organization explained the problem as follows:

> If material assistance was all that was needed, if the families seeking it could in all cases be relied upon to use it in such a way that they would quickly become self-supporting, the work of this department would be easy. Unfortunately, the large majority of applications for relief are caused by thriftlessness, mismanagement, unemployment due to incompetence, intemperance, immorality, desertion of the family and domestic quarrels. In such cases the mere giving of relief tends rather to induce pauperism than to reduce poverty, and it is upon such cases that the five visiting agents of the department spend most of their time. Relief and adequate relief is nearly always necessary for the sake of the children in this cold climate, but society must make sure that the giving of it does not simply make it easier for the parents to shirk their responsibilities or lead a dissolute life.[29]

In this absurd task of separating the worthy from the unworthy poor, the Associated Charities Bureau served as agent for the city's Relief Department and all requests for aid were screened by it. Needless to say, their approach left a vast number of Winnipeg's poor untouched.[30] They were thus forced to learn to cope as best they could with the economic system on a personal basis, by friendships and aid from relatives.

Another example of the commercial elite's attitude toward the city's working class is an exchange that took place between the Winnipeg Ministerial Association and E. F. Hutchings in 1911.[31] Severe comments had been made about the working conditions at the Great West Saddlery Company owned by Hutchings and at the request of several employees the Ministerial Association had consented to talk with the owner. The issue at stake was not only the working conditions but also the fact that ten employees had been dismissed when they refused to sign a statement that they would have nothing to do with a union. The *Winnipeg Saturday Post* of 4 November 1911 told what happened to what it termed "ministerial meddlers":

> That super-serviceable body, the Ministerial Association, has been rushing in again upon a matter which was none of its business, and has again made itself ridiculous in the eyes of sensible persons. ... Unfortunately for the fulfillment of its promises (to the dismissed workers) the Ministerial Association had figured without

its host—no less a person than President E. F. Hutchings of the Great West Saddlery Company. Mr. Hutchings has no use for labour unions. He has built up and conducted a large business successfully without union labour, and is quite outspoken in his intention to keep on in the same old way. When the committee [met with him] to ask what he was going to do about the ten long straw workers, they were told that it was none of their business, but that if they really wished to know, he did not propose to do anything, except manage his own business without help from labour agitators or the Ministerial Association. . . .

The *Saturday Post* went on to criticize the ministers for "condemning a reputable business firm" and to suggest that the value of the Ministerial Association's voice in public affairs was "in exact ratio to the infrequency with which that voice is heard." Given this attitude, it is hardly surprising that Hutchings did not eliminate from his conditions of work the ban on labour unions.[32]

There are several factors which should be considered in explaining the commercial elite's failure to deal with Winnipeg's social problems in a progressive manner. First of all, the city's businessmen were obsessed with the need for growth and discouraged financial support for any institution which did not promote economic returns. The drain of both public and private capital into economic enterprises thus left little for community services. Secondly, the members of the elite were for the most part self-made men who resented bitterly any organization, such as a labour union, which seemed intent on restricting their freedom of activity. They were advocates of the philosophy of laissez faire which stated that prosperity would come if businessmen were left free to pursue their own interests.

The other factors which help explain the state of Winnipeg's social agencies were ones over which the elite had less control. One of these was the age-sex ratio of Winnipeg. The absence of a large older age group may well have relieved the pressure upon health and welfare institutions but it also removed the steadying influence of tradition and deprived the community of the leadership of those who were not strenuously engaged in making a living. Similarly, with relatively few children among the early settlers, extensive educational, medical, and recreational facilities were not required in the early years. But when the situation changed rapidly with the heavy influx of persons in the child-bearing age group, causing a high proportion of young children, problems of maternity and infant welfare quickly assumed considerable importance. Naturally it took time for the city's institutions to adjust, but in the interval many suffered.

Interestingly, aside from the age-sex ratio (which would in time correct itself), the causes of the city's poor response to social issues could only be overcome with considerable educational effort and it is in this area that several of Winnipeg's private charities provided their most useful service.

Fortunately, the process of economic adjustment (and assimilation) did not rely exclusively on the inadequate agencies of the civic corporation. Both were aided by a host of voluntary associations. Winnipeg's groups were legion. They included the Sons of England, the St. Andrew's Society, the Irish Association, the German Society, the Icelandic Progressive Society, the (Polish) St. Peter and Paul Society, the Zionist Society, the Ruthenian National Society, and numerous others.[33] Exclusive without being invidious, such clubs served as guideposts for the bewildered immigrant. They identified other residents with like traits and similar interests and encouraged contact on shared grounds and participation in common activities. Coupled with the churches and ethnic newspapers, membership in these organizations of a fraternal and benevolent nature alleviated economic insecurity by providing funds, assistance, and insurance in cases of destitution, illness, and death. Finally, political and commercial bodies promoted aspirations in matters involving municipal authorities and even the federal government. Hence, voluntary organizations often first introduced the immigrant to the community and afterwards linked him to it.

The importance of these voluntary organizations should not be over-emphasized, since they had several weaknesses. Because they were voluntary in nature such organizations had neither the inclination nor the means to help each immigrant, even if he did belong to a particular ethnic group.[34]

Winnipeg was fortunate in having several private agencies, led by what can only be called practical idealists. Two such agencies have been singled out for examination: the Margaret Scott Nursing Mission and All Peoples' Mission. Both deserve special attention for they were not only the best known of Winnipeg's private charities, they were led, staffed, and financed by Anglo-Saxons and thus serve as valuable correctives to the generalizations made about that group. The genuine commitment of both agencies to Winnipeg's poor (of whatever ethnic origin) clearly indicates that not all Anglo-Saxon Winnipeggers shared the commercial elite's overriding concern with economic growth. Rather, those involved in these agencies were dedicated to removing—or at least moderating–the depersonalizing and demoralizing aspects of urban life and to meeting the physical, social, and moral needs of the city's poor. In so doing they played the important role of communicating to the public at large the great need for caring for all the city's residents.

The development and early success of the Nursing Mission was largely the result of the influence of one woman, Mrs. Margaret Scott.[35] She had first become actively involved in private charitable work through her connection with the Coffee House, a Protestant unemployment relief centre, but during the period 1898–1904 her work with the city's destitute broadened considerably. Seeking out the needy by attendance at the city's police court, she personally investigated cases and delivered food and clothing. Naturally in her visitations she came into contact with the sick who could not afford medical care and although she was not a nurse herself, she did keep up with various nursing manuals. But the most important aspect of her work in this period was that she publicized the conditions she found and soon gained the support of many private charitable organizations.[36] She also became a valuable source of information to the Winnipeg Health Department and to the medical profession who cooperated with her in answering calls.

As a direct consequence of Mrs. Scott's example a group of women met in 1904 to discuss the possibility of establishing an organization to aid the "sick poor." At an informal gathering early in the year it was decided "to call together men and women who had shown helpful interest in Mrs. Scott's work and to ask the cooperation of the different churches in establishing a closer relationship between these churches and the homes of 'ignorant poor' and unfortunate in the congested areas of the city."[37] In response to this appeal at least forty-eight Winnipeggers met in May for an organizational meeting where it was decided to establish a nursing mission. The plan involved the securing of a building and the recruitment of nurses. The circular issued as a result of this first meeting explained:

> The proposed nursing mission would be the home and headquarters of the nurses, where all their supplies would be kept, and where they would have a small dispensary for outdoor patients, and as the city's needs still increased other nurses might be trained there in city mission work. The nursing mission would be interdenominational in character and practical in its working, not only tending the poor when sick, but instructing them as far as possible how to study prevention by following the rules of simple hygiene. Above all, seeking with Christian influence to raise their moral tone to all that is highest and best.[38]

Although the religious implications of the Nursing Mission were stressed by some of the workers and supporters, there is no evidence that it in any way deterred the agency from becoming most effective in more down-to-earth pursuits. Prior to 1914 a "central home" was secured and staffed and the Mission got directly to work. The practical application of the Mission's aims came in the form of bedside nursing and in 1905 over 7,000 visits to homes were made. This rose dramatically to 28,830 in 1913. In this aspect of the Mission's work Mrs. Scott's chief asset was her identification of needy cases. But besides this rather obvious function, the Nursing Mission supplied several other very useful services to the city at large. In 1906, for example, Mrs. Scott approached the Winnipeg General Hospital and requested that "district nursing" be added to their nurses' training. When such a program was instituted this meant a dual reward for the Mission. For it not only received the free assistance of nursing trainees but the program meant that the city would therafter be provided with nurses trained in this field. In view of the observation that "an almost complete lack of trained workers characterized the institutions of social welfare before the Great War," the role played by the Mission in bringing about a training program for district nurses ranks as one of its more noteworthy achievements.[39]

It was in the area of publicizing the needs of the poor, however, that the Margaret Scott Nursing Mission played its most important part. From the outset the Mission received much needed financial aid from all levels of government, although in the aggregate it still relied chiefly on private contributions. Yet what was more important in the long run than this lack of adequate financial assistance from government was the fact that in 1913 the City's Health Department hired two full-time child welfare nurses, and the following year expanded this work still further by establishing a Bureau of Child Hygiene.[40] In the slow development of a social welfare program in Winnipeg this marked a distinct break with past practice, for it signified a clear move away from the old belief that success and failure were the respective social rewards for individual virtue and vice. Certainly without the influence of the Margaret Scott Nursing Mission, and other similar private charitable organizations, the relationship between environment and poverty would have taken much longer than it did to infiltrate the thinking of many Winnipeggers.

While the Margaret Scott Nursing Mission attempted to meet the newcomers' physical needs and was only indirectly concerned with assimilation, the All Peoples' Mission sought to help solve this much broader adjustment problem. Founded in 1892, All Peoples' was an agency of the Methodist General Board of Missions. Prior to 1907, however, it made but a limited contribution to the area it served.[41] It was only with the acceptance by J. S. Woodsworth in 1907 of the superintendency of the struggling Mission that it became a force in Winnipeg. As a result of his efforts All Peoples' rose from just another charitable organization to become one of the city's—indeed Canada's— most noteworthy social welfare agencies. As Woodsworth's biographer has noted, "All Peoples' was a pioneer . . . in the attempt to reach and serve a section of the population which was largely isolated from the denominational churches; in its germinating of new and imported ideas; and in its attempt to close the gap between rich and poor, alien and native."[42]

Woodsworth's, and thus All Peoples', chief concern was not

sectarian religious activity but the provision of adequate facilities for the assimilation of foreigners and a decent social life for the young and old of Winnipeg's North End. Woodsworth believed that the crux of Winnipeg's social problem in these years was the tremendous influx of foreign-born and the resulting complicated problem of assimilating a new and very different population. To help solve this problem the Mission undertook a great many programs in the period 1907–14. Besides a dramatic increase in physical facilities, All Peoples' staff grew to twenty full-time workers and well over a hundred student and church volunteers. Moreover, in order to better serve the needs of a multilingual ethnic population, several workers endeavoured to learn Polish, Ukrainian, German, and other languages.

The actual work carried on by the Mission was remarkable, both in scope and the number of people reached. A partial listing of the program includes the running of two kindergartens; visits to immigrants' homes; girls' and boys' classes and clubs; a fresh-air camp; the provision of swimming and gymnasium facilities; night classes in English and "civics"; Sunday schools; free legal advice; pressure for a juvenile court (established in 1908); hospital visitation; welcoming immigrants at the federal immigration building; Mothers' Meetings; dispensation of relief; concerts; and numerous other activities.[43]

Two aspects of the All Peoples' Mission are of particular interest because of their departure from the established pattern of most charitable organizations in Winnipeg. In 1912 North End House was established as a residence for settlement workers and this action, coupled with the fact that Woodsworth and his family also lived in the area, can be recognized as something of a breakthrough in Winnipeg.[44] Formerly (with the exception, of course, of the Margaret Scott Nursing Mission) the poor and the sick had to seek out aid; now it was brought to their homes. This move is all the more noteworthy since it coincided with a vast exodus of "respectable" (i.e., Anglo-Saxon) Winnipeggers from the North End. To be sure the work of the Mission in the North End had obvious shortcomings in that it could contact only a small minority of Winnipeg's vast new population. It was, nevertheless, a significant attempt to halt the type of residential segregation that naturally led to social and cultural isolation.

The sponsorship of the Peoples' Forum was the Mission's other special contribution to immigrant adjustment. These Sunday meetings served a variety of purposes. Consisting of lectures and various ethnic groups' music and dancing, they brought together, often for the first time, all sections of the city's population, irrespective of race, religion, and class. The great educational value and popularity of such gatherings is apparent from their rapid spread to other Canadian cities.[45]

As in the case of the Nursing Mission, one of the chief values of the work of All Peoples' was the publicity its work gave to conditions in Winnipeg's "foreign ghetto." Winnipeg's three daily newspapers gave generous space to the activities of the Mission and until the war, when charges of catering to enemy aliens were laid, praised Woodsworth unreservedly.[46] But it was a mark of Woodsworth's great conviction about the seriousness of the immigrant problem and the need to increase support for social welfare policies that he did not consider such publicity enough. While he served as Superintendent of All Peoples', Woodsworth published numerous articles in the *Christian Guardian* and other periodicals and newspapers, as well as writing two books that dealt with immigration and the social gospel.[47] These efforts served the same basic function as the publicity engendered by Margaret Scott's efforts. It is true, of course, that neither this publicity nor that resulting from the work of other charitable agencies did much to change the dominant laissez-faire attitudes in the period before the war. On the other hand, the greatly extended area of available and verifiable knowledge about the conditions of the city's poor did lead to some changes.

These changes are most readily apparent in the shifting position of the civic corporation towards the broad problem of relief and immigrant adjustment. In one respect the work of All Peoples' received less consideration than did the Nursing Mission, for City Council never contributed more than $1,000 to its work, and some years gave only $500. Hence the Mission was forced to rely on private contributions and the support of the Methodist General Board of Missions to meet its average annual expenditure of $15,000. Yet, as Woodsworth himself recognized, the city was in this period slowly but surely broadening the scope of its involvement in the social welfare area. Through their actual work with the newcomer and in their effect upon established society, the Margaret Scott Nursing Mission and All Peoples' Mission helped in no small way to ease the impersonal materialism of the city, and, except for the tragedy of a world war in 1914, these efforts might have succeeded in preventing the great social conflict that was to divide Winnipeg during the general strike.

11 / The Immigrant Problem: Education and Assimilation

In the process of assimilation there must be some standard to which the newcomer is expected (and often desires) to conform. It has already been observed that in Winnipeg's case the dominant or charter group was made up of persons of British-Ontarian stock. The entry of Manitoba into Confederation in 1870 was followed by a mass influx of these people into the province and by 1880 the original social make-up of the community at Fort Garry—a balance of English, French, and Indian-Métis—was dramatically altered. The new majority of Anglo-Protestants quickly and effectively established their economic, social, political, and cultural mores; they became, in effect, the masters of the city and, indeed, of the whole province.[1]

This is not to say that the English-speaking majority was a completely homogeneous group. Encompassing English, Scots, and Irish elements, the charter group was at one level at least culturally diverse. Yet what is much more important than this diversity is the fact that the British group felt themselves to be no less a unity than was Britain itself. The diversity that existed was almost completely obscured by the fact that the various elements were bound together by their common language, Protestant religion, and British heritage.[2] The dominant group was further united in Winnipeg by its common experience; its members had all migrated to the province and had worked there together to build a new community at the confluence of the Red and Assiniboine rivers.

Even more significantly, those who came in the 1870s and 1880s had been a united group even before they emigrated to Manitoba. They were in large part the Clear Grits of Ontario and as such held several basic beliefs with utmost conviction, in particular their conception of the future of Manitoba and the Northwest. To them Manitoba was the next frontier; it was to be a second Ontario or, rather, a second Canada West. This meant that their ideas about the separation of church and state and the absolute need for no privilege for any group were extended to Manitoba. In other words, unlike some of their contemporaries in Eastern Canada—where sheer geographical propinquity, the presence of vocal minority groups, and the demands of political necessity dictated some accommodation between French and English—they neither believed in nor subscribed to a bilingual and bicultural view of Canada. On the contrary, cultural uniformity (based, of course, on British traditions) was to them the key to national strength.[3]

Thus, very early in Winnipeg's history, two fundamental facts had been established that were to affect the process of assimilation throughout the period. Firstly, the dominance of the British-Ontarian group meant that there was a fundamental difference between two categories of newcomers. Those who arrived in Winnipeg from Ontario and Britain quickly resumed familiar routines and easily merged in interests and activities with established residents. But for those who came from other countries and whose memories and traditions held no trace of recognition for their new surroundings, adjustment was achieved only with the utmost difficulty. Many of this group faltered, were overwhelmed and lost, because in the whole span of their previous existence they found no parallel to guide them in their new life. The sense of alienation experienced by the newcomer is clearly revealed in the following penetrating comment on the ethnic divisions of Winnipeg society made by a Winnipeg immigrant of Hungarian origin: " 'The English,' he whispered, '. . . the only people who count are the English. Their fathers got all the best jobs. They're the only ones nobody ever calls foreigners. Nobody ever makes fun of their names or calls them bologny-eaters, or laughs at the way they dress or talk. Nobody,' he concludes bitterly, 'cause when you're English it's the same as bein' Canadian.' "[4]

The second factor—that the dominant group believed Winnipeg (and Canada) was, and should remain, a British country—meant that the concept of cultural pluralism (or a cultural mosaic), used so often to describe Canadian society in later years, was not even contemplated in Winnipeg during this period. Rather, the charter group was determined to follow the melting pot approach of their southern neighbours, and it was the English majority who were to provide the recipe and stoke the fire. It matters not that in subsequent years it was found that the English majority's approach to assimilation, based primarily on the language aspect, did not produce a "Canadian" culture.[5] The important point is that throughout the period the attempt to achieve the goal of a unified society was paramount in the minds of the English majority in Winnipeg.

The question of whether the "conglomeration of non-British peoples could be fused with the British Canadian majority to make a real community which would preserve the salient features of the old British allegiance" affected Winnipeg with varying degrees of intensity.[6] It might seem incongruous that from 1874–90 the ascendant group accepted a dual French-English education system that recognized French as a language of instruction in provincial schools. But they did not do so out of conviction as to its merits; they lived with the dual system that had existed before their arrival only so long as it took them to settle and transplant in Winnipeg (and Manitoba) their own familiar institutions in church, state, and school. Also, the fact that the great majority of French in Manitoba lived in a single community (St. Boniface) meant that it was possible to develop two distinct sets of institutions with little conflict. The Anglo-Protestant's real feelings are nevertheless discernible even in this early period. They are readily traced in their rather hysterical reaction to the shooting of Thomas Scott during the first Riel insurgency and in the continuing shocks of Riel's execution, the Jesuit Estates' Act and D'Alton McCarthy's Equal Rights League. They succeeded, moreover, in 1890 in gaining the tool they sought for achieving cultural (or at least linguistic) uniformity in the passage of legislation that established a public school system that was secular and unilingual.[7]

Yet, in spite of these developments, the period before 1897 was one of relative calm in the matter of racial questions in Winnipeg. The changes in the School Act in 1890 effectively removed the question of "French privilege" in Manitoba and, in terms of other ethnic groups, the English majority found that they had little to fear in their pursuit of assimilation. Prior to 1897 the only significant ethnic groups that entered Winnipeg were the Scandinavians and Germans. These Northern Europeans, with their familiar Protestant religions, were easily and quickly absorbed. Speaking of the Scandinavians, one observer noted:

> In the melting process Icelanders have the foremost place among the adopted peoples. In the colleges and university they have forged to the front and asked favors of no one. They have a long line of hard-working and thrifty generations at their back, which is bound to develop men of value. . . . The Scandinavian races have proven to be the best of foreigners in Canada and in Winnipeg. . . .

Winnipeg's reaction to the Germans was equally laudatory:

> The German is of good stock, and therefore we expect good citizenship to display itself in this element of our foreign poulation. We look for the virtues of his sturdy Teutonic stock to manifest themselves in thrift, progressiveness, and prosperity.
>
> Like the Scandinavian, the Germans are of the same racial type and original stock as ourselves and have, therefore, kindered habits and institutions and similar ideals and moral standards. These all enhance the value of prospective citizens. Blood will tell and the law of heredity is still active.[8]

Several distinct changes took place in the years 1897–1914 that were to seriously affect and impede this assimilation process. In the first place the immigrants who arrived after 1897 did so in enormously greater numbers than previously, and the impact of so many in so brief a period was in itself enough to cause a disturbing shock. This shock was intensified when it was found that a large portion of the newcomers were Slavs and Jews, people who were feared as "strangers within the gates."[9] This apprehension stemmed from the fact that these people, along with the inevitable difference of background, language, and religion, brought with them a sense of ethnic nationalism, born at once of oppression and the teaching of their leaders, which was new in Winnipeg. Moreover, they tended to segregate themselves into foreign ghettos in the North End.

Having experienced so little difficulty in their pursuit of a common nationality in the pre-1897 period, the charter group was ill-prepared to meet the enormous challenges of the next decade. They were particularly unprepared for the large degree of group consciousness that the immigrants who came after 1897 possessed, and this cohesiveness provoked a secondary reaction among established Winnipeggers. The English majority rapidly became even more conscious of their own identity. The "old" society felt a severe sense of frustration because the new arrivals did not fit into its categories, and resentment because they threatened its desire to create a broad cultural uniformity. Uneasy, the charter group attempted to avoid contact with the immigrants by withdrawing even farther into a solid, but isolated group of its own. By 1914 Winnipeg was a partitioned city, separated on the basis of language and ethnic background.

Expressions of outright bigotry toward the Slav and the Jew were voiced frequently in Winnipeg newspapers after 1897. A Ukrainian wedding—that joyful expression of an intense sense of community— was attacked as a debased orgy. The immigrant's use of wine and spirits offended many, especially the ladies of the Women's Christian Temperance Union, who had no difficulty in linking foreigners, liquor dealers, and politicians in a chain of corruption and degradation.[10] Comments such as "the Slav has not thus far proved himself the equal of the northwestern European as an immigrant," or "They are the unfortunate product of a civilization that is a thousand years behind the Canadian," were both expressed and believed by the charter group.[11] Even J. S. Woodsworth, for all his progressive work among the foreigners, was obsessed with the difficulties facing Winnipeg in its attempt to absorb these immigrants who were "distinctly a lower grade."[12] Some Winnipeggers became so concerned over the presence of large numbers of Slavs and Jews that in a rare abandonment of the growth ethic they advocated a policy of exclusion or, at the very least, a strictly controlled quota system. Examples of this type of argument are reproduced below:

Increased population, if of the right sort, will be of great benefit. ... But we should be careful that we do not bring in an imported population of such a character as will be an injury, not a benefit to our people. . . . Anglo-Saxon, Germans, and Scandinavians in general we can take in any number, but we cannot assimilate more than a limited number of immigrants of a radically different race. The Galician is as yet an experiment; we do not know how he will turn out; and we cannot afford to make the experiment on too large a scale.

There are now few people who will affirm that Slavonic immigrants are desirable settlers, or that they are welcomed by the "white" people of Western Canada. . . . Those whose ignorance is impenetrable, whose customs are repulsive, whose civilization is primitive, and whose character and morals are justly condemned, are surely not the class of immigrants which the country's paid immigration agents should seek to attract. Better by far to keep our land for children, and children's children of Canadians, than to fill up the country with the scum of Europe.[13]

But such drastic statements were expressed only infrequently, and the majority of Winnipeggers were convinced that in spite of their great differences the Slav and Jew could be assimilated if a sufficient amount of energy and determination was invested in the task.

The key agent in this assimilation process was the public school system. Most Anglo-Saxon Winnipeggers looked to the public schools "as the mightiest assimilation force for elevating the immigrant to the level of Canadian life."[14] The city's elite felt strongly that on the school, "more than any other agency, will depend the quality and nature of the citizenship of the future; that in the way in which the school avails itself of its opportunity depends the extent to which Canadian traditions will be appropriated, Canadian national sentiment imbibed, and Canadian standards of living adopted by the next generation of the new races that are making their homes in our midst."[15]

From the standpoint of Winnipeg's charter group, however, there were serious problems associated with using the public school system as an assimilating agent. Firstly, there was the problem of providing adequate facilities and teaching staff to serve the rapidly growing student population. As Table 24 illustrates, this meant that the resources of the Winnipeg Public School Board and the provincial Department of Education were heavily taxed in an attempt to keep pace the city's growth.[16] Yet despite the impressive growth in the public educational facilities of Winnipeg it was estimated that almost ten thousand children between the ages of six and sixteen were not attending public schools in 1911.

But the second difficulty, that of language, was even more difficult to solve. The problem here was one of having a sufficient number of teachers trained who could speak both English and the language of the

Table 24 / Growth of Winnipeg Public School System, 1874–1914

Year	No. of teachers and specialists	No. of buildings	Value of buildings, sites and fixtures ($)	Enrolment
1871	1	1	–	35
1876	4	2	3,500	423
1886	49	11	220,000	2,831
1896	96	14	397,700	6,374
1900	119	16	487,000	7,500
1903	140	18	750,000	9,500
1904	168	19	774,500	10,308
1905	192	21	1,071,701	11,675
1906	220	26	1,213,931	13,445
1907	248	30	1,552,753	14,802
1908	266	34	1,971,479	15,449
1909	297	33	2,300,000	16,070
1910	340	33	2,800,000	17,738
1911	381	37	3,225,000	20,167
1912	456	40	4,135,000	21,112
1913	531	40	5,032,589	22,364
1914	566	44	5,620,619	25,814

foreign immigrants they faced in the classroom. The situation that developed was described by the principal of one North End school:

> Imagine if you can a young girl, herself only a few years out of school, facing a class of fifty children, none of whom could understand a word she said; nor could the teacher understand a word spoken by her pupils. The children could not converse with each other, excepting in small groups of those who had learned the same language in their homes. Obviously the first task was to get teacher and pupils to understand each other. None of our teachers could read, write or speak the language of their pupils. They had, of necessity, to teach the children to speak as well as to read and write the English language.[17]

The members of Winnipeg's elite realized, moreover, that they had to reach more than school-age children if the process of assimilation through education was to be successful. Accordingly, Mayor Ashdown was instrumental in having the Winnipeg School Board establish a system of evening classes in 1907. During that year ten English-language evening classes were opened for foreigners and six more were soon added, twelve of the total being north of the CPR tracks. To attract students to the classes advertisements were run in the city's numerous foreign-language newspapers and handbills in five languages were printed and widely distributed.[18]

The efforts of the Winnipeg School Board to use the educational system as an assimilating agent were frustrated by problems other than facilities and language. One of these was the tendency of the city's foreign groups to take upon themselves the task of educating their children in the language and culture of their particular group. This was true for almost every nationality, be it Scandinavian, German, Slavic, or Jewish. It was estimated that in 1911 at least three thousand foreigners were attending private or separate schools in Winnipeg. Moreover, thousands more attended evening or weekend classes conducted by the religious and cultural organizations of the various ethnic groups.[19] In short, it was apparent to all but the most casual observer that many foreigners were either not being "Canadianized" at all, or they were being assimilated at a rate deemed unsatisfactory to the city's Anglo-Saxon elite.

There were still other problems faced by the charter group in Winnipeg, however, which eventually caused the whole education-assimilation question to become a major issue in the post–1897 period. For the Public Schools Act of Manitoba permitted bilingual schools and did not provide for compulsory attendance; and it was to be these two issues which led to a kind of open racism on the part of the Anglo-Saxon establishment that did little to improve ethnic relations in Winnipeg.

The views of one influential Winnipegger on the problem of "Canadianizing the foreigner" through the use of the public school system as an agent of assimilation may be taken as typical. J. W. Dafoe, editor of the *Manitoba Free Press* from 1901, had for years been carried away with enthusiasm for more and more settlers. But increasingly after the turn of the century he became concerned with the effect the growing number and diversity of aliens was having on what he termed the "emerging Canadian nationality."[20] What bothered him was the variety of unfamiliar languages he heard on the main avenues of the city, the creation of linguistic ghettos in the North End, the growing numbers and varieties of religious sects, and the pattern of group settlement in various parts of the province where language became a barrier to communication, a wall around an ethnic fortress. Perhaps he realized as well that as time passed and the tide of foreign immigration decreased it would be from these rural areas that the ethnic communities within the city would attract new members. Dafoe, and others, also noted that Winnipeg's problem was more serious than that of other Canadian cities. Toronto, for example, had in 1911 over 91 per cent of its population born in the British Empire and only 5 per cent born in Europe.

Winnipeg, on the other hand, had only 75 per cent in the former category and over 19 per cent in the latter.

Turning to the question of how these foreigners could best be Canadianized, Dafoe saw the only possible approach was through the English language and the education system. Although he recognized that many of the adult immigrants would never learn English he believed that their children should be forced to by the simple device of compulsory attendance at public schools, in which the language of instruction would be English. Dafoe "saw the necessity of compulsory education as a self-evident truth, a law of right reason, an inescapable conclusion, a point of view that no intelligent citizen could oppose, a proposition that only the apathetic would fail to support."[21]

Dafoe and his many supporters were correct in maintaining that language was a major factor in the assimilation process. Their mistake lay in assuming that through unilingualism the alien problem could be easily solved. Part of the reason for this assumption on the part of the charter group can be found in their impression of what was happening in American cities. It seemed to them that there, where compulsory attendance in unilingual, non-sectarian schools was widespread,[22] a national spirit had developed almost spontaneously as the immigrants felt themselves freed from the dead weight of conventions and prejudices of the older societies from which they had come; it was as if the great human potential in them was released to coalesce, almost automatically, into a new and better society. Little did they realize that such was not the case; that the process of assimilation was complex and affected by many varying and often intangible factors. Had they searched deeper and attempted to understand how assimilation operated they would have been surprised to learn that it was not an automatic process and that the speaking of English did not necessarily make one part of a homogeneous society. It was not recognized, for example, that the non-British ethnic groups were responding to the environment in which they found themselves; that the actions of minority groups in clustering together stemmed from basic social needs and was not very much different from the actions of the various people of British origin who made up the majority group. The only real solution then was one which had a broader base and took into consideration housing, economic opportunity, and social services—that is, all the factors that played so large a part in the newcomers' attachment to or rejection of the majority groups' way of life. Unfortunately, this kind of enlightened approach to assimilation was not adopted, and the enthusiasm for the Canadianization of foreigners soon led to the growth of myths such as those quoted above—myths that confused and distorted the conditions being experienced by Winnipeg's immigrants and stressed hereditary factors.

Perhaps the strident feelings of superiority on the part of the charter group would have been a great deal more restrained had they been able to implement their ideas on compulsory attendance and unilingual public schools rapidly and without outside interference. But the tragedy of the Manitoba Schools Question was that it could not have been settled by Winnipeg alone. Indeed, it became an issue in both provincial and federal politics. Moreover, the sheer numbers of new arrivals in Winnipeg in this period meant that plans for compulsory attendance could only be achieved by a massive expansion of physical facilities and teaching staff. But, paradoxically, few Winnipeggers were prepared to provide the necessary public funds.[23]

The chief obstacle preventing the use of the public school as the instrument of immigrant assimilation, however, was the compromise of 1897. Forced on Manitoba by the realities of national and provincial politics, this settlement weakened considerably the legislation of 1890. The compromise legislation provided that "when pupils in any school spoke French or any language other than English, the teaching of these was to be in French, or such other language, and English upon the bilingual system."[24] In the first few years of operation this clause worked as it was intended, to allow French children to be taught in the speech of their homes. But since even this compromise was less than satisfactory to most Winnipeggers it became intolerable when bilingual instruction was sought not only by the French but by the Ukrainians, Poles, and others. Dafoe noted, with unconcealed horror, that this had led by 1907 to some thirteen different languages being used in the provincial schools as languages of instruction. There is no question that the demands for bilingual instruction were often stimulated by the French Roman Catholic clergy, hopeful of obtaining among their Polish and Ukrainian co-religionists allies for the overthrow of the school system, and by political organizers of both parties seeking to curry favour with newly enfranchised voters. But whatever the source of the demand, the provincial Department of Education was hard pressed to supply teachers, let alone bilingual or multilingual teachers, to the increasing number of schools.[25]

The attempt to supply such teachers, however, made Winnipeg's Anglo-Saxons furious. The provincial government established at least two special training schools for bilingual teachers during this period in Winnipeg: a Polish Teachers' Training School and a Ruthenian Training School. Indeed, much to the consternation of the charter group, the Ukrainian teachers even established their own teachers' organization, held conventions in the city and published a Ukrainian weekly newspaper,[26] a journal which the *Winnipeg Tribune* described in June 1914 as being "subversive and destructive of Canadian citizenship and Canadian nationality."

The chaos latent in the loose phrasing of the bilingual clause was compounded by the lack of a school attendance law. Many Winnipeg children were receiving little or no education. To make matters even worse, this was particularly true in the case of new immigrants who, because of economic need or just plain ignorance or fear, kept their children away from classes. Faced with this situation, there arose in Winnipeg a demand for compulsory education as an absolute necessity. The problem was explained as follows:

> [Immigrant] children are growing up without an education, save in wickedness. Every day they are becoming a serious menace to the country. The future, if this continues, is very alarming. There must be compulsory education. There must! The party, the parliament, the government which permits a venerable obstacle to stand in the way of this absolute necessity to the very safety of the Dominion, which permits love for office or power to delay the enactment or proper enforcement of proper legislation whereby every child shall be compelled to attend school had forefeited all right to the respect of the people, and whatever its merits, must be replaced by those who have vision and courage to discern and do what is imperative.[27]

The opinions expressed here received widespread support among the English community in Winnipeg. In 1902, for example, a delegation headed by Mayor Arbuthnot met with members of the provincial government "and strongly urged the necessity of compulsory education."[28] And in 1909 a Citizen's Meeting, attended by such well-known Winnipeggers as ex-mayors Ashdown and Ryan and Alderman Riley, reported that "thousands of children never attend a school and were growing up absolutely illiterate and that such a condition will work as a menace to the community. The opinion prevailed that the solution of the question . . . lay in the immediate passage by the provincial government of a compulsory education bill."[29] This demand for compulsory education was also supported by such organizations as the Canadian Club and the Orange Order. The latter organization even arranged a mass meeting to protest the provincial government's lack of a school attendance law. The Grand Master of the Orange Lodge in Winnipeg, ex-alderman J. Willoughby, was especially vociferous in his attempts to obtain compulsory education.

J. S. Woodsworth also raised his voice and used his pen with growing insistence for a compulsory school law. In a 1912 report on the educational needs of children employed in shops and factories, he concluded with the blunt statement that "in nearly all cases the workers have very little education. . . ." And in an address to the Local Council of Women he stated:

> One-third of all the children in Manitoba do not attend school, only 25% pass through the entrance, 5% pass through the high school, and 1% go through college. All the rest are practically

unprovided for as far as education is concerned. There are few free lectures, concerts and reading rooms. The only public amusements in North Winnipeg are the saloon, the pool-room, theatre and dance hall. The public schools should be put to larger use.[30]

The feelings of Winnipeg's Anglo-Saxon majority were perhaps best summed up, however, in the reaction of the city's school board to the Coldwell amendments of 1912. These amendments, if implemented, would have resulted in a startling change in Winnipeg's public school system. The first amendment provided that for the purpose of the bilingual clause of the Public Schools Act, every classroom was in fact a complete "school," thus allowing almost every individual class in the public schools of Winnipeg to claim a bilingual teacher. Previously there had just been one or two bilingual teachers in each school. The next amendment compelled the school board to provide space for all children of school age in the city. This clause was intended to force the school board to assume the expense of running existing private schools. Finally, the third amendment would have allowed the segregation of children according to religion even during secular school work. This last section would have led to a system diametrically opposed to that established in 1890.[31]

Reaction to the Coldwell amendments was predictable. The *Manitoba Free Press* and the Orange Lodge denounced them, while the Winnipeg School Board stated bluntly and publicly it would not implement the measures in the schools of the city. The strength of the feeling over the issue of bilingualism had come to the point of open defiance of provincial law.

Given this apparently unanimous agreement on the need for compulsory education and unilingual schools among the English majority in Winnipeg, it is necessary to explain why their views were not met by the provincial government. This is not the place for a detailed analysis of the complicated state of provincial politics in Manitoba in this period, but a few basic facts can be stated.[32] The Conservative government, headed by Premier Roblin, drew heavily on the ethnic vote to maintain its hold on office.[33] Indeed, Roblin had virtually made a compact with the Roman Catholic Archbishop of St. Boniface that stipulated he would not disturb the status quo in return for the relatively small but powerful (in terms of provincial seats) French vote. The agreement was a good one for Roblin and served him well until 1915. The government's only efforts to appease the rising tide of protest in Winnipeg against this attempt to curry favour with the minority groups were the unsuccessful attack on truancy in the city by tightening the enforcement of the provincial Children's Act, and by the passage, in 1906, of flag legislation that symbolically required all provincial schools to fly the Union Jack during school hours.

At the time, in a cynical reference to the lack of a school attendance law, the latter action was treated as a measure designed to make the ensign more visible to the young by not requiring that the flag be inside the school where it could not be so easily seen.[34] The inadequacy of such measures in dealing with the main issue of non-attendance was revealed in 1911 when it was discovered—and widely publicized—that the percentage of illiteracy among foreign-born males in Manitoba (23.3) was the highest in Canada except Quebec, and that Winnipeg stood in eighth place among all cities over seven thousand in its illiteracy rate.

In the face of this unsympathetic attitude on the part of Premier Roblin and the Conservatives many in the city turned to the provincial Liberal party and its leader, T. C. Norris, who took a firm stand on the education question. And, shortly after a Liberal victory in 1915, the new provincial government established a "national" school system and passed a compulsory attendance law. Although the matter of bilingual schools has since remained an issue of some importance in Manitoba, the settlement achieved in 1916 is still in effect. In general, the legislation had the desired effect so far as the English majority were concerned and in subsequent years all immigrants of school age learned English as a matter of course. On the other hand, the heated rhetoric of the campaign itself impeded cordial social interaction in Winnipeg. While the merits of compulsory education and the utter absurdity of multilingual instruction (though not bilingual) are obvious, the controversy aroused in achieving these aims served to intensify racial divisions in Winnipeg for decades.

By all external indices Winnipeg had not succeeded by 1914 in assimilating the foreigner to any great extent. In the matter of political representation even the Scandinavians and Germans did not make any great advances in this period, although their record is noteworthy in relation to that of the Slavs or Jews. As far as residential segregation was concerned the same general pattern prevailed; the Northern Europeans, while segregated, were not nearly so isolated as were the other non-English ethnic groups. But the most telling fact in illustrating that the charter group had a long way to go in achieving their coal of a common Canadian nationality was to come during the crisis years of 1914–18 and 1919. During the war, for example, it was seriously proposed by a well-known Winnipeg minister that the property of foreigners be seized at grossly undervalued prices and distributed to returning veterans of Anglo-Saxon stock.[35] And when labour troubles erupted into a general strike in Winnipeg in 1919, popular hysteria blamed it on Bolshevik revolutionaries and foreign agitators, despite the fact that almost every leader of the strike had come out of the British trade union movement.

12 / The Commercial Elite and the Water Supply Problem

Since Winnipeg was governed by a growth-conscious commercial elite, it is not surprising that the city's municipal services were affected by their particular outlook. Indeed, the history of Winnipeg's waterworks system provides an excellent opportunity to illustrate how City Council's concern with economic matters affected the day-to-day affairs of the city. For, immersed in the often mundane details of Winnipeg's water supply question, are several important themes. There is, first of all, the disinclination on the part of the municipal corporation to care for all citizens, shown in its refusal to extend complete waterworks facilities (domestic water supply, fire protection, and sewers) to all parts of the city. A second theme is found in the comparison of water services in the various wards, for this adds another dimension to the city's geographic divisions and further illustrates that Winnipeg was in this period a severely divided community. The following account also illuminates the elite's overriding concern with financial matters, for their attempts to solve the water supply question were continuously directed toward finding the type of solution that could be justified in financial terms. They were little concerned with the high social costs inflicted by their intransigent attitude. Finally, and perhaps most important, an analysis of Winnipeg's water supply question indicates that the story of the failure of the city's governing group to create a humane environment for all citizens is a complicated one. It does not separate itself nicely into good and evil, times of victory and times of defeat. Rather, it is the story of ordinary men and commonplace events that accumulated over time to produce Winnipeg's great social problems.

Private Enterprise versus Public Weal: 1874–1900

At the time of incorporation most residents of Winnipeg received their supply of water from men who delivered river water to their homes or businesses. One such waterman, James Irwin, had started business in 1872 when he raised a scaffold out in the Red River, sunk down a pipe, and pumped water into barrels which were then loaded onto horse-drawn carts and delivered to customers in the city. A similar system, conducted on a grander scale, was employed by George Rath. His carts, drawn by a team of oxen, carried eleven barrels of water and were equipped with forty feet of hose, "by which means the water can be introduced into the houses of citizens without the pail system." This travelling "hauley system" of water service was kept full each night in case of fire. As the city's population increased so did the number of watermen until by 1876 there were at least six men employed full time in this occupation.[1]

As far as domestic supply was concerned this system (supplemented by private wells and collected rain water) met the city's needs well enough until 1880 when demands arose for a more sophisticated and dependable water supply. Although well supplied in summer, most residents could not obtain nearly enough water in the winter months when the ice of the river was several feet thick. Some concern was also being expressed about the purity of the water. In 1876 the city had constructed a sewage system that emptied into the Red and Assiniboine rivers and local doctors were quick to condemn the rivers' continued use for domestic water supply. But in spite of a continuing high number of cases of "Red River Fever" (typhoid), it was not the purity question that precipitated demands for a new system; rather, it was concern over fire protection.

Winnipeg obtained its first fire engine in November 1874 and, until the organization of a full-time brigade in 1881, relied on a volunteer force. Despite all efforts these early years were marked by extraordinarily high fire insurance rates due to the absence of water mains and hydrants and the very limited capacity of the self-contained steam fire-engines. Several serious fires occurred, including one on Christmas Day, 1875, that destroyed the fire hall and all the equipment in the building.[2] The susceptibility of Winnipeg to major fires was, of course, further increased by the poorly planned and constructed wooden buildings that dominated the city at this time.

Whatever the reason for the high losses suffered by the city's residents, there was almost unanimous agreement that only a modern water supply system could remedy the problems. To this end some citizens had urged that a municipal system be built and in 1880 $40,000 had been appropriated for this purpose. But in the carefree atmosphere of the boom this money had been spent for other projects. Instead, in what would later prove to be a hastily conceived agreement, City Council gave a franchise to supply water to a privately owned company. The reasoning behind this move was simply that the city would thus obtain a modern water supply system without the necessity for any large capital outlay of public funds.

The terms of the act incorporating the Winnipeg Water Works Company passed by the provincial legislature in December 1880 were generous, to say the least. The company was granted an exclusive right to supply water both to the City of Winnipeg proper and for one-half mile around the city limits. In return for this franchise, which was to run for twenty years, the WWW Company was to begin operation by July 1882 with two miles of water mains. It was also obligated to provide fire hydrants and "furnish free of charge to the city, to the full extent of the resources and powers of their works, all water requisite for the extinction of accidental fires." Finally, the company agreed to supply water for sewer flushing, street watering, and other public purposes at a reduced rate.[3]

Construction of the new system began in the spring of 1881 and by July 1882 six miles of mains had been laid and several score connections made. Water was drawn from the Assiniboine River by a large pump located at Armstrong's Point. Before entering the mains, the river water went through a crude settling and filtering process that removed some of the impurities.

During the first several years of operation few complaints about the quantity or quality of water supplied or about service were voiced in the press or in Council. Apparently the new system was so superior over the previous "hauley system" of water service that a kind of honeymoon period occurred. This spell was abruptly broken, however, in November 1886 when the city engineer presented a report to City Council that stated that the company was not honouring the terms of its act of incorporation.[4]

Among the many points mentioned in City Engineer Ruttan's report, two caused grave concern. The company had agreed to erect hydrants five hundred feet apart on all streets where mains existed and from which water could be drawn for "fire, sewer flushing, and other public purposes." Ruttan estimated that there should have been seventy hydrants while in fact there were only thirty-four. Moreover, of these thirty-four only one had a "drip" connection that allowed it to be used in winter, and only eight were in fact "hydrants." The remaining twenty-six were merely "valves in the water pipes which are enclosed in man-holes built from the pipes to the surface of the street." Before being used these valve connections had to be fitted with standpipes and this entailed considerable loss of time in emergencies such as fire.

As serious as the hydrant problem was thought to be, it was the matter of water quantity that occasioned the most attention. Ruttan pointed out that the supply to the city should have been based on the requirements of a population of forty thousand. Yet the system did not even meet the needs of a population of half that number. Instead of basing the quantity of supply on an "average domestic consumption per day" of sixty gallons, the company was using a figure of twenty-five gallons. In short, the volume of water being supplied by the company was simply inadequate to meet the needs of Winnipeg.[5]

When City Council made these inadequacies known to the water-works company, the latter simply replied that as far as it was concerned it was meeting its obligations. The www Company then pointed out that if Council wanted more hydrants and an increased water supply, it would have to compensate the company for the additional outlay. It suggested, for example, that if Council made water connections compulsory on all houses in the city, the company would then consider increased service.[6]

Meeting in January 1887, after civic elections in which the water supply question was one of the major issues, City Council did not immediately take up the proposals of the company. Instead, Council considered the options that were open to it in the effort to obtain an adequate water supply. The cheapest and most obvious solution was to convince—or compel—the www Company to meet what Council considered were the obligations imposed upon it in the original agreement of December 1880. The second option was to buy the company's franchise either by direct negotiation or by arbitration; the latter had been provided for in the original agreement. Finally, if these courses of action failed, Council could build its own waterworks system to operate in direct competition with the private company.[7]

While Council was discussing the various ways and means of dealing with the water question, it was becoming increasingly apparent that some course of action would have to be decided on quickly. Several prominent doctors warned that a continued water shortage would have disastrous effects on the health of the city. The local business community argued that the lack of adequate fire protection caused such exorbitant fire insurance rates that many of their businesses were threatened. The local press also demanded immediate action. Significantly, in all these arguments, and in the discussions of City Council, it was apparent that by the spring of 1887 all agreed that the city would eventually have to own its own system.[8] But, as was also pointed out, something had to be done immediately to deal with what was considered a critical situation.

Council's response to these pleas for action was to enter into negotiations with the waterworks company with a view to buying it out and establishing a municipal system. Negotiations got underway in August 1887 and continued off and on for over three years. But in 1890 the two parties were still a long way apart; the company asking $630,000 and the city countering with offers of never more than $350,000.

In light of the continuing complaints of Winnipeg residents about the inadequacy of the water supply this lack of concrete results requires explanation. If, as the city maintained, the company was not living up to the terms of the original agreement Council should have been prepared to put the matter before the courts. Indeed, the company

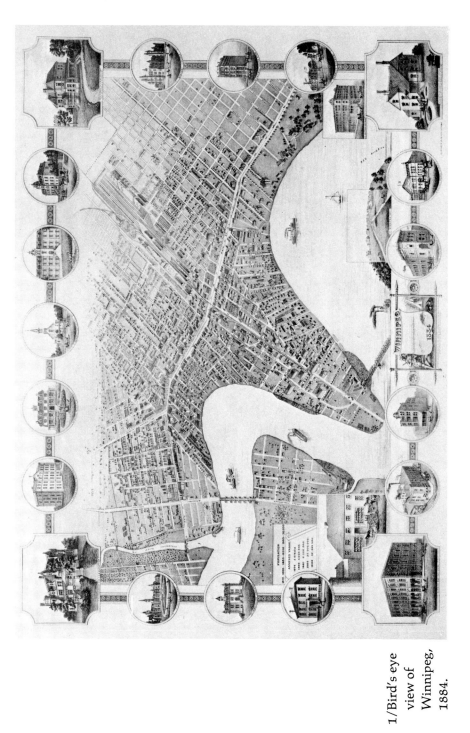

1/Bird's eye view of Winnipeg, 1884.

2/*Upper* Main Street, 1876.   3/McDermot Avenue, Ward 4, 1881.

Manitoba

AND

NORTH-WESTERN RAILWAY
LAND DEPARTMENT,
OFFICES - 622 MAIN STREET, WINNIPEG,

OFFER FOR SALE, WITHOUT CULTIVATION OR SETTLEMENT RESTRICTIONS,

2,750,000 ACRES OF LAND
IN THE WELL KNOWN

Park Lands of the Fertile Belt.
GOOD SOIL. GOOD TIMBER. GOOD WATER.

TERMS OF PAYMENT.—If paid for in full at time of purchase a discount will be allowed; but the purchaser may pay one-sixth in cash and the balance in five annual instalments, with interest at six per cent. per annum.

IMPROVED FARMS along the line to rent or for sale; a list of which can be seen at the Offices of the Company.

TOWN LOTS FOR SALE along the Manitoba & North-Western Railway in the following places: Arden, Neepawa, Minnedosa, Newdale, Strathclair, Shoal Lake, Solsgirth, Birtle, Fox Warren, Binscarth, Harrowby, Langenburg.

Maps showing settlement and lists of free Government Land open for entry. Folders (in English and foreign languages). Maps, &c., and any further information can be obtained at the Offices of the Company, or by letter addressed

A. F. EDEN, Land Commissioner M. & N. W. R.,

622 MAIN STREET, WINNIPEG.

Representatives from Minnedosa, Birtle and other districts along the line can be interviewed at the above address.

4/A typical land advertisement, 1887.

5/*Upper* Main Street subway under CPR tracks, 1905.

6/The CPR yards, 1884. "The longest railway yards in the world."

7 / Arrival of harvest excursionists at CPR station, 1897.

8/*Upper* Official opening of Winnipeg Electric Street Railway, 5 September 1892.

9/Broadway Avenue, Ward 2, 1910.

10/Portage and Main, 1910.

11/*Upper* "New Jerusalem" in Winnipeg's North End, 1908. This particular scene is on Dufferin Avenue.

12/Tenement houses in North End, 1909. These structures were on Jarvis Avenue.

13/*Upper* Delivery wagon in Winnipeg's North End, 1910. This milkwoman worked for the International Dairy.

14/The "Foreign Quarter," 1904. The photograph was taken on Dufferin Avenue.

15/*Upper* Winnipeg City Hall on Main Street, c. 1902.

16/Kennedy Street, Ward 2, 1900.

17/Main Street and City Hall Square, c. 1897. This view looks south toward Portage and Main.

18/*Upper* Main Street, c. 1897. This view looks north toward City Hall.

19/Cross section of Greater Winnipeg Water District Aqueduct to Shoal Lake. Construction commenced in March 1914.

Foote, Photo.

20/Prime Minister Wilfrid Laurier aboard the *Winnitoba* for the official opening of St. Andrew's Locks in 1910.

21/Andrew G. B. Bannatyne, one of Winnipeg's earliest businessmen and community leaders.

22 James H. Ashdown, Winnipeg's "merchant prince." He served as mayor in 1907 and 1908.

23/William Sanford Evans, leading member of Winnipeg's commercial elite. He served as mayor from 1909 to 1911.

24/Thomas Russ Deacon, founder of the Manitoba Bridge and Iron Works. He served as mayor from 1913 to 1914.

challenged the city to do just that. The problem confronting the city, however, was that strictly speaking the company's legal position was unassailable. In the matter of quantity of supply, for example, the original act clearly stated that the company was required to supply only twenty-five gallons per capita per day. The city's case rested on the doubtful ground that this had been a clerical error in the original act and should have read sixty gallons.[9] In fact, the www Company had the city in a position where it had to agree to increased compensation to buy the company out at its price, initiate arbitration proceedings, or wait until the company's franchise expired. Clearly, the very real problems present in the city in 1890 as a result of the inadequate water supply called for some action. But despite these problems, Council greeted every company offer with scorn and indignation. By the spring of 1890 any hopes for an amicable and negotiated settlement had disappeared completely.

During 1890 and 1891 the waterworks question was continually before Council, but it was not until July of 1892 that the city decided to establish a municipal waterworks system, to operate in competition with the www Company.[10] Plans for the system were hastily drawn up by the city engineer and a bylaw to raise $400,000 was submitted to the electors in December 1892. To the surprise of Council and the delight of the *Manitoba Free Press* the measure was defeated.[11] The latter had opposed the contemplated construction of a municipal system on the grounds that there would be too long a period of delay in the actual building of the works. It also pointed out that the city's right to build their own system was not altogether clear and the www Company had threatened legal action if the city attempted such a move. And, even if the city could prove its power to build works of its own, the delay caused would mean more time without adequate water for fire protection, sewers, and even domestic use.[12] In brief, the *Free Press* and the electorate demanded that Council reach an agreement with the company since this was the only immediate solution. Once this was done, it was argued, long-range plans that might include a separate municipal system could be contemplated.

Aside from questions raised about the quantity and pressure of water available for fire protection and sewer flushing, concern was growing over what many considered to be an even more serious question—the purity of the water itself. In response to this concern, City Council finally ordered the city engineer to prepare a report on the sanitary condition of the water supply. His report, published in November 1893, flatly rejected the use of the Assiniboine River as a source of anything more than a temporary supply. Instead, he recommended that the city look to artesian well water which was better in every respect than river water. This finding, which coincided with the recommendations made earlier in the year by Dr. Agnew, added a new dimension to the whole question of acquiring the works of the www Company. Since it drew its water from the river, purchase would mean that the city had only a distribution system on its hands; it would not solve the question of a proper source of supply.

Council interpreted this new evidence as support for their refusal to buy out the www Company. But if the commercial elite's adamant position in respect to the private company could be justified by the use of such evidence, it could just as easily be condemned from another point of view. For if the city refused to deal with the company there was no other course of action open to it other than waiting until the company's franchise ran out in 1900. Then, and only then, could a municipal system be built. In the meantime, water would continue to be drawn from the polluted Assiniboine and the quantity of water available for fire-fighting and sewer flushing would remain inadequate. Yet, despite the severe consequences, this was the course of action the Council decided to take.

The decision to wait until 1900 and then proceed with a municipal system was taken in 1896.[13] City Council, in a mood of uncharacteristic haste, ordered the city engineer and several doctors to make a report on the sources and cost of a new system. They recommended in October 1896 that the city draw its water from artesian wells and estimated the cost of a new system at $650,000. Council promptly prepared a money bylaw which was to be voted on in December. But even before the measure came to a vote it was apparent that it would be defeated.[14]

The opposition to the bylaw to raise money for a new waterworks system did not centre on the need for such a system. Everyone in Winnipeg—with the exception of the www Company's directors—had conceded or, rather, demanded this. What bothered the citizens was the haste Council displayed. It was a well-known fact that no action could be taken until 1900 and yet Council acted as if there was no time to lose. No specific plans had yet been drawn up for the new system and there was little evidence that the sum of money asked for would be used properly or efficiently. A wiser course of action, it was argued, would be to call in an expert, have him consider the sources available for Winnipeg's water needs, and then draw up specific plans for a new system. Only then should the ratepayers be asked to approve of any expenditure.

The defeat of the bylaw forced Council to accept this advice and early in 1897 an engineering expert was appointed to report on a future water supply for the city. The expert, Rudolph Hering, an engineer from New York, presented his report in September. Hering unequivocally recommended the adoption of an artesian well system as a source of supply. He noted that this water would be "not only cheaper, but safer to use, than that obtained from the Assiniboine River." As far as quantity was concerned the engineer felt there would be no great difficulty in obtaining all the water required for the city.

The report met with the unanimous approval of City Council and shortly after it was received a general election committee was chosen to see that the bylaw to raise the $700,000 required for the municipal system would be passed. Support for the project was received from the Board of Trade, which worked closely with Council to ensure that everyone who could vote on the measure was aware of its advantages. There was even a plan proposed to hire "agents, canvassers, and scrutineers" to publicly campaign for the passage of the bylaw, but such actions on behalf of Council were found to be illegal. No such legal niceties forbade the www Company from actively opposing the measure, however, and the day before the vote was to be taken it published an open letter threatening to raise its water rates by $16 a year if the measure passed. Undoubtedly, such rash action on the part of the company did not help its case. But even without such threats the measure probably would have passed, since the actual vote was 1346 for to 83 against. Following the vote Council took the added precaution of having the bylaw ratified by the legislature. This amendment to the Municipal Act also gave the city the right to commence construction immediately although they were not at liberty to sell water until they either bought out the www Company or until that company's franchise expired on December 23, 1900.

The passage of the bylaw and its confirmation by the legislature meant that for the first time since 1880 the city enjoyed an advantageous position in its dealings with www Company. Faced with the prospect of competition in a few years the company decided that it was to its advantage to sell its franchise and property to the city. During the months following the passage of the waterworks bylaw, the civic authorities entered into negotiations with the private firm and by August 1898 a satisfactory agreement had been made. Some objections were raised by city taxpayers that the price of $237,000 was too high, but City Council pointed out that the settlement meant that Winnipeg could "secure at a much earlier period than could otherwise be hoped a good supply of water in the north end of the city, and on certain important streets in other sections, where there is now no water."[15] In other words, if the city had not bought out the company it could not have sold any water from its new system until the expiration of the company's franchise in December 1900. With the settlement, municipal service could begin as soon as new mains, et cetera., were installed.

Following the agreement with the www Company, Council acted quickly. In April 1899 "An Act resting in the City of Winnipeg the Property, Franchises, and Effects of the Winnipeg Water Works Company" was passed by the provincial legislature and rates were immediately reduced. In May a water commissioner was appointed and construction of the new system was immediately undertaken. And, finally, in October 1900 water from artesian wells began flowing through Winnipeg's municipally owned water works system.

After twenty-six years Winnipeg finally obtained what was considered to be "an inexhaustible supply of pure water." The long delays experienced in reaching that goal, however, had inflicted heavy losses on the city, for the continued lack of an adequate and pure supply of water had adversely affected the city's health and had caused severe fire losses and high insurance rates. The inflexible position of Council is impossible to justify. In the first instance, most aldermen were businessmen themselves and should have had no problem accepting the company's argument that it was going to abide strictly by the obligations of the original agreement. If more was wanted or required by the city it expected compensation. But instead of accepting the original mistakes inherent in the agreement of 1880, Council refused to consider the company's proposals; rejected arbitration as provided in the Act; and insisted on putting forward impossible plans for building a duplicate municipal system in the face of doubtful legal authority and continued rejection of these plans by the electors.[16]

These observations, however, do not take into account one other factor that had a great deal to do with the elite's intransigent position. Throughout the long controversy with the private company the central portions of the city (wards 2, 3, and 4)—where most of the commercial elite lived and where most of their businesses were located—had adequate domestic supplies of water and at least elementary fire protection. It was in the North End (wards 5 and 6), where almost no water mains were laid, that the most severe problems were experienced. But since these districts included large numbers of foreigners and workingmen, few of whom had the vote or could influence the governing commercial elite in any way, Council could afford to take an inflexible stand. In so doing, however, their lack of genuine social concern was clearly revealed. It was, moreover, to show up again in their attempts to deal with the water supply question when it was once more thrust upon them in the years 1900–14.

A Case of Priorities: 1900–14

Unlike the experience of the www Company, which operated for six years without any major complaints, the new municipal system came under criticism less than a year after it had begun operation. Reports claiming that Winnipeg was faced with a water shortage appeared in the local press in January 1901 and were confirmed shortly thereafter by the city engineer in a report to Council. Ruttan reported that although Artesian Well No. 1 was living up to all expectations as to the amount of water supplied, the rapid growth of the city and the lack of a "waste prevention" system required that Council consider an extension of the artesian well system.[17]

Ruttan's recommendation that the artesian well system be enlarged was shared by the health authorities and by many businessmen. The former group noted that the heavy demands made on the city's single artesian well meant that water from the Assiniboine River was being used to supplement the domestic supply and the results were being registered in an alarming increase in typhoid cases. And, they added, should a serious fire occur, the amount of river water used would have to be increased greatly, causing even more problems. The businessmen's concern came as a result of a report issued by the Manitoba and North-West Fire Underwriters' Association which severely criticized the inadequacy of the water supply and stated that unless new wells were immediately sunk and the fire-fighting equipment of the city increased and updated, insurance rates would have to be raised substantially.[18]

It was not until August 1902, however, that Council responded to these proposals by calling in R. Hering once again to give them advice on the best course of action to take. Hering recommended in September that a second well be sunk. He estimated that this would give Winnipeg all the water it required. After considerable discussion of the report by the aldermen, the city engineer was ordered to carry out tests and report back to Council.[19] Following this brief flurry of activity Council moved slowly and it was not until 1905 that drilling for the new well started. This long delay, the reasons for which were never explained, proved to be one of the most costly in the city's history.

In the fall of 1904 a severe typhoid epidemic broke out in Winnipeg and although its causes were complex, a large part of the blame for the dramatic spread of the dreaded "Red River Fever" could be—and was—attributed to the city's inadequate water supply. This news could hardly have come as a surprise to City Council, for the deficiencies of the city's system had been pointed out to them many times. The provincial Board of Health, for example, had made known its opinion on the water supply situation in a strongly worded document that had been brought to the attention of both city engineer and the aldermen. Dr. R. M. Simpson, chairman of the Board of Health, stated that:

Purity of water supply bears a vital relation to public health. In cities where a pure and plentiful supply prevails, the general good health of the community is most noticeable. . . . [But] in our Province we have two cities with a sewage and water system, i.e., Winnipeg and Brandon, [that is inadequate]. In the former, the supply is obtained from artesian wells drawing water from underground streams. The supply is limited and . . . entirely inadequate even for present requirements. The chief danger of a well supply . . . is the consequent temptation on the part of officials to supply the demands from an auxiliary pumping station, such, for instance, in the City of Winnipeg, from the Assiniboine River pumping station. . . . In the city of Winnipeg some speedy action is necessary to procure an abundant supply of water, otherwise disease will continue to thrive, and . . . the citizens will be face to face with water famine. . . . There is no question of such vital importance to the people of Winnipeg as its water supply and speedy action should be taken. . . .[20]

A more detailed critique had also been presented to Council in October 1904 by the Fire Underwriters' Association. This report calculated that in the event of a serious fire the city would find itself deficient to the extent of over three million gallons of water.[21] The alarming fact about this estimate—one that was apparently lost on the city's aldermen—was that these figures were based upon the population then being supplied with water, which amounted to approximately 35,000, that is, less than half the actual population of the city. The report went on to point out that if the entire city had been supplied with water, the deficiency would be eight million gallons. It should also be emphasized that all these calculations included supplies to the extent of four million gallons from the Assiniboine River and only two and a half million gallons from the single operating artesian well.[22]

A serious fire had, in fact, occurred earlier in October and the city had been forced to pump river water into the mains or face a general conflagration that could conceivably have destroyed several blocks of businesses and homes.[23] The consequences of their action, however, proved to be even more serious, for shortly after typhoid fever broke out all over the city, whereas prior to this time it had been concentrated in the North End. And there was little doubt in the minds of the special-

Table 25 / **Distribution of Waterworks by Wards, 1905**

Wards	Habitations	Waterworks	
		No.	%
1	935	624	66.7
2	1,538	1,354	88.2
3	2,038	1,667	81.8
4	2,622	2,008	76.6
5	2,825	1,266	44.8
6	1,932	743	38.5

SOURCE: *Winnipeg Tribune*, 23 June 1905.

ists called in to investigate the epidemic that the culprit was the polluted river water.[24]

But while the outbreak of typhoid in Winnipeg's South End was attributed to the use of river water, the high incidence of that disease in the North End was just as clearly the result of a general lack of water connections. Indeed, as Table 25 clearly illustrates, less than half the dwellings in the North End (wards 5 and 6) were connected with the city's waterworks system. A total solution to Winnipeg's problems called for a massive and immediate increase in the number of households with water and sewer connections. But, as in the years before 1900, Council seemed little concerned with the disparities that existed between the North End and the rest of the city. From their viewpoint, other matters took priority.

It is a measure of Council's economic orientation that their first response to the fire and the typhoid epidemic was to decide upon the construction of a high-pressure system for additional fire protection. This entailed construction of high-pressure water mains in the central business district. Although it was pointed out that with the separate mains directly connected with the Assiniboine River pumping station there would be no possibility of mixing the supplies of the river and the artesian well, there is little doubt that Council's main concern was increased fire protection. The health aspect was only an added bonus. But at least the cost of the new system, some $380,000, was to be paid for by an assessment on the property that stood to benefit from the system, and not by a general assessment.[25]

No such easy solution was found for the city's inadequate domestic supply. A proposition received from a private, unincorporated company to supply Winnipeg with all the water it needed from the Winnipeg River, sixty miles northeast of the city, was quickly rejected on the grounds that the cost was too great. Council's attention then turned to supplementing the water supply by sinking two additional wells to tap the artesian source. Well No. 2, which had been under consideration since 1901, was finally put into operation in May 1905 and from then until June 1906 furnished the entire supply of the city. This was because when the second well had been put into use, Well No. 1 had dried up. Wells No. 3 and 4 were put into operation in July and December, respectively, of 1906. But with all this activity it was found that the overall capacity of all the wells at the end of 1906 amounted to a mere four million gallons daily, while an estimated supply of nine million gallons would be required in 1910, and fifteen million gallons in 1915.[26] Moreover, it was again pointed out that the entire city was not yet serviced with sewer and water connections and that consumption was at a rate of thirty-two gallons per capita while it should have been eighty-five.[27] In other words, even as the city attempted to increase the overall water supply by sinking more wells, the amount of water actually supplied per person decreased, until in 1906 it was less than half of what it had been in 1900.

These facts caused considerable disillusionment with the artesian well system, but it was only after repeated calls for action by the press and the Board of Trade that City Council appointed a water commission in July 1906. The Water Supply Commission, made up of the mayor, the chairman of the provincial Board of Health, four aldermen, and three citizens, did not take any concrete steps toward a "permanent solution" to the city's water problem until the spring of 1907. At that time they appointed a number of "expert engineers to advise fully as to the selection of a permanent and adequate system of supply of water for the City."[28]

In contrast to the Water Supply Commission, the experts appointed by it wasted no time in preparing and presenting a detailed report. Dated 29 August 1907, the ninety-six-page report consisted of six parts and made a total of twenty-two recommendations. It contained a review and forecast of Winnipeg's population growth and water supply requirements, an analysis of the artesian well system, and analyses of three other sources of supply—the Red River watershed, the Winnipeg River watershed, and Shoal Lake (Lake of the Woods) watershed. Finally, the report compared the different supplies as to quantity, quality, hardness, tastes and odours, and time and cost of construction.[29]

After a detailed consideration of the three available sources of supply, the engineers strongly recommended that the city plan to draw its water from the Winnipeg River.[30] They explained that their choice was not made on the basis of quality alone, for "Shoal Lake water is unquestionably the best source of supply." Rather, the choice was made because the Winnipeg River supply would be easier and thus less expensive to tap, could be in operation a year earlier, and would be cheaper to operate once completed. Having made this choice, the report proceeded to describe the work required to reach the supply and gave a total cost estimate of $17,084,000.[31] The engineers strongly emphasized, however, that the new water supply system should be built in stages and that an initial outlay of $6,050,000 would supply twelve million gallons daily, and this water could reach Winnipeg in three years if construction was started immediately.

After considering this report for three months, the Water Supply Commission accepted its proposals and recommended to City Council that "a start be made toward accomplishing this work without delay." The commission, however, was careful to point out that since the project would take three years to complete, Council should extend the artesian well system as rapidly as possible to provide for the temporary requirements of the city. The commission concluded by stating: "We desire to clearly point out that such extension of the wells should not interfere with the policy of providing for the permanent supply from the Winnipeg River being immediately determined upon and carried into effect."[32] Shortly after acceptance of the Water Commission Report City Council ordered the Board of Control to proceed with the construction of an additional well (No. 7). The more important recommendations, however, were left over to be dealt with by the 1908 Council.

During the years 1908, 1909, and through most of 1910, Council did absolutely nothing as far as dealing with the recommendations of the Water Supply Commission. This non-action can only be understood by reference to the water power question that was so important in terms of civic politics during these years. The financial difficulties occasioned by the proposed municipal water power development and Mayor Ashdown's concern about the credit of the city resulted in a firm policy of retrenchment that was not lifted until 1910. In this atmosphere, the recommendation that from $6 million to $17 million be spent on a new water supply was simply shelved. Indeed, during 1908, Council actually cut back on waterworks expenditure by closing the water softening plant in order to save a sum of $35,000 per year.[33]

As rational as this policy may have been to the business-minded City Council and Board of Control, it could hardly be justified on social grounds. Ignoring Winnipeg's water shortage did not solve the questions raised in 1907. Between that year and 1910 the amount of water supplied per day rose from 4.5 million gallons to 5.9 million gallons, while the per capita consumption rose from 41 to 45 gallons per day. In view of the opinion stated in the engineer's report—and agreed to by the Water Supply Commission—that the city required at least 9 million gallons daily and a per capita consumption rate of 85 gallons per day, these figures point out the continued seriousness of the problems.[34] Moreover, when it is realized that four of the eight members of the commission that had recommended "immediate action" were members of Winnipeg's civic government in 1908, the question of ignorance of the facts cannot be raised.[35] The flurry of activity occasioned by the typhoid epidemic of 1905 resulted, then, in no substantial action on the water question other than the publication of a report whose recommendations were ignored.

The water supply question was not raised again until August 1910 when City Council received from the provincial Board of Health a resolution in regard to "the present insufficient water supply in the City of Winnipeg." In response, Council asked for and received a report from the city engineer on the "present and future possibilities" of supply from the artesian system, as well as a comparison of that system with the Winnipeg River supply. Ruttan, comparing the two systems as to quantity, quality, and cost, left no doubt that he favoured an extension

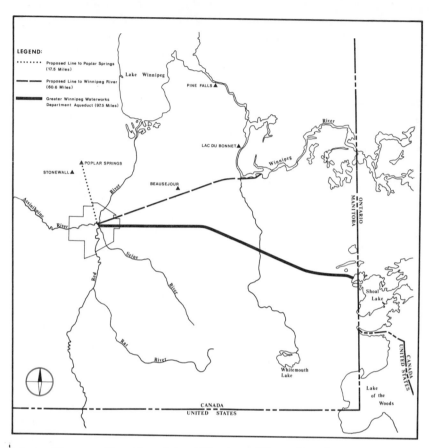

Map 7/Sources Considered for Winnipeg Water Supply

of the artesian system. This source, he pointed out, could supply up to twenty million gallons of pure water at a cost "only one sixth of that necessary to develop the Winnipeg River."[36]

Despite continued pressure from the public for action, Council still continued to procrastinate and it was only in August 1912 that a bylaw was prepared calling for the creation of a debt of $1.8 million to extend the artesian well system to Poplar Springs. As it was a money bylaw, it was to be submitted to the electors on 13 September. This done, Council proceeeded to arrange for yet another study of water sources admitting, in effect, that the Poplar Springs extension was at best a stopgap measure in that its estimated supply of twenty million gallons would not long be adequate for the city as its present rate of growth.

Like its predecessor of 1907, the 1912 report was extremely critical of the city's artesian system. And as for the Poplar Springs extention, the report stated that the project merely "temporizes with the whole subject of an adequate water supply." When this evidence was made public, only a week before the vote on the bylaw to raise $1.8 million for the Poplar Springs extension, there was little hope that the measure would pass, and it did not. Council was thus left with little choice but to carry out the recommendations contained in the report. After it had dismissed the artesian well system and the Poplar Springs extension, the 1912 report had gone on to recommend that Winnipeg take its supply from the Shoal Lake arm of the Lake of the Woods.[37] With no other course of action open to it, Council decided to accept this recommendation and during the remainder of 1912 and throughout 1913 the civic authorities at long last got down to some serious activity. Plans for a new water supply from Shoal Lake moved rapidly ahead and construction for the aqueduct to the lake began in late 1913. Because of the large expenditure involved in tapping the Shoal Lake supply ($13.5 million) the city decided to make the project a joint one, and in May 1913 the Greater Winnipeg Water District was established. The agreement between Winnipeg, the city of St. Boniface, the town of Transcona, and the surrounding municipalities of Assiniboia, Kildonan, Fort Garry, and St. Vital called for a cost-sharing program in the development of the project. Six years later, in 1919, water from the Indian Arm of Shoal Lake finally flowed into the water mains of GWWD members. To this date the district still receives its entire water supply from Shoal Lake, ample evidence of the wisdom of the decision to build the costly 97.5-mile aqueduct.[38]

It is revealing to note that once the decision to go ahead with the Shoal Lake project was finally made the governing elite of the city, who for so long had refused to act constructively on the water question, found ample reason for reassuring themselves that they had made a wise choice. But, not surprisingly, their case was made up almost entirely of statistics relating to economic savings. A pamphlet, published by the Board of Trade in 1919 in an effort to boost the city, contained the following:

WITH THE ADVENT OF SHOAL LAKE WATER
Less soap will be required and washing powders for softening purposes unnecessary.
CISTERNS WILL BE DISPENSED WITH representing a saving to citizens of $58,000 annually.

CHEMICAL SOFTENING PLANTS WILL BE DISPENSED WITH and a saving of $1,161,600 will be made annually.
Corrosion in old pipes will be removed and new pipes kept

clean. This will save Winnipeg citizens $115,000 yearly.
$27,600 will be saved in the maintenance of hot water heaters.
The life of boilers will be five times as long, and the saving in this respect will be $31,000 annually.
$500,000 annually will be saved in the reduction of present loss caused by scale in pipes. . . .
Thousands of dollars will be saved in fire salvage. . . .
NEW INDUSTRIES MADE POSSIBLE. . . .[39]

Significantly, neither this pamphlet nor any other made mention of the fact that the "inexhaustible supply" of pure water finally met Winnipeg's water needs from a health standpoint.[40] Certainly since 1874 the majority of Winnipeg's citizens had been refused their right to an adequate and safe water supply by civic officials who were so concerned with money matters that the human dimension of the water shortage rarely was considered. And, given the nature of civic politics during this era, there was little hope that those who suffered most could force the municipal government to act. Though recognizing serious inadequacies in the city's water supply, successive City Councils and Boards of Control took over thirty years to obtain a pure and inexhaustible supply. Here, as in the case of Winnipeg's water power development, the successful competition of a worthwhile public project came only after every attempt had been made to find a cheap, short-term solution to a problem that demanded an expensive and long-term answer.

13 / Public Health *versus* the Private City

Between 1874 and 1914 Winnipeg's public resources were directed almost exclusively towards growth-producing programs. A more logical allocation of municipal resources, one that would have ensured a healthy as well as a rapidly growing city, came about only slowly. Indeed, the development of an active civic health department was undertaken only in 1905, in the wake of a severe typhoid epidemic.

City Council's lack of concerted effort in regard to public health questions was not the result of an absence of serious health problems. Throughout the period such diseases as typhoid fever, smallpox, tuberculosis, venereal disease, scarlet fever, and diphtheria were not only prevalent, but often reached epidemic proportions.[1] This prevalence of disease was reflected in Winnipeg's high death rate which was frequently the highest in North America.[2] Thus the municipal corporation's lack of action on matters affecting public health must be attributed to other causes.

The most important reason for the lack of a responsible public health program was the disparity that existed between actual conditions and attitudes. The great majority of Winnipeggers, including the governing commercial elite, came from rural areas or small urban centres. With dispersed populations and plenty of open space, these areas only infrequently faced problems of sanitation, waste disposal, overcrowding, or disease spread by close contact. Accordingly measures designed to safeguard public health were not an essential service.[3] The fact that all these problems rapidly appeared in the booming city of Winnipeg, and that public health thus became a fundamental and essential service of the municipal corporation, was not quickly realized. Instead, a large part of the blame for the toll of disease in Winnipeg was placed on incoming immigrants. There is, of course, no denying the fact that immigrants did include a significant number of diseased persons. But in blaming all problems on immigrants, and in refusing to accept responsibility for the city's public health, the governing commercial elite was guilty of distortion and evasion. It is true that certain sanitarians recognized the city's responsibilities early and attempted to force Council to act, but outmoded attitudes died slowly and were re-

Table 26 / Death Rate per 1,000 Population: Winnipeg, 1884–1914

Year	Population	Total Number of Deaths	Rate Per 1,000
1884	16,694	469	28.0
85	19,574	310	16.0
86	19,525	400	20.5
87	21,257	522	24.6
88	22,098	524	23.7
89	21,328	534	25.1
1890	23,000	458	19.9
91	24,068	417	17.3
92	29,182	551	18.8
93	32,119	581	18.2
94	34,954	571	16.3
95	37,124	452	12.2
96	37,983	431	11.4
97	38,733	530	13.6
98	39,384	547	13.8
99	40,112	769	19.2
1900	42,534	908	21.3
01	44,778	820	18.3
02	48,411	1,094	22.6
03	56,741	1,304	23.0
04	67,262	1,449	21.5
05	79,975	1,471	18.4
06	100,057	2,093	23.2
07	111,729	1,741	15.6
08	118,252	1,500	12.7
09	122,390	1,740	14.2
1910	132,720	2,103	15.8
11	151,958	2,088	15.3
12	185,000	2,236	13.4
13	201,000	2,204	11.9
1914	203,000	1,955	9.6

placed even more slowly with modern ones. In general, City Council approached any and all public health matters in a piecemeal and often callous fashion.

These observations notwithstanding, an important reason for Council's obdurate stand on health matters stemmed from the fact that those who suffered most from overcrowding, disease, and inadequate sanitary facilities were those who lived in the North End. The distinction between that area and the other parts of the city in respect to housing and general sanitary conditions was so sharp and so often commented on, there was no possibility that Council was ignorant of the facts. But the existence of such conditions was usually attributed to the ignorance, laziness, and immorality of the North End's foreign population, and publicly sponsored programs designed to improve the area were few and inadequate.

Of all the city's various departments that of health suffered most from neglect in the years preceding 1900. Winnipeg obtained her first health officer only in 1881 and even then he was not a full-time employee. The first man to hold this position, Dr. J. Kerr, was simultaneously a practising private physician, a surgeon to the CPR, and Health Officer to the Province of Manitoba.[4] Prior to 1900 three other men held this post but their duties never seem to have gone much beyond presenting an annual report, which was usually ignored by Council. One report made by Dr. M. S. Inglis in 1895 even tried to appeal to Council's business instincts:

> I am fully aware that the adoption of measures requisite to all sanitary improvements at once meet with two great and serious objections, viz. expenditure and collision with personal interests. Whilst upon the other hand, a great many of the citizens, who are to be benefited and protected by improved sanitary measures, are remarkably indifferent to such labors on their behalf and their apathy is only as a rule awakened when their own home surroundings become the site of an intolerable nuisance, or epidemic sickness under their immediate notice startles them into activity. Yet whatever measures are taken to prevent loss of life and epidemic sickness, are essentially also measures of sound economy, equally effective in protecting the pockets of our citizens, and that in this as in any other business we cannot make bricks without the straw.

Evidence supporting the contention that matters of public health were considered to be of little importance is abundant. In 1887–88, when over $17,000 was allocated to the Police Department, only $2,810 was provided for the Health Department, and of this sum $1,200 was the salary of the health officer.[5] Also, in November 1886 Council amalgamated the Health and Relief Committee with the Market, License, and Police Committee to form the Market, License and Health Committee; apparently there was not enough work to keep both committees busy. Prior to 1900 only a few very general health bylaws were passed by Council for reasons best stated above by their own health officer. A typical measure was that passed in 1890 to "provide for the sanitary condition of Buildings." This bylaw made it incumbent on the builders of all new structures in the city to have plumbing installed "in accordance with the most improved measures." However, as the city engineer pointed out, this did not solve the problem with buildings constructed before the bylaw was passed. The measure, moreover, was effective only in those areas where sewers and waterworks existed, and in 1890 this was only about 10 per cent of the entire city.

A further illustration of Council's irresponsible stand on public health is the attitude it adopted on sewage and drainage, one of the city's most serious health hazards. Complaints about Winnipeg's lack of a proper sewage and drainage system were frequently voiced in the press, and City Council was beseiged by petitions from the medical profession, as well as by official communications from the provincial Board of Health. One petition that dealt with the matter of drainage gives some indication of the problems encountered:

> We desire respectfully to draw your attention to the state of the streets and lanes in the thickly settled portion of the City. Many of the streets running north and south have never been graded, and consequence being that in the spring and after all rains they are almost impassible, to the inconvenience, annoyance and loss of the residents on those streets, the carters and dealers who have to deliver goods, and all who require to use them to get to their homes. The water becomes stagnant, and with the accumulation of decaying vegetable matter, breeds the various diseases such as typhoid fever, scarlet fever, diphtheria, etc., with which we have been so much afflicted in these districts of the City. While, as just said, some of the streets are in very bad shape, the lanes are very much worse. . . . The natural fall is so slight that the slightest obstacle obstructs the drainage and the result in hot weather is a most disgusting and dangerous amount of poisonous and offensive gases. . . . A thorough system of drainage will have to be applied to the lanes. . . . [for] if something is not done at once, one of two results must happen; either we will have an epidemic, or the houses in these districts will be vacated. Upon the Council must rest the responsibility of refusing or neglecting to take the necessary precautions to prevent great loss of life and property.[6]

Council's reply in this case was typical. It noted that conditions were intolerable, but it neither proposed nor attempted to provide a remedy and maintained the position that its hands were tied by a lack of funds, a position that was hardly tenable in light of the financial commitments so freely made for railways and advertising. This irresponsible position is even more serious when it is realized that the sewer system, inadequate as it was, did not even cover a large area of the city. It was principally South and West Winnipeg (wards 1, 2, and 3) that were being serviced, while the North End (wards 4, 5, and 6) often had no service whatsoever. Even in areas where there were sewers, connections with houses were hardly universal. In 1890, for example, there were only 553 sewer connections in the entire city.[7] And although by 1902 this had increased to 2,600 connections it still represented only 33 per cent of the houses in Winnipeg.

Council's lack of concern did not go unnoticed. The *Manitoba Free Press* made this comment in April 1893: "It appears that members of Council have not only failed to realize the tremendous responsibility they have already assumed in regard to the neglect in taking prompt measures to meet the crying necessity for improvements in the sanitary condition of the city—a responsibility which is daily increasing—but they fail to realize that they are, by their policy of continual delay, tampering with the probability of an epidemic of disease, the contemplation of which is appalling."

Complaints such as this, combined with pressure exerted by the Board of Health,[8] finally resulted in Council taking its first constructive step in 1899 with the passage of a comprehensive health bylaw. This piece of legislation provided for the appointment of a full-time medical health officer whose duties included examining into nuisances, and cases of infectious disease; carrying out a program of vaccination; making an annual report to Council; and recommending action to be taken. The most important clause, however, was the one that ordered the MHO to "collect and make a return" of detailed mortuary statistics. Moreover, in providing for the appointment of a health inspector "and such number of assistants as may be deemed necessary by the Market, License, and Health Committee" the act held out the promise of an adequate city health staff for the first time in Winnipeg's history.

The importance of the order to provide complete mortuary statistics lies in the fact that prior to 1899 the figures that made up the city's death rate were not broken down as to causes or age groups. This situation allowed Council to pay little attention to those who argued that the city had an intolerable infant mortality rate. The health bylaw changed this and although expenditures increased only slowly— from $30,000 in 1898 to $36,000 in 1903—the ammunition gathered by the city's health department provided one of the main catalysts for the drastic changes that were soon to take place in public health matters.

Despite the continued efforts of the strengthened city health department, it was only in the years after 1905 that Council adopted a constructive stand on most questions of public health. And even then it was only after the city had suffered from the drastic effects of a typhoid epidemic. Typhoid, of course, was not a novel disease in Winnipeg and in the early days had been commonly called "Red River

Fever," since it was then attributed to the drinking of raw Red River water.[9] Outbreaks of this dreaded disease occurred frequently, the worst prior to 1904 taking place in 1893–94. At that time the Board of Health had pointed to Winnipeg's inadequate water supply and "filthy sewers" as the major causes but Council's response did not go beyond utterances of condolence to the victims. By 1900, with the start of operation of the municipal water system, it was felt that the conditions complained of were remedied and Council seemed content to ignore all evidence that this was not in fact the case. The consequences of this stance were to prove tragic.

Beginning in 1900 the revamped health department provided City Council with figures relating to Winnipeg's death rate that should have warned Council that all was not as it should have been in public health matters. The figures showed that typhoid was most prevalent during the months of July, August, and September and for the years 1900–1904 the number of reported cases for these months were high, being 339, 205, 107, 221, and 538, respectively. The figures for the entire year were even more startling. The number of cases and deaths were as follows: 1900—582 and 34; 1901—349 and 36; 1902—356 and 29; 1903—489 and 46; and 1904—1,276 and 133. Commenting on these statistics the medical health officer stated that he was particularly concerned over the large increase in 1904 and urged that immediate steps be taken to remedy the situation. He called for the passage of a law compelling sewer connections since he had observed that "when typhoid breaks out there were always more cases in districts where the majority of houses are not connected with the city sewers than in other sections of the city."

Replying to Dr. Douglas, City Council promised to see if it had power under its charter to enforce sewer connections, and it also instructed the Board of Health to "investigate the conditions underlying the present epidemic of typhoid fever."[10] The result of the latter motion was a report, presented in October, that gave a detailed account of the typhoid cases reported in 1904. Two possible causes (the city water and milk supply) were quickly and definitely excluded. The report then turned to other possible causes, noting that "certain areas of the city had escaped almost entirely, while others seemed to have suffered unduly." The two extremes were, respectively, the district between Broadway Avenue and the Assiniboine River (part of Ward 2), and that immediately south of the CPR tracks westward from Main Street (parts of wards 4 and 5). In their investigation of the latter district, the three doctors who were conducting the investigation found that "the general sanitary condition of this territory . . . was bad in the extreme." On one street, for example, they found a continuous line of outdoor toilets only a few feet apart. These were allowed to drain freely into a ditch on either side of the roadway and "there being little or no soakage into the ground," the ditches were practically a long open latrine. The report continued:

There seems to be no way for this to drain off, and a more congenial place for the breeding of the typhoid germ cannot well be imagined. Should this mass of filth be polluted by the stools or urine of a typhoid patient, a conveyance of the infection to the closely crowded houses, only a few feet away, must be considered as a certainty, when one thinks of the swarms of flies that must breed in the heaps of manure and other putrescible matter that abounds on every side. Practically the same state of affairs exists over the greater part of this district, and it was aptly compared by one medical man to that which must have obtained in an European Village of the Middle Ages.[11]

Turning to the city as a whole, the doctors recorded some startling statistics. Excluding the suburbs, Winnipeg had over 6,500 "box closets"; even in "no inconsiderable numbers" on such thoroughfares as Main Street and Portage Avenue. And in the North End, "the filth, squalor, and overcrowding among the foreign elements is beyond our power of description." Finally, the report suggested that the city immediately undertake remedial measures. Those suggested were enforced sewer connections; the abolition of box closets and their replacement by iron pail closets where connections were not possible; the abolition of all public wells; an increase in the scavenger service; and the frequent flushing of sewers under adequate water pressure.[12]

Council's response to this critical report was entirely in character with its previous record on public health matters. It passed a bylaw making it necessary to have a permit to erect outside privies, and then promptly dropped the whole question since with the coming of cold weather the cases of typhoid dropped dramatically. But others refused to let the matter stand, as they were convinced that the following spring would see a repetition of the typhoid epidemic. The city health officer, Dr. Douglas, pointed out that he concurred completely with the Board's findings. Indeed, he added, they had recommended measures he had been urging for years. The city's newspapers were also full of letters from irate citizens demanding action, including a particularly critical one from the former city health officer, Dr. Inglis, that censured Council for its lack of action. Added to this chorus of criticism were pointed remarks from the Board to the effect that only immediate action on their recommendations could remedy the typhoid situation.[13]

Certainly the intention of all these protests and opinions was to compel Council to take remedial action immediately, rather than to serve as a personal attack upon the aldermen and mayor. The Board of Health especially took pains to refrain from placing blame on anyone or any specific body.[14] But Council, and in particular its vibrant mayor,

Thomas Sharpe, promptly interpreted these comments as a personal attack and set out to prove the experts—that is, Dr. Douglas and the Board of Health—wrong. (Council seemed to forget that they had ordered the typhoid investigation themselves). Early in January Council solemnly proclaimed that the report of the Board of Health and the opinions of Dr. Douglas "did not adequately explain the causes of so much fever" and therefore they were forced to seek more information. They seemed especially concerned with the outbreak in late October 1904 (after the report had been completed), of a rash of typhoid fever in the southern areas of the city. And while it must be admitted that Dr. Douglas could not explain this phenomenon (they did not ask the Board of Health for its opinion), this so-called "mystery" hardly excuses their lack of action. Indeed, many in the city pointed out that even if the Council wanted outside opinions it could in the meantime still act on the earlier recommendations. This advice, however, was ignored and Council instead ordered two more investigations to be undertaken: one by a sanitary engineer and the other by a prominent American medical authority. Perhaps the best explanation that can be given to these actions was that Council probably felt that charges of unsanitary conditions might be an adequate explanation for outbreaks of typhoid in the North End but it would hardly do when the wealthy and predominantly Anglo-Saxon Ward 2 was involved.

Coincidentally these two reports, along with a report of Mayor Sharpe's trip to Ottawa as a delegate to the 1905 meeting of the Canadian Municipal League, were all tabled at the same Council meeting on February 20th.[15] Sharpe's report is interesting in that he expressed opinions that varied but little from those of either the Health Board or Dr. Douglas and it thus raises questions about his motive for calling in outside investigators. On his trip east Sharpe had "made it a point to visit a number of large cities [both in Canada and the U.S.] and enquire particularly into their system of sanitation." He now felt qualified, he reported, to make a series of recommendations among which were the following: the need for an immediate increase in the water supply; the abolition of box closets and the enforcement of compulsory sewer connections; and a vast increase in the annual appropriations to the city health department. He noted, for example, that the city of Toronto, with a population only slightly more than twice that of Winnipeg's, spent more than six times the amount of money on scavenging than did Winnipeg on all the activities of the Market, License, and Health Committee combined. As might be expected, the mayor failed to mention that all these points had been emphatically put forward countless times prior to his last-minute conversion.

Similarly, the other two reports, while more detailed, added little to the information already presented to Council by Dr. Douglas and the Board of Health. Professor Hazen, a sanitary engineer from New York, covered all the problems facing Winnipeg in dealing with sewers and drainage and his recommendations were remarkably parallel to those made as early as 1882 by another "outside expert." He noted the alarming lack of sewer and water connections and the equally serious problem faced by an inadequate water supply. For although the number of connections had increased from 2,600 in 1902 to 7,000 in 1905, the number of homes not supplied with water had remained virtually the same: 5,351 in 1902 and 5,140 in 1905. In short, Hazen pointed out the overwhelming need for an abundant and well-used water supply and recommended steps to be taken to provide for both.[16]

The second report, made by Dr. Jordan of the University of Chicago, began by comparing the typhoid situation in Winnipeg with that of other cities. He noted that Winnipeg's typhoid death rate for 1904 stood at 24.85 per 10,000 population and was higher than any other major North American or European city. Of thirty-two cities listed by Jordan none had typhoid death rates over 6 per 10,000 except one. Winnipeg's rate for 1900–1903 was as follows: 11.75, 11.83, 9.50, 8.46.[17] Jordan then turned to a consideration of the possible causes of the epidemic and dealt, in turn, with the following matters: contact infection, milk supply, lack of sewer connections, water supply, and "other considerations." The first two, while considered serious, were not blamed in any major way for the high number of cases. The lack of sewer connections, however, was "undoubtedly favourable to the maintenance of typhoid fever, and in the past has been largely responsible for the prevalence of the disease during the warmer months of the year."

Then, in a statement of public healthy policy that had still to be absorbed by Winnipeg City Council, Dr. Jordan pointed out that:

> It must be remembered that in sanitary matters the welfare of one section of the city is inseparably connected with that of another. The interests of the community so far as public health is concerned are not restricted by geographical or social boundaries. The presence of a large amount of infectious material from typhoid fever patients in the open privies of Wards 4 and 5 is a distant menace to the health of the whole city, and, as recent events have shown, is likely sooner or later to involve even distant districts.[18]

Turning to a consideration of the city's water supply Dr. Jordan stated that although there was no question about its purity, much could be said about its abundance. He noted that the two occasions in 1904 when "raw Assiniboine water was turned into the city mains to eke out the inadequate supply and meet the emergency caused by large fires" had been followed by a rapid rise in the amount of typhoid fever. Here, then, was the solution to the mysterious appearance of the dreaded fever in South Winnipeg. Jordan, however, was careful to point out that his earlier admonition concerning the general health of an entire city being affected by specific areas was no less valid because of this factor. Finally, Jordan concluded his report by recommending remedial measures that were almost identical to those proposed by the Board of Health and Dr. Douglas.[19]

At the first council meeting following the reception of the Jordan report Winnipeg's aldermen, in a display of newly found social concern, enacted sweeping reforms. Bylaw 3148, setting up a separate Public Health Committee, was passed in a single sitting (necessitating a suspension of rules). In supporting this measure Mayor Sharpe noted that "there is something incongruous in mixing up the issuance of dog tags with the care of public health." The setting up of this standing committee, it was hoped, would enable the medical health officer to have a distinct section of Council informed on public health problems. Also, with this clear apportionment of responsibility on Council, the objections of those who expressed concern over not being able to report health violations to a distinct segment of Council would be met. Finally, this new committee would have the power to appoint members of the medical profession to their number.

Other matters dealt with at this meeting included recommendations for the inauguration of a better system of street cleaning, the passage of an interim appropriation of $30,000 for scavenging (to cover the period to 30 April 1905), the addition of several new members to the staff of city health department, and the recommendation that legislation be passed to compel sewer and water connections throughout the city. Of all the measures taken to combat typhoid the latter was to prove to be the most contentious since it involved, in some people's eyes at least, a severe restriction on private property. Yet this was undoubtedly the keystone in the fight against typhoid and without its passage and strict enforcement all the other measures taken to improve Winnipeg's sanitary situation could only be partially effective.

The question of compulsory connections went back many years. It had been recommended as early as 1882 by the Winnipeg Waterworks Company and E. S. Chesborough, and it had formed a major part of the remedial measures suggested by Dr. Douglas, the provincial Board of Health, and Professors Hazen and Jordan. Throughout the years Council had always refused to act on this matter since it claimed it did not have the power under its charter (granted by the provincial government) to enforce connections. The fact that Council never applied for an amendment, however, suggests that a more likely explanation would be that in the interests of common law rights they did not desire to force property owners to have to make improvements. But with the dangers of the typhoid menace only too evident in the fall of 1904, Council had applied for the necessary powers and, despite some opposition, had succeeded in gaining the power to enforce connections in the "first class fire limits, or any extension of such limits."[20] Hence bylaw 3149, passed 6 March 1905, made it compulsory for any building "heretofore or hereafter erected" in the first class fire limits to have sewer and water connections. As far as the rest of the city was concerned, the law stipulated that all new buildings constructed on streets where sewers and mains existed would have to be connected, while all new buildings on streets without mains and sewers would have to install "pit-closets lined with cement so as to be perfectly water-tight." Thus the new law, while tackling the problem of unsanitary conditions in the centre of the city, left much to be desired in its approach to the rest of Winnipeg. By stipulating "new buildings" it meant that all the buildings then existing with box-closets had to do nothing whatever. As a result the new law soon came under attack.

Even before the inevitable barrage of criticism it became evident that enforcing the new regulations would be a difficult task. Indications that the new law was being flagrantly ignored appeared as early as May and continued steadily thereafter, with the major case being made by the Board of Health. In a strongly worded report to the premier that was published in the *Tribune*, Dr. Simpson charged that he knew "from reliable sources" of many buildings being erected in Winnipeg without compliance with the new bylaw. These general charges were shortly followed by specific facts and figures. Following an investigation, Simpson reported at least 391 box-closets still existing within the first class fire limits, while in the rest of the city there were countless cases of new buildings constructed in violation of the bylaw.

Council's response to these serious charges was anything but convincing. They stated that they had ordered the owners of the 391 houses to make connections and had, in some cases, prosecuted the violators. The fact that violators were being fined "as a rule one, two, or three dollars and sometimes only the [court] costs" made it possible for people such as Dr. Simpson to doubt their sincerity.[21] Council then argued that the legislature had given them the most difficult section of the city (i.e., the first class fire limits) to introduce the reforms for "the district is not a residential one . . . and the premises in it . . . are either old houses, few of which are worth improving, or small stores or restaurants, standing on valuable property which may be held for speculation or upon which the owner proposes to erect a fitting building in the near future."[22] But to argue that the province was at fault for giving the city a particular section in which to enforce the bylaw was absurd. The province had simply granted the civic corporation the power it had requested; it was Council who chose the first class fire limits. This fact did not go unnoticed by the press, as Council was accused of introducing a red herring issue.

It must be pointed out, however, that the city health department was encountering genuine problems in enforcing the new regulations, and these at least partially explain their tardiness. Persons constructing new homes on streets earmarked for sewer and water mains were naturally reluctant to bear the added expense of building pit-closets and argued that they would replace box-closets with sewer connections as soon as the lines were completed. There was also the problem of expense. In many of the areas of the North End people simply could not affford the money necessary to make the required improvements and Council hesitated to prosecute in these cases. On the other hand, if some homeowners were not inclined to obey the regulations, the fines levied did not prompt them to do so. Fines for the evasion of regulations were ridiculously low as, for example, when one owner was charged with non-compliance at his properties at 287, 289, 293, 295, 299 and 301 Nena Street. He was fined $3 and costs.[23] Many landlords circumvented the new regulations in ingenious manners. One merely connected his properties to sewer and water mains but did not install toilets or basins; another, in this case an apartment owner, connected the outdoor privies to sewers.[24]

While all this controversy was taking place the typhoid epidemic had continued unabated. Statistics released in the fall of 1905 showed that the only difference between 1904 and 1905 was that the area of the city affected most adversely had moved northward into wards 5 and 6. And when the final figures for the year were in they showed that there had been 1,606 cases (an increase of 330 over 1904) and 133 deaths (exactly the same as 1904). In the final analysis it was these alarming figures that finally overcame any objections the aldermen may still have harboured. In November 1905 Council passed a motion that allowed those who could not pay for connections outright to spread the cost over a period of five years. This measure was perhaps one of the most important in Winnipeg's public health history for it put sewer and water connections within the reach of all householders. Nothing was done, however, to overcome the problems faced by apartment dwellers or tenants until April 1906, when with the passage of bylaw 4143 it was stipulated that all buildings in the city situated on streets where sewer and water mains existed had to be connected. It was further ordered that in "all sewer-connected, occupied buildings" there was to be at least one water-closet and one sink for twenty persons. In places where sewer connections were impossible, concrete pit-closets had to be constructed according to detailed specifications as set down in the bylaw. Although these standards may now seem low, they were a distinct improvement over a simple box-closet for an entire apartment block.

The effect of this new legislation, coupled with increased inspection by an enlarged health department, can be seen in Table 27. With the demise of the outdoor privy, one of the symbols of the frontier

Table 27 / **Reduction of Outside Closets in Winnipeg, 1905–1914**

Date	Box-closets	Earth-pits	Brick-pits	Total
June 30, 1905	6,153	186	—	6,339
Dec. 31, 1905	3,182	80	1,020	4,912
June 30, 1906	2,255	747	1,325	4,327
Dec. 31, 1906	1,105	662	1,626	3,393
Dec. 31, 1907	80	201	1,535	1,816
Dec. 31, 1908	25	108	1,492	1,625
Dec. 31, 1909	—	53	1,432	1,485
Dec. 31, 1910	—	52	1,300	1,352
Dec. 31, 1911	—	47	1,171	1,218
Dec. 31, 1912	—	31	1,014	1,045
Dec. 31, 1913	—	39	838	877
Dec. 31, 1914	—	18	648	666

town, typhoid fever cases and deaths dropped dramatically.[25] In 1906 the number of cases stood at 1,174 while there were still 111 deaths. But in 1907 this had dropped to 347 and 35 respectively, and from that date until 1914 there were never more than 360 cases and 47 deaths in a single year.[26]

In retrospect the typhoid epidemic, while tragic in itself, did have positive effects. After 1905 the city health department began to receive the support, both financial and public, necessary to enable it to deal with some of the city's public health problems in an aggressive and positive manner. Appropriations for the department rose dramatically from a meagre $36,000 in 1904 to $65,000 in 1905, and then to almost $130,000 in 1906.[27] This large infusion of funds resulted in large staff increases. The number of employees more than doubled in a year, rising from fourteen in 1905 to thirty-four in 1906. Most of these new employees were health inspectors whose duty it was to collect statistics and ensure compliance with health bylaws. As a result hundreds of citizens were annually taken to court, fined, and ordered to bring their property or business establishment up to required standards.[28]

Even more important than these attempts to achieve the aim of public health through the power of the state was the discernible shift of emphasis towards a positive, educational approach to public health. This is not to say that the enactment into law of preventive legislation relating to contagious diseases and sanitary conditions in general was not a significant step in an age where social legislation of any sort was relatively alien to municipal, provincial, or federal governments. But it was one thing to enforce proper sanitary regulations and another to actively promote such things as proper infant and maternal hygiene. This was the problem that faced civic health authorities after 1905 in their desire to develop healthy practices in the daily life of the individual. The new attitude called for public education in the field of communicable diseases. The old scourges like typhoid had been brought fairly well under control, but the remaining diseases to be fought, such as tuberculosis and venereal disease, were only eradicable by the education method. Thus during the period 1905–14 greater and greater emphasis was placed on preventive medicine in a broad sense. Its aim was not only to develop facilities for detecting illness in its earliest stages but also to scan critically the material and social environment for possible bad effects upon the public health. Malnutrition, poor and crowded housing, and ignorance were gradually accepted as causes of illness. And although society was in these years very far from making the link between good public health and such potent forces as minimum wages and adequate housing for all (forms of the welfare state) some progressive measures were nonetheless being taken.

Two areas that provide examples of these new efforts are infant mortality and overcrowding. Although efforts were under way during this period to improve public health by such programs as massive extensions of sewer and water mains, frequent inspections of dairies, butcher shops, stables, and so on, and the formation of an active public pressure group that went by the name of the Sanitary Association of Winnipeg, it was in these two fields that one can most readily observe the effectiveness of a combined program of rigid inspection and education.[29]

It had long been recognized by health officials in Winnipeg that while Winnipeg's overall death rate was high it was low in comparison with the city's infant mortality rate. Statistics on this subject were first publicly recorded in the city health department's first annual report in 1908 and thereafter this aspect of the city's health received a high priority. As Table 28 makes clear, there was good reason for concern.

The first steps taken to meet the high mortality rate took place in 1909 and 1910. Since it was known that most of the deaths of infants were caused by gastro-intestinal diseases that could be directly traced to improper feeding and a contaminated milk supply, action was concentrated in these areas. The city health department distributed booklets of instruction on infant feeding and "exercised as much vigilance as possible over the milk supply." In 1910 the department established a depot for the production of "modified milk" for infants which went by the name of the Winnipeg Free Dispensary. Finally, the department encouraged the Margaret Scott Nursing Mission in their program of visiting homes and instructing mothers on proper infant care. Indeed,

Table 28 / Winnipeg's Infant Mortality Rate per 1,000 Births, 1908-1914*

Year	Births	Deaths	Rate
1908	3,738	535	143.1
1909	3,898	513	131.6
1910	3,890	628	161.4
1911	4,614	762	165.1
1912	5,041	1,006	199.5
1913	5,577	947	169.8
1914	5,789	729	125.9

Source: City Health Department, Annual Reports, 1908–14
*Includes children under one year of age, and excludes still births.

throughout the period the health department fully recognized the value of this private agency and vigorously encouraged its work.

Despite these activities the mortality rate rose sharply in 1910 and accordingly the department stepped up its activities the following year. Pamphlets were for the first time printed in several languages and distributed in the North End. Most important, however, was the fact that the department recognized "that economic conditions are responsible for a large proportion of the infantile mortality"; this belief that many people were sick because they were poor can be recognized as a major breakthrough in the thinking of the time. Unfortunately, the city's medical officer did not follow up his own analysis immediately, for he also stated that "we feel that no matter how bad the economic conditions, a very large number of children's lives could be saved if mothers only know proper infant care. . . . It is along educational lines that the most important work in preventing infantile mortality is to be done."[30]

Three educational programs were inaugurated in 1911: the Little Mother Movement, the publication of a monthly health bulletin, and a series of illustrated lectures. In the first instance a program supported by the School Board was set up in the city's schools whereby nurses instructed girls of school age in proper infant care. The second program, however, received most of the department's attention. A monthly bulletin, distributed throughout the city, was begun in August 1911. Its philosophy was clear from the statement each issue carried on its opening page: "No sanitary improvement worth the name will be effective whatever acts you pass or whatever powers you confer on public officers unless you create an intelligent interest in the public mind."[31]

Following this philosophy, the bulletin carried articles on all phases of public health such as "Hints to Householder," "Proper Ventilation," "Food Storage and Preparation," "Rats—A Warning," and so on. There was even an article appealing to the material instincts of the population entitled "The Cash Value of Sanitary Investments." Naturally, several articles a year were aimed directly at the mother, such as one in April 1912 entitled "The Reduction of Infantile Mortality by Child Training." Essentially this article expanded the thesis that the principle cause for the many "unnecessary deaths" of infants was ignorance and urged the city school board to expand programs such as the Little Mother Movement.[32] Finally, members of the health department gave illustrated lectures under the auspices of All Peoples' Mission which were directed at instilling habits of proper infant care.

Despite all these efforts the statistics for 1912 showed another alarming increase in infant mortality. It was found, moreover, that the tragedy of such deaths was concentrated in a specific geographical location in the city and struck hardest those of foreign origin. Throughout 1912 and 1913 statistics were collected separately for three areas and it was found that District No. 1 (southern city limits to Portage Avenue) accounted for only 21 per cent of the infantile mortality rate while containing 27 per cent of the city's population; District No. 2 (Portage Avenue to the CPR tracks) 25 percent with 39 per cent of the population; and District No. 3 (CPR tracks to northern city limits) 54 per cent with 34 per cent of the population. In 1913 the situation had worsened with the percentages being 12, 26, and 62 respectively.[33] Equally alarming was the rate according to the nationality of the mother, for it showed that deaths per 1,000 births among central and southern Europeans stood at 372, while for British (English, Irish, and Scotch) it was 125, and for Canadians 118.[34] Clearly the civic health department had to step up their efforts, particularly in the northern sections of the city.

Searching for a solution to the high death rate the city health officer noted that the best results were being obtained by the Margaret Scott Nursing Mission with their program of home visiting. He felt that while continued encouragement had to be given to such private agencies, more was needed. Thus he recommended in his 1912 report that the city set up a child welfare division composed of "one or two nurses who would visit mothers at their homes, both before and after birth of the baby, instructing and furnishing aid in the many ways that this might be needed." Early in 1913 this department was established with a staff of two nurses and during that year over two thousand visits were made. This department also started a program of free medication, clothing, and food in needy cases. In 1914 two more visiting nurses were added to the staff, while a house was set up in the North End with two resident nurses to which mothers were encouraged to bring infants for lessons on proper feeding and care. One of the major reasons for this large increase was the discontinuance of the Margaret Scott Nursing Mission's work in this area in late 1914; but the new efforts on the part of the city also showed a growing awareness of their responsibility in this area. The results of these new programs appeared almost immediately; in 1914 the infant mortality rate dropped to its lowest level in seven years.

Of all the programs instituted by the department in this period this one was certainly the most successful and progressive. But it must also be recognized that a large part of the impetus for these enlarged efforts came from the Margaret Scott Nursing Mission, without whose example it is unlikely that so much would have been done. It is significant, moreover, that the department's best efforts came in this area, for undoubtedly it was here that few would attempt to criticize. Only the most callous individual would begrudge public money being spent for helpless children and as a result the department was able to move far ahead of the times in its child welfare division as apathy gave way to prevention and genuine social concern and action. However, in other areas, such as housing, the activities of the health department did not go much beyond the use of the police power of the state. It was one thing to provide free medication, clothing, and food for infants; it was entirely another to even think of supplying adequate housing for all the city residents.

One of the major reasons given for the need for an expanded health department staff in 1904–1905 was Winnipeg's serious and ever-growing housing problem. Indeed, many in the city feared Winnipeg would soon be plagued with slum conditions, if such was not already the case. Thus, in an attempt to find the extent of the problem and to exercise some degree of control over it, the department's inspection staff was increased to fifteen in 1906. Several of these new employees were able to speak languages other than English and the department also took the step of hiring an interpreter. The investigations carried out by this staff revealed the worst; Winnipeg did have slum conditions in many areas of the city. The actual dimension of the housing crisis could not, of course, be thoroughly documented, for the inspectors admitted they could not keep up with the city's rapid population growth. Yet what they did turn up in their work was proof enough that the dimensions of the housing crisis were staggering.

In general, the department found that there were three major aspects to the housing problem. First, there were the single-family dwellings that were unsanitary. In many cases the cause was basically a lack of sewer and water connections, but the problem did not end here. The demand for housing in the city after 1900 had become so great that speculative builders had begun a vast program of building cheap, unsubstantial houses. Whole blocks of houses were literally thrown together on small and inadequate twenty-five-foot lots and then quickly rented to the newly arrived immigrants. Often tenants moved in before the building was even completed. "One family was found sleeping in the stable and cooking their meals in the cellars of an unfinished house. Another family was living in a shed intended for a garage and a third in a house with only the rough framework constructed, no roof, no plaster, and of course no plumbing."[35] Cheap construction also caused problems of frozen plumbing. This was sometimes a result of "the careless manner in which plumbing has been installed in many buildings, some plumbers caring nothing for what may happen to the pipes or fixtures once they have completed their work." But "in other instances the owner is at fault for neglecting to provide heat in the case of the poorer class of house," or for refusing "to allow the necessary room or space for properly installing the plumbing." Whatever the reason, frozen plumbing was common in Winnipeg during the period and gave rise to frequent instances of fires being built under the water-closets before they could be used.[36]

The second major area of difficulty was that, even with the vast increases in housing starts, the city simply could not properly accommodate its residents. Overcrowding became a common occurrence; in 1912 there were 2,752 reported cases.[37] This problem was complicated by factors other than the lack of available housing: cultural and economic factors also played a major role. In the first instance, the fact that a large proportion of the city's immigrants in this period were of non-Anglo-Saxon origin meant that the foreign ghettos already in existence in wards 5 and 6 received a disproportionate share of the newcomers. Ukrainians, Poles, Russians, Germans, and Jews tended to settle in the North End and it soon had some of the worst cases of overcrowding. Many of the city's elite felt unsanitary conditions were natural among foreigners but the reasons for the deterioration of these wards were economic, rather than cultural.[38] For while there was a severe lack of housing available anywhere in Winnipeg, it was also true that even if there had been small, inexpensive dwellings for sale most of the newcomers could not have afforded to buy them. The average cost of a modern frame house (with concrete foundation and plumbing) in 1908 was $3,000, while the average non-skilled labourer was fortunate if he earned over $500 a year—hardly enough to allow him to save money to buy a home.[39] Thus, most newcomers were forced to turn to renting homes, or, if single (as in the case of Winnipeg's large floating population), to a boarding house.

Once a labourer found a suitable home for rent (and this was no easy task) his problem was still not solved. Renting for an average of $20 per month, few workingmen and their families could afford to live there unless they made at least $1,200 a year. In desperation they sublet rooms in the house to other families in order to make ends meet. The result was described by a health inspector:

> A house of ten rooms was found occupied by five families, also roomers—20 adults and two children. Three of the families had only one room each. There were eight gas stoves, and none of these had hoods or pipes for carrying off the products of combustion and the odors of cooking. Two girl boarders occupied a portion of the cellar. . . . There was one water closet, one sink, a bath, and a wash basin. Two faucets had been fitted on the water-service pipe, and buckets placed under same in lieu of sinks.[40]

Yet the dimensions of the problem were still larger than this, for in most cases the owner of property would find out that the lessee was living rent free, or nearly so, on account of the profits he made from sub-tenants. "This leads to a further rise in rents, both to the lessee and the sub-tenants, or single roomers, and the last state of the house as regards overcrowding and also rents is worse than the former, the net result being overcrowded tenements utterly unfit for the purpose and rented at exhorbitant rents, having regard to the accommodation provided." Furthermore, for every lessee who was forced out of economic necessity to sub-divide a single-family dwelling there was a landlord who made a business of building houses, dividing them, and then renting separate rooms to whole families.

There were also those who went into the boarding-house or rooming-house business, providing accommodation for single males and crowding as many as possible into dwellings originally intended for single-family homes. One such rooming house is described below:

> A ten-roomed house was found to have nine separate tenants (only one of whom had two rooms) each living independently and doing their cooking on gas stoves and eating and sleeping in one room. To make matters worse, not one of the gas stoves had a hood or pipe to carry off noxious gases. Imagine these rooms . . . in winter with double sashes on. There was only one water closet and one sink in the house. We have reason to believe that this is not an isolated case, and that many places are to be found. . . .[41]

While accommodation for single males was generally a problem, it was particularly difficult for non-Anglo-Saxons. The Men's Own, a privately supported organization, served the social needs of many Anglo-Saxons, providing sleeping quarters, gospel hall, reading room, laundry, "fumigating room," dispensary, and even a free employment bureau. No such organization existed for foreign-born labourers. "The consequence is that they are received into premises either already fully occupied by families . . . or else are taken into some of the Ruthenian boarding houses, mostly frame buildings utterly inadapted for the purpose, and frequently in a poor state of repair and with very poor sanitary conveniences."[42]

Besides these problems of unsanitary premises and overcrowding of buildings originally designed as single-family dwellings, there was yet a third aspect to the housing crisis—the problem of the multiple-family unit or tenement.[43] It was, perhaps, natural that with such a shortage of housing in Winnipeg tenements would be built. The surprising thing is that most of those built prior to 1914 were, at first, rented by "a well-to-do class of tenants." Moreover, because of the abundance of unoccupied land within the city limits no district sprang up consisting principally of tenements and causing problems of high population density.[44] Yet despite these conditions, the city health department still saw reason for concern. They envisioned (quite accurately, as it turned out) an exodus of the well-to-do tenants to the suburbs with a resulting rapid deterioration in the tenement buildings. Hence they set out to ensure that all tenements met strict standards when first built, as an insurance against future deterioration. They noted, for example, that many tenements of "first-class design" were crowded onto small lots with single-family dwellings on both sides.[45] This not only caused problems of lighting and ventilation in the apartment blocks, but virtually shut off the light from the small houses. This "lack of healthful conditions," the report stated, "is responsible for the low vitality of many of the occupants, a slaughter of infants, the propagation of tuberculosis and other diseases; degeneracy of the body, morals, and intellect, and many other evils that may be attributed directly and indirectly to the badly constructed, faultily designed, inadequately ventilated, poorly lighted, and badly kept tenement house."[46]

In its attempt to cope with Winnipeg's housing problem, the city health department set out a four-point program designed to deal with the crisis. The first step, of course, was to gain "an exact knowledge of the conditions." This task was carried out by the large staff of health inspectors who made house-to-house inspections throughout the city. In many instances it was found necessary to inspect premises in the early morning hours; for it was only at that time that accurate surveys could be taken, since most tenants were careful to conceal evidence of overcrowding during the day. "The innocent looking couch by day is opened out at night and becomes a bed for two boarders. This disappearance of beds and bedding in the day time is one reason why day inspections for overcrowding are not sufficient unless supplemented by night inspections."[47] This problem, combined with that of the city's rapid population growth rate, led to repeated requests for a larger inspection staff but the department's demands were never fully met. Moreover, the hopes raised by the City Planning Commission's planned survey into housing conditions were also dashed when that body was refused the necessary financial support by City Council. Nevertheless, the inspection staff did turn up enough evidence to allow it to recommend legislation to deal with nearly all the conditions they found in the housing area.

Prior to 1909, housing problems were dealt with under powers granted by the general public health bylaw of 1899 (and amendments thereto) which gave the department the right to "abate nuisances" and deal with "unsanitary premises." After 1908, the department asked for more specific powers and by 1914 most of their requests had been granted. Only two of the bylaws passed in this period were of any great significance, however.[48] In 1909 the "tenement bylaw" was passed "to regulate the erection, ventilation and safety from fire or accident, of Tenement Houses hereafter erected or altered." This law, which defined tenements as dwellings housing two or more families, required that building permits were required before erection of or alterations to tenements could be carried out. And it set down numerous regulations concerning tenements that had to be fulfilled: percentage of lot occupied, fireproofing, fire escapes, restrictions on wooden tenement, height, area of courts, sizes and height of rooms, window areas, water-closet accommodation, and a host of other stipulations. The main drawback of the act was that it dealt only with buildings constructed after 1909; no control was asserted over the thousands of single-family dwellings that had been converted to tenements in the years prior to the passage of this bylaw.

The comprehensive "building bylaw" passed in 1913 was the second significant piece of legislation. Its purpose was to regulate "the construction, repair, removal, and inspection of buildings" and it set out a lengthy set of requirements that had to be met. As far as the city health department was concerned, however, this bylaw had an important omission. It failed to directly mention that permits would be required for the conversion of buildings from single- to multiple-family dwellings. In buildings so converted to tenements, "the offenders had to be reached in a round about way by prosecutions for inadequate plumbing, or overcrowding, or else to serve notice on the ground of insufficient lighting, ventilation, etc." The department asked for amendments to the bylaw to cover this area but their request was turned down. What this meant in terms of the department's work was that while they had sufficient power already, this could be exercised only with a great deal of effort, while the new legislation would have made their task easier. And since the department, although large, was continually understaffed, this extra effort often could not be applied.

Generally, however, the legislation passed by the city during this period was progressive in that it recognized the relation between living conditions and the general public health and brought the power of the state to bear on several of the problem areas. But here, as in the area of box-closet removal discussed above, it was only a partial step to pass legislation. Strict enforcement of the bylaws was an entirely different manner. The very rapidity of the city's growth caused the major problem of enforcement, but language differences were also an important factor. The great diversity of languages spoken in the North End made it necessary to employ interpreters who could explain the laws to the foreign immigrants. The laxity of penalties inflicted on offenders also did not make the department's work any easier and it continually urged stiffer fines. But it was "the scarcity of houses and the high rents" that most of all made it necessary for the department to proceed with caution in enforcement.[49] Indeed, the recognition by the medical health officer that many boarders were forced by economic necessity to break the law led him to make some pretty daring proposals between 1910 and 1914.

After stating that he knew of "no question of more vital importance to the future welfare of the city than the housing problem," Dr. Douglas noted that he hoped the annual reports on the existing conditions would make public opinion ripe "for a step forward in the housing problem."

> It will cost money—such reforms generally do come high. It may become necessary, for instance, for the City to show by practical example what can be done in the way of Municipal Lodging Houses erected and equipped on sanitary lines. Such a building in North Winnipeg would at least remove one excuse offenders put forth, viz: that their boarders have nowhere to go if they refuse to take them in: or a model tenement house might be erected to show that such buildings can be erected in accordance with the laws of sanitation and still be a paying investment.
>
> The main point is that we cannot stop at simply abating gross overcrowding . . . but must be prepared to go much further and ensure that every place occupied as a dwelling within the city —no matter how humble it may be—is perfectly sanitary and a fit and proper place in which to bring up Winnipeg's most valuable asset—her children.[50]

In other articles Dr. Douglas suggested that if the city itself would not get into the house building business it could possibly be done by "some philanthropic individual or society." He was careful to point out that it was feasible to do such "a great and much needed work" and at the same time receive a reasonable return on the investment.[51]

But true to the traditions of privatism and the growth ethic, the city's governing commercial elite rejected these suggestions and the destructive and costly (both in human and material terms) private building process continued well beyond 1914. Indeed, the grossly substandard living conditions of the mass of Winnipeg's labourers was to be a major cause of the Winnipeg general strike of 1919. The irony of this situation was only too evident. For while private enterprise could persuade the municipal corporation to invest heavily in attracting railways, building a city-owned hydro-power plant, and even in attracting the very immigrants who caused the housing problem, it would not allow it to invest in the most vitally important question affecting the city's welfare—housing—no matter what the later public costs of the private real estate market might be.

14 / Red Lights in Winnipeg: Segregated Vice, Moral Reformers, and Civic Politics

There was only one important issue that caused any serious conflict within the ruling commercial elite between 1874 and 1914. Not surprisingly, it was a moral issue rather than an economic or social one. What is noteworthy about Winnipeg's prostitution question, however, is that a majority of the city's voters supported those civic leaders who argued that the protection of Winnipeg's reputation was more important than the suppression of organized vice. This policy was defended on the grounds that constant and vigorous attempts to suppress prostitution caused bad publicity and this in turn adversely affected outside investors and immigration. It was thus to be avoided at all costs. Indeed, this group went so far as to implement a program of controlled and, one might argue, legalized prostitution. Thus, while Winnipeg's prostitution problem is colourful and interesting in itself, discussion of it serves a more important purpose. It shows that economic growth and prosperity were by far the most important goals of a majority of Winnipeg's voters. To achieve these ends they were content to have their city labelled the "vice capital of Canada."

Although the most dramatic upsurge in prostitution occurred after the turn of the century, Winnipeg had been faced with a serious problem much earlier. In March 1874 City Council had received a petition from a resident of Notre Dame Avenue asking for the removal of "Houses of Ill-Fame."[1] Other complaints followed this one and between 1874 and 1883 the problem of prostitution was periodically raised in the local press.[2] Finally, in 1883, Winnipeg was forced to endure the first of many "Anti-Social Evil Crusades," vigorously launched by the city's Ministerial Association. Significantly, during this first campaign four different approaches to the problem of prostitution were put forward and for the next thirty years the arguments changed little.

The most unpopular approach to the problem of prostitution was the argument that it was a result of socio-economic conditions and could only be eradicated, or minimized, by socio-economic solutions. Interestingly, this view was held by Winnipeg's official labour spokesmen and by the keepers and inmates of the houses themselves. Labour argued that a major part of the problem was caused by the great imbalance in the city that existed between males and females, an imbalance, they pointed out, that was a direct result of the city's campaigns to attract immigrants. Moreover, with the glutting of the labour market with vast numbers of workers, wages were kept at a minimum and consequently single men could not afford marriage, while married men could not bring their wives or families to Winnipeg. Despairing of their soreful lot, these men turned to drink, gambling, and "women of easy virtue." In short, organized labour argued that if the standards of living were raised, a large part of the problem would disappear.[3] While labour thus attempted to explain the male side of the problem, the prostitutes themselves also blamed their state on others. They argued that for the immigrant woman or one caught in the transitional process from country to city, prostitution sometimes offered the only hope of surviving in the urban environment. With any kind of security at a premium, and separated from their parents and family, with no money, education, or skills, women frequently turned to prostitution in a desperate attempt to cope. The prostitutes argued that they were "unfortunate women cruelly condemned" by society to a life of crime and shame.[4]

The public in general, however, were not prepared to accept the fact that other than basically evil women or men could be involved in the "scarlet sin." Accordingly, various groups set out to rid Winnipeg of the "evil" entirely, or at least officially deal with it by forcing the business to be carried on in a certain, usually undesirable, location in the community, referred to colloquially as the "red light district" or, in a more official language, the "segregated area." Those who would accept no compromise whatever took the former approach and were largely the city's religious leaders, especially members of the Methodist, Presbyterian, and Congregationalist churches.[5] The ministers who were involved in the various campaigns to drive out the prostitutes argued that it had to be opposed since it was not only a crime, but a dreadful sin as well. The only choice open was "vigorous and persistent measures" to drive "sinful women" out of Winnipeg. Indeed, they were so strongly opposed to prostitution that they time and time again raised the question in public in an attempt to "arouse public sentiment" against the evil. In a city and an era where Sunday School classes were segregated and where not even streetcars could operate on Sunday, this was indeed a drastic measure. Some did, however, take the precaution of never mentioning the subject in "mixed congregations."[6]

The vast majority of the population, on the other hand, were content to ignore the problem as long as it did not affect them directly. They were, for the most part, satisfied to let their elected officials and police deal with the problem in any way they saw fit. Only when "houses of ill-fame" depreciated the property values in their neighbourhood did most citizens take a stand. In other words, they were all for segregation, but not in their neighbourhood.

The distasteful task of dealing with the problem was, of course, ultimately in the hands of City Council and the city police department. The latter publicly stated that they would do whatever was asked of them in dealing with the problem but they were also quick to point out the great difficulty of gathering sufficient evidence to make a case against the prostitutes. One first had to gain entry to a brothel and then, somehow, prove that sexual intercourse for money actually took place. Certainly policemen could not be asked to carry out such undercover work and there were precious few public-spirited citizens who would be willing to take the witness stand with such evidence.

In formulating the official city policy, Council undoubtedly took these views into consideration. In fact, they went much further, for they virtually adopted the philosophy of an "unnamed gentleman" (possibly an alderman) who made his views public during the scandal of 1883:

> I really cannot see what good can be accomplished by agitating this question. The clergy may denounce the social evil from their pulpits Sunday after Sunday; the Chief of Police may make raid after raid until he and his men are tired, the newspapers may write leader after leader, and after all has been done there will not be one of the houses the [prostitutes] inhabit closed. The social evil is as old as humanity, it began with the human race and it will not cease until the last man is dead. It is a necessity, just as much a necessity as air or food, and the most we can expect to do is to hide its most hideous features and keep them from public gaze.
> It is a mistaken policy to hunt those women from house to house and from street to street. It has been tried in a thousand different cities and always with the same result, utter failure.

Given the inevitability of prostitution and Council's strong desire to preserve the city's reputation from adverse publicity, the aldermen were left with two choices in dealing with the matter. The first course was to institute a licensing and tax system, like that in vogue in "Germany, France, New Orleans, and St. Louis." This would enable medical inspections to be carried out and would also "contain an avowal that the trade was one that ought to be pursued only under conditions of supervision and restriction." There were, however, objections to this approach, the chief of which was that "it implies only that a certain revenue must be raised—it indicates nothing immoral, nothing wrong. . . . It legalizes the crime by taxing it."[8] The second alternative was then considered and accepted. This policy of segregation was in effect a tacit agreement between the prostitutes and the city that the activities of the houses would be confined to the outskirts of Winnipeg; there would be no soliciting in the settled portion of the city; they would be allowed to ride only in closed carriages; and the segregated area would be regularly patrolled by police. The prostitutes were also probably told that it was to their benefit to carry on a quiet business for there was no telling what might happen if the clergy learned of the arrangement, for "clergymen are not the most intelligent men, nor yet do they reason the best."[9]

The problem of prostitution first became a matter of public concern in the fall of 1882. Council did not respond quickly, however. Rather, "an armistice was granted for the purpose of allowing the [prostitutes] to withdraw gracefully. . . . It was denounced as cruel to begin an attack at a season when the women . . . would be subjected to the vigors of a Manitoba winter, in quarters much less comfortable than those they had perforce abandoned. It was demanded and conceded that reasonable notice should be given and proceedings stayed in the meantime. This has been done."[10] But early in April 1883 the campaign against the houses of prostitution located on Portage Avenue was renewed by the Ministerial Association and a number of other citizens. In a petition sent to Council twenty-three persons deplored the fact that the prostitutes should have been allowed to remain "in a part of the city so near the centre, and affording such desirable sites for private residences." Moreover, in so allowing the houses to exist after March 31 in this area the License and Police Committee was "breaking the promise" made the previous fall. But the problem was soon solved, for by July 1883 the police were being instructed to patrol the houses in their new location on Toronto Street (in the western portion of Ward 3).

Following this flurry of activity in 1883 prostitution was mentioned only sporadically in the press during the next eighteen years, and it seems that the segregation policy was successful. At least part of its success during these years was attributable to the fact that the prostitutes cooperated with the police. In 1894, for examples, a deputation from Ward 3 approached Council and complained that houses of ill-fame were depreciating their property values and asked that they be moved. Accordingly, on the advice of the police the prostitutes moved farther west, this time to Thomas Street (now called Minto), where their thriving business was soon re-established.

One other development that is worthy of note took place during this period of relative calm. Prior to 1884 the city police department had been under the direct control of City Council, a situation that proved all too embarrassing during the controversy of 1883 when many clergymen quite rightfully blamed Council for not vigorously urging the department to drive out the prostitutes. To circumvent this touchy question, in 1884 Council decided upon an ingenious scheme. By an amendment to the provincial Municipal Act, Council was empowered to appoint a Board of Police Commissioners, consisting of the mayor, the judge of the county court, and the police magistrate. This board was to have "sole charge and control of the police department of the city and the persons therein employed. . . ." In effect, the board "was to remove members of the force from political influence and interference, whether municipal or otherwise," a condition which undoubtedly appealed to members of Council. For although "the people" were represented by the mayor, he could claim in any embarrassing situation that he had been out-voted. In short, the creation of the board took the administration of the segregation policy out of the hands of Council.

By 1900 the city of Winnipeg was in the midst of the greatest period of growth it had ever known. One writer described it as a "lusty, gusty, bawdy frontier boomtown roaring through an unequalled economic debauch. . . ."[11] The rapid population growth of this period, for all the benefits it gave to the city as the "exploiter" and "tollgate" of the West, caused prostitution to once again be thrust onto the Winnipeg political scene. Apparently the fact that the rapid spatial growth of the city had caught up with the houses of prostitution was the cause for the renewed complaints. Residents of the affected area of Ward 3 complained, as had others before them, that the existence of the segregated area exposed their families to lewd and indecent behaviour; that the noise, drunkenness, and general debauchery were disruptive to their peace of mind; and, most importantly, that the area was a cause of decline in property values. But, given past experience, this problem should have been easily solved by resorting to the tactic of having the houses moved again to the outskirts of the city. The failure of this procedure testifies to the fact that Winnipeg, and its citizens, had changed since 1894.

One of the basic changes that had occurred was that the surplus of males over females in Winnipeg had increased dramatically from 1,200 in 1891 to more than 11,000 in 1906. Also, in the period between 1896 and 1911 more than 500,000 immigrants found their way to Western Canada and nearly all passed through Winnipeg; indeed, almost one-tenth stayed. Thus, besides the great imbalance in the city's resident population, Winnipeg had countless more men, a floating population, that did much to aggravate the prostitution problem.[12] Moreover, after fifteen years of continuous and trouble-free operation, the word had got around that Winnipeg was a safe place for prostitutes to operate and they flocked to the city in droves.[13] The combination of a ready market and an eager supplier proved too much, for with the vast increase in the number of bawdy houses, control slipped out of the hands of the police. Such a thriving business was suddenly too big to hide from public view for any great length of time.

A second major factor that worked against the Board of Police Commissioners' attempt to solve the prostitution problem by a continuance of the segregation policy was that this time, when the Protestant clergy raised the issue of the "scarlet sin," they received a far greater degree of public support than they had in 1883. A reformist mood was fast gaining momentum in this period and although it was mainly concerned with the questions of alcohol and education, some of its zeal naturally spilled over into the arena of civic politics.[14] This reform movement was at least partially a result of the reaction among the settled members of the community to the radically changing social conditions of an urbanizing and rapidly expanding population. The challenge to the traditionally accepted values and ways of life of the heretofore predominantly Anglo-Saxon community of Winnipeg presented by the vast influx of non-British newcomers added to the general feeling of social malaise. It was, then, "not surprising that the first reaction of the churches was to see the new urbanism as a challenge to moral standards."[15] At the same time, however, the social gospel preached by the clerical reformers had deep roots in the puritanical spirit of the early Ontario settlers who had founded and built Winnipeg. Indeed, one observer has noted that "one can with some plausibility interpret the crusading zeal of the period not as a response to a new threat but as a dramatic effort to complete a process of moral reformation that had been going on since pioneering days."[16]

But whatever the cause of this spirit of reform it swept throughout Canada and the United States during this period and organizations of citizens, usually dominated by clergymen, sprang up to combat prostitution. In Winnipeg this reform movement took hold dramatically and at least three "reformist" organizations played important roles in the prostitution controversy. These were the Women's Christian Temperance Union, the Citizens' Committee for the Suppression of Vice, and the Moral and Social Reform League. The WCTU, which was, of course, mainly involved with the question of prohibition, did not become especially active in the segregated prostitution question. But it did do much to allow women to overcome traditional, and often imposed, inhibitions about getting involved in public questions; so much so that by 1910 discussions and meetings were held on the subject. They went so far as to endorse candidates for the municipal election according to their stand on the segregation issue, and since women then had the vote in municipal elections this was a potent force.[17] The Citizens' Committee (also called the Civic Social Purity Committee) never exceeded one hundred and fifty in strength and was mainly an ad hoc group organized to present local citizens' complaints to the civic authorities. But by virtue of some of the personalities included in the group, its size is illusory. Yet it was the Moral and Social Reform League, formed in 1907, that proved to be the strongest advocate of the anti-segregation policy. A contemporary weekly tabloid sponsored by the organization characterized the group as a "federation of the religious and social reform bodies for consultation and cooperation with respect to legislative reform growing out of their common Christianity." Groups affiliated with the league, at one time or another, were the Trades and Labor Council, the Icelandic Lutheran Synod, the WCTU, the Unitarian Conference, the Scandinavian Anti-Saloon League, the Polish National Catholic Church, the Ruthenian Catholic Church, the Russian Orthodox Greek Church, plus, of course, the Methodist, Baptist, and Congregationalist churches. The league's activities revolved around all aspects of the prostitution question, including liquor, traffic, gambling, and the white slave trade. Significantly, in view of the league's later failure in their anti-segregation crusade, such powerful groups as the Winnipeg Board of Trade, the Grain Exchange, the Builders' Exchange, the Winnipeg Development and Industrial Bureau, and the Real Estate Association did not affiliate themselves with the league. As a matter of fact, they took a very dim view of this mixture of religious zeal and civic politics and worked hard to overcome the pressures exerted by the league.[18]

The final element present in the years after 1900 that had not been there in 1883 was the personage of Thomas Sharpe. Elected as alderman in 1900, this Presbyterian contractor was not only in complete agreement with the aims of the Moral and Social Reform League, he was willing and able to take up the whole question of segregated vice.

The second crusade against prostitution in Winnipeg started quietly enough. As in 1883 it was a group of affected citizens who raised the subject clearly as a matter of self-interest rather than a moral issue. But these petitioners soon received support from the City Ministerial Association which presented itself as a delegation before City Council, demanding the complete abolition of the segregation policy. Mayor Arbuthnot, speaking for Council, stated that if the association would aid "in the gathering of evidence the place complained of would be cleared out in 24 hours." A special committee of Council was then appointed to consider the matter and the delegation withdrew. By October 1901 it was apparent that Council's special committee had indeed acted, for it was reported that the Thomas Street Colony was ordered to "remove to more remote quarters."[19]

Council did take one significant step in late 1901, however. On a motion of Alderman Sharpe it was decided to enlarge the Board of Police Commissioners to include two aldermen, thereby giving control of that body to Council. The motion passed by a "silent vote" and there were even attempts to have its enactment into law blocked in the legislature, but early in 1902 the newly composed board was appointed. Although Alderman Sharpe failed of election to the new board, it was apparent that if sufficient public pressure should arise Council could no longer say they had no control over the matter.

The prostitution problem was not openly discussed again until November 1903 when "in accordance with a concerted action decided upon by the Ministerial Association," a public campaign was launched. A number of sermons were preached that included severe criticism of the police commissioners.[20] The tactic of merely moving the prostitutes to a new area whenever there were complaints was not acceptable to the ministers; they would not be satisfied until the segregation policy was abandoned. Following the opening of the campaign on Sunday, 15 November, a public meeting was called for Monday evening. This gathering went predictably enough; prostitution was denounced as sinful and as a crime and a complete abolition of the segregation policy was called for. Those present at the meeting also formed the Civic Social Purity Committee and pledged their support only for those candidates for City Council who agreed with their platform.

Despite these efforts City Council, and in particular Mayor Arbuthnot, refused to direct the City Police Department to discontinue the policy of segregated prostitution.[21] Of all the Council members only Alderman Sharpe publicly allied himself with the anti-segregationists.[22] The latter were thus hopeful that Sharpe's election as mayor in December 1903 would lead to a change in the prostitution policy of the city.[23]

The anti-segregationist's expectations were fulfilled when in January 1904, at the first session of the Board of Police Commissioners, Mayor Sharpe was able to obtain passage of a resolution that stated "that hereafter the law relating to disorderly houses will be rigidly enforced." Within two hours of this decision the "colony of a dozen houses were closed up and eighty-four women were in police court." "Keepers of houses were fined $40 and inmates $20" and they were told that henceforth they had to either cease practice, leave the city, or suffer the full penalty of the law. Thus in one dramatic measure Winnipeg's official policy of segregated prostitution was abolished.[24]

Although this policy of rigid enforcement was pursued throughout the administrations of Mayor Sharpe (1904–6) and Mayor Ashdown (1907–8), it by no stretch of the imagination solved Winnipeg's prostitution problem. With the continued rapid growth of the city prostitution in fact thrived and although the Ministerial Association could no longer complain of connivance on the part of the civic authorities, there were nonetheless frequent complaints from all over Winnipeg that houses of ill-fame were all too prominent. The city's police force also voiced complaints early in 1909. It stated that with over one hundred "known" houses of prostitution in the city the department could not spare the men or the time required to control the social evil.[25] Faced with complaints from both sides the Board of Police Commissioners decided that some action was required.

Following a discussion of the prostitution question at a Board of Police Commissioners' meeting in April 1909, the commission rescinded the 1904 resolution, replacing it with the following: ". . . that all matters relating to the question of houses of ill-fame and dealing with immoral women be left to the Chief of Police, he to act in accordance with discretion and best judgement."[26] The commission's action, in effect, meant that the police chief was to set up a police-regulated segregated district along the line of the old Thomas Street area. Chief of Police McRae in fact later admitted that it was at this time clearly understood by both the commissioners and himself that the new policy would be to locate the prostitutes in one section of the city. The plan was, he stated, "that these people were to be got together if possible, in order that there might be more effective enforcement of the law."[27]

Following the tradition of efficiency that had been established in the 1883–1903 period, Chief McRae wasted no time in setting up the new red light district. Shortly after the passage of the new resolution he went to see Minnie Woods (popularly known as the "Queen of Harlots") because, he later said, she had been a "house-keeper" in the segregated area of Thomas Street and presumably "knew all the ropes." Hs asked her if she thought segregation was possible and when she replied in the affirmative, he told her that the selection of a suitable location was entirely up to her: "The responsibility is all yours. I have nothing whatever to do with that."[28] Subsequent developments, however, strongly suggest that McRae and, implicitly, the Police Commission, were not as disinterested as they claimed, for when Minnie Woods suggested a site in Point Douglas as being appropriate because it was within easy walking distance of the CPR Station and the Main Street hotels, McRae contacted a real estate dealer by the name of J. Beaman and asked him if he would make arrangements for the move.

Beaman, of course, accepted the offer, as he correctly perceived that it could be a very lucrative proposition. With a demand for houses in the area as inelastic as it was bound to be in a district where prostitutes had little choice but to buy, the supplier could reap a fantastic windfall and this the real estate agent promptly proceeded to do. He bought as many of the properties in the area as he could and then re-sold them to the prostitutes at exorbitant prices. Some of the women paid as much as $12,000 for property that would normally have sold for no more than $3,000. And although Beaman was considerate enough to give a $1,000 discount for cash payments, he was later to admit to having bought twenty-two houses in the area in the summer of 1909 on which he made a profit of about $70,000.[29] In a subsequent investigation of this whole series of events no evidence turned up to indicate that these transactions yielded anything but personal profits for Beaman. On the other hand, gossip alleged that Beaman was a relative of McRae. Even more suspect, however, was the fact that according to the *Henderson Directory*, Beaman had arrived in the city in 1909 and stayed for only one year, facts that suggest he was probably just a front man for the entire operation. Finally, the fact that Beaman was clearly a novice in the real estate business (he was not listed in the *Directory* as being a member of any real estate firm) who probably had neither the capital nor the know-how to carry out such an operation, further suggests that the available evidence yields something less than the whole story.[30]

The area chosen for Winnipeg's vice district comprised two streets in Point Douglas known as McFarlane and Rachel (the latter is now called Annabella), and the pocket of houses concerned were north of the CPR main line. When the area was selected, the district was occupied by perfectly respectable, hard-working families. A study carried out by the All Peoples' Mission in 1909 indicated that the area was largely composed of "working people, foreign immigrants, and children—a comparatively helpless group."[31] Of course, nobody consulted these residents about turning their district into a red light area. And although it was ideal from the standpoint of the prostitutes, it was equally desirable to the police chief and police commissioners. The area was geographically isolated from the rest of the city, especially from well-to-do, established Winnipeggers, being bounded on the north and south by the Red River, on the west by a huge and odoriferous artificial-gas cooking plant, and on the east by a power station. Moreover, the large foreign element in the area could be expected to make little trouble as most were tenants, rather than home owners. This undoubtedly helped the transactions move speedily, as the absentee owners of the property could be expected to ask few questions when the right price was offered. In any case, the area developed quickly since by October 1909 twenty-nine houses of prostitution had been established in the area, and this grew to more than fifty during 1910.

True to established precedents, the segregated area was subject to a number of regulations. The houses would be allowed to operate only if they remained as inconspicuous as possible. McRae stated that the regulations imposed by the police were that the prostitutes were "not to parade on the streets, to solicit on the street, . . . or to call on the downtown district; that they were not to have any manifestations of disorderly conduct; that all outward manifestations of disorderly conduct would be suppressed."[32] Loud music and distinctive markings on the house such as bright lights or enlarged house numbers were prohibited, although the women were allowed to go uptown as long as they reported their visits to the madam and returned by eight o'clock. Furthermore, on these occasions they "must behave themselves and dress quietly." In short, prostitutes were allowed to conduct business only so long as they did so politely and quietly. McRae later claimed, however, that he never indicated to their spokeswoman, Minnie Woods, that they would be "undisturbed" in the district. The morality officers of the Police Department were responsible for seeing that adherence to these regulations was maintained. The women would be subject to apprehension for "disorderly houses, thefts, robberies, and admission of persons who should not be there, etc."[33] The latter qualification probably referred to minors. Obviously, if the regulations were intended to be strictly enforced the women would probably have never bothered to move to the area in the first place. As a matter of fact, what developed was that the women received summons regularly each quarter from the courts and they were not disturbed for another three months. In other words, they paid a licence of $400 a year for their business, since the law stipulated that a fine of up to $1,000 for each offence could be charged.

The establishment and operation of the segregated area involved a great number of individuals, some of whom had a financial interest in the venture. Besides the police department, the police commissioners (three of whom were on City Council), and the courts, the provincial Liquor Licensing Department, the liquor business interests, and even the telephone company were involved. In the former case it was later proved that both the province and city received substantial profits from "licences" granted to sell liquor in the houses, while the liquor business did a booming trade as "deliveries were made frequently" to the keepers of the houses. Even more interesting, however, is the situation respecting telephones. By the end of 1910 over forty-three pay telephones had been installed in the area, a development that had "involved new telephone construction on the streets in question." The "house-holders" guaranteed a revenue of $40 per month for the phones, while the telephone company took "any surplus that may be found in the cash box." An indication of the utility of the phones is given by the fact that in October 1910 one phone paid a revenue of $526.15 in one month. This wide involvement of so many facets of the city's administrative structure and service industry is important to bear in mind in view of subsequent developments.

If City Council—with the important exceptions of Mayor Evans, Alderman F. J. C. Cox, and Alderman L. McMeans, all of whom were members of the Police Commission—were at first unaware of these significant developments they did not remain so for long. Reports stating that a segregation policy had been decided upon began appearing in the local press as early as May 1909 and these were, of course, quickly followed by appropriate actions on the part of the Moral and Social Reform League.[34]

The league undertook a determined and vigorous program designed to have the segregation policy abandoned. Sermons, mass meetings, advertisements in local newspapers, delegations to City Council—all demanded an end to the "herding of immoral women."[35] The tone of the league's arguments is perhaps best revealed by a pamphlet it sponsored in 1910. Entitled "The Problem of Social Vice in Winnipeg," this document provided a host of arguments against the policy of segregated prostitution.[36] Written by Rev. Dr. F. DuVal, a Presbyterian minister prominent in the social reform movement in Winnipeg, the pamphlet was a passionate indictment of the commission's policy. DuVal prefaced his discussion with the pretentious observation that "After thirty-five years of meditation upon medico-moral subjects relating to the purifying of the springs of human well-being . . .," he had concluded that prostitution was an evil that had to be completely exterminated. In similarly elaborate language, he proceeded to deal extensively with the arguments proposed for and against segregation. He dismissed the policy of unofficial segregation as being just as detrimental to the moral health of the community as legal toleration.[37] "Noxious weeds grow just as well under passive permission as official. Human lust does the same." He contended that the police had assumed the right to legislate, execute, and enforce the laws regarding prostitution since the appropriate political authorities had shirked their duty. This was a flagrant violation of the sacred traditions of Western Christian civilization. DuVal then charged that ". . . a minority who choose to degrade the sacred powers of generation, and by the use of aphrodisiacs [liquor], and the cultivation of filthy imaginations, bring themselves into a pathological debasement, that seems to themselves a permanent institution of sexual vice, have no right, Divine or human, to maintain such an institution to the injury of the commonwealth." The pamphlet concluded by exhorting the citizens of Winnipeg to fight the growing evil: "As virtue in this city has still the vantage ground, in God's name, and in the name of all that we expect to bequeath to our children, let us hold that vantage. As Winnipeg goes, so goes the coming West, and the springs from which future generations shall drink in their character, will be purified or poisoned here." In short, according to DuVal's "domino theory," the struggle in Winnipeg was far more than a local issue; it was a holy war to save Western Canada, indeed, the whole country, so that it might yet prove to be the "noblest edition of national life" in the world.

Other anti-segregation arguments were based on more down-to-earth sentiments and probably were more effective in influencing public opinion. J. M. Fraser, an official of the league, pointed out that the segregated district could not be compared (as it often was) to a smallpox area in quarantine. People were not allowed to enter or leave at will in a smallpox district as in a red light district, nor did police ensure that every "affected" person move into the segregated district as they did with smallpox victims. He also attacked the argument that prostitution could never be eradicated, just as thievery was impossible to totally eliminate, as fallacious. Whenever a thief is detected, he noted, especially in the neighbourhoods of Armstrong's Point or Wellington Crescent, the police always managed to find the means to remove him.[38]

Despite the league's extensive efforts, the Police Commission persisted in its policy of segregated prostitution. The fact was that City Council, and especially Mayor Evans, refused to be put on the defensive and simply ignored the Moral and Social Reform League and their supporters. Even more important, however, the great mass of the citizens either did not want to get involved or could not find the time to do so. It is true, of course, that the reformers had a fairly wide following and their efforts to elect an anti-segregation mayor—in the person of E. D. Martin—in the 1910 civic elections may yet have proved successful. It was equally true, however, that powerful and influential groups like the Board of Trade were probably supporters of the segregation policy. At least by staying out of the controversy they implicitly implied acceptance of the status quo.

This situation was sharply changed early in November 1910 with the publication of the following sensational headline in the Toronto *Globe*:

SOCIAL EVIL RUNS RIOT IN WINNIPEG

VICE DISTRICT GROWING

EVERY DEN AN ILLICIT LIQUOR DIVE

SUMMONSES ISSUED QUARTERLY

FINES OF ONE HUNDRED DOLLARS IMPOSED

The ensuing story was based on an interview with Rev. Dr. J. G. Shearer, general secretary of the national Moral and Social Reform League and a respected Presbyterian minister known for his role in persuading Parliament to pass the Lord's Day Act in 1907. Dr. Shearer had just returned from a month's tour of western Canada, under the auspices of the International Purity Federation, reported the *Globe*:

"They have the rottenest conditions of things in Winnipeg in connection with the question of social vice to be found in any city in Canada." With the above sentence as preface, Rev. Dr. J. G. Shearer . . . launched a strong indictment against the police officials in the prairie city. He detailed circumstances which he believed to be strongly suggestive of graft. Not the least telling of his points against segregated areas for a certain class of women, was the fact that it offered a ready market for the White Slave Trade. He gave instances of this. . . . Dr. Shearer said, "Two years ago they had no vice district in Winnipeg. One year ago they had 29 houses in a restricted area. Now they have 52 houses, with probably 250 inmates. Everyone of these is a criminal under the terms of the Code of Canada, yet they are permitted to exist, and instead of the Criminal Code certain rules and regulations are established for them. Here are some of them: they must not play the piano too loudly. They must not make noise enough to attract attention on the street. They must not have white female cooks. They must not solicit from the windows and doors. All these regulations are, of course, from time to time violated. Everyone of these criminal dens is also an illicit liquor dive. . ." Speaking of the white slave traffic, Dr. Shearer said: "Some half a dozen of white slave victims have been marketed within the past year in the vice district of Winnipeg. . . ."

Another Toronto daily, the *Toronto Star*, also printed a report of an interview with Dr. Shearer prefaced with the headline, "Wicked Winnipeg Wallows in Vice."

These and other similar reports in eastern newspapers triggered a violent reaction among "respectable Winnipeggers" and particularly in City Council, the main target of the allegations. That Winnipeg should be vilified as the "rottenest City in Canada" by the eastern establishment was too much for the adolescent pride of the growing western community to bear. Perhaps even more important, public attacks such as this would certainly not help in the city's efforts to attract immigrants and industry from the east.

In the weeks following the Toronto reports, prostitution became the major issue of the upcoming mayoralty election. The *Free Press* noted that Shearer's charges were being "hotly commented upon in Winnipeg." The same paper went on to add that City Council felt that the charges were only a part of the campaign of Mr. E. D. Martin, the anti-segregation mayoralty candidate supported by the reformers. "The impression is general around the city hall that Dr. Shearer's aspersions are simply a portion of a campaign organized with the intention of boosting the chances of the anti-segregation candidate for the mayoralty chair."[39] Given this interpretation, Evans and his supporters adopted a policy of "no comment" on Shearer's charges. But within a week this "calm in the face of the storm" was shattered when the *Telegram*—owned by Evans—began running angry editorials denouncing Shearer as a "monomaniac" and a "liar and a slanderer."[40]

The anti-segregationists were quick to defend Shearer. The Presbyterian Synod published a statement calling the *Telegram*'s charges "slanderous and cowardly," and urged Winnipeg's electors to vote only for those who supported an anti-segregation policy—that is for the league's candidate, E. D. Martin.[41] The league also held several meetings in the days following the *Globe* report. At a Sunday meeting in the Winnipeg Theatre, Adjutant McElheny of the Salvation Army addressed the audience and claimed that Dr. Shearer's charges were not only true but moderate. From his work in the area he had found "216 girls in 51 houses. . . . There are some from this city; but the great majority of them have been driven out from other cities and have found a refuge down here." He noted that in two and one half hours on one night after nine o'clock, 292 men had been observed to enter fourteen houses. And this, "on the dullest night of his investigation!" McElheny concluded his speech by pointing out that the Salvation

Army provided a home (Rescue Home) for the women "to help them back to hopefulness and cleanliness, and purity and godliness." Others spoke as well, of course, but the above speech proved to be the highlight of the gathering.[42]

During the same weekend the civic election campaign moved into high gear in what, the *Free Press* observed, "promises to be one of the most severely contested campaigns ever fought in Winnipeg's municipal history." At a meeting held in North Winnipeg (Ward 5), the focus of all the candidates' remarks was the segregation issue. E. D. Martin, the reform mayoralty candidate, declared that the vice district should be abolished and the women sent back to the United States from whence the majority of them came. Controller Waugh, who along with Controller Harvey constituted Martin's opposition, claimed that this was a negative attitude. "It is useless to go to the women and say, 'Go elsewhere, go to Portage la Prairie, or go to h - - - [sic], if you like, so long as you clear out of Winnipeg!' " Another candidate up for re-election, Alderman Gower, in a rather weak attempt to exonerate himself from the inaction in Council in regard to the segregated area, said very judiciously that "it was useless to keep on speaking in the council, so he had kept his ammunition to use when the time was ripe."

At the first Council meeting following these stories of gatherings, the aldermen finally decided that some action would have to be taken to stem the growing criticism that was bound to effect their chances of re-election. Accordingly, in a long resolution prefaced with a statement of Dr. Shearer's charges, Council "memorialized the Lieutenant Governor-in-Council to appoint a Commission to investigate fully into all charges made by said J. G. Shearer and others, respecting all matters hereinbefore referred to."[43] Council also agreed to pay all the expenses of the commission including lawyers—one representing "persons or parties making the charges," one for the Police Commission and one for City Council.

That same night a raid was made by the police on some of the houses on McFarlane Street. Unfortunately for the Police Commission, the desired effect of persuading the public that the authorities were making a conscientious effort to enforce the law was not achieved. The *Free Press* reported that the police officers were met with protests by the inmates such as "But I paid my licence a little while ago." By the "licence", the *Free Press* explained, "they probably meant 'fine', having recently been summoned and convicted on the same charge."[44]

The royal commission, presided over by Justice Hugh A. Robson, Judge of the King's Bench, commenced the investigation on November 23 with almost indecent haste. Mayor Evans contended that speed was essential to produce the full facts of the case before the coming election. But as it was highly unlikely that any report could be completed in two or three weeks, it must be assumed that Evans and his associates on Council and the Police Commission thought it was to their political and personal advantage to appear to be eager to proceed with the hearings.[45]

The evidence given at the commission hearings largely corroborated the main charges of the social reformers—that a segregated district had been set up on Rachel and McFarlane streets and thus clearly violated the law. Once this fact was established, the main attention of the hearing centred on Police Chief McRae, who was singled out as the main villain of the piece. An inordinate amount of time was spent on the issue of Winnipeg's character, in particular the charge that the social reformers had done the city a great disservice by making a public issue out of so delicate a subject. Most significant of all, the royal commission virtually ignored any examination of the role of Winnipeg's elected officials in the whole prostitution question.[46]

As expected, the final report of the royal commission did not reach Council until 7 January 1911, three weeks after the mayoralty election. The report concluded that a segregation policy had been in force and that illicit liquor conditions "had been general." But Judge Robson also "definitely" concluded that Winnipeg was not the "rottenest" city in Canada. Other than these unremarkable findings, the main role the commission played in the whole prostitution issue was a diversionary one. For by focusing the attention of its investigation on the "defamatory" charges of Dr. Shearer, the commission confused the issue in the public mind so effectively that even before it made its report—that is, before civic elections of December 13—the electors were ready for some clear-cut issue to base their vote. This Mayor Evans and his supporters quickly provided.

The civic campaign had, of course, continued apace during the hearings, reaching a peak early in December when Mayor Evans announced his decision to run for a third term. The election campaign was called the most strenuous and hotly contested in the history of municipal politics. Evans emerged as a master of political strategy. His campaign was highly polished, well-organized and ruthlessly efficient. With the active and strongly partisan support of the *Telegram*, and the more passive support of the *Free Press*, the mayor succeeded in pushing the issue of segregation to the background and replacing it with the issue of Winnipeg's "good name."[47] Martin and his followers, on the other hand, operated a more plodding campaign which was rather conventional in all respects but in the issue itself. They displayed little of the political *savoir faire* of Sanford Evans.

Upon announcing his candidacy, Evans accused his opponents of conducting a campaign of "reeking publicity and cruel defamation" against the good name of the city. In another speech he reaffirmed his "sincere belief" that Winnipeg was both sound and moral. He denounced the reformers as mere agitators and continuously harped upon the topic of Winnipeg's good name.

> As citizens of our community, we should be, if possible, even more jealous of the good name of our city than of our homes. . . . It is patent that those who have the welfare of the city at heart would not advertise it abroad as the rottenest city on the continent. I stand for the best and cleanest and purest city in the world—for Winnipeg to have the reputation of such.[48]

Evans furiously attacked the reformers as "yellow pulpiteers" who "have preached defilement in its visionary state to hundreds of virgins and young men whose minds were pure before." Unquestionably the members of the Moral and Social Reform League were quite surprised to find themselves portrayed as the propagandists of illicit sex.

Evans' tactics had the desired effect of putting Martin and his supporters on the defensive. The anti-segregationists diligently presented their arguments against segregation, but this issue had been overshadowed by their need to repudiate the various charges levelled by Evans and company. In one speech, for example, Martin devoted the majority of his time to defending himself from Evans' charge that he was a candidate of foreign agitators. Of course, Martin and the reformers were not naive about Evans' strategy. It was evident that they realized the "reputation of the city" issue was a red herring. As Martin stated, ". . . . he [Evans] tries to hide himself behind the good name of the city [but] it is not the good name of the city that is on the trail at this election; [it is] the action of men who, in defiance of the law, set up conditions which inevitably reflected upon the city's good name." Martin's efforts to bring the "real issue" into sharp focus, however, were largely unsuccessful.[49]

Yet Martin's election campaign was good by usual standards. He had the vigorous support of many church groups and ministers, plus three ex-mayors, Thomas Ryan, Thomas Sharpe, and James Ashdown. There was also extensive advertising in the newspapers (often in foreign languages to attract those immigrants who could vote), personal canvassing, and distribution of campaign literature. He was reported to have issued 100,000 pamphlets.[50] It is, then, necessary to somehow account for Evans' overwhelming success in terms other than mere propaganda efforts. The most likely explanation was made by the *Free Press*, which suggested that the entire provincial Conservative party's election machinery was placed at Evans' disposal.[51] And even though this paper's motives in making the charge could partially be explained by its avowed Liberal connections, other evidence supports this view. In the first place Evans was a strong Conservative supporter, one who was often mentioned as a possible candidate for provincial office. It would not do for him to step down from the mayor's chair under the controversy that surrounded that office in 1910. An election victory, on the other hand, would save his name for future provincial campaigning.[52] Secondly, the *Telegram*, which Evans owned, had long been an unquestioning supporter of the Roblin regime and the support of the Conservative party in 1910 could be regarded as a partial payment for that support.[53] Finally, the extent of Evans' campaign in 1910 suggests outside help. He had an extensive ward organization with at least fifteen committee rooms scattered at strategic locations throughout the city. And at a large meeting for Martin in North Winnipeg, the proceedings were interrupted by the entrance and consequent commotion of forty or fifty drunken "hooligans" who appeared to be led by one well-dressed but unidentified man—a tactic that had never before been used in civic elections but was common enough in provincial contests.[54]

Evans was amply rewarded for his skillful campaign when the results were declared. He was elected by a vote of 7,364 to 5,744, winning 57 of 72 polls. Every incumbent alderman and controller who ran for office was also returned. Interestingly, in view of evidence already presented about the nature of the municipal franchise in Winnipeg in this era, Evans won Ward 5 by a majority of 475 votes. This can probably be accounted for by the fact that with the plural vote and with the large degree to which Ward 5 was a tenant-occupied area, the vote was at least partially an expression of voters' preferences from other areas of the city. But Martin was sufficiently astounded by the results that he contested the election on the grounds of illegal voting practices (one could vote in every poll where one owned property but only in every ward for a mayor). The suit, however, was eventually dropped, apparently because of a lack of funds, since Martin had to provide all the evidence on his own behalf. No royal commission, with city-paid counsel, was appointed in this case.

In the ensuing years the social vice issue was mentioned only infrequently and the brothels on Rachel and McFarlane streets continued to operate openly for a full thirty years until "the trade fell victim to amateur competition."[55]

The significance of the prostitution issue in Winnipeg in terms of the overall view of the city in this period does not lie in the demonstration it gives of the zeal of the social reform movement, or the apparent indication that Winnipeg was a "typical frontier town" in its ambivalent moral attitudes, or even in the illustration of the effect of the operation of a skillful and shrewd politician such as Mayor Sanford Evans. These are, of course, all important aspects of the issue. But far more significant is the fact that even though there was a very real conflict within the dominant social, commercial, and political elite of Winnipeg over this issue, the status quo (and in particular the overwhelming argument of economic stability) was preserved. The *Tribune* summed up the issue neatly:

It is true that [Mayor Evans] had a large following: [he] had many very respectable citizens, men of means representing prominently the money power . . .; men who were too busy to pay any attention to what they called "That nasty little question," and who deplored any discussion of it as detrimental to business interests. The respectability of these men is not called into question, [but their motives are]. And, besides these respectable citizens, and hand in hand with them, the advocates of loose law or no law, and the unclassified riff-raff and moral flotsam that fattens on the products of vice in every form. And this is the following that tolled up the Mayor's majority, and, in the words of the city solicitor, "rebuked" that large body of citizen reformers. . . . It is to be anticipated that they will feel sufficiently rebuked. Yes, viewing the majorities from the purely numerical standpoint, it was a glorious victory for the officials concerned, and for officialdom in the mass; a victory which no one will begrudge them, and no self-respecting citizen will envy them. Set out in this true light, it was an achievement to be proud of. The campaign organization of the city hall, comprising as it did, the party machines . . ., the liquor interests, and every other special interest or privilege, was a distinctively Boss organization, a spectacle to put even Tammany to the blush. . . . There is no reason [we] should fail to recognize the perfectly obvious trend of events at city hall so exemplified once more by this latest [campaign].[56]

In other words, given a choice between "prosperity" and "theories of social and moral reform" (in Mayor Evans' words), a majority of Winnipeg electors decisively opted for prosperity. Growth-producing programs such as railway and river development, hydro-power projects, and advertising came before issues of morality. And since the social reformers of 1910 could offer no economic returns and Mayor Evans could (or claimed he could), there was really no choice at all.

part six

toward urban maturity

It is as clearly a dictate of common sense to
plan a city as it is to plan any other intricate
and important structure.
City Planning Commission Report, 1913

15 / The Rise and Demise of a City Planning Movement

City planning did not become a matter of public interest in Winnipeg until 1910. Prior to that date the only concern for the physical development of the city was expressed in the setting aside of land for several parks and in a boulevarding and tree-planting program. The desirability of establishing a program of park development and tree planting had been enunciated many times in the local press prior to substantive steps being taken in 1892. It is clear, however, that these early pleas for aesthetic development were not taken seriously in an era when most of those involved in the building of the city were interested solely in quick profits. Indeed, the growth of a "park movement" in Winnipeg after 1892 was even then not so much a response to the haphazard development of the city or even its unfinished appearance, as a reaction to the prospect that all the land in the city would soon be occupied. This would have meant that when parks were eventually planned the cost of acquiring suitable sites, both as to size and location, would have been either impossible or too costly. It was largely in response to this feeling of the high cost of each year's delay that action was taken late in 1891.

Since the provincial Municipal Act, by virtue of which Winnipeg received its legal authority, did not include any mention of public parks the first step had to be taken at that level. Following a campaign of editorials and public meetings,[1] a delegation headed by Alderman Carruthers approached the provincial government with a draft proposal for a public parks act and succeeded in having the Public Parks Act for Manitoba passed in April 1892. This act provided for "the establishment and maintenance of public parks" and was based on similar bills which existed in other Canadian provinces and in the United States. It stipulated, subject to approval by a majority vote of the ratepayers, that an annual tax levy "not to exceed one-half mill on the dollar upon the assessed value of all rateable real and personal property" could be levied by City Council. It also provided for an appointed board to manage and control the parks.

Immediately following the passage of the act, "interested citizens" took steps to ensure that City Council would apply the new powers granted to it. Acting on a section in the act that stipulated that Council had to submit a bylaw to the voters upon being petitioned to do so by three hundred ratepayers, a petition with more than the required number of signatures was presented in May 1892. Council then proceeded to draw up a bylaw "providing for the adoption of the Public Parks Act by the city" and at the municipal elections in December of 1892 it was passed by a decisive majority (1,129 to 185).

With these preliminaries disposed of, a Public Parks Board was appointed in January 1893. This first parks board included such prominent Winnipeggers as ex-alderman E. L. Drewry, ex-mayor A. Macdonald, aldermen G. H. West and Thomas Gilroy, and Mayor T. W. Taylor. E. L. Drewry, in particular, took an interest in the development of the city's parks and served on the board well past 1914.[2] During his term as chairman, from 1893-1897, the board set about the task of establishing "small urban parks, ornamental squares, or breathing spaces, throughout the city."[3] During the next few years no less than eight parks were established at a cost of $74,000. Thereafter the board's efforts were concentrated on developing and maintaining the city's new properties.[4]

Even while these first parks were being established there was some discussion about developing a large suburban park "so that suitable spaces could be set aside for playgrounds, ball, tennis, cricket, etc., [and for] a pavilion."[5] Due to protracted wrangles over a suitable site and over land values, however, it was not until 1904 that Assiniboine Park on the banks of the river of the same name was established. This 282-acre site proved to be one of the most popular in the Winnipeg area. Although several other parks were established prior to 1914, Assiniboine Park remained one of the most gratifying investments the city made.

Besides this commendable development of parks, the city's Park Board also concerned itself with the "great handicap" they felt Winnipeg laboured under. It was pointed out that except for the two rivers running through the city there were "few natural advantages wherewith to court the visitor's eye." To deal with this condition a program of "boulevarding" and tree-planting along streets was undertaken in 1896 in a limited way, with work being conducted on two or three thoroughfares in the city. The program proved so popular that in 1900 full authority was granted the Parks Board by City Council to carry on an extensive program throughout the city. Under the procedure adopted the board supervised the work and then charged the city. Council, in turn, assessed the owners of the property upon which the boulevards abutted. This was the beginning of the "city of trees," so called by surprised visitors who expected no verdancy in the gateway to the prairies. Indeed, the city came to be so proud of its trees that it actually kept a running count on the number planted on streets and in 1905 boasted a total of 12,072.

In general, Winnipeg's leaders—and probably a majority of citizens as well—were completely satisfied with the city's beautification program. Comments congratulating the Parks Board for making "a garden out of a desert" were frequently heard.[6] Moreover, as the parks and boulevarding program progressed it was noted with some degree of satisfaction that besides providing aesthetic enjoyment, these developments did much to increase property values. Indeed, many property owners in the city looked on boulevarding and tree-planting as a form of landscaping for their own private benefit, rather than as a project designed to serve the city at large.

This program for beautifying the city was not accepted by all, however, for at least one editorial appeared in this period that criticized Winnipeg's approach to aesthetic development. The main criticism made was that the city "was not laying her foundation broad enough and deep." It was pointed out, for examples, that in the one-mile circle from the corner of Portage Avenue and Main Street, the only open green spaces that would not eventually be built upon were Central and Victoria Parks.[7] "These are excellent in their way but not one of them are large enough to permit of that feeling of freedom which is half the pleasure of recreation." The article then lamented that "it was too often taken for granted that valuable land in the vicinity of a busy district or in the line of an incoming railroad is of little use for park purposes. In reality the opposite is the case." The destruction, "for commercial purposes," of Upper Fort Garry in the early 1880s was cited as an example of Winnipeg's tendency "to mortgage her future to luxuriate in the present." It was further observed that a large central park would more than compensate for its cost in the enjoyment it would give to the city's citizens. Instead, Winnipeg, "brimful of business, greedy for gain, and optimistic to a fault, built, drained, paved and expanded without the imperfections of the city and its inconsistences" being given anything but "scant attention." Prophetically the article stated that the city's physical development would "be regarded as a burden . . . by the citizens of another century."[8]

The proposals made in this article were not to be acted upon prior to 1914, but the thrust of the whole argument is nevertheless significant since it indicated that a new—and to Winnipeg hitherto almost unknown—critical spirit was developing amongst some of the city's elite. And this new manifestation of critical self-examination blossomed forth in 1910 in the form of a city planning movement.

There are many factors that have to be considered in explaining the sudden popularity of city planning in Winnipeg around 1910. On the one hand, the movement can be viewed as an outgrowth of the broad spirit of reform that was sweeping North America during this period. Just as this reformist impulse affected Winnipeg's attitudes towards civic government and social vice, it was also an important element in the new attitudes that appeared concerning the physical development of the city. In the United States the City Planning Movement had grown steadily and surely since the Chicago Exposition of 1893, reaching a high point with the calling of the first conference on City Planning at Washington in 1909.[9] This civic awakening in the United States reached Winnipeg by means of magazines, newspaper accounts and, of course, by the personal experiences of the Winnipeg residents who travelled in the States during this period and who often attended various municipal conferences. By 1911, for example, the Winnipeg Development and Industrial Bureau was both a member of the American Civic Association and a subscriber to the *American City Magazine*. Thus most of the originators of Winnipeg's City Planning Movement had been exposed in one way or the other to the various manifestations of the American movement.

Besides the American example, Winnipeggers could draw on European inspiration. Following the example of Germany, the desire for the "orderly planning" of cities had swept Europe after the turn of the century and when it reached England in the form of the Garden City Movement, repercussions were sure to be felt in Winnipeg.[10] Indeed, the founder of the Winnipeg movement, William Pearson, was born in England and had kept close connections there ever since emigrating to Canada. He often referred to the progress being made in England and urged Winnipeggers to follow that country's example.[11] British influences were also felt in other, more direct ways. The WDIB subscribed to the *Architectural Review* of London, England, the *Garden City Magazine*, and sponsored talks on such things as "The Model Towns of England." In short, outside influences—whether American or European—were strong factors in prompting some form of a city planning movement in Winnipeg and the founders of the local movement readily admitted this fact.[12]

The foreign inspiration of Winnipeg's planning movement is further confirmed when it is noted that similar city planning movements sprang up all across Canada around 1910. Almost every large Canadian city was affected by a new spirit of "great civic pride and responsibility" and quickly took steps to become involved in the "noble ideal of city planning."[13] In fact, the stereotyped and simultaneous response to the idea of city planning all across the country was so widespread (and also so short-lived) that one suspects that the concept of planning was often accepted simply because it was a new and exciting idea, rather than as a sincere response to local conditions. Involvement in "planning the city beautiful" was suddenly the acceptable thing to do. In Winnipeg, for example, the list of names and associations who so readily "sent in their names as being ready to assist and do all in their power to further the work" of civic planning reads like a social register of the city.[14]

This critical view of the whole movement was later confirmed when the city plans drawn up in response to the movement disintegrated when it was found that recommended developments threatened the interests of individual members. Indeed, this assessment of the whole planning phenomenon was recognized, in Winnipeg's case at least, even before that city's plan had been drawn up. Stating that many Winnipeggers were "humbugging" themselves, the superficiality of the city's commitment to planning was pointed out in the following statement early in 1911:

> Enthusiastic citizens orate on town planning, and the possibilities of a City Beautiful, our real estate exchanges resolves in a most resolute fashion and, but, or notwithstanding the people who do things permit a railway to come into the city with level crossings in its most congested and populous quarters. Why? Because of a hoped-for, a sectional commercial advantage. And that reason is paramount. Its consequences may involve desperate inconvenience . . . but when the dollar is against the city Beautiful the dollar wins.[15]

But to suggest in an unqualified and simplistic manner that the city's elite joined the planning movement only because they wanted their city—and themselves—to be part of a widespread movement would be a distortion. For if they were quickly repelled by the costly mechanics that were later found to be a part of "planning the City Beautiful," there is little doubt that in the early stages they were sincerely attracted to the idea of efficient and orderly planning. Indeed, given the following arguments that were advanced as a reason for supporting the movement, the growth-conscious leaders of Winnipeg could hardly be expected not to have been interested:

> City planning along the lines of improving the present layout of a city would seem to some to incur an expenditure which is not warranted by the improved beauty of the streets. More beauty, they say, is not worth spending so much money upon. Nevertheless, if one looks further than the immediate results of civic improvements, one can see how the material prosperity of the community would be increased.
>
> City planning, in its narrowest form, means the improvement of city streets and beautifying of the city all round. This attracts residents, who create a demand for the products of industry, and therefore create industry, and these residents in many cases bring industries with them. Another phase of the city planning question is the improving of health conditions by the providing of boulevards, parks, and other breathing spaces. These, in turn, attract strangers to the city and accordingly the city prospers.[16]

In short, while the concept of city planning only attracted the attention of Winnipeg's elite because of developments outside the city, they were quick to find in it many aspects that appealed to them.

This analysis of the popularity of the City Planning Movement in Winnipeg does not preclude the fact that there were those in the city who were genuinely interested in planning for reasons other than ones motivated by concern for economic growth. By 1910 the city health officer and his staff had realized as a result of their experiences in the North End that something needed to be done to prevent the great waste of human life that was daily occurring because of a lack of planning. Of similar opinion were such individuals as Dr. Simpson of the provincial Board of Health and, of course, J. S. Woodsworth and Margaret Scott. Organized labour, too, had for many years been calling for "sane community sense" to be exercised in the physical development of Winnipeg. Also important in this core group was F. J. Cole, whose commitment to city planning stemmed from professional interest. Finally, several professors from the University of Manitoba became involved in the planning commission and their expertise was an important element in the production of the Planning Report. This group was made up of Professors Feather-Stonhaugh, Broderick, and Brydone-Jack.[17] In the final analysis, it was these individuals and groups who succeeded in preventing the movement from becoming just another means of encouraging economic growth in the city.

The actual initiation of the planning movement in Winnipeg is reported to have taken place at a banquet held at St. Luke's Church in Fort Rouge, sometime in late 1910. Following an address by W. Pearson on "Good Citizenship," a committee to deal with the matter of town planning was formed on the spot, consisting of Pearson as chairman and six other members.[18] After one or two meetings this committee decided to cooperate with a town planning committee of the Industrial Bureau which that body had also recently appointed. Together, the two committees started a reference library of current periodicals which dealt with city planning and also sponsored a series of talks on various aspects of city planning and beautification. But the most important result to come out of the cooperative efforts of these two committees was their successful attempt to interest City Council in the formation of a City Planning Commission.

Winnipeg's City Planning Commission was established by bylaw on June 5, 1911. The commission was not given power to prepare a plan but was instructed to make a report to the City Council. While its terms of reference were quite broad, namely "to consider and report to the City Council upon a city planning scheme," the commission approached their task in a specific, businesslike manner. Six committees were appointed to study and report on the following subjects: social survey—"general social and health conditions"; housing; traffic and transport: river frontage and dockage; aesthetic development; and physical plan. The latter was to incorporate the recommendations of the first five committees, "having in view the eventual production of such a physical map of the city as would be demanded by an expert called in to prepare a comprehensive plan for Greater Winnipeg."[19]

The formal membership of the commission was made up of the mayor, Sanford Evans, as chairman, six aldermen, the Municipal Commissioner of the Province of Manitoba, and one representative each from the Architects' Association, Builders' Association, Real Estate Exchange, Trades and Labor Council, Board of Trade, Industrial Bureau, University of Manitoba, Provincial Board of Health, Winnipeg Parks Board, and the Winnipeg Electric Railway Company. It was from this basic group that the chairmen for the six committees were selected but, significantly, the chairmen were authorized to invite citizens to act upon their committees. Generally they were very successful in persuading experienced professionals to serve and it was this fact which gave the commission's report its impressive character.[20] A further demonstration of the breadth of outlook of this initial commission was that it realized the metropolitan nature of its task and therefore invited and accepted as honorary members representatives from the adjacent municipalities of St. Vital, St. Boniface, Kildonan, Springfield, and Rosser.

Commission members were aware from the outset that although the "vital importance of improved housing and city planning schemes is today everywhere acknowledged," it was still difficult to obtain definite guidance as to the best methods to be followed. They pointed out that their instructions were broad and indefinite and that Manitoba did not yet have any general framework of legislation, "such as exists in England . . . and in the Provinces of Ontario, New Brunswick, and Nova Scotia," which could create powers and indicate general and constitutional methods of procedure. Accordingly the commission "relied upon its own judgement as to the methods and plan of action which best suited its own resources and special conditions existing in [Winnipeg]." Quite reasonably it was decided that the first step should be to investigate actual conditions in the city and collect the many and varied facts which could then "form the basis for a plan that will correct existing defects and properly provide for future development." It was also recognized that it would be necessary to submit the final drafting of a plan to experts of world-wide experience.

At its organizational meeting in October 1911 the City Planning Commission set forth the general principles they felt should be followed in their work:

The ideal city must be so laid out as to assure for all the citizens proper light and air, recreation spaces and sanitary facilities, and must in addition have such restrictive regulations and such equipment for inspection as will tend to secure to all the citizens the maximum of good health. The ideal City must be as convenient as it is possible to make it, and this will involve the proper width and direction of main highways and subsidiary streets, . . . etc. and these questions must be studied with a view to the present and probable future movements of the people between their work and their homes and the places of recreation, and would involve ultimately the planning of zones which would bring about an economic distribution of places of work and places of residence. In respect to all changes the aesthetic consideration must be kept in view, for all elements of beauty in architecture, in the arrangement of streets, bridges, boulevards and parks, in the proper treatment of focal points and the creation of attractive vistas, as well as in the detail of street lamps and of everything else allowed upon the streets is a most important factor, in educating the taste and stimulating the pride of citizens and in attracting the better classes of those who travel and of those who seek homes.[21]

In short, the main objects to be served by a city planning scheme were to be health, convenience, and beauty.

In spite of the statement of these worthwhile and energetic aims it was apparent from the outset that there was a division within the commission. On the one hand there was a distinct group—most notably represented by Dr. Simpson, Dr. Douglas, the Trades and Labor Council, William Pearson, and Professor E. Brydone-Jack—who were completely sincere in their support of city planning. On the other hand, the City Council members, and probably the bulk of the other membership, looked on the planning commission's work as a distinctly business proposition, as just another means to boost Winnipeg's image outside the city's borders.[22] This analysis is confirmed by a number of developments that took place following the formation of the City Planning Commission in June 1911. In the first place, the commission was refused an adequate appropriation of funds to carry out its work. Asked to make an estimate of required costs, the commission had requested $15,000, but the total amount made available to them by City Council was only $7,119. And out of this sum a full-time secretary (F. J. Cole) had to be paid.

It must be remembered that of the eighteen official members of the planning commission seven were members of the civic government. Three of these representatives—Mayor Evans and controllers Harvey and Waugh—had the power as members of the Board of Control to recommend expenditures to Council; but despite their position of power they refused to grant the $15,000. Moreover, the four aldermen on the commission were all committee chairmen who probably wielded a good deal of influence on Council, but they, too, did not choose to take up the commission's case. What these actions indicate is that despite their public position of support for the concept of city planning, the city's representatives were in fact not sincerely committed to the very commission they had appointed and on which they served.

As a consequence of the parsimony of City Council, the commission reported that it had been impossible for them to carry out the full plan it had formed and problems such as river frontage and dockage and the provision for future railway facilities had to be ignored. Also, the Aesthetic Development Committee's work, "needing the expenditure of money on data and photographs for the guidance of the Commission as to precedents, etc., was considerably hampered."[23]

Council's parsimony also extended to another area which some commission members felt was essential to the success of their work. Since the commission was so short of funds it annually made a request to City Council to send two or three of its number to attend the annual International Conference on City Planning which had been inaugurated in 1910. In view of the commission's stated concern over their lack of guidance and inexperience in the whole field of city planning these conferences were looked on as excellent opportunities to learn what was being done in other cities. But despite their explanations the commission's requests were turned down by City Council.

Council's refusal to adequately support the commission was certainly not a result of a lack of available funds. This is made clear by their sponsoring of the "First Canadian Conference on Town Planning" held in Winnipeg in July 1912. No exact figures on the cost of this three-day gathering are available but the Industrial Bureau did hold a banquet on the final day of the conference and since that body received the bulk of its funds from Council, there is little doubt that the Winnipeg business community was more interested in publicity than in the actual workings of their own planning commission. The bureau ensured that the conference received wide publicity and held it up as an example of Winnipeg's progressive spirit. But despite the presentation of many highly professional papers at the gathering and the passage of resolutions urging action on the part of municipal authorities, Winnipeg City Council continued to give their own planning commission much less than total support.[24]

Further evidence of the civic authorities' lack of genuine interest in the commission's work is their poor attendance at that body's meetings. The secretary of the commission, F. J. Cole, reported in late 1912 that of the seven city government members who were on the commission, "two have never attended a single meeting and the rest have only attended one." Cole also pointed out that with the exception of the session of the planning conference at which the Governor General spoke, no Council members attended any of the meetings.[25] Finally, the city of Winnipeg was not represented at the first convention of Western Canada building inspectors held in Calgary in the fall of 1912. This gathering's aim was to deal with building bylaws and problems of enforcement, both of which were current issues in the city. Yet despite the timeliness of such a conference, Council refused funds for a delegation.[26]

Despite Council's lack of support—and in one instance interference[27]—the commission succeeded in producing the most concise, objective and far-reaching document to come out of Winnipeg in the first forty years of its history. There were, of course, some indications of the lack of financial support present in the commission's findings. Maps, diagrams, charts, and tables which the commission had hoped to include were omitted, and the report itself was presented in what could only be described as "rough" form. Notwithstanding these omissions, the report was an impressive document consisting of a committee-by-committee account of their work and findings, a summary by the chairman, and a series of recommendations for future action.

The findings and recommendations dealing with public health were the most damning and progressive in the report. The social survey and housing committees found that there was overcrowding in many quarters, much poor construction leading to discomfort and insanitary conditions, and that many rows of houses were so arranged on narrow (usually twenty-five or thirty-three-foot) lots as to prevent the "proper access of light and air to certain rooms."[28] What was most alarming about these conditions was that there was little reason for them. For, as the committees observed, they were largely a result of inadequate and non-enforced building and health bylaws, coupled with under-manned and financially starved building inspectors and health departments. It was recommended that Winnipeg consider the development of "model suburbs for workmen" and, to overcome the lack of sufficient accommodation for seasonal workers, the erection of "suitable lodging houses." Significantly, the committee did not shy away from stating that if these projects could not be developed by private capital "the city should in its own interest erect them." It was also emphasized that "the most immediate results for bettering some of the conditions" indicated in their report could be obtained by City Council and the Board of Control "assuming a more sympathetic attitude towards the Health Department, and at once making a much larger appropriation for materially increasing the staffs of both the Health Department and the Building Inspector's Department."

The housing committee took notice of the fact that the city's lack of zoning had lead to the encroachment of business structures into residential areas and this had been followed by increasing land prices and the tendency of buildings that were once private residences and "good class" apartment blocks to degenerate into crowded, low-class tenements. In addition, the high and uneven infant mortality rates clearly showed that the city's child welfare program had to be dramatically stepped up. Finally, it was pointed out that the city's park program was inadequate and it was recommended that since the most marked deficiency was in the central district, more playgrounds or "neighbourhood centres" should be quickly established.

As far as convenience was concerned, the report wasted little time in dealing with the city's obvious lack of planning in regard to roads, street railways, and railroads and instead recommended that a comprehensive plan be drawn up and thereafter strictly adhered to.[29] It would have to include, they noted, provision for the entrance of new railroads, the proper placement of new street railway tracks, and the prohibition of the erection of office buildings too high for the width of the streets on which they were situated. In short, the commission did not set out any magical solution to the complex problems of city transportation but it did lay down general guidelines and stressed the need for long-term planning. It was careful to point out that the civic authorities' enthusiasm for attracting industry and railroads should not, as it so often had in the past, result in the making of exceptions to guidelines that were established for the long-term benefit of the city.

In respect to aesthetic development the commission observed that the city had thus far neglected its rivers and that action had to be taken immediately so that the great natural opportunity of adding to the city's beauty would not be lost forever. Here, as elsewhere, the commission stressed the need for long-term planning.

In short, the commission concluded, there were "unquestionably . . . serious defects in the present conditions and many dangerous tendencies which must be corrected to provide properly for the development of the city." Before dealing with recommendations for future action, the commission pointed out the great logic of city planning:

It is as clearly a dictate of common sense to plan a city as it is to plan any other intricate and important structure rather than trust to the partial and divergent views of individual workmen; . . . it is a saving of money to work to the comprehensive plan, for it does not mean that the complete conception shall be put under contract at once or that more should be done at any one time than the community can well afford, but it does mean that every bit of work carried out is done in the right place and in the right way, so that it need not be undone in the future and loss through waste is largely eliminated, even if no account be taken of the greater value in public convenience created by the expenditure; . . . in other respects it is also the highest economy, for in addition to producing the maximum of convenience with its saving of time and effort it will conserve and promote the health of the citizens and will enlarge and elevate the spirit of the common life.

Turning to the course of action that they felt the civic authorities should pursue in the future, the commission took pains to note that their job was far from complete. They suggested that their work be continued by appointing a new commission with powers that, as a result of their report, could be readily defined. However, "in view of the great amount of detailed labour involved and the need for expert advice," it was urged that the new body be composed of expert town planners who would be engaged to draw up a comprehensive city plan. With this completed the municipal authority should be approached with the view to the passage of a Housing and Town Planning Act which would give official sanction to the plan drawn up by the local authorities. Finally, it was suggested that City Council encourage, by its approval and by the active participation of Council members, the formation of a strong voluntary organization "which could lend support at all stages and assist in educating public opinion. It is believed to be important that the planning and the gradual realization of the ideal city should enlist the active interest of the citizens, manifested through an organization formed for that purpose."[30]

Reaction to the commission's report varied from high praise by the Trades and Labor Council and the *Free Press* to an attitude of complete indifference on the part of City Council. Both of the former commented on the commission's great achievement in the face of less than satisfactory support and urged that Council make "adequate provision for the fulfillment of the task that has been begun."[31] But Council's attitude was clear when the report was simply tabled with a minimum of discussion and with no provision for its printing and distribution. Indeed, the only recommendation that was acted on was the increase in the staff of the health department. Moreover, in at least one other instance, the commission's recommendations were more than ignored when the city allowed the T. Eaton Company "not only to erect buildings nearly twice as high as provided for in its own by-law but bridge Graham Avenue."

Faced with this official indifference a group of citizens led by such men as William Pearson formed the Winnipeg Housing and Town Planning Association in March 1913.[32] This voluntary organization had as its objective the urging of the carrying out of the commission's recommendations, public education, the promotion of governmental housing and town planning legislation, and the improvement of local housing by encouraging progressive building bylaws and by promotion of a model housing project. For the first year of its existence little success beyond the cultivation of a few vacant lots was achieved, but in 1914 and 1915 two more significant successes were registered. Following a great deal of lobbying the association succeeded in having Council appoint a Greater Winnipeg Planning Commission whose duty it was to prepare a comprehensive street plan of the city.[33] And although the six members of this new body were to serve without salary, Council did grant a sum of $5,000 for operating expenses. Also in 1915, largely through the efforts of the Planning Association, the provincial legislature passed a Town Planning Act for the Province of Manitoba. This enabled any municipality or combination of municipalities to bring any plan they wished to have adopted under the protection of provincial law.

Aside from these developments the great aims of constructive city planning that had been raised in 1910 produced no concrete results in Winnipeg and subsequently, until the later years of the Second World War, planning activities lay dormant.[34]

Council's actions in respect to the Planning Commission and city planning in general were—as were so many other of that body's activities— a result of its overriding commitment to growth. Through 1911 and part of 1912 the setting up and support of a city planning commission and even the hosting of a planning conference had been considered useful moves, actions that could be pointed to as examples of the city's coming of age. But with the first intimation in 1912 that many of the commission's findings showed that Winnipeg was far from a progressive city it was decided to strangle their activities by cutting off funds. The fact was that while Council was "daily publishing to the world the great totals of building permits" many commissioners were criticizing nearly every aspect of the city's building boom and, even more importantly, placing the responsibility for the city's growing problems (particularly in the field of housing) squarely on the shoulders of City Council. In short, the charge laid by the *Voice* that the Planning Commission "was too little in sympathy with the real estate interests that are overwhelmingly represented on the Council" was not far from the truth.[35] To a body as concerned with economic growth as was Council, the type of publicity being presented by the commission was less than satisfactory and Council thus refused to accede to that body's repeated requests for financial support.

Yet as easy as it may be to dismiss the City Planning Movement in Winnipeg as an exercise in non-productive enthusiasm on the part of a few, it must be said that the whole experience does indicate that at least some of the city's elite were willing and able to approach the fundamental problems of their own time. Indeed, the great attractiveness of the City Planning Commission's report lies in the fact that it enunciated, both explicitly and implicitly, a set of basic premises that were felt to be of great importance for urban society. It was noted that the community had to be built for social and personal well-being as well as for economic-technological-physical growth and that the city's organization (or reorganization) in these terms could be partially guided, unified, and enhanced by comprehensive planning. It was also recognized that such planning required the collaboration of experts and citizens and that it could be achieved by no magical wand waving but rather by a slow and gradual process whose success depended largely upon education. The fact that the discovery and elaboration of these ideas was not accompanied by their implementation (and that even their discovery was confined to only a few) should not deter one from an appreciation of their significance. They were important because of the prospect they offered for the growth of such ideas as a departure from laissez-faire attitudes of the past, rather than in any dramatically evident humanization of the city of Winnipeg.

conclusion

the end of an era

The Winnipeggers of the old era lived on terms of intimacy which grew out of the pioneer spirit. They seldom passed one another in the street without pausing for more than a greeting. The older inhabitants of the Winnipeg of today remember easily the time when they were acquainted with every person of respectable appearance in the town. That was when Winnipeg, though it had outgrown its early youth, was still a small place, before the great inflow of settlers began to spread over Western Canada in the closing years of the century, before the city had begun to grow with extraordinary rapidity, before . . . the old conditions of life changed and passed away.
W. J. Healy, *Winnipeg's Early Days*

Conclusion / The End of an Era

The collapse of the real estate market in 1913 and the outbreak of war in 1914 both had a profound impact on Winnipeg. After a long period of persistent and prodigious growth, immigration halted, land sales subsided, and commercial activity contracted.[1] The "continuous joy-ride" was over as Winnipeg entered a new era; one in which the city was to face the major consequences of the boom, the unresolved questions of race and class relationships, and the agony of a great war. Yet these disruptive events did not diminish Winnipeg's prior material progress; in terms of population and productivity it stood well in the forefront of Canadian cities in 1914. Nor did they obscure Winnipeg's unique character. With regard to landscape, economic base, society, and government, it was the culmination of the aspirations of the dominant commercial elite.

1914 can be viewed as an important terminal point in the city's history. Compared to the struggling, pre-railway city of 1881, or the compact and ethnically homogeneous city of 1896, Winnipeg in 1914 was an established, sprawling, and heterogeneous metropolis. Behind lay forty years of existence as an incorporated city, time enough to provide the perspective necessary to determine how effectively the commercial elite had reconciled their ambitions for a great city with the more important dimension of effective community life for the great majority of citizens.

The commercial elite's desire to make Winnipeg the West's metropolis was more than met by 1914. Winnipeg was—and had been for some time—Canada's third largest city. In terms of industrial output Winnipeg stood in fourth place, surpassed only by Montreal, Toronto, and Hamilton. Winnipeg accounted for one-half of the prairie provinces' manufacturing output in 1911, and was firmly established as that region's banking, jobbing, and shipping headquarters. In short, Winnipeg had all the ingredients necessary to make it the undisputed metropolis of Western Canada. The city had access to a rich hinterland and had developed within its boundaries the services necessary for control over a region. These included such resources as financial institutions, manufacturing establishments, large, diversified wholesale houses, transportation facilities, administrative agencies, and even specialized services such as firms of architects and consulting engineers. But the most spectacular, and to the city's businessmen the most satisfying, element in the growth of this period was the surpassing of Minneapolis, Chicago, and other famous American cities, and the crowning of Winnipeg as the greatest grain centre on the North American continent. This occurred in 1909 when Winnipeg handled 88 million bushels of wheat compared to 81 million for Minneapolis, 61 million for Buffalo, 56 million for Duluth, 30 million for Montreal, 26 million for Chicago, and 23 million for New York.

The story such statistics told Winnipeg's businessmen was perhaps best summed up by the *Canadian Annual Review* of 1912:

> Of the future of Winnipeg little need be added to a narrative which indicates the certainty of greatness. Geographically it is the heart of the continent and of Canada; it is the gateway of a West which must grow to splendid proportions in production, population, and wealth; it is the capital of a Province where public prosperity and individual opportunity are manifest. As the Canadian West and North unfold their almost limitless wealth in lands and forests and mines and fisheries; as their railway facilities increase to meet the new and greater output of rich commodities; as the demands of life and trade weave an ever-growing fabric of production over an ever-widening area of settlement; so the importance must grow and the fundamental resources of Winnipeg expand.[2]

What is particularly noteworthy about this economic success story is the role played by Winnipeg's commercial elite in bringing it about. For among the many factors involved in Winnipeg's rise to metropolitan status was the indispensable confidence of the commercial elite that their city was destined to become one of the great cities of North America—the "Bull's Eye of the Dominion" and the "Chicago of the North." The hard-headed businessmen who directed Winnipeg's growth in this period constantly and confidently used every tool at hand to ensure the city's dominance. The powerful Winnipeg Board of Trade constantly sought assistance from the federal and provincial governments while City Council, itself dominated by the elite, used public funds to promote the growth the businessmen desired.

This high degree of boosterism among the city's businessmen was primarily a result of the fact that the commercial elite considered Winnipeg a permanent home. The city's advancement thus implied enlargement of their own business and profits. In the postwar period, this condition was no longer so clearly evident as branch offices became more and more dominant in Winnipeg's economy. The aggressive individuals employed in these firms had no permanent roots in Winnipeg since they were almost certain to be transferred in due course to eastern Canada. In contrast to the prewar city which had a large number of commanding businessmen who individually had built up major business organizations and collectively had made the Winnipeg Board of Trade a power to be reckoned with in western and national affairs, postwar Winnipeg had few outstanding entrepreneurial figures. As a result, the years after 1914 saw a diminution of Winnipeg's commanding position. The city's days of rapid growth and ever-increasing importance were over.[3]

The great success of the commercial elite's economic programs in the period 1874–1914 must be balanced by Winnipeg's obvious shortcomings. Politically, the city was governed by a select group of successful businessmen who, by means of a restricted franchise, plural vote, and centralized form of government, excluded Winnipeg's labour and ethnic groups from political office, thereby ensuring that only their conception of desirable public policy would prevail. The city's failure was also physical. The inattention of Winnipeg's builders and civic officials to the fragmentation of the city's community life had far-reaching results. Although a few of the city's leaders were impressed with plans for a more efficient, orderly, and attractive community, the great majority of the commercial elite were too devoted to development to accept restrictions on private enterprise. As a result, Winnipeg's environment developed into distinctive and mutually exclusive neighbourhoods, marked by unequal social services and amenities; these conditions were clearly unfavourable to the development of meaningful community life. It is true each district had its own church groups, clubs, and specialized societies of all kinds, but the city lacked any effective agency that could deal with the problems of the metropolis as a whole. Even the municipal corporation, dominated as it was by a small, growth-conscious business elite, could not conceive of the urban environment as belonging to and affecting all citizens.

In the final analysis it was the overriding commitment to growth that provides the most profound reason for Winnipeg's failure to develop an all-encompassing community life in the first forty years of its history. With economic growth the unquestioned priority, few public resources were left over to guarantee for all in the city a satisfactory standard of living. In 1914 the poor of Winnipeg lacked steady, well-paid work, adequate housing, and decent medical care. They were segregated into one-third of the city, ill-protected from crime, their children without good schools or adequate recreation. The vast majority of Winnipeggers, the working and middle class, lived in adequate but ugly shelters and were over-regimented by the conditions of work and the constraints of their urban environment. Despite the protection of unions for some and affluence for others, the mass of Winnipeggers lacked any effective means to humanize their lives. The city's notoriously high death rate—and especially its infant mortality rate—and the rising tide of strikes in the years after 1900 revealed most clearly that an exclusive commitment to "bigger and better" was not the way to build a vibrant community.

Yet in the longer perspective, it is clear, the possibility of co-existence between Anglo-Saxon and foreigner, management and labour, rich and poor, never vanished entirely. There were always a precious few in every group who recognized the community of interests which transcended the particular divisions in Winnipeg's population. If they were not much heeded in Winnipeg's first forty years, they nevertheless carried forward into subsequent decades constructive ideals, the roots of which extended back to an older Winnipeg that included such public-spirited organizations as All Peoples' Mission, the Margaret Scott Nursing Mission, and the Town Planning Association.

appendixes

Appendix A/*Elected Officials, City of Winnipeg, 1874-1914*

Mayors of the City of Winnipeg, 1874-1914

Andrews, Alfred J. 1898-99	Logan, Alexander 1879-80, 1882, 1884
Arbuthnot, John 1901-3	McCreary, William F. 1897
Ashdown, James H. 1907-8	McMicken, Alexander 1883
Conklin, Elias G. 1881	Macdonald, Alexander 1892
Cornish, Francis E. 1874	Pearson, Alfred 1890-91
Deacon, Thomas R. 1913-14	Ryan, Thomas 1889
Evans, William S. 1909-11	Scott, Thomas 1877-78
Gilroy, Thomas 1895	Sharpe, Thomas 1904-6
Hamilton, Charles E. 1885	Taylor, Thomas W. 1893-94
Jameson, Richard W. 1896	Waugh, Richard D. 1912
Jones, Lyman M. 1887-88	Wesbrook, Henry S. 1886
Kennedy, William N. 1875-76	Wilson, Horace 1900

Aldermen of the City of Winnipeg, 1874-1914

Adams, F. W. 1908-11	Ashdown, James H. 1874, 1879
Alloway, William F. 1876-77, 1879-80	Baker, George W. 1888, 1897-98
Andrews, A. J. 1894-97	Bannerman, A. J. 1895-96
Andrews, G. A. F. 1890-91	Banning, W. W. 1876
Arbuthnot, John 1897-98	Barclay, R. 1900-1903
Archibald, Heber 1885	Bathgate, William 1882

Bawlf, Nicholas
1883-84

Bell, H. T.
1889

Bell, W. G.
1897-98, 1900

Black, Alexander
1887-90, 1896

Blanchard, Sedley
1879

Bole, D. W.
1893-94

Bond, A. L.
1912-14

Bredin, John
1876

Brown, Alexander
1877-79

Brown, George
1884

Brydon, William
1883

Burridge, James
1883

Burrows, Alfred W.
1877

Calder, A.
1892-93

Callaway, Joshua
1884, 1886-91

Cameron, John R.
1875, 1882-83

Campbell, Chris.
1900-1907

Campbell, C. H.
1889

Campbell, George H.
1885-86

Carruthers, George F.
1885, 1892-94, 1900-1901

Cass, E.
1909-11

Chaffey, B. E.
1894-97, 1901-2

Clark, Willoughby
1875

Cockburn, J. W.
1891-92, 1901-6

Conklin, Elias G.
1877-80

Cornish, Francis E.
1876, 1878

Cowan, Thomas
1899

Cox, F. J. C.
1904-9

Craig, George
1895-96

Crotty, Henry S.
1885

Crowe, George R.
1885, 1912-14

Currie, Hugh
1889

Davidson, A. T.
1906-7

Davidson, F. H.
1912-14

Davis, Matthew
1875

Dawson, A.
1892-94

Doidge, Edwin
1881

Douglas, W. G.
1908-11

Drewry, Edward L.
1883-84

Dyson, D. J.
1897, 1900

Eden, Arthur F.
1879

Eggertson, Arni
1907-8

Finkelstein, Moses
1905-6

Fletcher, Joseph
1888-90

Fonseca, William G.
1874-78, 1880

Fowler, F. O.
1908-1914

Fortune, Mark
1879-81, 1883

Frederickson, A.
1892

Fry, Henry
1898-1901, 1904-5

Gibson, J. G.
1903-8

Gilroy, Thomas
1891-94

Gowler, J. R.
1907-1912

Gray, H.
1911-14

Grundy, William
1887-89

Hackett, John
1875

Ham, George H.
1883-84, 1887

Hargrave, John G.
1889

Harkness, Peter
1886

Harvey, J. G.
1883, 1899-1906

Henderson, J. B.
1893-94

Hespeler, William
1876, 1878

Higgins, John
1874

Hislop, Charles
1896-97

Horne, J. W.
1898-1901, 1904-5

Hutchings, Elisha F.
1887-88, 1894-95

Jackson, Samuel J.
1877-78, 1880

Jameson, Richard W.
1892-95

Jarvis, Edward W.
1876

Jones, Lyman M.
1886

Kennedy, C. W. N.
1894-99

Latimer, J. G.
1901-6

LeCappellaine, John O.
1881

Lewis, L. M.
1889

Logan, Alexander
1874-78

Long, W. J.
1913-14

Lustead, Thomas
1875-76

Lyon, William H.
1878

McArthur, Alexander
1879-80

McArthur, Archibald A.
1906-7

McBain, D. G.
1883

McCalman, Peter
1906-7

McCarthy, J. H.
1902-3

McCharles, Alexander
1904-5

McCreary, William F.
1884, 1895-96

McCrossin, Thomas
1883

Macdonald, Alexander
1887-88

McDonald, Duncan
1886-89

Macdonald, K. N. L.
1884

Macdonald, R. C.
1909-14

McDonald, Stuart
1884-85

McDougall, Horace
1878, 1891

Mackenzie Kenneth
1889-90

McLean, D.
1907-10

McLenaghan, James
1874-75

McLennan, A.
1913-14

McMeans, L.
1909-10

McMicken, Alexander
1875, 1881-82, 1890-91

McMicken, H. G.
1876-77

McMillan, W. W.
1881-82

McNabb, James M. M.
1882

McNee, Archibald
1877, 1886

McVicar, George D.
1883

Manning, R. A. C.
1907-8

Martin, E. D.
1898-99

Mather, John B.
1890-91

Mathers, T. G.
1898-99

Midwinter, Charles
1908-12

Miller, M. H.
1887

Milton, W. R.
1909-14

Mitchell, J. F.
1897-99

Monkman, Albert
1881-82

Montgomery, C. C.
1878, 1880-83

Moore, E. D.
1886

More, John B.
1874, 1877-81

Muir, R.
1892

Mulvey, Robert
1874

Mulvey, Stewart
1883-88

Munroe, J. G.
1911-14

Nares, L. A.
1893

Newton, William
1906-7

Nicholson, J. S.
1892

Nixon, Thomas
1883

Owens, William J.
1882-83

Pearson, Alfred
1885-86

Pearson, John H.
1880

Penrose, James
1886

Phillips, T. G.
1885

Polson, Alexander
1887-88

Polson, Samuel
1884

Potter, J. A.
1908-12

Pulford, A. H.
1906-7

Rice, James
1877

Richards, A. E.
1894-96

Richie, D. A.
1902-3

Rigg, R. A.
1914

Riley, Robert J.
1887-88, 1908-9

Roblin, Finlay P.
1876

Ross, D. A.
1889-93, 1899-1900

Ross, I. M.
1895-96

Russell, John
1901-4

Ryan, Thomas
1885-88

Sandison, H.
1905-6

Scott, Thomas
1874

Sharpe, Thomas
1900-3

Shore, R. J.
1910-14

Sinclair, Dugald
1875, 1877

Skaletar, A.
1913-14

Smith, Daniel
1890-91

Speirs, J. T.
1899-1900

Spencer, George B.
1885

Sproule, J. C.
1893-96

Stefanik, T.
1912-13

Strang, Andrew
1874, 1881

Strang, Robert
1878-81

Stuart, James
1897

Sutherland, Donald
1882-83

Swimford, Herbert
1874

Taylor, T. W.
1890-91

Thibadeau, W. B.
1874

Villiers, John
1875

Walker, S.
1891

Wallace, J. J.
1910-14

Wells, John L.
1902-3

West, G. H.
1892-93

Willoughby, J.
1908-11

Wilson, C. H.
1897-98

Wilson, George M.
1881-84

Wilson, Horace
1895-99

Wilson, John T.
1890-91

Wilson, R. A.
1883

Wilson, Thomas
1907-8

Wishart, Charles
1884

Wolf, Joseph
1890

Wood, D. D.
1901-4

Woods, Alexander
1886

Wright, Archibald
1874-76, 1879-80

Wright, J. A.
1882

Wyatt, R.
1892-93

Wynne, J. R.
1904-7

Young, David
1879

Young, George H.
1885

Controllers of the City of Winnipeg, 1907-1914

Baker, J. W.
1907-8

Cockburn, J. W.
1907, 1909-14

Douglas, W. G.
1912-13

Evans, W. S.
1908

Garson, William
1907

Harvey, J. G.
1907-12

Latimer, J. G.
1908

McArthur, A. A.
1909-12

McArthur, F. J. G.
1914

McLean, D.
1913-14

Midwinter, Charles
1913-14

Waugh, R. D.
1909-11

Appendix B/*Schemes for Governmental Reform, City of Winnipeg*

Part I/*Property Owners' Association Scheme Presented in May, 1883.*
(Winnipeg Times, *29 May 1883*)

PROPOSED AMENDMENTS TO CHARTER

The committee recommend that the following plan be proposed to be embodied in the amended charter now about to be applied for as calculated to remedy some of the very grave evils now existing in the management of the affairs of the city.

It is proposed:–

1st. That on a day to be affixed in the amended act the present Council be dissolved and a new election held as hereafter provided for, of Mayor and Aldermen.

2nd. That the election be for two members for each ward—making a council of twelve Aldermen. That the Alderman getting in each ward the highest number of votes remain in office until December, 1884. That the Alderman receiving the smallest number of votes go out of office at the annual election in December, 1883. That thereafter one Alderman retire in each Ward at the annual election in January of each year. This will ensure an annual election of one Alderman in each Ward, and give each Alderman after election two years in office.

3rd. That the duties of the Council shall be legislative, and that they shall be elected under the the present franchise for the election of Aldermen, but that the voting shall be by ballot.

4th. That the Mayor, a Treasurer, and Commissioner of Works shall be elected for a period of two years and that the persons entitled to vote for these three officers shall be those who are entitled to vote for the issuing of debentures to be charged as, and deemed to be, a mortgage upon the whole city, and that the votes shall be counted as follows:

The last preceding assessment roll duly authorized shall be the list of voters.

That every holder of property to the value, according to the last assessment roll, of not less than $500 shall be entitled to one vote.

That every holder of property of more than $2,000 and less than $10,000 shall have two votes.

That every holder of property of the value of $10,000 and less than $25,000 shall have three votes.

That every holder of property of the value of $25,000 and less than $50,000 shall have four votes.

That every holder of property of the value of $50,000 and less than $100,000 shall have five votes.

That every holder of property of more than $100,000 in assessed value shall have not more than six votes.

That the voting for these three officers shall be over the whole city, irrespective of wards, and the election shall be on a different day from that for the aldermen.

5th. That the Mayor shall preside at all meetings of the Council and shall be the principal official representative of the city; that he shall be charged with the duty of supervising the police system, the fire brigade, the health department and the licensing arrangements.

6th. That the Treasurer shall have charge of the finances of the city; be responsible for the due receipt of all incomes received by the city, and of all payments made on its account; that he shall be required to see that all monies paid out are on account of and within the limits of specific appropriations properly passed by the Council; that he shall see that all accounts are properly certified, and are in accordance with the foregoing rule; and that it shall be his duty to refuse to pay any account presented to him which he considers wrong or improper, giving his reasons in writing for such refusal and such account refused by him shall not be paid unless so ordered by two thirds of the whole Council of the twelve members after full consideration of the treasurer's written reasons for refusing such payments.

7th. That the Commissioner of Works shall have the charge and superintendence of all works carried on in the city, including sewage, roads and roadways, sidewalks, waterworks and buildings.

That he be held responsible for seeing that all works are properly submitted wherever practicable to public competition by contractors upon carefully prepared plans and specifications. That all work done, either by contractor or where it cannot otherwise be executed, by day work, under competent foremen, is well and faithfully executed, and that proper economy and supervision is exercised in the carrying on of all works executed for the city.

8th. That the Mayor, Treasurer and Commissioner of Works shall form the Executive Committee of the City Council, and that it shall be their duty to submit recommendations to the Council who shall have the right to discuss and decide upon the various matters so brought before them by the Executive Committee.

9th. That the present system of ward appropriations be abolished.

10th. That the Executive Committee prepare and submit to the Council not later than the month of February in each year a complete statement of the estimates of the city expenditure during the year, showing the items of each outlay and the means of providing for the same, whether from loans or ordinary civic income.

That said estimates shall not exceed the total of the estimated receipts, and shall bear as close a resemblance as possible to the annual statements of revenue and expenditure, according to the system in force in Parliament. That it shall be the duty of the Council to carefully consider such estimates, and to reduce the sum if they see fit, but that they shall not have the power to increase any item or to insert any not included in the scheme brought before them.

11th. That it shall be the duty of the executive committee to prepare and submit not later than the 10th day of each month a full synopsis of the receipts and payments for the preceding month, and to show what temporary loans, if any, have been made with the rate of interest paid, and the total amount of interest incurred during such month, as well upon temporary loans as upon the funded debt of the city.

12th. That under this plan the Council will consist of 15 members, the Mayor having a casting vote only when the members are equally divided.

13th. That the Council will meet once a fortnight, during the afternoon that special meetings, when necessary, may be called by the Mayor, and that the Council shall have the right to appoint committees for any special purpose they desire. That upon receiving a requisition to that effect from five members of the Council it shall be the duty of the Mayor to call a special meeting for the purpose named in such requisition.

14th. That the Mayor, Treasurer, and Commissioner of Works shall be paid salaries of not exceeeding $———— each per annum.

15th. That in the event of the death or resignation of any member of the executive committee or aldermen, a new election shall be held in accordance with the foregoing rules, and the person so elected shall hold office for the same period as would have been the case with the person who had died or resigned.

Part II/*Legislative Committee Recommendations, Presented in December, 1892.* (City Council Minutes, *14 December 1892*)

That there be the Mayor and two Commissioners to be elected by all the citizens for a term of three years who will form an Executive Committee, and to be known individually as

THE MAYOR,
THE COMMISSIONER OF FINANCE,
THE COMMISSIONER OF WORKS.

They will retire from office in rotation, the order of retirement to be decided in the first instance by the number of votes received. There will be a Council constituted and elected as at present. The Commissioners, who will also be members of Council, to be paid as follows:—

The Mayor	$3000 per annum
The Commissioner of Finance	2000 " "
The Commissioner of Works	2000 " "

and to be entitled to an increase of emolument upon some equitable basis as the population increases.

The Mayor will be the chairman of the Executive Committee and his general duties will be as now laid down in the Rules and Regulations governing Council. The Standing Committees to be as at present, the Commissioner of Finance to act as chairman of the Finance Committee and of the Market, License & Health Committee, and the Commissioner of Works as chairman of the Committee on Works and the Fire, Water & Light Committee.

The Commissioners to have the control, management and dismissal of all the civic officials, except the Comptroller who will be responsible directly to Council; transact all business now done by the Standing and Special Committees and prepare their reports for submission to the said committees before presenting them to Council.

A two-thirds vote of the Council to be necessary to veto a report or recommendation of the Commissioners.

The Commissioners to have daily stated hours, say one hour in the forenoon and one hour in the afternoon, Sundays and public holidays excepted, during which they will be in their offices at the City Hall for the purpose of interviews, but will be required to clear off all detail work brought before them whether it can be disposed of in the time that they may be specified or not.

The Council's duties will be of an advisory and legislative nature. The Aldermen will be relieved of all detail work, but will meet as at present for the purpose of having laid before them from time to time the policy of civic government as formulated by the Commissioners, passing of the estimates, &c, &c, and which, before being carried into effect must be approved of by them in Council.

Part III/*Special Committee on Legislation, Report on Civic Government, Presented in August, 1893.* (City Council Minutes, *28 August, 1893*)

Your Committee on Legislation begs leave to report that it has had under consideration the matter of civic government and would submit the following for the consideration of Council:

(1) The Commissioners who shall form an Executive Committee shall be appointed and shall be composed of

1st ——— The Mayor and Commissioner of Finance.

2nd ——— The Commissioner of Works.

3rd ——— The Commissioner of Public Affairs.

(a) The Mayor shall be the Head of the Corporation and the chairman of the Executive Committee, and shall also take charge of those duties at present discharged by the Finance Committee, and other duties as now laid down by law and by-laws of the Council.

(b) The Commissioner of Works shall take charge of the department at present administered by the Committee on Works and Property.

(c) The Commissioner of Public Affairs shall take charge of those departments at present administered by the Fire, Water & Light and Market, License & Health Committees.

(2) The Mayor shall be elected as at present, but for a term of four years.

(3) The council shall consist as at present of twelve members and shall be elected for three years. Each ward shall elect one alderman, the other six members shall be elected from the City at large.

(4) The council so formed shall be ballot elect from among themselves at their first meeting:–

1st ———— A Commissioner of Works.

2nd ———— A Commissioner of Public Affairs.

who shall hold their respective positions for the time of their term.

(5) At the first meeting of Council after qualification, members shall proceed to elect a Commissioner of Works from their number. If a clear majority cannot be obtained when the ballots are taken the lowest candidate or all the candidates having the same lowest number will then be dropped. Ballots will then be taken for the remaining candidates and the vote shall proceed until a majority is secured. If no majority is obtained before ten ballots the lowest candidate or candidates having the same lowest number are again dropped and so on until a clear majority is secured for a candidate. If a tie occurs on the tenth ballot or a multiple thereof, the Mayor shall decide.

The Commissioner of Public Affairs shall be elected in the same manner as the Commissioner of Works and at the same or an adjourned meeting.

(6) Each year four members of the council shall retire, two of whom shall be ward representatives, and two elected from the City at large.

(7) Such retiring members shall be eligible for re-election with this proviso, that should a commissioner or commissioners be amongst the number, he or they being desirious of re-election to council must be so re-elected by the whole City.

(Note) (Though in the first instance it might be desirable to select a commissioner from amongst the ward representatives, it is evident that should such commissioner desire a continuance of office at the hands of the council, he should re-enter that body with his official course approved of by the citizens generally).

(8) The order of retirement to be from wards in rotation commencing with No. 1 and No. 2 and from amongst the other six aldermen for the first two years in accordance with the number of votes polled, those having the least going out first. In case of a tie the order of precedence to be decided by lot.

Emolument

(9) The emolument of the commissioners shall be as follows:–
1st ——— The Mayor and Commissioner of Finance $3,500
2nd——— The Commissioner of Works   2,000
3rd ——— The Commissioner of Public Affairs   2,000
based on the present population of 30,000 persons and to be subject to an increase of $500. for each additional 10,000 until the population has increased to 60,000.

General Outline of the Duties of Council

(10) The duties of the council will be principally of a legislative and advisory character, such as, approving of and passing the estimates and all interim appropriations, passing by-laws, except such as are hereinafter provided for. Approving and confirming such contracts as are contemplated under section 501 of the Municipal Act and all other contracts exceeding in amount the sum of $25,000. Rearrangement of ward limits and other duties of a like nature.

(11) The council by a two-thirds vote on those present shall have the power of deposing from office either the Commissioner of Works or Commissioner of Public Affairs. The Council by a two-thirds vote may decide to submit a by-law to the people at the next ensuing general municipal election for deposing the Mayor. The said by-law must receive two-thirds of the total vote polled to have effect.

Duties of Commissioners

(12) The commissioners in full commission assembled, (of whom two shall form a quorum) to have the entire control, management, appointment, and dismissal of all civic officials except the comptroller who shall be responsible directly to council. Shall have the expenditure of the estimates, shall prepare and submit to council for approval all new by-laws or amendments to existing by-laws except such as relate to the appointment or dismissal of civic officials. Shall have full powers to prosecute local improvements as provided for under the Municipal Act and of entering into necessary contracts and for the carrying out of the same; also of entering into contracts for supplies of all kinds; provided always, that contract for such supplies as are contemplated under section 501 of the Municipal Act hereinbefore referred to and all contracts exceeding the amount of $25,000. shall be subject to the approval and confirmation of the council.

(13) The commissioners to have daily stated hours, Sundays and public holidays excepted, during which they will be in their offices at the city hall for the purpose of interviews, but will be required to clear off all detail work brought before them whether it can be disposed of in the time that may be specified or not.

(14) The commissioners shall, at least once per month, lay before the council in writing a report of their proceedings up to date.

(15) Your Committee on Legislation would recommend that the above outline be adopted and that the city solicitors be instructed to immediately prepare the necessary legislation to give effect to the foregoing report.

Part IV/*Plan of Civic Government Reform, Presented in January 1896, by Citizen's Committee on Civic Government Reform* (Council Communication, *Series II, No. 3212, read 3 February, 1896*).

Winnipeg,
January 20th, 1896.

To the Mayor and Council
of the City of Winnipeg.

Gentlemen:–
At a meeting of the Citizen's Committee on Civic Government Reform held in the Committee Room, City Hall, on the evening of the 25th of November last the following motion was carried:– "That the resolution adopted by the Committee be presented to the City Council at their first business meeting in January 1896 by the Chairman and Secretary of the Committee, requesting the Council to cause the recommendations contained in the said resolutions, or any amendment thereto, to be framed into an amendment to the Municipal Act; which amendment shall be submitted to a joint meeting of the City Council and the Citizens General Committee, and if approved by said joint meeting the Council to ask authority from the Legislature to submit said amendment to a vote of the people within three months after obtaining such authority. Should a majority of electors declare in favor of the amendment, said amendment shall become law and take effect on a date to be named by the Lieutenant Governor in Council. For the purpose of the plebiscite the municipal voters list of 1895 to be used."

In accordance with the terms of the foregoing motion we beg to hand in herewith for your consideration and action the resolutions re Civic Government Reform referred to.

We have the honor to be
Gentlemen
your obedient Servants,

J. H. Ashdown
Chairman of Citizens Committee

George F. Carruthers
Secretary of Citizens Committee

Plan of Civic Government Reform

(1) The Committee recommends the appointment of one chief officer to be appointed by resolution of the Council, who will have charge or supervision of the general management of civic affairs under such direction of the Council as may hereafter be defined and who shall be called the general superintendent.

(2) The mayor and the chairman of the finance and works committee shall be an executive of the council.

(2A) It shall be the duty of the executive to meet at intervals with the general superintendent, whose recommendations and reports shall be submitted to them for their consideration, action or report.

(3) The superintendent shall have the right to sit at all meetings of the council and committees, with the right of discussion but no vote. Notwithstanding anything heretofore recommended the executive may meet at any time without the presence of the superintendent.

(4) The superintendent shall be responsible for the proper execution of all by-laws within the jurisdiction of the Council.

(4A) The head of any department shall upon the request of the superintendent or executive furnish to him or them forthwith any information desired in relation to its affairs.

(5) The superintendent shall report promptly on all petitions claims and other matters of importance, but shall deal with all minor details as he deems best; reporting his action to the Executive.

(6) All heads of departments shall be appointed by Council on the recommendation of the superintendent, except the comptroller, who shall be appointed direct by Council. The superintendent shall appoint all other employees.

(7) He shall have power to discharge any official or employees, except the comptroller, for cause, but the discharged may appeal to the executive, and if sustained by that body the question shall be referred to the Council where a two-thirds vote will be necessary to sustain the appeal. Should the decision of the executive be adverse to the appellant, he may appeal to the Council where a two-thirds vote shall be necessary to sustain him.

(8) The dismissal of the superintendent shall require a majority vote of the whole Council.

(9) The superintendent shall pass in review and certify to the correct-

ness of all contracts. He shall also certify to and submit for approval to the executive, all payrolls and interim estimates, and the executive may authorize their payment.

(10) He shall have the power to stop work on any contract not being carried out in accordance with its terms and conditions, and the executive may authorize him to have the work continued by day labor until such time as the matter has been decided upon by the Council.

(11) All reports to Council shall come through the executive.

(12) The executive may at any time appoint a competent person or persons, not exceeding three in number, to examine, or may themselves examine, without notice, the affairs of any department, official, or employee, and for the purpose of such or any other examination into civic affairs the executive shall have the power to summon witnesses, examine the same under oath, and compel the production of all books or papers bearing on the case; their powers in all respects to be as full as those of a justice of the peace. The result of any examination shall be transmitted to the Council without delay.

(13) The executive may call a meeting of the Council or of any committee therof, at any time, (subject to the usual notice required by by-law) for the purpose of submitting for consideration business requiring immediate attention.

(14) The executive shall have all the powers of the various committees of council as laid down under by-law 511.

(15) The executive shall be a Board of arbitration for the settling of such disputes as may arise between any employer and employee doing work for the City, either by contract or by day labor, within the City limits.

All of which is respectfully submitted

J. H. Ashdown   George F. Carruthers
Chairman.   Secretary.

Part V/*Amendments to Winnipeg Charter Dealing with Board of Control. (Statutes of Manitoba, 1906, Chap. 95.)*

27. Said Charter is hereby amended by adding thereto the following sections:

268A. (1) Notwithstanding anything in this Act the Council of the City of Winnipeg shall consist of the mayor and four controllers, to be elected annually from the City at large, and fourteen aldermen, two of whom shall be elected from each of the seven wards of the City, and the four controllers so elected, together with the mayor, shall be the board of control for the said City and the mayor shall be the chairman thereof.

(2)   Each elector entitled to vote for mayor shall also be entitled to vote for four persons to be elected as controllers, or for one or more thereof, and the aldermen shall be elected in the manner at present provided by law by the municipal electors entitled to vote in each of the wards in which they may be qualified so to vote.

(3)   The candidates for the office of controller shall be nominated at the same time and place, and in the same manner, as candidates for the office of mayor are nominated, and the provisions of this Act providing for the nomination and election of a mayor, including election by acclamation, and the filling of any vacancy that may occur in the said office, shall except as otherwise provided herein, mutatis mutandis apply to the nomination and election of controllers.

(4)   Any person desiring to vote for a controller or for controllers shall do so by placing a cross opposite the name or names of the candidates for whom he so desires to vote.

(5)   The Council may fix by by-law the salaries to be paid to the members of the board of control, but the same shall not exceed, for mayor, five thousand dollars, and for each controller, four thousand dollars, per annum. The salary that the mayor shall receive as member of the board of control shall not be in addition to the salary received by him as mayor.

(6)   Where, at any such election in the City, less than four controllers are to be elected, then each elector shall have the right to vote for as many candidates as are to be elected.

(7)   All powers, duties and obligations given, conferred or placed upon aldermen in the City shall be possessed and exercised by, and shall be binding upon, any controller provided for under this section.

268B.   (1)   It shall be the duty of the board of control—

(a)   To prepare an estimate of the proposed expenditure of the year and certify the same to the council for its consideration. The council shall not appropriate or expend, nor shall any officer thereof expend or direct the expenditure of, any sum or sums not included in or provided by such estimates, or in or by any special or supplementary estimates duly certified by the board to the council, without the affirmative vote of a majority of the members of the council, authorizing such additional appropriation or expenditure. But this prohibition shall not extend to the payment of any debenture or other debt or liability lawfully contracted and payable, nor to the interest thereon;

(b) To prepare specifications for and award all contracts, and for that purpose to call for all tenders for works, material and supplies, implements or machinery or any other goods or property required, and which may lawfully be purchased, for the use of the corporation, and to report their action to the council at its next meeting. Upon the opening of any tenders, the chairman or board shall require the presence of the head of the department or sub-department with which the subject matter of such is connected, and of the city solicitor when required. Such head of department may take part in any discussion at the board relating to such tenders, but shall not be entitled to vote. The council shall not, unless upon an affirmative vote of at least a majority of the members of the council, reverse or vary the action of the board of control in respect of such tender and decision of the board thereon, when the effect of such vote would be to increase the cost of the work, or to award the contract to a tenderer other than that one to whom the board of control has awarded it;

(c) To inspect and report to the council monthly or oftener upon all municipal works being carried on or on progress with the city;

(d) To nominate to the council all heads of departments and sub-departments in case of any vacancy, and after a favorable report by the head of the department, any other officer of the corporation required to be appointed by by-law or resolution of the council, and any other permanent officers, clerks; and no head of department or sub-department or other permanent officer, clerk or assistant as aforesaid shall be appointed or selected by the council in the absence of such nomination without an affirmative vote of at least a majority of the members of the council; but the council may, by a majority vote, refer such nomination back to the board of control for reconsideration;

(e) To dismiss or suspend any head of a department and forthwith to report such dismissal or suspension to the council. Where any head of department has been dismissed by the board, he shall not be reappointed or reinstated by the council unless upon an affirmative vote of at least two-thirds of the members of the council present.

(2) In the absence of any by-law of the council prescribing the mode of appointment of all or any other subordinate officers, clerks, assistants, employees, servants and workmen, not included in clauses (d) and (e) of the preceding sub-section, and required by any department or sub-department for the due and proper discharge and performance of the duties and

work thereof, the board may by regulation or resolution direct by whom and in what manner such subordinate officers, assistants, employees, servants or workmen shall be appointed, engaged or employed.

(3) The board may from time to time submit proposed by-laws to the council and, where in the opinion of the board it is desirable, may amalgamate departments or sub-departments.

(4) The board may appoint a secretary or clerk, whose duty it shall be to keep minutes of all proceedings of the board and prepare all reports and other proceedings of the board, and he shall perform such other duties and services as may be assigned to him from time to time by the board, the mayor or the council.

(5) The council may by by-law or resolution impose upon or assign to the board of control such other duties as to the council may seem meet; and the board shall, when so required by resolution of the council, and upon one week's notice, return to the council copies of the minutes of its meetings, and any other information in their possession, which the council may require.

(6) Nothing in this section contained shall prevent the council (by vote of the majority of the members of the council present and voting) from referring back to the board of control any report, question, matter or thing for consideration.

(7) In all cases where it is sought in council to reverse, set aside or vary the action of the board of control, or where a majority vote of the members of the council present and voting is required for any purpose, the vote by yeas and nays shall be recorded in the minutes of the council.

(8) The public school board, the board of police commissioners and the public parks board, or any other board that may hereafter be constituted, respectively shall furnish to the said board of control, on or before the first day of March in each year, their several and respective annual estimates.

(9) Clause (d) of sub-section (1) of this section shall not apply to any member of the fire department of the city, except the head thereof, nor to any assessor, except the assessment commissioner; and nothing in this section contained shall deprive any head of department of the power which he possessed on the first day of January, 1906, under any by-law or otherwise, to dismiss any subordinate officer, clerk or employee.

(10) Notwithstanding anything in the Winnipeg Charter contained, the duties herein assigned to the board of control shall be discharged exclusively by the said board, except in the cases provided for in sub-section (3) of this section.

Appendix C/ *A Comparative Profile of Winnipeg's Occupational Structure, 1881 and 1911*

Table C1 classifies Winnipeg's occupational structure by the function of the occupation. The data for this table come from the Second Census of Canada, 1881; *and the* Fifth Census of Canada, 1911.

Table C1/ *A Comparison of Some Elements of the Work Structure of Winnipeg, 1881–1911*

Classification	1881	1911
Trade and commerce	14.9	24.9
Manufacturing	23.9	17.5
Building trades	14.2	17.1
Transportation	2.1	13.7
Domestic and personal service	11.8	10.5
Professional	6.3	7.5
Government employees; all levels	.7	5.2
Agriculture	22.7	1.0
Hunting, fishing, logging	.6	.1
All other categories	2.8	2.5
	100%	100%
Total classified	5,029	62,265

Studying the proportions of the employed work force in the various sectors of the economy, it is possible to locate the major changes that accompanied Winnipeg's rapid growth between 1881 and 1911. The basic and perhaps most significant change occurred in agriculture. The sharp decline in the percentage of the work force engaged in agricultural pursuits is not surprising when it is realized that Winnipeg had grown in this period into a major urban area. By 1911 land was simply too valuable to be used for agricultural pursuits. The agricultural workers still in Winnipeg in 1911 were florists, commercial gardeners, and farm owners and labourers. In the latter case many merely lived within the city's boundaries and travelled to surrounding farms to work.

The picture that emerges from the changes in the agricultural category is one that reinforces the contention that the old Red River Settlement, with its river lot farms, had been almost totally engulfed by a thriving commercial centre. Indeed, if one uses a widely accepted definition of an urban area—the residence of non-agrarian specialists—the changes indicate that Winnipeg was clearly a city by 1911.

Another major change occurred in the transportation category. The sharp rise in transportation employees points to Winnipeg's growth as the distribution centre for Manitoba and the Northwest. In the 1870s and early 1880s goods and people had moved by steamboat and cart brigade and Winnipeg had only a few teamsters, boatmen, and railway employees. But with the completion of eighty-five miles of railway track in Manitoba in 1878 a new age of the locomotive was begun and expansion continued at a rapid rate. By 1911 three transcontinental railway systems were completed and east-west traffic on all of them was routed through Winnipeg. All three established yards, shops, and terminals in the city, as did a number of other smaller railways. The Red River Settlement of 1870, centre of a small community of settlers and the channel through which furs flowed east, now became the "Gateway to the West" and the commercial centre for the vast farming regions that were on the railway lines. The organization of the Grain Exchange in Winnipeg established control of the grain trade in western Canada and the city inherited its place as the metropolis of an area in excess of one hundred million acres suited primarily to cereal production.

Besides railway employees, a significant portion of the rise in the transportation category is made up of street railway employees. As Winnipeg's spatial growth continued apace with its economic growth, intra-urban transportation became a necessity; by 1911 Winnipeg had over 78 miles of street railway track serviced by over 750 employees.

Agricultural expansion and activity in Winnipeg's hinterland produced demands for goods and services. To serve these Winnipeg competed against the older metropolitan centres of eastern Canada and the younger urban centres which emerged in the hinterland itself. Advantages of size, location, and discriminatory freight rates, coupled with an active and growth-conscious elite group, enabled Winnipeg to compete successfully against both. This success revealed itself in the 10 per cent rise in the number of trade and commerce employees. This was in large part taken up by the growth in the number and size of wholesale and retail firms. Increases in the professional and building trades category were also the result of demands for more services in the hinterland, as well as in the city itself. The other major increase was in government employees. Over half the increase can be accounted for by the growth of the provincial civil service along with some federal government personnel; the remainder was taken up by municipal government employees such as firemen, policemen, clerks, and officials.

The only other major change was the decline in the percentage of persons employed in manufacturing. This can be explained by two developments: advances in industrial organization and machine processes freed men and women for other occupations; and with the growth of efficient railway transportation goods could be imported more cheaply. Whatever the cause, Winnipeg by 1911 was characterized by a very mixed work force, with no one job category dominating all others.

The changes outlined above clearly show that the work forces of the small community of 1881 and the large, complex, and commercialized city of 1911 are markedly different from each other. The fur trader, farmer, and small businessman that dominated Winnipeg society in the 1870s and 1880s were all individualists who laboured alone, with their family, or with a partner or two. But as the amount and rate of industrialization increased significant changes took place in the arrangement of economic activities. The frontier egalitarianism of the 1870s was replaced by a hierarchy of owners, managers, foremen, tradesmen, and labourers. Naturally such changes were reflected in the city's spatial growth with the rise of residential segregation according to income. Thus, as Chapter 9 shows, certain districts in Winnipeg became working-class areas while others were dominated by upper or middle-class elements.

A related change occurred in what can be termed the group organization of work. As manufacturing establishments, railway shops, and wholesale and retail businesses grew, more and more of the city's work force was brought into a hierarchical structure. In manufacturing, for example, only 30 per cent of the employees worked in establishments of fifteen or more persons in 1891. But by the First World War this had increased to 80 per cent (15,152) of the manufacturing work force.* In the simplest, most general sense this transformation in the organization of work had the effect of creating a new lattice of loyalities and social relationships in Winnipeg. The work group became a source of discipline, loyalty and culture in its own right. It taught co-operative life and action to many artisans and labourers who had formerly worked in virtual isolation in their own homes or fields or with one or two men. Also, work associations at times cut across ethnic lines and replaced to some extent family and neighbourhood associations. Thus work groups could probably be given some credit for modifying the tensions of assimilation and urban living in general.

Paradoxically, these same changes made labour organization and the use of the strike as a weapon possible. Large work groupings made it impossible for one man to supervise all his workers, to channel through himself the daily flow of information, socialization, and psychological orientation needed by the workers. The result was the establishment of a middle group (management): a "they" who, without direct or continued contact with the workers, set their tasks, determined

*These figures have been taken from the *Third Census of Canada*, 1891; and F. H. Kitto, *Manitoba*, p. 101.

the hours and wages, approved piecework rates, allowed the vacations, imposed the lay-offs and short weeks. As a reaction to this growing depersonalization of the worker's life, labour organizations sprang up in Winnipeg; in the Labour Day parade of 1899, for example, twenty-seven unions took part. This development set the stage for class conflict and in 1899 and 1906 Winnipeg was forced to experience two fierce strikes. Yet, in the aggregate, labour organization in the years prior to the war remained diverse and uncoordinated, and its most significant role probably remained the modifying, rather than the fostering of tensions. Unfortunately, until the whole subject of the relationship between work groups and social order is subjected to more detailed and systematic study by historians, only such limited observations can be made.

Appendix D/J. S. Woodsworth Report on Living Standards, City of Winnipeg, 1913

Part I/A Workingman's Budget. (The Christian Guardian, 11 June 1913.)

The Guardian has recently given considerable space to a discussion of the important question of preachers' salaries in relation to the cost of living. Incidentally, several farmers' budgets have been produced. Why not widen the discussion to wages in general and the cost of living in cities where incomes and expenditures can most easily be stated in dollars and cents. Others than preachers may need a minimum wage. In this article we confine ourselves to the cost of living as shown by a suggested budget for a working man's family. In subsequent articles we hope to treat the question of wages, and show in what ways the ordinary family endeavors to "make both ends meet," and, possibly, later to suggest some practical way out. We would venture to suggest that such articles are particularly valuable as "Sunday reading," especially for employers who are anxious to carry out, under modern conditions, the second great commandment, "Thou shalt love thy neighbor as thyself."

FOOD. The Labor Gazette, April, 1913, publishes a table showing the typical weekly expenditure on staple foods for a family of five. The quantities indicated in the budget are slight modifications of those employed in similar calculations by various official bodies. At Winnipeg retail prices, as given by the Gazette, this food budget amounts to $8.16 a week, or $424.32 a year. Mr. Frank Kerr, Winnipeg License Inspector and Relief Officer, working on an altogether different basis, estimates the food expenditure as follows: Groceries, $15 a month; bread, $4 a month; milk, $4 a month; fruit and vegetables, $4 a month; meat, $12 a month, a total of $39 a month, or $468 a year. I have carefully compared these budgets with the actual expenditures of working men's families. There is considerable variety in kinds of foods and quantities of each kind but one may safely conclude that the estimate of the Department of Labor is not too high. Food, then, $424.32 a year.

CLOTHING. It is very difficult to determine the amount needed for clothing. Individual taste enters very largely. Better clothing has been worn of late years. The expenditure of those who can afford to buy is very heavy. In Winnipeg, as Chapin in "The Standard of Living" has noted in New York, "a large proportion of the families on the lower incomes depend upon gifts to keep up such standards in regard to dress as they maintain." Again, in this northern climate special clothing for certain seasons (for instance, woollens and furs for winter) becomes a necessity. Mr. Kerr's estimate is as follows:

"The least a man can dress on is $72 a year. A working suit at $15 and a better suit at $20 will be $35; two pairs boots are $8; underwear for summer and winter, to last two years, will be $5 a year; linen adds another $5; head and hand covering, $3; and rubbers and overshoes, $4. Furs are a necessity in Manitoba, and a fur coat at $60 will, with care, wear five years, that is $12 a year. (Cloth coats would come to about the same.)

"A woman, if she is clever with her needle, can dress on $80 a year. A winter coat at $50 will with care, wear four years, that is $12.50 a year. Hand covering will be $3 a year, and hats, if she has some skill at millinery and is content with two a year, will cost $10. A suit at $20 will last two years—$10 a year. Dresses, one good for the summer season is $5, one for winter $12; three shirt-waists at $1.50, $4.50; separate skirt, $5. Footwear, two pairs of boots at $3, overshoes at $1.50, is $7.50. Underwear will be $10 a year. Total $74.50. (Mr. Kerr apparently leaves $5.50 for extras, and thus shows that he knows what he is talking about!)

"The children will take $50 each. Anyone acquainted with young Canada's talent for going through shoes and stockings will accept that estimate as made by an optimist!"

Total for clothing, then, $302. In comparing these figures with actual family budgets it would appear that Mr. Kerr has been too generous with the wife and children. If the wife "makes over" garments for the children, does her own sewing and laundry, and wears her last year's hat, she could cut down the clothing bill from $50 to $100. Put the clothing at the lowest possible figure, $200.

HEAT, LIGHT AND WATER. These are the other "fixed charges." Fuel is absolutely essential in a cold climate. Four tons of anthracite coal, at $11 a ton, is $44. (During the past year I burned coal in my furnace for nearly seven months.) Wood, for cooking purposes and supplementary heating, six cords, at $7 a cord, $42. (At this figure a man must buy at a certain season and himself cut and split and store his wood.) This makes the total fuel bill $86.

Light, at 50 cents a month for eight months and $1 a month for four months is $8. In Winnipeg electric light is as cheap as coal oil, having dropped when the city plant was established from ten cents to three cents, and from a minimum charge of $1 a month to fifty cents a month.

Water, cost about $8 a year. This makes a total for heat, light and water of $102 a year. (It may be noted that in its statement of rents and fuel for Winnipeg the *Labor Gazette* is decidedly in error.)

CAR FARE. This should perhaps be included in the fixed charges, as in the city the workingman must use the street car in getting to and from his work. Two trips a day during "red ticket" hours, with an occasional shopping trip down-town for the wife, bring the street car fare to $25 a year.

HOUSE FURNISHING. House furnishing is difficult to estimate. Furniture is sometimes inherited, lasts for years, is often bought cheaply second-hand, yet involves heavy expenditures when it must be replaced. Bedding, dishes, household utensils, need to be frequently replaced. We will be well within the mark if we put this item at $250 for ten years or $25 a year.

HEALTH EXPENDITURES. Health expenditures, including doctor's, nurse's and dentist's fees, medicines, etc., should probably be placed at $4 a month, or $48 a year. This must include periods of serious illness, operations, childbirth and children's diseases. Few who do not receive help from charitable institutions escape with a smaller expenditure than this.

RECREATION AND EDUCATION. Here we touch what have been termed "cultural wants." Surely they are necessities, too, for man cannot live by bread alone. Church collections, lodge dues, union fees, concerts and lectures, books and newspapers, school supplies for the children, music lessons, better not mention an organ or a piano, holidays, perhaps beer and tobacco—all cost. The family's range of interests would not need to be very extensive to induce them to expend $1 a week, or $52 a year. Remember, we are dealing with minimum expenditures!

INSURANCE. Insurance should properly be reckoned as a necessity. Our study of actual workingman's budgets shows, as a rule, only small expenditures to cover "sick benefits." A straight life insurance policy for $2,000 would cost $50 a year. If a man began at twenty years of age and paid $50.05 a year till he was sixty, he would then receive a Government annuity of $500. Surely $100 a year ought not to be too much to put into insurance and savings. That could hardly be called adequate insurance.

HOUSEHOLD HELP. It will be noted that in this budget the wife and mother is supposed, in addition to caring for her children, to do her own cooking, sewing, housework and laundry. But many women, and all women at times, are not strong enough to accomplish all these tasks alone. It costs in Winnipeg $1.50 to $2 a day to secure a woman for a day's washing or cleaning. To this should be added one or two meals and probably car tickets. Household help costs $18 or $30 a month, plus $50 a year for an additional bedroom, and $150 to cover food, laundry, breakages and waste. From $400 to $500 is a conservative estimate for household help; but, of course, this is altogether beyond the ordinary income. So we leave the "house mother" to struggle on alone—fortunate, indeed, if she is not forced to "go out working," to supplement her husband's earnings. Well, what have we?

RENT. A "five-roomed" cottage on a surface foundation, without bathroom or furnace, but with water and sewer connections, costs $20 a month, or $240 a year. A six-roomed (small rooms) house is a workingman's quarter, the standard adopted by the Department of Labor, cannot be procured for less than $25 a month or $300 a year. A local study based on actual rentals paid per room, confirms these figures, secured from rental agents. Minimum rent, then $240 a year.

Budget for Family of Five

Food	$ 424
Clothing	200
Heat, light and water	102
Car fare	25
House furnishings	25
Health expenditures	48
Recreation and education	52
Insurance and savings	100
Household help	—
Rent	240
Total	$1,216

Where can we cut down our budget? Study the items again, and we find that already we have cut them to a minimum—that is, the minimum needed to maintain an ordinary, "decent" Canadian standard of living. But throw off, if you will, still another $16, which will cover any item that may seem to someone to be too high. We still have a family budget of $1,200. What about the man who receives less than $100 a month? What about the workman who receives less than $50 a month? How work out his problem?

Part II/*A Normal Standard of Living* (The Christian Guardian, *9 July 1913.*)

The National Conference of Charities and Correction, meeting at Cleveland, Ohio, in June, 1912, agreed upon the following standards of living:

"The welfare of society and the prosperity of the state require for each individual such food, clothing, housing conditions, and other necessaries and comforts of life as will serve and maintain physical, mental and moral health.

"A living wage must include enough to secure the elements of a normal standard of living; to provide for education and recreation; to care for immature members of the family; to maintain the family during periods of sickness; and to permit of reasonable saving for old.

"Social welfare demands for every family a safe and sanitary home . . . privacy, rooms of sufficient size and number to decently house the members of the family."

Are these too high for Canada?

Yet it is difficult to find an actual working man's family budget which maintains a normal standard. We give in detail conditions found in one home in which the man is receiving so-called fair wages. In this case the man's wage of $720 is supplemented by the earnings of the wife to the extent of about $200, which brings the income over $900. The family is larger than usual—six children—but clothing cost practically nothing, being supplied by private charity.

The man is a painter in the railroad shops, is paid 36 cents an hour, eight hours a day, one-half day Saturday, that is 44 hours a week. Holidays off. Also nine days at Easter. Last summer many laid off, but he was fortunate in holding his job. Income averages $60 a month. No prerequisites except the chance of a railroad pass, which is valueless, as he could not afford to lose the time. Occasionally he makes a little extra by mending broken china. Has wife and six children, none old enough to work. Rent, $23 a month for six-roomed house in very poor condition, in poor locality, beside railroad tracks. Saved street car fare. When I called the man was kalsomining, as "landlord wouldn't do a thing."

Light, 50 cents to $1.97 during December.

Water, $2.10 a quarter.

Coal, four tons at $11, $44 (much less than in winter, when it cost $70.)

Wood, almost three cords at $7, supplemented by old boxes, which he bought cheap and broke up.

Groceries, $20 to $25, including butter and eggs, vegetables and flour (wife bakes her own bread.) Also condensed milk (cannot afford to buy "cows' " milk, which, too, was sometimes adulterated.)

Meat, $8 to $10 a month.

Clothing: Had fair stock when they came to this country. Man had only two suits in six years and one pair of shoes in two years. Some of the children were then without shoes. Wife did her own sewing. Her own clothes and those of children were "made over" from old clothing obtained from a "mission."

Man was a member of a fraternal order, and carried a sick benefit costing $10 a year. Union fees were 85 cents a month.

Sickness: Youngest child, five months old, doctor's bill not yet paid; hope to be able to save enough now that the warmer weather was coming. Little girl's eyes had been bad. Had been examined at hospital; given glasses. Eyes grew worse. Consulted specialist at cost of $10. Specialist said child should not have had glasses, and would be permanently blind. Now in an institution at Government expense.

Wife does some dressmaking: averages perhaps $2 a week. Could not work for some time after the baby came.

Tried boarders, but no money in it. Takes roomers when she can get them. Income from this source irregular. (Little girl sleeping on couch in parlor-sitting-room when I called.)

Here is a man who doesn't drink, isn't lazy, a skilled mechanic, getting fair wages. His wife isn't extravagant, works hard, cares for six children, does dressmaking, keeps lodgers.

Yet the family is dependent on charity for clothing, is making absolutely no provision for old age, and had no prospect of anything better.

This man's outlook may be of interest. He was particularly concerned about his fellow-employees who are receiving, not like himself, 36 cents per hour, but many $17\frac{1}{2}$ to 20 cents, with a possible rise to 27 cents an hour. There was little chance of obtaining a foreman's position, as foreman's jobs were limited, the advancement was through favor. Public affairs were largely in the hands of those looking for "graft." The church was not a factor in the situation. It was supported by wealthy men. Where, then, any hope? A change of system (he produced *Cotton's Weekly*); do away with rent, interest and profits.

What would you do if you were in this man's shoes?

Part III/*How Make Both Ends Meet?* (The Christian Guardian, *12 July 1913.*)

A workman's income is not reckoned by the year or month, but by the day or by the hour. It becomes necessary, then, to translate so many cents an hour into so many dollars a year. Further, Sundays, holidays, "off-days," and slack seasons must be reckoned with. Three hundred working days a year may be considered full time. Many unskilled workers have only 200 working days in the year.

Let us keeping the following table in mind:

20¢	hour, 10 hours a day, 300 days	-	$ 600
17½¢	hour, 10 hours a day, 200 days	-	350
45¢	hour, 9 hours a day, 200 days	-	810
45¢	hour, 9 hours a day, 300 days	-	1,215

To maintain the normal standard of living, at Winnipeg prices, as given in our first article, would take full time, at 45 cents an hour. Let each reader figure it out on the basis of local wages and local prices.

The following is the fair wage schedule of the Manitoba Provincial Government:

Trade or class of labor	Rate per hour (cents)	Hours per week
Bricklayers and masons	70	48
Carpenters	55	50
Stone cutters	65	48
Plumbers	55	48
Steamfitters	55	48
Plasterers	65	48
Lathers	56½	54
Painters	40	54
Electricians	45	48
Sheet metal workers	45	54
Structural ironworkers	50	54
Portable and stationary engineers	50	60
Marble workers	65	54
Tile setters	55	54
Asbestos workers	50	54
Builders' laborers	27½	60
Team and wagon	60	60
Excavators	25	60

N. B. – The painters' scale has been advanced to 42½ cents.

Several considerations must be kept in mind:

1. Many receive wages much below the fair wage schedule. At the present time (May, 1913) many builders' laborers, for instance, are receiving only 17½ to 20 cents.

2. The building trades are better paid than some other forms of labor.

Packing house employees are receiving 19 cents for skilled labor; railway employees, 18 cents; foundry workers, 20 cents; teamsters are working eleven to fourteen hours a day for $2 a day, their pay having been reduced from $2.25 during the winter of 1912-13.

Wholesale houses are generally "bad pay." Here is an instance vouched for by one of our ministers. The man is a member of his church. "P. applied at a warehouse of a prominent Methodist layman, and was taken on as an experienced packer. He worked for two weeks and received a pay envelope containing $16. He pointed out to his employer that he could not possibly keep himself and his wife and four children on such a wage. The employer told him that this was all he ever paid, but added kindly, 'Brother, as you are one of ourselves, we will do something better for you.' Two weeks later he opened his envelope and discovered $17! Fifty cents a week increase! Yet this employer contributes large sums annually for the conversion of the Jews!" If this work were continuous (which it is not), and no time were lost by sickness or holidays, the sum of $442 for the support of a family of six would be all the "brother" could win by his toil.

3. Many unskilled laborers and skilled workmen in outdoor trades work only eight months in the year, having to spend the winter in enforced idleness.

Thus large numbers of workmen are receiving under $600 a year, many under $500, half what is necessary to support a family according to a normal standard.

How is the difference made up?—for nature's laws are inexorable. Differences are always made up somehow. The small wage of the husband often means that the wife and mother is forced to go out working. Our washwomen and scrubwomen are largely married women with families. The effect? The hospitals report that in many cases the women are "run down." Overwork, if not the direct cause of disease, often complicates and aggravates the disease.

And the homes? From juvenile courts and reformatories come the cry of the mother's care.

Again, the small wage of the father often means the children must go out to work at an early age to supplement the family income. The principal of a Winnipeg school gave evidence before the Government Commission on Technical Education: "In connection with my school work I have noted during the past five years that many children leave school to go to work long before they are physically fit or have any adequate preparation for their life-work. Very few children in our district complete the eighth grade in school. They go to work in stores, box factories, breweries, and as messenger and office boys. Many boys and girls are kept at home to mind younger children while the parents are out working. These form probably the largest class of child workers. It is a sad fact, but it seems necessary that in order to maintain the existence of a family the mother must go out to work rather than care for her children. This is the source of much truancy and juvenile crime."

Let the family save on food and we have under-nourished women and children. It is pathetic that in February and March, before work starts again, the children of many families show very decidedly the effects of under-nutrition.

Save on rent and we have overcrowding, which means insanitary conditions and often immoral conditions.

Save on education. Here is the case of a little girl sent out at twelve years to earn her board so that she could stay at school. At fifteen she is out of school, having reached only grade six. Her father, who is "working in the city" at 25 cents an hour, could not afford even to buy her school books. So we are developing another generation of unskilled workers! Yes, sooner or later the community pays the bill.

Here is an example given by the minister of a Methodist church in a working-man's district: "D. is a member of my church, a local preacher of considerable ability. He has been in the employ of a railway company for ten years, starting with a wage of 15 cents and finally reaching 26½ cents. He has a wife and three boys, the eldest of whom is now fourteen. This man's income was at no time adequate. Attempts were made by both mother and father to increase it. Overwork, poor fare and imperfect housing have at length done their work. D. has been six months at Ninette, having contracted tuberculosis. He has just been allowed out of the infirmary, and must be retained for at least another year. The youngest boy is in the Children's Hospital. His tubercular hip has been twice operated upon, and he has been six months in bed. The doctor thinks one and a half years must intervene if permanent good is to result before he can be discharged. Each of the other three members of the family have been under medical treatment during the winter, one as an in-patient, the others as out-patients, of the General Hospital. Besides this, the community must help support the family during the bread-winner's incapacity. The mother, a skilled needlewoman, lost her position, her fellow-employees refusing to work by her side for fear of tubercular infection. The eldest boy, of whom his teachers spoke in highest terms as the most brilliant pupil they had under their charge, is taken out of school to earn $20 a month, while the second boy is alone from 7:15 a.m. to 6:45 p.m. each day, without proper mid-day meals such as growing boys need. What will the family ultimately cost the community?" There are hundreds of persons now being supported at public expense whom adequate wages would have maintained as effective producers.

Part IV/*Wage-Earning Girls and Homeless Men* (The Christian Guardian, *16 July 1913*).

So far in this series of articles we have been considering the family as the unit, and comparing the family budget with the wages of the one who, in the phraseology of the olden time, was known as the "bread-winner."

Two other classes of workers have their own peculiar problems, and at the same time complicate the family situation, i.e., "wage-earning girls" and "homeless men." Is it possible that to a certain extent each of these classes is responsible for the existence of the other, or that they are both victims of common economic conditions?

WAGE-EARNING GIRLS. First there is the case of wage-earning girls. Here is a clipping from the *Guardian* of May 14th:

"Professor Derrick, of McGill University, read a paper before the National Council of Women, held in Montreal last week, in which she dealt with this matter. She claimed that there are 72,571 women working in this country for an average wage of $261 a year, or $5 a week. From the year 1900 to 1910 the number of women earning an average of $447 a year rose from 2,151 to 6,375; but during the same period the number of women earning an average of $261 a year increased from 61,220 to 72,751. This means that while we have a little over 6,000 women who average about $8.50 a week, we have over 72,000 who average only $5, i.e., for every woman who earns $8.50 a week there are twelve who get only $5 a week."

Take the girls in the employ of the Provincial Government. The minimum wage up to June 1st has been $24 and the maximum $40 per month. This is now increased to a minimum of $30 and a maximum of $47 a month.

In an investigation made by a special committee two years ago in Winnipeg it was found that out of 118 store representatives and factory girls, while 25 received over $7 a week, 93 received less, 18 being under $3 a week. Yet competent authorities assure us that it takes $8 to $9 a week for a girl to live as she should.

Again, how is the difference made up? Under-nutrition, the temptation to make "easy-money," and then finally weakness passed on through the mother to another generation.

Of course it is said, and rightly, that many of these girls live at home. Yes, that often saves the situation. But let us come to clear thinking. Economically, either the girl is a help or she is a burden to her parents. The employment of young girls is justified, on the one hand, on the ground that they live at home and thus receive help from home. For the employer it seems to be a case of "Heads I win, tails you lose."

THE HOMELESS MAN. Such large numbers of our immigrants belong to this class that they cannot be overlooked. Their wages and standards of living have a direct bearing on family life.

Many laborers on construction work are receiving $60 a month. Board and incidentals cost $25 a month, which leaves them $35 a month. But this is for only seven months in the year, or $245 a year for many of them. Put aside $45 for clothing, and the homeless man has only $200 to keep him for five months. As a farm hand he would receive about $35 for seven months, or, if he worked all year, $240, which would mean a saving of $200 a year. Mr. Bruce Walker, Commissioner of Immigration, stated recently: "The wages for farm laborers have never been better than they are at present, and farmers are offering $300 to $350 per year for experienced help, with board and lodging." This is from $60 to $100 a year higher, but only for an experienced man. Very well, so long as he remains unmarried. And unmarried the unskilled laborer, and many a skilled laborer, must remain, unless he is willing to maintain his family below a decent standard.

Last year in Cleveland, at the National Conference of Charities and Correction, at the section meeting of the Committee on Standards of Living and Labor, J. W. Magruder, general secretary, Federated Charities of Baltimore, told the following story:

"Joseph Heberle was a German who had become interested in the free public drinking fountains. Though, to use his own expression, he was 'nothing but a common Dutchman,' he succeeded in accomplishing a great work in Cincinnati, and indeed throughout Ohio. 'Heberle,' said Mr. Magruder, 'had come to my home to enlist me in this fight. We were in the midst of an earnest discussion of the plan of campaign, the persons to be seen, the points to be argued, and all the rest, when into the room there toddled a baby girl. Instantly the man of one idea forgot me, forgot drinking fountain, forgot everything except the child. He crooned over her, fondled her, talked baby talk to her.

" 'Heberle,' I finally interrupted, 'why don't you get married?'

"I ought to have known better. The man's face fell; he turned upon me almost fiercely, and, with eyes flashing, fairly hissed at me: 'I'm nothing but a teamster. I earn only ten dollars a week. The most I can ever hope to earn is eleven dollars. And I'll never ask any woman to undertake the responsibilities of a family.'

"I awoke to the fact that I was looking into the face of a middle-aged man of warm domestic nature, who, rather than subject a wife and children to the privation and slow torture of less than a living wage, was subjecting himself to involuntary bachelordom, and suffering in his own domestic soul a daily martyrdom."

Not only is there a menace here to morality, but the "homeless man," the man who has only himself to support, fixes the standard for wages. Our wage scales are based largely on this standard, and wives and children must support themselves or suffer.

The situation in Canada is complicated by our large foreign immigration. The immigrant's standards of living are lower than Canadian standards. But the Canadian must compete with the immigrant. It would seem that low standards bid fair to win out, for even though the immigrant may be ambitious to attain Canadian standards—and, in spite of economic laws, actually attempt to adopt them—he must in turn compete with his later arrived brother-immigrant, who, anxious only to gain a foothold, is willing to take the lowest wage and put up with almost any privation or injustice. The low standards of the most backward countries of Europe are the base line. So long as standards of living in Canada are even a little above the line immigration will continue, and, as waters find their level, the tendency is for the standards to approximate. That's orthodox political economy! And that, to be candid, is the only reason that I'm a bit suspicious, here, of my own reasoning!

abbreviations

CW City of Winnipeg, City Clerk's Office

HSSM Transactions Historical and Scientific Society of Manitoba Transactions

MFP Manitoba Free Press

PAC Public Archives of Canada

PAM Public Archives of Manitoba

SC Statutes of Canada

SM Statutes of Manitoba

WCIA Western Canadian Immigration Association

WDIB Winnipeg Development and Industrial Bureau

W. Telegram Winnipeg Telegram

WT Winnipeg Tribune

notes

1/The best analysis of the subject of conceptualization and methodology in urban history is Gilbert A. Stelter, "A Sense of Time and Place: The Historian's Approach to the Urban Past," unpublished paper presented to Canadian Historical Association, Queen's University, June 1973.

2/For an account of these facets of Winnipeg's history see Ruben C. Bellan, "Relief In Winnipeg: The Economic Background" (M.A. thesis, University of Toronto, 1941); and Bellan, "The Development of Winnipeg As a Metropolitan Centre" (Ph.D. thesis, Columbia University, 1958).

3/The following sources are useful for determining what literature in Canadian urban history is available: F. H. Armstrong, "Urban History in Canada," *Urban History Group, Newsletter*, No. 28 (December 1969), pp. 1–10; Armstrong, "Urban History in Canada: Present State and Future Prospects," *Urban History Review*, No. 1 (February 1972), pp. 11–14; Yves Martin, "Urban Studies in French Canada," in M. Rioux and Martin, eds., *French-Canadian Society* (Toronto, 1967); Paul-André Linteau, "L'histoire Urbaine au Québec: bilan et tendances," *Urban History Review*, No. 1 (February 1972), pp. 7–10; and Gilbert A. Stelter, *Canadian Urban History: A Selected Bibliography* (Sudbury, 1972).

4/Sam B. Warner, Jr., "If All the World Were Philadelphia: A Scaffolding for Urban History, 1774–1930," *American Historical Review*, Vol. 74, No. 1 (October 1968), pp. 26–43.

5/See, for example, introductory comments of Michel Brunet in his article

entitled, "The British Conquest: Canadian Social Scientists and the Fate of the *Canadiens*," *Canadian Historical Review*, Vol. XL, No. 2 (June 1959).

6/J. M. S. Careless, "Nationalism, Pluralism, and Canadian History," *Culture*, Vol. XXX, No. 1 (March 1969). See also Careless, "Somewhat Narrow Horizons," Canadian Historical Association *Papers*, 1968, pp. 1–10.

7/Armstrong, "Urban History in Canada," p. 2. See also Armstrong, "Metropolitanism and Toronto Re-Examined, 1825–1850," Canadian Historical Association *Papers*, 1966, p. 29.

8/The following books and articles are useful in outlining the historian's task in regard to urban studies: Sam B. Warner, Jr., "If All the World Were Philadelphia: A Scaffolding for Urban History, 1774–1930"; H. J. Dyos, ed., *The Study of Urban History* (London, 1968), passim; Eric E. Lampard, "American Historians and the Study of Urbanization," *American Historical Review*, Vol. LXVII, No. 1 (October 1961), pp. 49–91; O. Handlin and J. Burchard, eds., *The Historian and the City* (Cambridge, 1963) passim; W. Stull Holt, "Some Consequences of the Urban Movement in American History," *Pacific Historical Quarterly*, Vol. XXII (November 1953), pp. 337–351; N. H. Lithwick and G. Paquet, eds., *Urban Studies: A Canadian Perspective* (Toronto, 1968), passim; L. F. Schnore, ed., *Social Science and the City: A Survey of Urban Research* (New York, 1968), passim.

9/See Sam B. Warner, Jr., "A Local Historian's Guide to Social Statistics," in

Streetcar Suburbs (Cambridge, Mass., 1962), pp. 169–178; and John Porter, Ca-nadian *Social Structure: A Statistical Profile* (Toronto, 1967), pp. 1–38.

CHAPTER 1/*The Origins and Incorporation of Winnipeg (pages 7–19)*

1/The history of Manitoba during the years prior to 1870 has been the subject of numerous books and articles. The standard work is W. L. Morton, *Manitoba: A History* (Toronto, 1957). Some of the more important specialized studies are: A. S. Morton, *A History of the Canadian West to 1870–71* (Toronto, 1939); J. M. Gray, *Lord Selkirk of Red River* (Toronto, 1963); E. E. Rich, *The Fur Trade and the Northwest to 1857* (Toronto, 1967); A. C. Gluek, *Minnesota and the Manifest Destiny of the Canadian Northwest* (Toronto, 1965); and G. F. G. Stanley, *The Birth of Western Canada* (Toronto, 1960), pp. 1–74. See also H. C. Klassen, "The Red River Settlement and the St. Paul Route, 1859–1870" (M.A. thesis, University of Manitoba, 1963); A. M. Henderson, "From Fort Douglas to the Forks," *HSSM Transactions*, pp. 15–32; and A. Artibise, "The Crucial Decade: Red River at the Outbreak of the American Civil War," ibid., pp. 59–66.

To avoid confusion in the following pages the use of several terms must be explained. Prior to 1862 there were two distinct groups of buildings within the borders of present-day Winnipeg. The homes and farms of a few original Selkirk settlers were located on Point Douglas. To the south, at the confluence of the Red and Assiniboine rivers, was located the Hudson's Bay Company post of Upper Fort Garry. Both are designated on Map 4. See also the map and account of the establishment of Forts Douglas and Upper Fort Garry in G. Bryce, "The Five Forts of Winnipeg," *Transactions of the Royal Society of Canada*, pp. 135–145.

These two settlements, however, made up only a part of the larger Red River Colony. Up and down the Red River and along the banks of the Assiniboine were located the river lot farms of Scottish, French, and halfbreed settlers. A good map of the entire Red River Colony is contained in Morton, *Manitoba*, p. 89. Thus, when reference is made to the Red River Colony, it is meant to include more than just Upper Fort Garry and Point Douglas.

2/J. Steen and W. Bryce, *Winnipeg, Manitoba and Her Industries* (Winnipeg, 1882), pp. 8–10; and William Douglas, "The Forks Become a City," *HSSM Transactions*, pp. 73–75.

3/G. F. Reynolds, "The Man Who Created the Corner of Portage and Main (Henry McKenney)," *HSSM Transactions*, pp. 5–40.

4/M. McWilliams, *Manitoba Milestones* (Toronto, 1928), pp. 88–89.

5/Henderson, "Fort Douglas to the Forks," p. 24. See also Douglas, "The Forks Become a City," pp. 73–75. Douglas names some of the other business establishments which located around McKenney's store in the years after 1862.

6/There is little record of the growth of Winnipeg between 1863 and 1870. See, however, Steen and Boyce, *Winnipeg and Her Industries*; Douglas, "The Forks Become a City," pp. 73–75; Reynolds, "The Man Who Created the Corner of Portage and Main"; and George Bryce, "The Illustrated History of Winnipeg," Chapter XIII. The latter source is a series of forty articles that were run in the Saturday editions of the *MFP* during 1905. Also useful, particularly for the maps of Winnipeg in 1869 and 1872, is H. A. Hosse, "The Areal Growth and Functional Development of Winnipeg from 1870 to 1913" (M.A. thesis, University of Manitoba, 1956).

7/W. J. Healy, *Winnipeg's Early Days: A Short Historical Sketch* (Winnipeg, 1927), pp. 14–15.

8/George Young, *Manitoba Memories* (Toronto, 1897), pp. 63–64. For other contemporary descriptions of Winnipeg around 1870, see A. Begg and W. R. Nursey, *Ten Years in Winnipeg* (Winnipeg, 1879), Chapter 1, and George Bryce, "Early Days in Winnipeg," *HSSM Transactions*, pp. 1–8.

9/J. E. Steen, *Winnipeg: A Historical Sketch of Its Wonderful Growth, Progress, and Prosperity* (Winnipeg, 1903), p. 5. See also W. T. Thompson and E. E. Boyer, *The City of Winnipeg* (Winnipeg, 1886), pp. 16–21.

10/Morton, *Manitoba*, p. 166.

11/Ibid., pp. 165–173; Begg and Nursey, *Ten Years in Winnipeg*, Chapters I to IV; Bellan, "The Development of Winnipeg as a Metropolitan Centre," pp. 19–22; and *MFP*, 9 Nov. 1872 and 30 Nov. 1872.

12/A short history of many Winnipeg merchants is contained in Steen and Boyce, *Winnipeg and Her Industries*.

13/Ibid.; and Morton, *Manitoba*, pp. 167–168.

14/Bryce, "History of Winnipeg," Chapter XXII; Steen and Boyce, *Winnipeg and Her Industries*, pp. 17–42; and Morton, *Manitoba*, p. 168. The stories of Winnipeggers who made fortunes in real estate are numerous. For one example see Thompson and Boyer, *The City of Winnipeg*, pp. 26–28.

15/Steen and Boyce, *Winnipeg and Her Industries*, pp. 11–13.

16/Begg and Nursey, *Ten Years in Winnipeg*, p. 53.

17/Winnipeg's role as the chief western metropolis is a very important part of its history. However, since this story has already been told in some detail, only passing reference will be made to it in this study. See Bellan, "The Development of Winnipeg as a Metropolitan Centre."

18/See P. F. W. Rutherford, "The Western Press and Regionalism, 1870–1896," *Canadian Historical Review*, pp. 287–305.

19/See J. M. S. Careless, "The Development of the Winnipeg Business Community," *Transactions of the Royal Society of Canada*, pp. 239–254.

20/George H. Ham, *Reminiscences of a Raconteur* (Toronto, 1921), pp. 29–30.

21/Bryce, "History of Winnipeg," Chapter XXIII.

22/A. D. Phillips, "The Development of Municipal Institutions in Manitoba to 1886" (M.A. thesis, University of Manitoba, 1948), Part II, Chapter 1.

23/Begg and Nursey, *Ten Years in Winnipeg*, p. 52. See also Bryce, "History of Winnipeg," Chapter XX.

24/There is no evidence available to suggest that this view was a mistaken one. There seemed no reason why the legislature should have refused Winnipeg's request, unless, of course, members representing other incipient "commercial emporiums" felt, as Begg did, that incorporation was the key to rapid progress.

25/Bryce, "History of Winnipeg," Chapter XX; Begg and Nursey, *Ten Years in Winnipeg*, p. 53; *The Manitoba Gazette and Trade Review*, 4 May 1872; Healy, *Winnipeg's Early Days*, p. 25; and *MFP* 14 Dec. 1872.

The Hudson's Bay Company and the four other property owners had good reason to oppose incorporation. In 1874 the assessment on these properties was as follows: HBC—$595,312; Bannatyne—$84,225; McDermott—$78,876; Macaulay—$44,500; and Alexander Logan—$53,000. See Thompson and Boyer, *The City of Winnipeg*, p. 19.

26/*MFP*, 21 Dec. 1872 and 4 Jan. 1873; and Bryce, "History of Winnipeg," Chapter XX.

27/*MFP*, 8 March 1873. Manitoba at this time had an appointed Upper House of seven members, and an elected assembly of twenty-four.

28/Begg and Nursey, *Ten Years in Winnipeg*, pp. 80–81.

29/*MFP*, 15 and 29 March 1873.

30/Ibid., 15 March 1873. See also Bryce, "History of Winnipeg," Chapter XX.

31/*MFP*, 8 March 1873. This is a quote of Francis Evan Cornish, who was to become Winnipeg's first mayor in 1874.

32/*MFP*, 1 and 15 Nov. 1873; Bryce, "History of Winnipeg," Chapter XX.

33/*SM*, 1873, Chap. 7; and *MFP*, 15 Nov. 1873.

34/*MFP*, 25 Oct. 1873. See also the issue of 22 July 1874 in which Winnipeg's incorporation is referred to as "an event of importance and will be hereafter looked upon as a noteworthy landmark in the path of British American progress."

35/For a more detailed discussion of Ontario influences on Manitoba's municipal development, see Phillips, "The Development of Municipal Institutions." It should be noted that the Bill of Incorporation was framed by F. E. Cornish, a lawyer who received his training in Ontario.

36/From the date of incorporation in November 1873 until 1886 the government of Winnipeg was carried on under the powers of a special charter of incorporation granted by the provincial legislature. In the latter year this special charter was repealed, and from that time until 1902 the city's affairs were administered under the provisions of the Manitoba Municipal and Assessment Acts. In practice this change signified no reduction in the city's powers. In 1902 the city again obtained a special charter, which arrangement lasted until the present-day.

37/Begg and Nursey, *Ten Years in Winnipeg*, pp. 110–111.

38/*MFP*, 19 Sept. 1874; *The Manitoban*, 15 Aug. 1874.

39/Begg and Nursey, *Ten Years in Winnipeg*, p. 101;*The Manitoban*, 28 Feb. 1874.

CHAPTER 2/*The Dominance of a Commercial Elite (pages 23–42)*

1/A. R. M. Lower, *Canadians in the Making: A Social History of Canada* (Toronto, 1958), p. 364. When Professor M. Prang reviewed John Porter's, *Vertical Mosaic: An Analysis of Social Class and Power in Canada* (Toronto, 1965), she lamented that Canadian historians had done so little work in the study of elite groups. She suggested that such groups needed to be studied from a regional approach in order to confirm or disprove Porter's comments concerning the low degree of social mobility in Canadian society as a whole. See *CHR*, Vol. XLVII, No. 2 (June 1966), pp. 156–158. Hopefully, this chapter will answer some of the questions raised in her review.

2/This chapter is concerned with why Winnipeg's businessmen were able to implement their growth ethic so easily. Other chapters—3, 4, 5, 6, and 7—will show how they did so.

3/Data for these tables has been drawn from a variety of sources: local newspapers; PAM, the *Manitoba Biography Collection;* CW, Election Records; *Who's Who in Western Canada* (Winnipeg, 1911); and Manitoba Library Association, *Pioneers and Early Citizens of Manitoba* (Winnipeg, 1971). A complete list of mayors, controllers, and aldermen, and the dates they held office, can be found in Appendix A.

Unfortunately, I have not been able to locate sufficient biographical data on enough office holders to attempt a comprehensive collective portrait, including such things as place of origin, religious and political affiliation, racial origin, time of arrival, place of residence in city, and so on. Thus, until a great deal more work is done on this subject, any conclusions offered must be of an impressionistic nature.

4/The Board of Control was established in 1907 as a kind of executive committee and was designed to bring "business efficiency" to local government (see Chapter 3). See also H. Carl Goldenberg, *Report of the Royal Commission on Municipal Finances and Administration of the City of Winnipeg* (Winnipeg, 1919), Chapter 3. This work is useful for background on the structure of Winnipeg's civic government since 1874.

5/The following sources contain some discussion of who governed other North American cities: Guy Bourassa, "The Political Elite of Montreal: From Aristocracy to Democracy," L. D. Feldman and M. D. Goldrick, eds., *Politics and Government of Urban Canada* (Toronto, 1969), pp. 124–133; M. S. Donnelly, "Ethnic Participation in Municipal Government: Winnipeg, St. Boniface and the Metro Corporation of Greater Winnipeg," ibid., pp. 61–70; N. E. Long, "Political Science and the City," in L. F. Schnore, ed., *Social Science and the City* (New York, 1968), pp. 243–262; R. A. Alford, "The Comparative Study of Urban Politics," ibid., pp. 263–302; S. B. Warner, Jr., *The Private City* (Philadelphia, 1968), pp. 79–98 and passim; and S. P. Hays, "The Politics of Reform in Municipal Government in the Progressive Era," in A. B. Callow, ed., *American Urban History* (Toronto, 1969), pp. 421–439.

6/Good accounts of postwar municipal politics in Winnipeg can be found in Paul Barber, "Class Conflict in Winnipeg Civic Politics: The Role of the Citizens' and Civic Elections Organizations" (PAM, unpublished paper, March 1970); and A. B. McKillop, "Citizens and Socialists: The Ethos of Political Winnipeg, 1919–1935" (M.A. thesis, University of Manitoba, 1970).

7/Labour's weakness in municipal politics is also revealed by the 1902 civic election. They attempted to unseat Mayor Arbuthnot and elect J. F. Mitchell, a businessman considered more friendly to their point of view. They failed, however, with Arbuthnot winning the upper and middle class districts of the city (wards 1, 2, 3, and 4), and Mitchell taking only wards 5 and 6. (For a detailed discussion of ward differentiation, see Chapter 9). Moreover, labour probably would have done even more poorly had they run an artisan or workingman, for Mitchell was a prominent Winnipegger and a former member of the provincial legislature.

8/Besides the sources listed in note 3, I have used biographical data contained in H. Huber, "Winnipeg's Age of Plutocracy: 1901–1914," unpublished paper.

9/Information on the clubs which are mentioned in the following sketches can be found in The Clubs, Societies and Associations of Winnipeg (Winnipeg, 1908).

10/F. R. Munro, "Winnipeg's New Mayor," Busy Man's Magazine, Feb. 1909, in PAM, W. S. Evans Papers.

11/W. Telegram, 10 Oct. 1906; and MFP, 12 Dec. 1906.

12/W. Telegram, 29 Jan. 1910.

13/See Chapter 11.

14/See, for example, Bourassa, "The Political Elite of Montreal: From Aristocracy to Democracy."

15/W. Telegram, 29 Jan. 1910.

16/Two of the many examples are J. W. Cockburn and J. G. Harvey. Together they served a total of twenty-nine years as aldermen and controllers (see Appendix A). Cockburn made his fortune in real estate speculation, Harvey in the grain business.

17/Almost any number of examples could be given to show the national and regional interests of Winnipeg's commercial elite. Who's Who in Western Canada provides a ready reference.

18/The role of individual and group decisions in the rise of Winnipeg is discussed in Careless, "The Development of the Winnipeg Business Community," and Bellan, "The Development of Winnipeg as a Metropolitan Centre."

19/See Town Topics, passim; and Civic, Social and Athletic Association, Souvenir of Winnipeg's Jubilee, 1874–1924 (Winnipeg, 1924), pp 131–145.

20/Morton, Manitoba, p. 415. See also M. K. Mott, "The 'Foreign Peril': Nativism in Winnipeg, 1916–1923" (M.A. thesis, University of Manitoba, 1970), pp. 99–100.

21/See McWilliams, Manitoba Milestones, pp. 169–170; Representative Men of Manitoba (Winnipeg, 1902), pp. xviii–xx; and Jubilee, 1874–1924, pp. 101–105, 123–125.

22/Careless, "The Development of the Winnipeg Business Community," pp. 247–248; Morton, Manitoba, p. 193; George Bryce, "Treasures of our Library," HSSM Transactions; and George Bryce, "A Great City Library," ibid.

23/Representative Men of Manitoba, pp. xix–xx; McWilliams, Manitoba Milestones, pp. 168–170; Morton, Manitoba, pp. 191, 265, 321–323.

24/Mrs. G. Bryce, "The Charitable Institutions of Winnipeg," HSSM Transactions. See also chapters 10 and 12, below.

25/MFP, 16 Nov., 28 Dec. 1912, and 1 March 1913. See also W. Kristjanson, The Icelandic People in Manitoba (Winnipeg, 1965), pp. 288–296, 428–434; A. Chiel, The Jews in Manitoba (Toronto, 1961), pp. 168–181; and P. Yuzyk, The Ukrainians in Manitoba (Toronto, 1953), pp. 200–202. For discussions of the election of Mayor Steve Juba in 1954, see Donnelly, "Ethnic Participation in Municipal Government"; and D. C. Masters, "The English Communities in Winnipeg and in the Eastern Townships of Quebec," in M. Wade, ed., Regionalism in the Canadian Community (Toronto, 1969), pp. 130–159

26/For brief biographical sketches of the losers see Huber, "Winnipeg's Age of Plutocracy."

27/Good accounts of Winnipeg's labour organizations can be found in M. Robin, *Radical Politics and Canadian Labour, 1880–1930* (Kingston, 1968), pp. 21–118; and Leo Heaps, *The Rebel in the House* (London; Niccolo Publishing Co., 1970), pp. 1–12.

28/Robin, *Radical Politics and Canadian Labour*; and A. R. McCormack, "Arthur Puttee and the Liberal Party, 1899–1904," *CHR*, pp. 141–163.

29/See comments to this effect in cw, *Council Communications*, Series II, No. 1428, read 10 March 1890.

30/All the information on electors' qualifications, etc, is taken from the *SM*; in particular from the Manitoba Municipal Act and the Winnipeg City Charter.

31/cw, *1906 Election Records*.

32/Progressive in the sense that such a step was not taken at the provincial level until 1916, and even later at the federal level.

33/*W. Telegram*, 28 Jan. 1914.

34/*MFP*, 28 Jan. 1914.

35/*WT*, 23 Dec. 1910. See also yearly editions of *Lists of Electors*.

36/*WT*, 23 Dec. 1910.

37/Ibid., 31 Dec. 1910, 21 Jan. 1911, 10, 13, and 16 Feb. 1911.

38/It could perhaps be argued that service as alderman did not require an inordinate amount of time. However, the important and powerful positions of chairman of the Finance Committee, etc., did. Also, in the case of mayor, the time required to do an effective job was a crucial question throughout the period. See, for example, *MFP*, 22 Nov. 1894.

39/J. A. Jackson, *The Centennial History of Manitoba* (Toronto, 1970), pp. 164, 156–176.

40/Ibid. See also "Our Elections, Impressions in a Foreign Ward," (newspaper clipping dated Nov. 1911) in pac, *J. S. Woodsworth Papers*, M. G. 27, Series III C7, Vol. 29.

41/See, for example, discussion of a municipal power project in Chapter 6.

42/See Mott, "The 'Foreign Peril': Nativism in Winnipeg"; and McKillop, "Citizens and Socialists: The Ethos of Political Winnipeg."

CHAPTER 3/*Civic Politics: The Search for Business Efficiency in Municipal Affairs (pages 43–58)*

1/See D. A. Young, "Canadian Local Government Development: Some Aspects of the Commissioner and City Manager Forms of Administration," in *Politics and Government of Urban Canada*, pp. 207–218; W. B. Munroe, "Boards of Control and Commission Government in Canadian Cities," Canadian Political Science Association, *Papers and Proceedings* (Ottawa, 1913), pp. 112–123; and Hays, "The Politics of Reform in Municipal Government in the Progressive Era."

2/*MFP*, 24 Oct. 1893.

3/Population statistics can be found in Chapter 8. For a general discussion of municipal development during the years 1874–81 see Phillips, "Development of Municipal Institutions in Manitoba to 1886"; Charles R. Tuttle, *The Civic Situation, Including a*

Brief History of the Corporation of Winnipeg from 1874 to the Present Time (Winnipeg, 1883); Begg and Nursey, *Ten Years in Winnipeg*; and Alan C. Ewart, "Municipal History of Manitoba," *University of Toronto Studies*, Studies in History and Economics, pp. 131–148.

4/*Winnipeg Times*, 20 Oct. 1894.

5/*Manitoba Sun*, 7 Dec. 1886.

6/Begg and Nursey, *Ten Years in Winnipeg*, pp. 101–102. The latter two bond issues are discussed at length in Chapter 4.

7/*MFP*, 25 Dec. 1882; and Tuttle, *The Civic Situation*, pp. 31–33. The 1882 Council also increased the number of aldermen from twelve to eighteen.

8/*Winnipeg Times*, 12 April 1883; Tuttle, *Civic Situation*, pp. 31–79; and G. B. Brooks,

Plain Facts about the New City Hall (Winnipeg, 1884), passim.

9/*Winnipeg Times*, 16 April 1883.

10/Ibid., 26 April 1883.

11/Ibid., 16 April 1883.

12/Bellan, "The Development of Winnipeg," pp. 60–70.

13/For short biographies of the millionaires, see "Winnipeg's Millionaires," *W. Telegram*, 29 Jan. 1910. Other biographical information can be found in *Pioneers and Early Citizens of Manitoba*; *Manitoba: Pictorial and Biographical* (Winnipeg, 1913); and Peter Lowe, "All Western Dollars," *HSSM Transactions*, pp. 10–25.

14/*Winnipeg Times*, 15 May 1883; and *MFP*, 15 May 1883. One of the interesting facets about this citizens' meeting, and the scores of others that were held in ensuing years, was that nearly all were attended only by businessmen. In this case, for example, it would not be out of place to call the gathering a Board of Trade meeting. This is not to say that Board of Trade members were not citizens. But, conversely, this meeting does not deserve the connotation that the word "citizen" implies. Rarely did the so-called "mass" or "citizen's" meeting contain a representative cross-section of the Winnipeg populace. A list of those present at this particular meeting is contained in above references.

15/*MFP*, 15 May 1883.

16/Ibid.

17/The reaction of the local press to the POA was most favourable. See, for example, ibid., 16 May 1883.

18/*Winnipeg Times*, 29 May 1883. The fifteen amendments are reproduced in full in Appendix B, Part I.

19/*Winnipeg Times*, 1 June 1883.

20/Ibid., 30 Oct. 1883.

21/*Winnipeg Times*, 12 Nov. 1883; *MFP*, 16 Nov. 1883; and Tuttle, *The Civic Situation*, pp. 66–69.

22/*Winnipeg Times*, 11 Dec. 1883. For a detailed account of Logan's civic career see

A. F. J. Artibise, "Alexander Logan of Winnipeg," *Beaver*, pp. 4–12.
Alexander McMicken, Logan's opponent in the 1883 election, had been born in Queenstown, Upper Canada, in 1837. He arrived in the Red River Colony in the early 1870s and established the first bank in the city. He was one of the promoters of the incorporation of Winnipeg and served as alderman in 1875, 1880, and 1881. He was elected mayor for 1883. McMicken's unpopularity with the POA seems to stem from the fact that during his term as mayor he acted as banker for the city. Also, when a bond issue of $1,250,000 was authorized early in 1882, he personally sold these in New York. In other activities, McMicken promoted a racetrack in Winnipeg and organized the first cricket club in the city. He was a Presbyterian.

23/CW, *City Council Minutes*, 7 Jan. 1884; and *MFP*, 8 Jan. 1884.

24/*MFP*, 6 March 1884.

25/*Winnipeg Times*, 7 May 1884. See also issue for 5 Dec. 1884; and *MFP*, 5 April 1884.

26/*Winnipeg Times*, 23 Aug. 1884.

27/*MFP*, 30 Oct. 1884.

28/PAM, "Report of the Special Auditors," dated 9 June 1884.

29/*MFP*, 8 Oct. 1884.

30/Ibid. For example, Alderman Stuart Macdonald was re-elected in 1885 on the "Citizen's Ticket."

31/Ibid., 25 Oct. 1884.

32/Ibid., 24 Oct. 1885. See also ibid., 12 Nov. 1884.

33/Ibid. For a short biographies of J. A. M. Aikens, see J. K. Johnson, ed., *The Canadian Directory of Parliament* (Ottawa, 1968); and "Winnipeg's Millionaires," *W. Telegram*, 29 Jan. 1910. Like so many other prominent Winnipeggers, Aiken made his fortune in real estate.

Hamilton's opponents in the mayoralty contest were Alexander McMicken and E. G. Conklin. The latter was a partner in the real estate firm of Conklin and Fortune. He had served as alderman from 1877 to 1880 and as mayor in 1881. In other activities Conklin was organizer of the first rifle association in Manitoba, an early president of the St. Andrew's Society, vice-president of the first curling club, and a veteran member of the Masonic Order. He also served a term as MLA.

34/*MFP*, 12 Dec. 1891.

35/Ibid, 10 Nov. 1884.

36/Ibid., 9 Dec. 1884. It is interesting to note that while the 1884 Council had three aldermen who were members of the Board of Trade, the 1885 Council had eight. It should also be pointed out that the elections of 1883 and 1884 indicate that the backing of the Board of Trade was essential for success at the polls. Both McMicken and Conklin had impressive credentials, but neither received the support of the Board of Trade. Logan and Hamilton, the winners, did.

37/*Manitoba Sun*, 11 Nov. 1889. See also ibid., 18 Nov. 1889; and *MFP*, 12 Dec. 1891. An interesting sidelight to the election of 1884 and its aftermath was the reaction of organized labour. The 1885 Council and their successors quickly reduced public expenditures with the result that many workingmen engaged in public works projects lost their jobs. The Knights of Labor made strong protests to Council and listed five reasons why such programs should be continued. See *Council Communications*, Series I, No. 4710, read 19 Jan. 1885. Significantly, Council not only did not respond to these requests, but in the next few years the business-dominated Council did find considerable sums for a vacant lands program. See Chapter 7.

38/Munro, "Boards of Control and Commission Government," p. 112.

39/Ibid., p. 113. See also *WT*, 29 Oct. 1894.

40/All are reproduced in Appendix B.

41/Munroe, "Boards of Control and Commission Government," pp. 113-114.

42/*WT*, 9 Sept. 1892. Mayor Alexander Macdonald was typical of Winnipeg's mayors during this period. He had come to

Winnipeg in the 1870s from Ontario and had established himself in the wholesale business. He made a large fortune from this enterprise, as well as from real estate speculation. He was also involved in "mercantile establishments in the growing towns of the west." Prior to becoming mayor, he served as alderman in 1887 and 1888. He was one of the founding members of both the Board of Trade and the Historical and Scientific Society of Manitoba.

43/*MFP*, 19 Nov. 1895.

44/See H. Huber, "The Winnipeg Board of Control, 1907-1918; Good Business or Progressive Municipal Reform?," PAM, unpublished paper, March 1970.

45/Mayor Sharpe and Alderman Latimer were on the executive of the Union from 1904 to 1906. The delegates to the annual meetings of the Union always gave detailed reports of the proceedings to Council on their return. See, for example, *Council Communications*, Series II, No. 7338, read 17 Oct. 1904.

46/All these problems are discussed at length in succeeding chapters. See in particular chapters 6, 11, and 12.

47/See *MFP*, 5 April 1904, for an account of Sharpe's trip to Montreal and Toronto.

48/*W. Telegram*, 27 Sept. 1905. A good account of Sharpe's views on the Board of Control are contained in his address to the Canadian Club of Winnipeg, 10 Jan. 1906. See Appendix B for details of the Board of Control system.

49/*W. Telegram*, 27 Sept. 1905. The Board of Control had been instituted in Toronto in 1897. See S. M. Wickett, "City Government in Canada," *University of Toronto Studies*, Studies in History and Economics, pp. 1-24.

50/*W. Telegram*, 27 Sept. 1905.

51/*MFP*, 9 Nov. 1905. See also PAM, Winnipeg Board of Trade, *Annual Report for 1907*. All the local newspapers expressed support for the action taken by the business organization. See *MFP*, 9 Nov. 1905; *W. Telegram*, 9 and 13 Nov. 1905; and *WT*, 9 Nov. 1905.

52/See Appendix B.

53/See Chapter 6.

54/See, for example, *MFP*, 20 June 1906 and 23 June 1906; and *WT*, 22 June 1906.

55/*MFP*, 29 June 1906.

56/Morton, *Manitoba*, p. 304.

57/*WT*, 21 Sept. 1910. See also J. H. Ashdown, "Winnipeg's Board of Control," *The Canadian Municipal Journal*, Vol. 4, No. 10 (1908), pp. 445–446; and *Canadian Annual Review*, 1912, "Special Supplement," pp. 70–90.

The men who served on the Board of Control over the years were all outstanding businessmen. From 1909 to 1911, for example, the four members of the Board were J. G. Harvey, J. W. Cockburn, A. A. McArthur, and R. D. Waugh. The latter became mayor in 1912.

James Graham Harvey had moved to Winnipeg from Ontario in 1872 and made a fortune in real estate. He called himself a "gentleman" and a man of independent means. He served on the Parks Board in 1904 and on City Council in 1886 and from 1899 to 1906. He was a member of the Commercial Travellers' Club and the Masonic Lodge and was a Liberal and a Presbyterian.

John Wesley Cockburn was also called a "gentleman." An engineer by profession, he was engaged in politics almost full time from 1901 on. He sat as alderman in 1891 and 1892 and from 1901 to 1906. He was president of the Winnipeg Liberal Association in 1906. He had arrived in Winnipeg in 1882 from Ontario and was a Methodist.

Like Cockburn and Harvey, Archibald A. McArthur also came to Winnipeg from Ontario in 1882. He owned the McArthur Grocery Company. He served as alderman in 1906 and 1907. He was a member of the Masonic Lodge, the Liberal party, and the Baptist Church.

CHAPTER 4/*Winnipeg's Legacy: Geography, Railroads, and a Triumphant Growth Ethic* (*pages 61–76*)

1/General background for this chapter and for the broader question of transportation in the Northwest can be found in the following works: Morton, *Manitoba*, Chapter 7; J. B. Hedges, *Building The Canadian West* (New York, 1939), Chapter 1; R. England, *The Colonization of Western Canada* (London, 1936), Chapter 3; G. P. deT. Glazebrook, *A History of Transportation in Canada* (Toronto, 1964), II, Chapter 7; Begg and Nursey, *Ten Years in Winnipeg*, passim; Bellan, *The Development of Winnipeg as a Metropolitan Centre*, chapters 1 and 2; and Bellan, "Rails across the Red: Selkirk or Winnipeg," *HSSM Transactions*, pp. 69–77.

2/England, *Colonization of Western Canada*, p. 53.

3/Canada, *Sessional Papers*, 1870, No. 12, pp. 18–30.

4/*MFP*, 5 July 1873. See also ibid, 9 March 1873 and 18 July 1874.

5/PAC, Department of Public Works Papers, R. G. 11, Series III, Vol. 125, Reference No. 004033, 13 July 1874. A good account of the difficulties encountered on the Dawson Road is contained in Pierre Berton, *The National Dream; The Great Railway, 1871–1881* (Toronto, 1970), pp. 52–58. See also map of this route on pp. 54–55.

6/J. A. D. Stuart, *The Prairie WASP* (Winnipeg, 1969), pp. 31–33. For a contemporary account of the difficulties of the American route, see M. Fitzgibbon, *A Trip to Manitoba* (Toronto, 1880). The author travelled from Toronto to Sarnia by rail, then by boat to Duluth, rail to Crookston and, finally, by boat to Winnipeg.

7/Gluek, *Minnesota and the Manifest Destiny of the Canadian Northwest*, Chapters 1–3; and Klassen, "The Red River Settlement and the St. Paul Route."

8/C. M. Studness, "Economic Opportunity and the Westward Migration of Canadians During the Late Nineteenth Century," *Canadian Journal of Economics and Political Science*, pp. 570–584. Winnipeg City Council tried to redress this imbalance in immigration by attempting to have a federal government agent appointed to look after the interest of British subjects passing over the route. No such agent was appointed. See *City Council Minutes*, 13 April 1874.

9/*MFP*, 27 Dec. 1913. The belief that railroads were indispensable in the promotion of economic and population growth was one that was held by nearly everyone in North America. See, for example, R. W. Fogel, *Railroads and American Economic Growth: Essays in Econometric History* (Baltimore, 1964), pp. 1–16; and D. J. Boorstin, *The Americans: The National Experience* (Toronto, 1965), pp. 115–123.

10/See, for example, *MFP*, 8 March 1873 and 19 Dec. 1874.

11/A copy of this map, dated 1874, is contained in *Canada: A Handbook of Information for Intending Emigrants* (Ottawa: Department of Agriculture, 1877). Winnipeggers contended that this map was identical to the one published in 1872. The key point about these maps, however, is that both were based on "exploratory surveys." The federal government had not claimed that the maps indicated the final line. Clear evidence that Ottawa had not decided on the route of the main line before 1874 is contained in Canada, *Sessional Papers*, 1872, No. 33, pp. 4–5; and ibid., 1873, No. 2, pp. 53–55.

12/*MFP*, 24 and 31 Jan. 1874, and 9 May 1874.

13/Glazebrook, *A History of Transportation in Canada*, II, pp. 65–66; D. C. Thomson, *Alexander Mackenzie: Clear Grit* (Toronto, 1960), pp. 196–198; and *MFP*, 23 Jan. 1875. See also map of Fleming's route in O. D. Skelton, *The Railway Builders* (Toronto, 1916), p. 118.

14/Fleming's views on the question of flooding can be found in cw, "Documents in Reference to the Bridging of the Red River," City Engineer's Office.

15/Bellan, "Rails Across the Red," p. 70.

16/*MFP*, 19 Dec. 1874; *City Council Minutes*, 3 Feb. 1875.

17/PAM, "The Petition of the Citizens of Winnipeg and Inhabitants of Manitoba...." The pledges, according to Winnipeggers, took tangible form in maps issued by the Minister of the Interior and distributed by government officials of the Immigration

Department. Ibid.; and Canada, House of Commons, *Debates*, 4 April 1887, p. 1121.

18/"Report of Railway Delegation," *MFP*, 17 April 1875.

19/Mackenzie probably agreed to aid in the bridging of the Red River at Winnipeg because $25,000 had already been placed in the estimates toward building a wagon bridge as part of the Dawson Road. When he later learned that a railway bridge would cost as much as $500,000 he withdrew the offer. See cw, *Special Committees File*, "Report of the Mayor of Winnipeg re Railroad Matters," 8 Nov. 1875.

20/*City Council Minutes*, 15 Sept. 1875. Part of this money was to be taken from the funds raised for sewer construction in the city. *MFP*, 10 Aug. 1875.

21/"Report of the Mayor . . . ," 8 Nov. 1875.

22/*MFP*, 7 Feb. 1877.

23/Ibid., 17 and 22 Feb. 1877.

24/Ibid., 5 April 1877. See also issue of 27 April 1877; and Canada, House of Commons, *Debates*, 4 April 1877, pp. 1118–1126.

25/"Report of Special Committee to Wait on D. Mills," Special Committee File, 1 Oct. 1877.

26/*MFP*, 14 March 1878.

27/Ibid., 26 Feb. 1878 and 28 Feb. 1878.

28/The results of the election of 1878 in the federal riding of Selkirk were 555 votes for Donald A. Smith (Liberal) and 545 votes for Alexander Morris (Conservative). The important point, however, was that Smith's majority came from polls outside the city. In Winnipeg itself, the vote was 303 for Morris and only 210 for Smith. See Bryce, "Illustrated History of Winnipeg," Chapter XXXIV. Moreover, the election was later declared void and he was defeated in a by-election in 1880 by former mayor Thomas Scott. Smith (Lord Strathcona) never forgave the Winnipeg voters for this defeat at the polls. Despite the fact that he gave away $12 million during his lifetime and $20 million in his will, Smith donated no charitable dollars to Winnipeg schools or hospitals. He even went so far as to time his return from an inspection of the CPR's Rockies section in 1909 so that he would pass through Winnipeg at night, and he refused to talk to a deputation of citizens who were there to greet him. See *Canadian Directory of Parliament*; and Peter C. Newman, *Flame of Power* (Toronto, 1959), pp. 67–69.

29/"Report of Special Committee on Railways," Special Committees File, 4 Nov. 1878; *City Council Minutes*, 11 and 18 Nov. 1878.

30/*MFP*, 9 April 1879. See also House of Commons, *Debates*, 8 May 1879, pp. 1849–1852. The original intention of chartering the MSWR was proven correct, since in changing the course of the route the federal Minister of Public Works, Charles Tupper, explained that "he was disposed to concur in the views of the engineers and of his predecessor as to the best line for the Pacific Railway . . .; but when they came to consider the question, either of refusing a charter to [the MSWR], or of allowing them to establish a line which bade fair to come into competition with the Canadian Pacific Railway, it had been decided to deflect the main line south of Lake Manitoba." Ibid., p. 1850.

Despite this explanation by Tupper, designed to appeal to Winnipeggers, there was another more important explanation for the adoption of a more southerly route for the CPR. Ironically, it was the findings of John Macoun, a botanist who travelled in the Northwest with Sandford Fleming, that played the largest role in the route change. By proving Palliser and Hind wrong in their assessment of the land south of the Saskatchewan River, Macoun was able to convince Tupper, and eventually the men who built the CPR, that this area was not an arid plain but a fertile belt. For a discussion of Macoun's influence, see Berton, *The National Dream*, pp. 44–46; and Hedges, *Building The Canadian West*, pp. 35–36.

31/PAC, *Privy Council Records*, R.G. 43, Series A 1, Vol. 21, Subject 961, Reference No. 18871, dated 18 April 1879; and House of Commons, *Debates*, 8 May 1879, pp. 1849–1852.

32/*City Council Minutes*, 23 April 1879.

33/The city had considerable trouble getting a bylaw passed. Their first attempt, Bylaw 96, was declared illegal since under the terms of incorporation the city was not empowered to raise money for "bonusing." The second attempt, Bylaw 106, was read twice but it also had to be withdrawn since it had not been properly drawn up. Finally, on 5 Sept. 1879, Bylaw 110 was passed and allowed to stand.

34/See Map 1, and *Winnipeg Times*, 24 May 1879 and 5 July 1879.

35/CW, *Special Railway Committee Minutes*, 2 June 1879–25 July 1879; *City Council Minutes*, 16 Sept. 1879 and 22 Jan. 1880. It is interesting to note that two aldermen, J. H. Ashdown and D. Young, were directors of the MSWR. See *Winnipeg Times*, 24 May 1879.

36/*Council Communication*, Series I, No. 2040, read 2 Nov. 1880.

37/*MFP*, 11 Nov. 1880.

38/Bryce, "Illustrated History of Winnipeg," Chapter XXXIX.

39/*MFP*, 30 Nov. 1880.

40/*Council Communication*, Series I, No. 2278½, read 17 June 1881.

41/J. A. Jackson, "The Disallowance of Manitoba Railway Legislation in the 1880's" (M.A. thesis, University of Manitoba, 1945), Chapter 1. See also H. W. Winkler, "Early Manitoba Railroads," *HSSM Transactions*, pp. 5–13.

42/CW, Bylaw 148, passed 5 Sept. 1881. The directors of the MSWR did not suffer much of a loss, since they leased their line to the CPR in 1884. See Innis, *History of the C.P.R.*, p. 140.

43/The location of the transcontinental through Winnipeg was only one factor in the city's rise to metropolitan status. See Bellan, "The Development of Winnipeg as a Metropolitan Centre." On the other hand, the adoption of a more southerly route was certainly one of the most significant events in the history of Winnipeg. It also had a tremendous impact on the entire Northwest. Prior to the coming of railways, water routes had determined the location of settlements, while after 1881 it was the CPR.

44/Good accounts of the boom can be found in ibid., Chapter 3; J. Macoun, *Manitoba and the Great Northwest* (Guelph, 1882),

Chapter 27; W. J. Healy, *Early Days in Winnipeg* (Winnipeg, 1927), pp. 22–25; Pierre Berton, *The Last Spike: The Great Railway, 1881–1885* (Toronto, 1971), pp. 52–58; and J. H. Gray, *Booze* (Toronto, 1972), pp. 3–19.

45/For one example of the development of a local bank, see Lowe, "All Western Dollars."

46/The *MFP* reported that up to 1909 the tax exemption given the CPR cost the city $900,000. See *MFP*, 11 March 1911.

47/J. H. Gray, *The Boy from Winnipeg* (Toronto, 1970), p. 4.

48/"Traffic and Transportation Report," CW, *City Planning Commission Report*, January 1913. See also Chapter 9, below.

49/*WT*, 4 Dec. 1900.

CHAPTER 5/*Winnipeg: Port of the Northwest (pages 77–87)*

1/Gluek, *Minnesota and the Manifest Destiny of the Canadian Northwest*, pp. 137–140. Also, see map of steamboat routes in ibid., p. 141. Another map of the water routes of Manitoba can be found in Warkentin and Ruggles, *Historical Atlas of Manitoba* (Winnipeg, 1970), pp. 300–301.

2/Gluek, *Minnesota and the Manifest Destiny of the Canadian Northwest*, p. 138. See also H. Bowsfield, ed., *The James Wickes Taylor Correspondence, 1859–1870* (Altona, 1968).

3/For a more detailed account of trade between Winnipeg and St. Paul, see Klassen, "The Red River Settlement and the St. Paul Route." See also M. McFadden, "Steamboating on the Red," *HSSM Transactions*, pp. 21–29; Begg and Nursey, *Ten Years in Winnipeg*, pp. 101–102; Bryce, "Illustrated History of Winnipeg," Chapter XXII; Berton, *The National Dream*, pp. 220–229; and *MFP*, 17 Sept. 1877 and 6 April 1882.

4/*MFP*, 9 Jan. 1875.

5/In 1888 the *MFP* figured the value of this trade on the basis of 4,207 miles of track in Dakota, 4,789 miles in Wisconsin, 4,828 miles in Minnesota, and 5,539 miles in Michigan. It made no mention of the potential in Canada (*MFP*, 11 Aug. 1888.) More general arguments in favour of improvements to the Red River navigation system, as well as general information on the river, can be found in W. Murdoch, "The Red River," *HSSM Transactions*, pp. 1–3; and J. H. Rowan, "The Red River," ibid., pp. 5–11.

6/As an example of Winnipeg's concern over the monopoly the CPR enjoyed in Manitoba and the problems it caused for the city,

see "Petition To Dominion Government Re Control of Railways," CW, Miscellaneous File. It was forwarded to Ottawa in April 1887.

7/"Red River Memorial . . .," *Council Communications*, Series II, No. 2017, read 7 March 1892.

8/*MFP*, 31 Oct. 1893. The most extensive arguments presented by the city in regard to the iron ore deposits are contained in *Council Communications*, Series II, No. 5085, read 11 Sept. 1899. This was a report to the members of City Council and the Board of Trade of a committee appointed to conduct a survey of the resources of the Lake. It also contains comments on the fishing potential of the region.

9/*MFP*, 25 Jan. 1888. See also Stanley, *The Birth of Western Canada*, pp. 184–185. Stanley tells of the formation in 1880 of the North West Navigation Company, with a fleet of five vessels, for the transport of freight and passengers between Manitoba and the settlements on the Saskatchewan.

10/*W. Telegram*, 14 Jan. 1899. The arguments for this water route to the Bay increased in direct proportion to the declining fortunes of the Hudson Bay Railway project. On the latter, see L. F. Earl, "The Hudson Bay Railway," *HSSM Transactions*, Series III, No. 14 (1959), pp. 24–32. The plans for a water route to the Bay ignored the fact that the Hudson's Bay Company had abandoned this system in 1859 because of the enormous difficulties it had encountered. See Gluek, *Minnesota and the Manifest Destiny of the Canadian Northwest*, pp. 140–142.

11/*MFP*, 19 and 20 June 1894.

12/*W. Telegram*, 16 July 1894.

13/Ibid. See also *MFP*, 9 May 1874, and 11 Nov. 1880.

14/This campaign can be followed in detail by consulting the following sources: *MFP*; *City Council Minutes*; *Council Communications*; and PAC, Department of Public Works Records.

15/PAC, *Department of Public Works Records*, R.H. II, Series IV, No. 139,821.

16/*MFP*, 16 April 1893.

17/*MFP*, 9 Oct. 1893. See also *WT*, 6 Oct. and 12 Oct. 1893. For a more general account of western alienation during this period, see Rutherford, "The Western Press and the Regionalism, 1870–96."

18/*WT*, 16 June 1894.

19/*City Council Minutes*, 8 Jan. 1894.

20/Ibid., 15 Jan. 1894. See also *MFP*, 9 Feb. 1894. Alderman Carruthers had come to Winnipeg in 1871 and in 1874 became managing director of the Canada West Fire Insurance Company and in later years became managing director of the Winnipeg Grain Exchange. He was a member of City Council for a number of years. He was a president of the Manitoba Rifle Association, president of the Board of Trade in 1906, and a life governor of the Winnipeg General Hospital. He was a Mason and a Conservative and belonged to the Manitoba Club.

21/*WT*, 20 Feb. 1894. This view was hotly disputed by the proponents of the scheme. See, for example, *MFP*, 24 Feb. 1894.

22/*Council Communications*, Series II, No. 2586, read 19 March 1894.

23/House of Commons, *Debates*, 19 June 1894, pp. 4622–4627.

24/Ibid., p. 4627

25/Ibid., pp. 4627–4628. See also *WT*, 26 June 1894.

26/PAC, "Memorial of the Town of Selkirk . . . ," Department of Public Works Records, R.G. 11, Series IV, No. 181,000.

27/*WT*, 13 Sept. 1895.

28/The negotiations can be followed in the *Annual Reports* of the Winnipeg Board of Trade for 1896, 1897, 1898, and 1899. The man elected as MP for Winnipeg in 1897 was R. W. Jameson. He had served as a Winnipeg alderman from 1892 to 1895 and as mayor in 1896. A lawyer who had come to Winnipeg in 1882, Jameson's main interests lay in real estate speculation. He had large financial interests in the city and he represented several British capitalists who invested money in Winnipeg and Manitoba. He belonged to the Board of Trade and was a member of the Manitoba Club.

29/*MFP*, 26 June 1900.

30/See, for example, Winnipeg Board of Trade, *Annual Report for 1904*.

31/*MFP*, 3 June 1909.

32/"Resolution of Council," *Special Committee File*, 4 April 1911.

33/*Council Communications*, Series II, No. 9365, read 21 Nov. 1911.

34/"Dockage and River Frontage Committee Report," *City Planning Commission Report*, January 1913.

35/"Memorandum to the Board of Trade by the Lake Winnipeg Shipping Company Limited in Regard to Obstructions to Navigation on the Red River," *Special Committees File*, November 1911.

36/"Department of Railways and Canals, Annual Report for 1915," *Sessional Papers*, No. 20a, p. 93.

CHAPTER 6/*The Search for Cheap Power (pages 88–101)*

1/J. W. Cockburn, "Power Plant of Winnipeg, Man.," *The Canadian Municipal Journal*, Vol. VIII, No. X (October 1912), p. 398. Winnipeg's waterworks system is discussed in Chapter 11, below.

2/*MFP*, 20 Dec. 1890.

3/The University of Manitoba was established in Winnipeg in 1877. See W. L. Morton, *One University: A History of the University of Manitoba* (London, 1957).

4/Cockburn, "Power Plan of Winnipeg," p. 400.

5/*Council Communications*, Series II, No. 648, read 13 Oct. 1887. See also *Manitoba Sun*, 13 Oct. 1887, and 12 July 1888.

6/*City Council Minutes*, 6 Feb. 1888.

7/H. N. Ruttan, "Water Power and Navigation of the Assiniboine River," cw, Report Presented to City Council, 5 July 1888.

8/J. T. Fanning, "Report on the Winnipeg Water Power of the Assiniboine in Manitoba," cw, Report presented to City Council, 18 June 1889.

9/*Manitoba Sun*, 19 July 1889.

10/*MFP*, 17 Oct. 1890.

11/*Manitoba Sun*, 19 July 1889.

12/*Council Communications*, Series II, No. 1234, read 22 July 1889. It is interesting to note that four of the five directors of the Assiniboine Power Company, who were at this time anxious to construct the water power privately, were influential members of the Board of Trade. They were W. F. Alloway, J. E. Steen, W. Bathgate, and A. Wright.

13/The course of these negotiations can be followed in the "Report of the Special Committee on Assiniboine River Water Power." See also *City Council Minutes, Council Communications*, and the *MFP*.

14/See, for example, "Memorial of Council of City of Winnipeg asking for permission to construct Water Power Dam . . . without locks," passed 20 Dec. 1890, *Special Committee File*. See the government's reply in *Council Communications*, Series II, No. 1836, read 13 July 1891; *MFP*, 31 July 1891.

15/See, for example, "Report of Special Committee . . . on Water Power," 26 July 1889.

16/*MFP*, 1 Oct. 1901; Warkentin and Ruggles, *Historical Atlas of Manitoba*, p. 303.

17/*MFP*, 17 Oct. 1901 and 10 Oct. 1901; *WT*, 27 Jan. 1903.

18/*Report of Special Committee on Water Power*, read 20 Sept. 1903; *MFP*, 22 Sept. 1903.

19/The negotiations can be followed in the following: *Report of Special Committee on Water Power; Council Communications*,

Series II, No. 7072, read 28 Dec. 1903; *MFP*, 22, 29, and 30 Dec. 1903; and *WT*, 31 Dec. 1903.

20/See, for example, *W. Telegram*, 24 March 1904; *MFP*, 1 March, 15 Aug., and 17 Sept. 1904.

21/A short history of the werc can be found in cw, *Historical and Financial Report, covering the years 1892 to 1918*. See also W. E. Bradley, "History of Transportation in Winnipeg," *HSSM Transactions*, pp. 7–38; *MFP*, 28 Nov. 1903; and *W. Telegram*, 27 Dec. 1913. The various companies acquired by the werc from the date of incorporation to 1906 are as follows, with the cost of acquisition in brackets: Winnipeg Street Railway Company, 1893 ($175,000 cash); Manitoba Electric and Gaslight Company, 1897 ($240,000 cash and $300,000 in stock of werc); Northwest Electric Company, 1900 ($126,947 cash); and Winnipeg General Power Company, 1904 ($250,000 in stock).

22/A fairly concise statement of Winnipeg's problem in connection with the werc can be found in cw, "Memo Re Taking Over the Winnipeg Electric Street Railway System," dated 18 March 1925. See also *MFP*, 24 Feb., 9 March, and 17 March 1906.

23/See, for example, the explanations of Alderman Cockburn, a strong supporter of municipal power, in "Power Plant of Winnipeg," pp. 398–401; and "Winnipeg's Hydro-Electric Power System," *The Western Municipal News*, Vol. 8, No. 12 (Dec. 1913), pp. 390–392. Cockburn subsequently became known as the "Father of City Hydro." See cw, "The 50th Anniversary of City Hydro," pamphlet published by Winnipeg City Hydro, 1961.

24/*City Council Minutes*, 23 Jan. 1905; *MFP*, 24 Jan. 1905. The committee included Alderman Cockburn who had already decided upon a public scheme. See *City Council Minutes*, 6 Feb. 1905.

25/pam, Winnipeg Board of Trade, *Annual Report for 1906*; *MFP*, 26 May 1905; *WT*, 26 May 1905.

26/*MFP*, 27 May 1905; *WT*, 27 May 1905.

27/E. S. Russenholt, "The Power of a City," unpublished manuscript in City Hydro

Office, Winnipeg. The site was actually granted in Cockburn's name and later turned over to the city at no cost to the latter.

28/*SM*, 1899, Chap. 24. This legislation came about when the city was considering the proposal to establish a municipal electric light plant for civic and commercial purposes. At the 1899 session of the legislature they requested legislation to enable them to do so. Their request was opposed by the WERC which by this time had a monopoly of lighting services in Winnipeg. The contention was put forward that it was unfair for the city to enter into competition with a private company. Premier Roblin agreed and stipulated in the legislation that the city had to acquire all existing plants before it could sell power. See *MFP*, 24 Feb. 1906.

29/Ibid., 16 Oct. 1905. Besides being prominent Winnipeg businessmen, all these men had experience as civic politicians. See Appendix A.

30/*MFP*, 3 and 13 April 1906. See also W. R. Plewman, *Adam Beck and Ontario Hydro* (Toronto, 1947).

31/*MFP*, 4 May 1906.

32/Ibid., 4 June 1906.

33/*Council Communication*, Series II, No. 7800, read 11 June 1906.

34/Russenholt, "The Power of a City"; *MFP*, 5 and 18 June 1906; *WT*, 19 and 22 June 1906; *W. Telegram*, 29 June 1906; and *The Voice*, 23 June 1906. It is important to note, however, that the *MFP*, in urging public ownership of electric power, was careful "not to put itself on the side of the socialist fanatics." See M. Donnelly, *Dafoe of the Free Press* (Toronto, 1968), p. 55. The fanatics referred to, of course, were the members of the Winnipeg Trades and Labor Council and the editors of *The Voice*.

35/"Power Prospectus," *Miscellaneous File*. This document was twenty pages in length and endeavoured to answer in advance the criticisms Council felt would be directed toward the scheme. The title page of the document appealed to the growth ethic of the city's voters by declaring "Vote and use

your influence to make Winnipeg a Manufacturing Center."

36/Russenholt, "Power of a City."

37/*W. Telegram*, 29 June 1906; Western .. *Municipal News*, Vol. 1, No. 7.

38/PAM, Winnipeg Board of Trade, *Annual Report for 1906–1907*. See also Mayor Sharpe's address to the Canadian Club on the Board of Control in *MFP*, 11 Jan. 1906; and PAM, Canadian Club of Winnipeg, *Annual Report for 1906*.

39/Russenholt, "Power of a City."

40/*MFP*, 29 June 1906.

41/This controversy can be followed in Russenholt, "Power of a City"; PAM, Board of Trade, *Annual Reports for 1907–1908*; City Council Minutes; Council Communications; and in the local press. See especially *MFP*, 26 Nov. 1907. Mayor Ashdown had Marwick, Mitchell, and Co., chartered accountants, compile a report on the accounts of the city from 1 May 1905 to 30 April 1907. This report, presented 6 March 1908, stated that there were several "serious circumstances present in connection with the City's finances." See CW, "Report of Marwich, Mitchell and Co. . . ."

42/*MFP*, 8 Jan. 1909. A brief history of the Winnipeg Hydro-Electric System from 1906 to the present can be found in the City of Winnipeg, *Municipal Manuals*. The latter are particularly useful for following the success of the project in terms of users and rate schedules. Equally useful up to 1939 is H. Carl Goldenberg, *Report of the Royal Commission on the Municipal Finances and Administration of the City of Winnipeg* (Winnipeg, 1939), Chapter VIII.

43/*MFP*, 10 May 1913. See also issue of 28 July 1913, and *WT*, 1 Sept. 1931. This latter reference is a special edition of the *Tribune* devoted to the hydroelectric system. The overwhelming success of the power project is also apparent from the fact that when the WERC began selling power from their Pinawa Plant in the city in 1906, City Council moved to have the courts block the transmission of the power into the city. They based their move on the terms of Bylaw 543, the original agreement between the WERC and the city. The case went all the way to the Privy Council and was finally decided in the company's favour. But despite the competition thus given to the city's power plant, the latter was able to compete suc-

cessfully. See cw, "Memo Re Taking Over the Winnipeg Electric Railway System," dated 18 March 1925. See also Goldenberg, *Report of the Royal Commission on . . . City of Winnipeg*, Chapter VIII.

44/*MFP*, 28 July 1913.

CHAPTER 7/*The Campaign for Immigrants and Industry (pages 102–125)***

1/*MFP*, 16 March 1904. See also *WT*, 20 Oct. 1906, for a similar expression of "truth" under the headline, "Each New Settler Means Increase in Wealth."

2/*MFP*, 16 March 1904.

3/There has been considerable general comment about the fact that "it was in real estate that the great fortunes of Winnipeg's leading citizens were made." See, for example, Morton, *Manitoba*, p. 168; "Winnipeg: The Gateway of the Canadian West," *Canadian Annual Review*, 1912, Special Supplement, pp. 83–84; and *W. Telegram*, 29 Jan. 1910. The latter is a study of Winnipeg's nineteen millionaires and it is worth noting that nearly all made considerable parts of their fortunes in real estate speculation. Unfortunately, as with so many aspects of Winnipeg's history, the real estate business still requires a good deal of painstaking research. For the purposes of this study, however, it is safe to say that many of Winnipeg's commercial elite had more than a passing interest in real estate, and hence in attracting immigrants.

It should also be noted that many members of the elite, while not directly involved in selling land, stood to make large gains from an influx of immigrants. One example of large profits stemming from population growth was that of a building contractor, John E. Wilson. During the boom period 1902–1905 Wilson made profits of $125,000 "in building and speculation." See *Manitoba: Pictorial and Biographical*, pp. 111–116.

4/*The Voice*, 24 Jan. 1902. See also the issue of 23 April 1903.

5/The early efforts of the federal government are dealt with in H. D. Kemp, "The Department of Interior in the West, 1873–1883" (M.A. thesis, University of Manitoba,

1950). See also A. S. Morton, *History of Prairie Settlement*, and C. Martin, "Dominion Lands" Policy (Toronto, 1938); and N. Macdonald, *Canada: Immigration and Colonization, 1841–1903* (Toronto, 1966).

6/*MFP*, 19 April 1873.

7/*Sessional Papers*, 1878, No. 9, p. 50. This was the Annual Report of the Winnipeg Immigration Agent, W. Hespeler. Hespeler was an alderman in 1876, so City Council was well aware of the efforts of the federal government.

8/Several of these requests are located in *Miscellaneous File "G."* They include letters from both American and Canadian points.

9/*City Council Minutes*, 5 Sept. 1892.

10/The pamphlet was entitled "Souvenir of the City of Winnipeg Presented to Members of the British Association for the Advancement of Science, 1884." A copy can be seen in the Rare Book Collection, Provincial Library of Manitoba, Winnipeg.

11/Hedges, *Building the Canadian West*, pp. 94–125.

12/Ibid., pp. 110–111. The *MFP* reviewed the work of the CPR over the years in a long editorial on 26 Aug. 1899.

13/See Stanley, *Birth of Western Canada*, pp. 177–193; M. Zaslow, *The Opening of the Canadian North* (Toronto, 1971), pp. 20–21; J. E. Page, "Catholic Parish Ecology and Urban Development in the Greater Winnipeg Region" (M.A. thesis, University of Manitoba, 1958), pp 99–105; and *MFP*, 15 Oct. 1901.

14/Ibid. The inhabitants of the lands along the Red and Assiniboine rivers in twelve of the Red River parishes enjoyed the exclusive right to cut hay on the outer two miles immediately in the rear of their river lots, and this outer belt became known as the "hay privilege." "Staked claims" were lands that had been surveyed just prior to the transfer of Rupert's Land to Canada. Of this class, some of the lands had been entered upon and occupied constantly since that time. The problem was caused by lands that had been little improved but the ownership of which had been recognized locally. See Kemp, "Department of the Interior," pp. 111–132. For a clear picture of the extent of land reserved for these purposes see Map 3, "Reserves and Settlements in Manitoba in 1881," in J. Friesen, "Expansion of Settlement in Manitoba, 1870–1890," *HSSM Transactions*, p. 42.

15/*MFP*, 13 June 1876.

16/*MFP*, 3 Feb. 1886.

17/Ibid.

18/*Council Communications*, Series II, No. 450a, read 4 April 1887. See also *MFP*, 5 April 1887.

19/This pamphlet, entitled "Winnipeg: Farm Lands! Cheap Lands! Good Lands! Best Markets! . . . ," can be found in the Rare Book Collection, Provincial Library of Manitoba. Facts about its distribution are available in PAM, Winnipeg Board of Trade, *Annual Report for 1888*.

20/The *MFP*, 28 Nov. 1888, made the following comment: "The supporters of the by-law outnumber the opponents 5 to 1, but this counts for nothing unless it is expressed at the polls."

21/CW, Report of Joint Committee on Vacant Lands, read 18 June 1888.

22/Ibid.

23/Winnipeg Board of Trade, *Annual Report for 1898*; *MFP*, 15 Sept. and 16 Nov. 1898.

24/Hedges, *Building The Canadian West*, pp. 126–169; England, *Colonization of Western Canada*, pp. 65–74; Bellan, "Development of Winnipeg . . . ," pp. 110–165.

25/Morton, *History of Prairie Settlement*, pp. 96–118.

26/After the turn of the century the expansionist railway policies of the Laurier government added to the lowering of the cost of transportation. See Glazebrook, *History of Transportation*, Vol. II, Chapter 10. See

also T. D. Regehr, "The Canadian Northern Railway: The West's Own Product," *CHR*, pp. 177–187.

27/Bellan, "Development of Winnipeg . . . ," pp. 110–111.

28/N. L. Gold, "American Migration to the Prairie Provinces of Canada, 1890–1933" (Ph.D. thesis, University of California, 1933); K. D. Bicha, *The American Farmer and the Canadian West* (Lawrence, Kansas, 1968); and P. F. Sharp, *The Agrarian Revolt in Western Canada* (Minneapolis, 1949), pp. 1–21.

29/Ibid., and Bicha, *The American Farmer*.

30/*MFP*, 22 and 23 Nov. 1895, and 24 Nov. 1895.

31/*MFP*, 23 Jan. and 20 Feb. 1896. See also *Daily Nor'Wester*, 21, 27 and 29 Jan. 1896.

32/*MFP*, 26 Feb. 1896. These men included Mayor Jameson, ex-mayor Gilroy, and aldermen Andrews, Sproule, and Wilson.

33/Winnipeg Board of Trade, *Annual Report for 1896*; *MFP*, 27 and 29 Feb. 1896. See also *Daily Nor'Wester* for same dates.

34/See "A Few Facts: Issued by the Western Canada Immigration Board, Under the Authority of Hon. Clifford Sifton, Minister of the Interior . . . 1897," PAC, Department of the Interior Papers, R.G. 76 PARC 74, File No. 26820.

35/Winnipeg did, however, continue to welcome and conduct tours for press excursions, etc., organized by the federal government and the CPR. See *Council Communications*, Series II, No. 5057, read 31 July 1899. This letter expressed thanks on behalf of the federal government for these activities. See also Hedges, *Building the Canadian West*, pp. 134–135.

36/Hedges, *Building the Canadian West*, 141–168; J. W. Dafoe, *Clifford Sifton in Relation to His Times* (Toronto, 1931), pp. 306–309; and Macdonald, *Immigration and Colonization*, pp. 235–256.

37/Bicha, *The American Farmer*, Chapter 5.

38/Hedges, *Building the Canadian West*, p. 165; Department of the Interior Papers, R.G. 76, PARC 181, File No. 294612, dated 12 April 1904.

39/Ibid. See also *Sessional Papers*, 1905, No. 25 pt. 2, pp. 32–35.

40/"Western Canadian Immigration Association: Its Origin, Organization, and Purposes," PAC, Department of the Interior Papers, R.G. 76, PARC 181. See also Winnipeg Board of Trade, *Annual Report for 1904*.

41/*WT*, 24 and 25 Feb. 1904; *W. Telegram*, 25 Feb. 1904; and Winnipeg Board of Trade, *Annual Report for 1904*.

42/*W. Telegram*, 25 Feb. 1904.

43/For example, in 1905 D. W. Bole was both president of the WCIA and MP for Winnipeg. He was also an ex-alderman. Also, the first vice-president, G. F. Carruthers, was an ex-alderman (1899–1901). Many members of the Board of Trade were also prominent in the executive of the WCIA.

44/See WCIA, *Annual Reports*, for 1904, 1905, 1906, and 1907.

45/WCIA, *Annual Report* for 1905, p. 23. The desirability of getting representatives from many districts was still being debated in 1907.

46/WCIA, *Annual Report* for 1906, pp. 33–34.

47/A copy of this pamphlet is in Department of the Interior Papers, R.G. 76, PARC 181.

48/WCIA, *Annual Reports* and WCIA, "Circulars," Numbers 1–40. These bulletins were mailed every six weeks or so to all the members of the WCIA and reported on the activities of the association. A complete set of these bulletins exist in Department of the Interior Papers, R.G. 76, PARC 181.

49/Ibid., File No. 294612, No. 475003, dated 22 Feb. 1906.

50/Ibid., No. 75003, dated 22 Feb. 1906, and No. 632236, dated April 1907.

51/Ibid., No. 476446, dated 24 Feb. 1906.

52/Ibid., No. 474955, dated March 1906. There are at least twenty other replies similar to this one in File No. 294612.

53/M. L. Hansen and J. B. Brebner, *The Mingling of the Canadian and American Peoples* (New Haven, 1940), p. 223.

54/Morton, *Manitoba*, p. 327.

55/*Council Communications*, Series II, No. 9248, read 5 June 1911.

56/Ibid., No. 9396, read 5 Jan. 1912.

57/*W. Telegram*, 13 Jan. 1912. See also *MFP*, 13 Jan. 1912.

58/*W. Telegram*, 14 Sept. 1906; *MFP*, 25 April 1906.

59/Winnipeg Board of Trade, *Annual Report for 1906*.

60/*WT*, 25 April 1906. It should be noted that on this subject, and many others, the *Tribune* was the avant-garde newspaper in Winnipeg during this period. Perhaps because of Dafoe's international reputation, built up during the 1920s and 1930s, the *MFP* is often regarded as the most cogent Winnipeg newspaper from the date of his assumption of the post of editor in 1901. But, on local matters at least, the *WT*, under the editorship of R. L. Richardson, was much more outspoken. This is not to say the *Tribune* adopted radical views on all subjects—on the question of assimilation, for example, it fell in line with the other newspapers—but it consistently provided the most far-sighted views on most local issues. See, for example, *WT*, 5 Nov. 1903.

61/CW, *Board of Control Communication*, No. 5541, dated 26 June 1911. Reviews of the work of the bureau are also contained in the following references; *MFP*, 4 May 1911; *Winnipeg Saturday Post*, 6 May 1911, p. 9; C. F. Roland, "Community Advertising," *The Canadian Municipal Journal*, Vol. VII, No. V (May 1911), p. 178; C. F. Roland, "The Modern Art of Advertising a City," *The Western Municipal News*, Vol. 5, No. 5 (May 1910), pp. 135–137; "Extracts from an Address . . . delivered by C. F. Roland . . . ," ibid., Vol. 6, No. 6 (June 1911), p. 192.

62/WDIB, *Annual Report for 1914*.

63/*Fourth Census of Canada*, 1901, Vol. III; *Fifth Census of Canada*, 1911, Vol. III; *Postal Census of Manufacturers*, 1916. For the census years 1881 and 1891 the number of employees include all establishments, regardless of size. For the census years 1901, 1911, and 1915 only establishments with 5 or more are included. The population figure for 1915 is an approximation; by 1921 it was 179,085.

64/"Souvenir of the Opening of the Winnipeg Industrial Bureau New Permanent Exposition Building," p. 3, WDIB Papers; and WDIB, *Annual Report* for 1913, p. 24.

CHAPTER 8/*Population Growth and Change in Winnipeg (pages 129–147)*

1/An excellent example is given by the protest the City of Winnipeg made over the federal census taken in 1896. At a council meeting the following resolution was passed: "Your committee believing the census of this city which was lately taken by the Dominion Government to be inaccurate and the figures shown as the population to be far below the actual numbers, and believing that such a statement going abroad would be an injury, it would recommend that an application be made . . . to have the census retaken." *City Council Minutes,* 22 July 1896. See also *Council Communications,* Series II, No. 3383, read 3 August 1896; and Table 6, below.

2/The attitudes of Winnipeg's dominant English-speaking majority will be discussed in Chapters 10 and 11. It should be emphasized at the outset that this chapter aims only to provide a statistical substructure for the entire study, and particularly for chapters 9–13. While this chapter suggests some of the ideas and insights that can be obtained from statistical sketches, the ensuing chapters will deal with their importance at greater length.

3/The federal census figures are taken from the respective censuses of Canada or censuses of the Prairie Provinces. A useful summary can be found in the *Seventh Census of Canada,* 1931, Vol. II, pp. 1–150. The City Assessment Office figures are taken from H. A. Hoose, "The Areal and Functional Development of Winnipeg From 1870 to 1913" (M.A. thesis, University of Manitoba, 1956), pp. 195–196.

4/Bellan, "Relief in Winnipeg: The Economic Background," p. 46. A discussion of the harvest excursions is also contained in Hedges, *Building the Canadian West,* pp. 110–112.

5/A colourful sketch of the employment bureau of the type that could be found in Winnipeg during this period is contained in E. W. Bradwin, *The Bunkhouse Man: A Study of Work and Pay in the Camps*

of Canada, 1903–1914 (New York, 1928), pp. 50–59.

6/For an extensive discussion of Winnipeg as a labour market see Bellan, "Relief in Winnipeg," pp. 46–62. See also Gray, *Booze,* pp. 1–20 and passim.

7/*Sixth Census of Canada,* 1921, Bulletin X, "Population of Canada, 1921." See also W. J. A. Donald, "The Growth and Distribution of the Canadian Population," *Journal of Political Economy,* pp. 292–312; N. Keyfitz, "The Changing Canadian Population," in S. D. Clark, ed., *Urbanism and the Changing Canadian Population* (Toronto, 1961), pp. 3–19; R. H. Coats, "The Growth of Population in Canada," *Annals of the American Academy of Political and Social Science,* Vol. CVII (May 1923), pp. 1–7; C. B. Davidson *et al, The Population of Manitoba* (Winnipeg 1938); and *The Winnipeg Tribune,* 24 January 1947. All these are useful in placing Winnipeg's population growth in a broad perspective. Unfortunately, because of a lack of statistical sketches of other Canadian cities, it is impossible to readily compare Winnipeg's growth with that of other urban areas. Two significant exceptions to the generalization are: Norbert MacDonald, "Population Growth and Change in Seattle and Vancouver, 1880–1960," *Pacific Historical Review,* pp. 297–321; and L. D. McCann, "Urban Growth in Western Canada, 1881–1961," *The Albertan Geographer,* No. 5 (1969), pp. 65–74.

8/*Sixth Census of Canada, 1921,* Bulletin V, "Population of Manitoba, 1921,"; ibid., Bulletin X, "Population of Canada, 1921;" and *Seventh Census of Canada, 1931,* Vol. II, pp. 1–150. It should be noted that the figures for the decade 1911–1921 reflect a great downward trend in growth rates. In a sense this is misleading for the downward trend did not start until the outbreak of war in 1914.

9/Details for this map have been gleaned from various sources. See especially *WT,* 28

May, 1914; and Hosse, "The Areal Growth and Functional Development of Winnipeg." Winnipeg's geographical size, expressed in acres, at different dates is as follows: 1873—2,000; 1882—12,750; and 1914—15,138.

10/This is an estimate. The population of Ward 1 in 1885, following the spectacular increase of the boom period, was 377. This area of the city includes all that portion south of the Assiniboine River and west of the Red River. See Map 4.

11/For further details regarding these three communities see Morton, *Manitoba*; Jackson, *Centennial History of Manitoba*; and Mary M. Ferguson, *A History of St. James* (Winnipeg, 1967).

12/The population figures are taken from Table 6. The birth and death statistics are taken from PAM, Manitoba Department of Agriculture and Immigration, *Annual Reports*; and cw, City Health Department, *Annual Reports*, 1908–1914.

13/cw, City Health Department, *Annual Report for 1908*.

14/*Second Census of Canada*, 1881, Volume I; *Third Census of Canada*, 1891, Volume I; *Fourth Census of Canada*, 1901, Volume I; *Fifth Census of Canada*, 1911, Volume I; and *Census of the Prairie Provinces*, 1916. Saskatchewan and Alberta are included in the territories for census years 1881, 1891, and 1901.

15/Ibid. For census years 1881, 1891, and 1901 Galicia and Bukowina (which were actually provinces in Austria) were included with Austro-Hungarians. See P. Yuzyk, *The Ukrainians in Manitoba* (Toronto, 1953), Chapter 2. The justification for placing these "provinces" in a separate category lies in the fact that their inhabitants were distinctly different from the rest of the populace of the Austrian Empire. In Canada they were called Ukrainians. Ibid., pp. 25–26. See also J. H. Syrnick, "Community Builders—Early Ukrainian Teaching," *HSSM Transactions*, pp. 25–34.

16/See, for example, L. O. Stone, *Migration in Canada* (Ottawa, 1916); M. V. George, *Internal Migration in Canada* (Ottawa, 1970); and W. E. Kalbach, *The Impact of Immigration on Canada's Population* (Ottawa, 1970).

17/L. F. Schnore, "Problems in the Quantitative Study of Urban History," in H. J. Dyos, ed., *The Study of Urban History* (London, 1968), pp. 189–208.

18/S. D. Clark, "The Prairie Wheat Farming Frontier and the New Industrial City," *The Developing Canadian Community* (Toronto, 1962), pp. 99–112.

19/The reasons for the small number of Quebeckers in Manitoba are discussed in A. I. Silver, "French Canada and the Prairie Frontier, 1870–1890," CHR, pp. 11–36. See also Stone, *Migration in Canada*, Chapter 5. The importance of the dominance of Ontarians in Winnipeg is discussed in Chapter 10, below.

20/See *Sixth Census of Canada*, 1931, Bulletin XVI, p. 19. While only 4.3% of Winnipeg's residents in 1911 were born in the U.S., 9.5% of Calgary's, 11.8% of Edmonton's, 4.8% of Regina's, and 8.7% of Saskatoon's were American-born. See also W. L. Morton, *The Progressive Party in Canada* (Toronto, 1950), pp. 36–38.

21/Morton, *Manitoba*, pp. 308–311.

22/*Second Census of Canada*, 1881, Volume I; *Census of the Province of Manitoba*, 1886; *Fourth Census of Canada*, 1901, Volume I; and *Census of the Prairie Province*, 1916. Figures are not available for the 1891 census. It is an understatement to point out that in the interpretation of origin statistics one must exercise extreme care. However, most of the problems have been delineated in an excellent article by L. B. Ryder entitled "The Interpretation of Origin Statistics," *Canadian Journal of Economics and Political Science*, Vol. 21, No. 4 (1955), pp. 466–479. See also V. J. Kaye, "The Problem of the Ethnic Name," in *Early Ukrainian Settlements in Canada, 1895–1900* (Toronto, 1964), xxiii–xxvi. Without going into the complicated problems involved with every group it can be stated that for the purpose of this study only two qualifications need be made. In terms of the German category the figures for 1916 fail to include all appropriate members. This reflects the status of German-Canadian relations. The outbreak of the First World War caused a statistical flight from the German ethnic group. Unfortunately, it is impossible to pinpoint the groups that benefited from the German loss but some research into the question would indicate that it would be the Austrian, Russian, Dutch, and British groups. Thus the figures for these groups in 1916 will tend to be inflated.

The second major problem is one that deals with the Ukrainian group. In general, this group was reported with the Austro-Hungarian group for the period up to 1916. At the latter date, however, a distinction was being made. Thus it should be noted that the vast increase in Ukrainians in 1916 is not all attributable to migration. Moreover, the decrease in the Austro-Hungarian group would have been even more were it not for the flight from the German group.

These qualifications, along with others made in the above-mentioned sources, made it fair to conclude that the usefulness in research of Canadian statistics on origins is limited. However, it is possible to divide the population into broad groups and since that is all I have tried to do in this study, there is little reason to doubt the conclusions drawn from Table 12.

Finally, it should be pointed out that since "origin" most commonly is understood as meaning a distinct cultural or ethnic group, some of the linkages made in Table 12 are not at all accurate. For example, there is obviously a distinction to be made between Russian and Polish cultures. The important fact, however, is that the dominant British group in the city would not make such a distinction. Indeed, they most often grouped the Russians, Poles, and

Ukrainians into the broad category of Slavs or Galicians.

23/See Tables IX and XI of the *Census of the Prairie Provinces*, 1916.

24/The Northern-European group includes Germans and Scandinavians while the Slavic group includes Russians, Poles, Ukrainians, and Austro-Hungarians. Precise distributions are, of course, given in Table 12.

25/See note 14. The classification "non-Christian" includes Buddhists, Confucians, Moslems, Sikhs, and Hindus. The classification "no-religion" includes pagans, agnostics, and atheists.

26/See Porter, *Vertical Mosaic*, pp. 98–104, for a discussion of the influences of ethnicity and religion. One result of the dominance of evangelical-fundamentalist Protestants in Winnipeg was a concern in Winnipeg over temperance. See Gray, *Booze*.

27/*Census of Canada*, 1891, Volume I; *Census of the Prairie Provinces*, 1916; Davidson, *The Population of Manitoba*, pp. 78–103. No figures were available for Canada in 1916 and those included in the table are for 1911.

28/George, *Internal Migration in Canada*, p. 153.

29/*Census of the Prairie Provinces*, 1916.

30/*Census of Canada*, 1891, Volume II; and *Census of the Prairie Provinces*, 1916.

31/Kalbach, *The Impact of Immigration on Canada's Population*, p. 44.

CHAPTER 9/*The Urban Environment (pages 148–173)*

1/Gray, *Boy from Winnipeg*, p. 4. It cannot be too strongly emphasized that the reader will be able to follow the developments discussed in this chapter only if time is taken to study Maps 3 and 4 thoroughly, and to refer to them frequently.

2/Reynolds, "The Man Who Created the Corner of Portage and Main," pp. 21–22 and passim.

3/The following sources deal wholly or in part with Winnipeg's spatial growth: Ibid.; *WT*, 10 June 1911; and Hosse, "The Areal Growth and Functional Development of

Winnipeg." I am particularly indebted to this latter study, especially the excellent collection of maps it contains.

4/Henderson, "From Fort Douglas to the Forks," pp. 15–32. See also *MFP*, 19 Aug. 1911; and cw, City of Winnipeg, *Urban Redevelopment Study No. 1: South Point Douglas*, pp. 1–4.

5/Begg and Nursey, *Ten Years in Winnipeg*, p. 118. They state that in 1875 there were over 5,000 people in Winnipeg while City Assessment Office figures show only 2,061.

6/McWilliams, *Manitoba Milestones*, p. 119.

7/Hosse, "The Areal Growth and Functional Development of Winnipeg," p. 100.

8/The boundaries of these wards are detailed in Begg and Nursey, *Ten Years in Winnipeg*, p. 77.

9/Ibid.; and Hosse, "The Areal Growth and Functional Development of Winnipeg," pp. 85–86.

10/The ward boundaries for the period 1882–1909 are those shown on Map 4. In 1909 and again in 1910 the boundaries for wards 2, 3, 4, 5, and 6 were changed. In 1909 Bylaw 5556 (passed 11 May) altered the boundaries from those shown on Map 4 as follows: Ward 2— western boundary moved to Maryland Street; Ward 3—eastern boundary becomes Maryland Street; Ward 4—northern boundary moved to centre line of CPR main line; Ward 5—southern boundary becomes CPR main line and northern boundary moved to Burrows Avenue; Ward 6—southern boundary becomes Burrows Avenue. In 1910 Bylaw 5895 (passed 4 Feb.) changed the boundaries of wards 2 and 3 as follows: Ward 2—western boundary moved to Spence Street. To avoid confusion all references to wards in this chapter will refer to boundaries as shown on Map 4 and will not take into account the changes of 1909 and 1910.

11/Another feature that distinguished the Winnipeg of 1881 from that of 1911 was the city's radically altered work structure. This aspect of Winnipeg's development will be discussed in Appendix C. I have chosen to comment on Winnipeg's changing occupational structure in an appendix, rather than in the main body of the text, for two reasons. First of all historians are only just beginning to become proficient in the use of occupation statistics, and they are still plagued by numerous problems of definition. Secondly, from what limited work there has been in this area it is clear that more detail is needed than I have been able to obtain. See M. B. Katz, "Social Structure in Hamilton, Ontario," in S. Thernstrom and R. Sennett, *Nineteenth Century Cities: Essays in the New Urban History* (New Haven, 1969), pp. 209–244. It can be pointed out, however, that the information contained in Table C1 is still useful in gaining some perspective on Winnipeg's development. Unfortunately an occupational breakdown by ethnic groups is impossible because of a lack of data.

12/A good illustration of the growth of Winnipeg's business district and its encroachment of residential areas is given in a series of maps produced in *MFP*, 4 March 1911.

13/Hosse, "The Areal Growth and Functional Development of Winnipeg," p. 118.

14/*Henderson's Directory of Winnipeg*, 1901.

15/Ibid., 1914.

16/Winnipeg's metropolitan role is discussed extensively in Bellan, "The Development of Winnipeg as a Metropolitan Centre."

17/*MFP*, 20 Dec. 1910.

18/Urban Renewal and Rehabilitation Board, *Urban Renewal Study No. 2* (Winnipeg, n.d.), pp. 3–5.

19/Ibid. The Midland Railway yards are not indicated on Map 4 since they were not constructed until 1911. They were located in the western part of Ward 4.

20/*Henderson's Directory of Winnipeg*, 1914.

21/The best description of this aspect of Winnipeg society can be found in Gray, *Boy from Winnipeg* and *Booze*. The latter contains a number of excellent photographs of the bars of this era.

22/Ham, *Reminiscences of a Raconteur*, pp. 53–55.

23/*WT*, 10 June 1910. In the trend to residential segregation according to class, four divisions have been consistently used. They are upper class, middle class, working class, and lower class. The divisions are based on occupations and social position. In terms of occupations the upper class would include successful professionals, grain brokers, financiers, manufacturers, real estate agents, etc. The middle class includes many of these same categories, although at a less successful stage. But it would also include managers, foremen, and some artisans and tradesmen. The working class includes the rest of the work force excepting only those with no skills. The latter, of course, are the labouring or lower class. Thus, as an example, in the category of railway employees all four classes would be found: managers and officials; foremen and superintendents; brakemen and trainmen; and labourers.

The social position of the residents of the various wards also provides clues to class differences. Thus, as Chapter 2 showed, Winnipeg's political elite tended to live almost without exception in the South and West Ends. Conversely, the city's disadvantaged immigrants (Slavs and Jews) generally lived in the North End, regardless of occupation.

It is obvious, of course, that no strict divisions can be made between the districts, and my comments are meant to be general observations only. They are, nevertheless, supported by contemporary newspaper accounts. Thus the *MFP*, 17 Aug. 1907, reported: "Wellington Crescent is now the most desirable residential portion of Winnipeg, and it is here that many of the city's merchant princes and financial men have their homes"; and "[Ward 7] is essentially a small house district, being chiefly peopled by workers in the manufacturing districts of Point Douglas and St. Boniface."

It should also be noted that these class divisions were balanced by many other factors: religious, ethnic, political, and so on. I have concentrated only on two of the more important ones here—class and ethnic distinctions.

24/*Manitoba Sun*, 1 Oct. 1887, and 8 Oct. 1887.

25/City of Winnipeg Health Department, *Report on Housing Survey of Certain Selected Areas*, 1918, p. 5.

26/It must be emphasized that the labelling of certain areas of the city at certain dates as "desirable" residential locations was a common habit of Winnipeg's newspapers. This was particularly true of newspaper advertisements. See, for example, *MFP*, 20 June 1903. See also an article entitled "The Progress of Winnipeg's Best Residential Districts from Point Douglas to Tuxedo in Sixty Years," in *WT*, 26 February 1930.

27/*Housing Survey*, 1918, p. 21

28/These statistics are taken from the annual reports of the City of Winnipeg Building Inspector. They are totals for the years 1900, 1904, 1908, and 1912 and do not include every year between 1900 and 1912. For Ward 7 there are figures available only for 1908 and 1912. In these two years there were 4 brick, 128 modern, and 192 non-modern frame homes built in this ward. It should be noted that these building reports contain a wealth of material, much more than could be included here. The difference between modern and non-modern frame homes is that the former have plumbing and concrete foundations, the latter do not.

29/The sources for this table, and similar ones on the North End and South and West Ends, are: *Census of Manitoba*, 1885–1886; *Census of Canada*, 1901; and *Census of the Prairie Provinces*, 1916. In 1886 and 1901 the figures for the central core are those for wards 2 and 4; for the North End, wards 5 and 6; and for the South and West Ends, wards 1 and 3. In 1916 ward statistics were not available and the figures for this date are not entirely accurate. However, the divisions used in the 1916 census—Winnipeg South, Centre, and North—follow the districts I discuss fairly closely.

My use of the word "foreigner" in this and other chapters closely follows its contemporary usage. All non-Anglo-Saxons (and Anglo-Saxons included British, American, and Canadian) were grouped together as "foreigners." The attitude of the Anglo-Saxons to Europeans—and particularly Jews and Slavs—was epitomized by the canvassers for *Henderson's City Directory*. When they came to a family with an unpronounceable name, or an "unspellable" name, they simply used the word "foreigner" which seemed to satisfy everybody. See Gray, *Boy from Winnipeg*, pp. 3–4.

30/G. F. Chapman, "Winnipeg: The Melting Pot," *The Canadian Magazine*, p. 410. Chapman notes that "The main line of the Canadian Pacific Railway ... is generally accepted as a division, the foreign section being to the north. The 'north-end' has become a significant definition in the city."

31/John Marlyn, *Under the Ribs of Death*

(Toronto, 1957), p. 11. Marlyn arrived in Winnipeg in 1912 as a young child and grew up in the city. He was a Hungarian.

32/Gray, *Boy from Winnipeg*, p. 3.

33/The growth of the CPR yards can be followed in the following sources: *MFP*, 17 Sept. 1898, 19 Dec. 1903, 26 Nov. 1904, and 9 May 1905. The detrimental effect of these facilities on the North End was at the time recognized by the *WT* (see Chapter 4, p. 75). The City Planning Commission which reported in 1913 also criticized the manner in which the CPR and other railways cut up the residential areas of Winnipeg.

34/"Tide of Winnipeg's Population Pouring Northward," *The Dominion*, Vol. 4, No. 1 (October 1912), pp. 13–14.

35/See, for example, G. F. Chapman, "Winnipeg: The Refining Process," *The Canadian Magazine*, Vol. XXXIII, No. 6 (Oct. 1909), pp. 548–554; and *WT*, 15 Sept. 1906.

36/See, for example, City of Winnipeg Urban Renewal and Rehabilitation Board, *Urban Renewal Study No. 5: Selkirk Avenue—C.P.R. Yards—Salter Street—Main Street* (Winnipeg, n.d.), passim.

37/V. Turek, *The Poles in Manitoba* (Toronto, 1967), p. 109.

38/*MFP*, 1 March 1913.

39/Ibid., 28 December 1912. See also H. Herstein, "The Growth of the Winnipeg Jewish Community and the Evolution of its Educational Institutions," *HSSM Transactions*, Series III, No. 22 (1965–66), pp. 27–66.

40/W. J. Sisler, *Peaceful Invasion* (Winnipeg, 1944) p. 13.

41/Gray, *Boy from Winnipeg*, pp. 2–4; and "Tide of Winnipeg's Population Pouring Northward," p. 13.

42/See Turek, *The Poles in Manitoba*, pp. 103–104. In reference to pre-1914 Polish immigrants Turek states that "no more than about a hundred . . . could secure employment of a higher standard, i.e. requiring some training and better remuneration. All the rest had to take up the most exacting kinds of manual work, and on that account the general visage of the Polish urban group

in Manitoba had to have an overwhelming working-class character of the lowest wage standard and most humble social class."

43/*A Handbook to Winnipeg . . . prepared for . . . British Association for the Advancement of Science* (Winnipeg, 1909), pp. 51–52; CW, WERC, *Annual Reports*, 1910–1915. See also H. W. Blake, *The Era of Street Cars in Winnipeg, 1881–1955* (Winnipeg, 1971).

44/Hosse, "The Areal Growth and Functional Development of Winnipeg," pp. 133–134.

45/*MFP*, 20 June 1903, and 13 Sept. 1902.

46/PAM, A. J. Lunty and K. C. Hurley, "Armstrong's Point: A Historical Survey," 1969.

47/Gray, *Boy from Winnipeg*, pp. 119–120

48/Marlyn, *Under the Ribs of Death*, pp. 64–65.

49/*MFP*, 6 Nov. 1909. See also the issues for 13 Nov. 1909 and 23 March 1912.

50/W. Kristjanson, *The Icelandic People in Manitoba* (Winnipeg, 1965), p. 212.

51/See Fromson, "Acculturation or Assimilation: A Geographic Analysis of Residential Segregation of Selected Ethnic Groups: Metropolitan Winnipeg, 1951–1961" (M.A. thesis, University of Manitoba), and Ed Reed, "The Beautiful People of Winnipeg," *The Manitoban*, 3 March 1970.

52/See H. W. Blake, *The Era of Interurbans in Winnipeg, 1902–1939* (Winnipeg, 1971).

53/*Census of the Prairie Provinces*, 1916.

54/The lots in the eastern portions of St. James, near Winnipeg's limits, were usually 100 to 110 feet wide and increased to 200 to 300 feet towards its western boundaries. See Hosse, "The Areal Growth and Functional Development of Winnipeg," p. 161. It should be noted that St. James was not actually incorporated as a municipality separate from Assiniboia until 1921. Thus, strictly speaking, it should not be included on Map 6. However, the distinct degree of urbanization in St. James as opposed to the generally rural character of Assiniboia gave the former area a distinct character well before 1921. Indeed, it was recognized in the federal census, for population statistics were given for both St. James and Assiniboia. It is impossible to say, however, what boundary lines were used for the division. In any case, as Map 3 illustrates, most of the development was along Portage Avenue.

55/For a fuller account of St. James' development see M. M. Ferguson, *A History of St. James* (Winnipeg, 1967).

56/Winnipeg Town Planning Commission, *Background for Planning Greater Winnipeg: Report No. 1* (Winnipeg, 1946), p. 31. Table 2 in this study details the population growth

of Winnipeg's suburbs to 1941. A ranking by size at this date is as follows: St. Boniface, St. James, St. Vital, East and West Kildonan, Transcona, Fort Garry, Assiniboia, Charleswood and Tuxedo.

57/See Fromson, "Acculturation or Assimilation: . . . Segregation in Winnipeg," passim.

58/For one account of Winnipeg's class and racial problems after 1914, see M. K. Mott, "The 'Foreign Peril': Nativism in Winnipeg, 1916–1923."

CHAPTER 10/*The Immigrant Problem (pages 177–194)*

1/Gray, *Boy from Winnipeg*, p. 2.

2/The typhoid epidemic of 1904–5 and Winnipeg's severe housing shortage were both indirect results of the city's rapid population growth. See chapters 11 and 12.

3/For a variety of reasons the phase of immigrant adjustment termed acculturation will not be analysed here. It takes place so gradually that it must be studied in a longer time period than this account embraces. And, because it is primarily a subjective matter rather than an objective, easily observable one, its study must await a great deal more research into the attitudes and feelings of the immigrants themselves. Indeed, a noted student of the city has stated that historical studies of acculturation are virtually impossible because of the lack of suitable records. See L. F. Schnore, "Problems in the Quantitative Study of Urban History," p. 197. In any case, from what limited work there has been in this area it would appear that acculturation hardly began prior to 1914, for at that date the various ethnic categories still dominated the city's social and cultural life. Winnipeggers had not yet reached that stage of development where a distinctive, all-encompassing Canadian nationality dominated other considerations. See, for example, R. D. Fromson, "Acculturation or Assimilation: A Geographic Analysis of Residential Segregation of Selected Ethnic Groups: Metropolitan Winnipeg, 1951–1961" (M.A. thesis, University of Manitoba, 1965). For more general comments on "Canadian"

nationality see A. Smith, "Metaphor and Nationality in North America," *CHR*, pp. 247–275; and J. M. S. Careless, "Limited Identities," ibid., pp. 1–10.

4/"Report of the Commissioner of Immigration at Winnipeg," Canada, *Sessional Papers*, 1900, No. 13, p. 107. Unfortunately, not all the reports of the Commissioner of Immigration contain statistical data on the number accommodated; particularly those reports dealing with the post-1900 period, the time of the greatest influx. But the growing numbers are indicated by the fact that from a yearly average of 4,382 immigrants between 1886 and 1896, the number rose sharply to 10,864 in 1897, to 27,857 in 1898, and to 36,175 in 1899.

5/Ibid., 1873, No. 9; *MFP*, 29 Nov. 1873; and *Manitoba Gazette and Trade Review*, 4 May 1872.

6/Hosse, "Development of Winnipeg," p. 68; *Sessional Papers*, 1905, No. 25, pp. 68–73. For exact location of immigration building see Map 4.

7/*Winnipeg Times*, 31 March 1883.

8/Department of the Interior Papers, R.G. 76, Box 16, File 179, letter dated 18 October 1892.

9/Canada, *Sessional Papers*, 1885, No. 8, p. 47.

10/City Council Minutes, 23 May 1877.

11/*Winnipeg Daily Times*, 31 March 1883. See also monthly reports of the caretaker contained in *Council Communication* files.

12/See *Miscellaneous File*, 1883–1887; *MFP*, 2 March 1888. The void created by the government's inadequate facilities and the city's apparent lack of concern was frequently filled by private organizations. Various associations of ethnic groups who had already established themselves aided in the form of accommodation and economic relief. See, for example, the account of the work done by the Icelandic Progressive Society in W. Kristjanson, *The Icelandic People in Manitoba* (Winnipeg, 1965), pp. 179–181; and the description of the efforts of the Jewish community in S. Belkin, *Through Narrow Gates* (Montreal, 1966), pp. 30–32.

13/*WT*, April 1906.

14/A detailed account of the epidemic is contained in Kristjanson, *The Icelandic People in Manitoba*, pp. 47–52.

15/cw, *Report of Medical Health Officer*, 4 June 1882.

16/*MFP*, 15 Aug. 1882.

17/*City Council Minutes*, 26 Oct. 1885. See also *MFP*, 26 and 29 Oct. 1885.

18/*MFP*, 13 Oct. and 9 Nov. 1892.

19/See Department of Agriculture Papers, R.G. 76, Box 16, File 169, dated 17 Aug. 1892. See also, R. Mitchell, "Public Health in Manitoba," in R. D. Defries, ed., *The Development of Public Health in Canada* (Toronto, 1940), p. 90.

20/Department of the Interior Papers, R.G. 76, Box 58, File #14205, dated 27 April 1894.

21/pam, *Health Department Correspondence*, Letter Book #1, dated 21 Dec. 1896. The controversy over the 1897 outbreak was still going on in 1902. See *City Council Minutes*, 7 April 1902.

22/Winnipeg Board of Trade, *Annual Report for 1898*. See also *MFP*, 24 Nov. and 1 Dec. 1898.

23/Winnipeg Board of Trade, *Annual Report for 1898*; and *MFP*, 7 Feb. 1899.

24/It must be emphasized that the economic adjustment of the newcomers cannot be completely divorced from the broader assimilation process. But, for reasons of clarity, I have chosen to discuss this "phase" separately, although I recognize that employment opportunities in Winnipeg prior

to 1914 were often directly related to the newcomer's "acceptability" or ability to speak English.

25/Bellan, "Relief in Winnipeg," pp. 46–61. See also Bellan, "The Development of Winnipeg," for a more detailed account of economic conditions in the city.

26/See Appendix D for this report. Chiefly as a result of his work with All Peoples' Mission Woodsworth became an accomplished publicist. These articles represent but one example of his attempt to broaden his base of support in the community. See McNaught, *A Prophet in Politics*, pp. 30–57.

27/For examples of such report see chapters 12 and 14.

28/*City Council Minutes*, 26 Feb. 1874, Bellan, "Relief in Winnipeg," pp. 58–61; and *MFP*, 7 Oct. 1910. Compare these sums to the amounts spent on attracting immigrants.

29/Ibid., 10 Feb. 1912.

30/Prior to 1896, when the city was relatively small, this haphazard approach was probably sufficient. After that date, however, with the mass influx of immigrants and the segregation of the city into distinct areas, many poor families were unnoticed by those who were in a position to help them.

31/E. F. Hutchings was a typical member of the commercial elite. Born in Ontario in 1855, he had come to Winnipeg in 1876. In 1878 he opened the Great West Saddlery Company. His other business interests included the presidency of the Scott Saddlery Company, the Royal Oak Saddlery Company, the Brick and Tile Company, the Capital Loan Company and the Bird's Hill Land and Gravel Company. He was also a director of the Canadian Fire Insurance Company, chairman of the City Sinking Fund trustees, and a member of the advisory board of the Great Western Loan Company. He served as alderman for four years. A member of the Commercial and Commercial Travellers' Clubs, he was a Conservative, an Anglican, and lived on Wellington Crescent. See *Who's Who in Western Canada, 1911*.

32/MacInnis, *J. S. Woodsworth*, pp. 81–83. See also *MFP*, 23 Oct. 1911.

33/It would be a tedious task to list them all. See the various ethnic studies cited above for a more complete listing not only of fraternal and benevolent societies, but ethnic newspapers, political clubs, churches, etc. A partial list of such organizations is also contained in a series of articles that were run in the *MFP* in November and December 1912 and March 1913. They dealt with the Germans, Slavs, Icelanders, Scandinavians, and Jews. See also *The Clubs, Societies and Associations of Winnipeg* (Winnipeg, 1908); and "How Winnipeg Welcomes the Immigrant," *The Dominion*, Vol. 4, No. 10 (July, 1913), pp. 15–16. To give some indication of the various associations formed by ethnic groups in Winnipeg prior to 1914, I have listed the organizations of the Poles. They included the Holy Ghost Fraternal Aid Society (1902–); St. Peter and Paul Society (1902–); Vladislav Jagiello Polish Society at Fort Rouge (1909–12); Polish Gymnastic Association "Sokol" (1906—); Polish Sokols Association (1907–10); Branch No. 1069 of the Polish National Alliance (1909–36); Polish Artisans Association (1910–); Polish Emigration Society (1908-11); Canadian Eleuthery Society (1910–12); Polish Canadian Club (1910–); Polish Patriotic Society of the White Eagle (1904–); Dramatic Guild of J. Slowacki (1913–); The Knights of St. George (1910–); I. Daszynski Society (1910–); Working People Association "Star" (1908–10); and Holy Ghost Parish School (1900–). As is readily apparent, these organizations covered the full range of social, cultural, educational, and political activities. See Turek, *Poles in Manitoba*, chapters VIII and IX. For a complete listing of newspapers and periodicals published in Winnipeg, see *The Canadian Newspaper Directory* for any given date. In 1909 it includes a total of fifty publications in the city.

34/For example, see H. Herstein, "The Growth of the Winnipeg Jewish Community," p. 32. Herstein states that the desperate state of the Jewish poor in Winnipeg forced them to seek help from non-Jewish agencies. See also, V. Turek, *Poles in Manitoba*.

35/See K. Pettipas, "Margaret Scott and the Margaret Scott Nursing Mission, 1904–1943," PAM, unpublished paper, Feb. 1970.

36/As an example of the publicity Mrs. Scott received, see *W. Telegram*, 24 Jan. 1903.

37/H. Macvicar, *The Story of the Mission* (Winnipeg, 1939), p. 17.

38/*MFP*, 10 May 1904.

39/S. D. Clark, *Social Development in Canada* (Toronto, 1942), p. 383.

40/City Health Department, *Annual Reports for 1913 and 1914*.

41/M. Curtis, "The Early Days of All Peoples' Mission," in PAC, *J. S. Woodsworth Papers*, M.G. 27, Series III, C7, Vol. 29. (Hereafter cited as *Woodsworth Papers* followed by vol. number.)

42/McNaught, *Prophet in Politics*, p. 42.

43/See *Annual Reports of All Peoples' Mission, 1907–14*, in *Woodsworth Papers*, Vols. 28 and 29.

44/North End House was located at 75 Robinson Street in Ward 5, while Woodsworth lived next door to the Stella Avenue Mission in the same Ward. The designation of "All Peoples' Mission" on Map 4 represents the Sutherland Avenue Institute of the Mission. The other major building run by the Mission was the Maple Street Church whose pastor, Rev. W. Somerville, did most of the spiritual work. See *Annual Report* for 1911–12 for a complete listing of various agencies run by All Peoples'.

45/McNaught, *Prophet in Politics*, p. 44.

46/See, for example, *MFP*, 28 Feb. 1905 and 20 Jan. 1910; *WT*, 29 Jan. 1908; and *W. Telegram*, 10 Dec. 1910.

47/See, for example, Appendix D. The two books were *Strangers Within Our Gates* (1909) and *My Neighbour* (1911).

CHAPTER 11/*The Immigrant Problem: Education and Assimilation (pages 195–206)*

1/See J. E. Rea, "The Roots of Prairie Society," in D. P. Gagan, ed., *Prairie Perspectives* (Toronto, 1970), pp. 46–57; Phillips, "Development of Municipal Institutions in Manitoba," passim; and Morton, *Manitoba*, Chapter 10 and passim.

2/See Smith, "Metaphor and Nationality."

3/See Rea, "The Roots of Prairie Society"; and V. Jensen, "The Manitoba Schools Question," unpublished paper in possession of author.

4/Marlyn, *Under the Ribs of Death*, p. 24.

5/Smith, "Metaphor and Nationality"; and Careless, "Limited Identities."

6/Morton, *Manitoba*, p. 311.

7/Ibid., Chapter 10. See also articles by W. L. Morton and Ramsay Cook in C. Brown, ed., *Minorities, Schools, and Politics* (Toronto, 1969), pp. 10–31.

8/G. F. Chapman, "Winnipeg: The Melting Pot," p. 412. See also *MFP*, 16 Nov. and 7 Dec. 1912; and *WT*, 10 Oct. 1903.

9/Germans and Scandinavians also came in increased numbers during these years. But the fact that both had well-established organizations to help their own kind and that Winnipeggers were used to them meant that they were rarely in the public eye.

10/See J. H. Thompson, "The Liquor Question in Manitoba, 1892–1956" (M.A. thesis, University of Manitoba, 1969); and Gray, *Booze*.

11/*MFP*, 1 March 1913; and Chapman, "Winnipeg: The Melting Pot," p. 413.

12/Woodsworth, *Strangers Within Our Gates*, p. 132 and passim.

13/*WT*, 29 Jan. 1900; *W. Telegram*, 13 May 1901.

14/*MFP*, 7 Dec. 1912.

15/"Public School Education in Winnipeg," Civic, Social, and Athletic Association, *Souvenir of Winnipeg's Jubilee*, p. 65.

16/Ibid., p. 71. See also W. H. Lucow, "The Origin and Growth of the Public School System in Manitoba" (M.Ed. thesis, University of Manitoba, 1950); and J. W. Chafe, *An Apple for the Teacher: A Centennial History of the Winnipeg School Division.*

17/Sisler, *Peaceful Invasion*, pp. 19–20.

18/Ibid., pp. 69–70; W. G. Pearce, *Winnipeg School Days, 1871–1950*, pp. 24–25; and Chafe, *Apple for the Teacher*, pp. 65–66.

19/See, for example, Herstein, "The Growth of the Winnipeg Jewish Community"; and

Turek, *The Poles in Manitoba*, chapters VII–IX.

20/For a detailed discussion of Dafoe and his attitudes, see M. Donnelly, *Dafoe of the Free Press* (Toronto, 1968).

21/Donnelly, *Dafoe*, p. 71. In the period 1911–15 Dafoe published a series of sixty-four articles on the education question in the pages of the *MFP*.

22/By 1890 compulsory attendance laws had been passed in twenty-six states. See McKelvey, *The Urbanization of America*, p. 170.

23/See, for example, Winnipeg Public School Board, *Annual Report for 1904*.

24/Morton, *Manitoba*, p. 271.

25/I do not propose to discuss all the issues involved in the Manitoba School Question over the years. See Morton, *Manitoba*; Lovell Clark, *The Manitoba School Question* (Toronto, 1968); G. L. Comeault, "Archbishop Langevin, Schools, and Politics in Manitoba, 1895–1915" (PAM, unpublished paper, February 1970); M. Spigelman, "Bilingual Schools in Manitoba and their Abolition" (ibid., unpublished paper, February 1970); and Brown, ed., *Minorities, Schools and Politics.*

26/See Turek, *Poles in Manitoba*, p. 220; and Syrnick, "Community Builders—Early Ukrainian Teachers," pp. 29–31.

27/*WT*, 22 Aug. 1908. For other representative opinions on behalf of the English majority, see ibid., 27 June 1912; and *MFP* 20 May 1909 and 8 Dec. 1913.

28/Ibid., 12 June 1909.

29/*WT*, 20 May 1909.

30/MacInnis, *J. S. Woodsworth*, pp. 65, 80.

31/Spigelman, "Bilingual Schools in Manitoba and their Abolition," pp. 14–15.

32/See L. Orlikow, "A Survey of the Reform Movement in Manitoba, 1910–1915," *HSSM Transactions*, pp. 50–61.

33/The ethnic minorities, particularly the Ukrainians and French, were opposed not only to the abolition of the bilingual clause but also to compulsory attendance legislation. The former were used to having sons and daughters help earn the family living, while the French were afraid such legislation would lead to "godless institutions." Moreover, the lack of an attendance law meant that any changes in the school laws that were obnoxious could be resisted, at the expense of the children, by refusing to allow them to attend school. See Morton, *Manitoba*, pp. 311–312.

34/Jackson, *Manitoba*, p. 173. The Children's Act had some serious shortcomings. No child could be forced to attend school unless he was a "neglected child" whose parents ignored their moral duties in rais-

ing him. Only parents who contributed to "juvenile delinquency" (whatever that meant) could be prosecuted. Finally, any child apprehended had to be treated, under the provisions of the law, in the same manner as criminals, thus tempting the truant officers to ignore rather than arrest young offenders. In short, despite Roblin's statement that the act was an effective alternative to a compulsory attendance law, it was only barely enforced in Winnipeg and not at all in rural areas.

35/Mott, "The 'Foreign Peril': Nativism in Winnipeg, 1916–1923," p. 13.

CHAPTER 12/*The Commercial Elite and the Water Supply Question (pages 207–222)*

1/W. J. Healy, *Winnipeg's Early Days* (Winnipeg, 1927), pp. 21–22; G. B. Elliot, *Winnipeg As It Is* (Winnipeg, 1874), p. 11; *MFP*, 26 April 1873, 24 April and 31 Oct. 1876.

2/See *MFP*, 24 Aug. and 30 Dec. 1882 for short histories of the Winnipeg Fire Department.

3/*MFP*, 14 Sept. 1882. The directors and executive officers of the company were A. Moffat, R. G. Elwes, R. F. Manning, G. H. Balfour, F. H. Matheson, Heber Archibald, S. A. Rowbotham, and T. H. McEwen. They were all "gentlemen well-known in the city and much respected." Archibald, for example, was alderman in 1885. See *Manitoba Sun*, 17 June 1887.

4/H. N. Ruttan, "The Water Supply of the City of Winnipeg; Reports of 2nd March and 12th of November, 1886" (hereafter cited as *Ruttan Report, 1886*).

5/Ibid. Included in Ruttan's report were comparisons between the waterworks in operation in Winnipeg and those of other cities of about the same population. In every category of comparison Winnipeg stood in last place.

6/See pamphlet by the company engineer, R. G. Elwes, "Winnipeg Water Works Company Report, October, 1886" (hereafter cited as *WWW Co. Report, 1886*).

7/See, for example, *MFP*, 13 December 1886. Throughout the campaign the desire for a municipally owned waterworks system

was frequently expressed by A. McNee, who won a seat on Council.

8/See, for example, Dr. Agnew, "Our Water Supply," *HSSM Transactions*, Series I, No. 2 (1883–84), pp. 1–4. It was repeatedly pointed out that 80 per cent of all North American cities owned their own water supply systems. See also *Manitoba Sun*, 16 March 1887; and *MFP*, 2 July 1887.

9/See *SM*, 1880, Chap. 7; and *Ruttan Report, 1886*.

10/*WT*, 26 July 1892. See also "Review of the Work of Council for 1892," *Council Communications*, Series II, No. 2224, read 27 Dec. 1892.

11/*MFP*, 21 December 1892. The vote on Bylaw 582 was 497 for and 83 against. In other words, it was defeated primarily because of a poor turnout. However, one must consider that the electors realized that simply refusing to vote was as effective as registering a negative vote. See, for example, ibid., 19 and 21 November, 1892.

12/*MFP*, 28 Nov. and 3 Dec. 1892. The company argued that their Act of Incorporation gave them a monopoly. Council, on the other hand, argued that the company's franchise was exclusive only insofar as other private companies were concerned. But Council's refusal to solve this question in the courts suggests that they used the threat of a municipal system only to gain concessions from the company. See *Council*

Communications, Series II, No. 2261, read 6 Feb. 1893. Moreover, the company's position was further strengthened when in 1893 it had legislation passed that stipulated the city could not build its own waterworks until the company's franchise expired in 1900. The city, of course, opposed such legislation but to no avail. See *SM*, 1893, Chap. 50; *MFP*, 7 March 1893; and *WT*, 9 March 1893.

13/Between 1893 and 1896 various proposals were debated but none of them resulted in any concrete developments. See *MFP* and *WT* for these years, especially a review of the "important incidents in the history of the Company," in *MFP*, 1 November 1894.

14/*WT*, 3 October 1896; H. N. Ruttan *et al*, "Report on the Assiniboine River and Artesian Wells as Sources of Supply and on a System of Water Works for the City of Winnipeg," October 1896. See also Province of Manitoba, *Sessional Papers*, 1897, No. 15, pp. 251–257. The latter contains a report made to the Board of Health on the use of the Assiniboine River as a source of supply. It strongly urged that Winnipeg obtain a new source.

15/*City Council Minutes*, 1 August 1898.

16/A good example of the absurdity of the city's position occurred in 1894. Council drew up and submitted a bylaw to the electors asking for permission to raise $250,000 to construct a system for fire protection and sewer flushing. They could not legally sell water at this time but expressed the view that in 1900, when the private company's monopoly expired, this system could be expanded. Yet when the voters rejected the bylaw, Council still refused to negotiate with the www Company on the matter of extending their services since it would "cost too much." See *MFP*, 26 and 28 Nov. 1894, 17 and 19 Dec. 1894; and *Nor'Wester*, 27 Nov. 1894.

17/The problem of waste arose from the fact that at this time water meters were not used. Rather, each household or business establishment was charged a fixed rate. Also, in a large number of poorly constructed houses it was necessary to run

water continuously in winter months to prevent freezing of water pipes.

18/*MFP*, 16 April and 16 Sept. 1901.

19/Ibid., 20 Aug. and 24 Sept. 1902.

20/Manitoba, *Sessional Papers*, 1906, No pp. 352–353. The typhoid epidemic will be dealt with in detail in the following chap

21/"Report on Municipal Fire Preventive Appliances in the City of Winnipeg as October 25th, 1904," in *Board of Control Papers*, No. 447.

22/The water from the Assiniboine Rive of course, would be used only in the cas of an emergency. It was not being used a this time for domestic supply, since the capacity of the artesian well was sufficie to supply the portion of the population then having water connections.

23/The fire, which became known as the "Bulman-Ashdown Fire," is discussed in Fire Underwriters' Report, cited above. occurred on 11 October 1904.

24/See *Hazen* and *Jordan Reports* cited a discussed in Chapter 13.

25/*City Council Minutes*, 3 April 1905; *MFP*, 4 April 1905. See also Board of Tra *Annual Report for 1905*. The quick actio of the Council on the matter of increase fire protection came largely as a result o pressure from the Board of Trade. With announcement of the proposed construct of the new system, the Fire Underwriter Association promised reduced insurance rates. See letter from CFU Association Winnipeg Board of Trade. A report on t Fire Service Water Works System, completed in 1908, can be found in H. N. Ruttan, "Winnipeg Water Works," *The Canadian Municipal Journal*, Vol. V, No. (March 1909), pp. 109–112.

26/These figures are found in "Report o New Water Supply for the City of Winni peg," dated 29 Aug. 1907 (hereafter cited *Water Report, 1907*). See also H. N. Rutt "Address to Canadian Club on Water Supply of Winnipeg," 31 March 1906, *Canadian Club Papers*.

27/In 1905, for example, only 60 per cent Winnipeg houses were supplied with wat connections. See *Hazen Report*, p. 6. See also Manitoba, *Sessional Papers,* 1906, No. 6, pp. 351–353.

28/*MFP,* 29 March 1907.

29/*Water Report,* 1907. The report was very critical of the city's artesian well system. The water was "chemically unsatisfactory" and "the quantity that can be depended on is uncertain." The report also noted that any extension of the city's artesian system, such as to Poplar Springs 17.5 miles northwest of Winnipeg, would meet with similar objections as to quality and quantity.

30/The development of a supply from the Red River was rejected largely on grounds of its undesirable quality both then and in the future. In other words, as the province became more settled, there would be a much higher risk of pollution of Red River water than at either of the two other sources. Ibid.

31/This compared with a total cost estimate of $26,407,000 for the Shoal Lake supply. Initial costs for this system would be $8,979,000. Ibid.

32/*Council Communications,* Series II, No. 8167, read 11 November 1907.

33/*WT,* 19 May and 3 July 1908. The water from the artesian well system was absolutely pure from a health standpoint but was extremely hard. The softening plant, which only processed some 200,000 gallons out of a total of almost 5,000,000 gallons was considered next to useless.

34/See R. Hering, *et al,* "Report on a Water Supply from Shoal Lake for the Greater Winnipeg Water District," presented 20 Aug. 1913, for figures on water consumption in Winnipeg from 1902 to 1912.

35/These men were Mayor Ashdown (chairman of the commission in 1907), Controller A. A. McArthur, Controller J. G. Harvey, and Alderman J. C. Gibson.

36/*Fire, Water, and Light Committee Correspondence,* No. 927, read 9 Aug. 1910, and 24 October 1910. In comparing the two systems Ruttan conceded that the Winnipeg River supply was superior only in that it required no softening.

37/See "Robson Report," *Fire, Water and Light Committee Correspondence,* No. 435. The report went to considerable length to justify its decision, especially in the light of the recommendation made in 1907 that the city should go to the Winnipeg River. It concluded its comparison of the two sources by stating: "I recommend the Shoal Lake supply solely for the reason that it is the best; it is not the cheapest. I do not believe that it is necessary at this time to weigh too nicely the cost of such a project."

38/It is estimated today that only in 1974 will the original aqueduct be used to its full capacity of 85,000,000 gallons. Thus studies are now in progress on means of augmenting that supply, probably by building an additional aqueduct.

39/Winnipeg Board of Trade, "Winnipeg Water Works: A World's Wonder."

40/The only sour note was sounded by the chairman of the Board of Health, who stated that it "will be a great boom to the city of Winnipeg to have an undoubted and plentiful supply of good water. The only regret is that this same step was not taken at an earlier date. It is no conceit on my part in stating . . . that annually for some years I urged, as strongly as could be urged, and in the face of strong opposition, action by the local authorities. . . ." See Manitoba *Sessional Papers,* 1915, No. 14, p. 683. See also ibid., 1914, No. 3. p. 314 for a similar expression of opinion.

CHAPTER 13/*Public Health* versus *the Private City (pages 223–245)*

1/Unfortunately complete and accurate statistics are not available for the period prior to 1900. There is ample evidence, however, that deaths from these diseases were numerous. See Ross Mitchell, "Public Health in Manitoba," in R. D. Defries, ed., *The Development of Public Health in Canada* (Toronto, 1940), pp. 87–98.

2/See Table 26. This table was drawn up from the following sources; Province of Manitoba, Department of Agriculture and Immigration, Reports, 1883–1889; H. N. Ruttan, "Reports on Sanitary Condition of City of Winnipeg. . . .," November 1893; and City Health Department, *Annual Reports,* 1908–14. To give meaning to this table some comparisons with other Canadian cities are essential. In 1891, when Winnipeg's death rate was at the relatively low rate of 17 per thousand, it was still one of the highest in Canada. The following rates were recorded in other centres: London, Ont., 13; Kingston, 14; Hamilton, 13; Toronto, 13; Ottawa, 18; and Montreal, 19. See *Census of Canada*, 1891. Another comparison was made by the *Winnipeg Telegram* on 5 Jan. 1905. Giving Winnipeg's death rate at 21.74, it noted that the average for all the cities in the U.S. was only 18.6.

3/A. E. Graeur, *Public Health: A Study Prepared for the Royal Commission on Dominion-Provincial Relations*, (Ottawa, 1939), p. 2.

4/R. Mitchell and T. K. Thorlakson, "James Kerr, 1848–1911, and Harry Hyland Kerr, 1881–1963; Pioneer Canadian-American Surgeons," *Canadian Journal of Surgery*, Vol. 9 (July 1966), pp. 213–220.

5/See cw, *City Comptrollers Report*, 1887. Following are further statistics on health expenditures during this period: 1880—$650; 1884—$5,774; 1890—$14,030; 1895 —$32,140; and 1898—$30,444.

6/*MFP*, 3 May 1889. For other complaints see ibid., 13 Jan. 1885, 8 April 1887, 18 Oct. 1888 and 9 Nov. 1892; *Winnipeg Daily Sun*, 10 Aug. 1887, 7 Jan. 1888, 14 May 1888 and 25 Nov. 1889; *WT*, 20 Sept. 1892, 30 Sept. 1892, and 1 April 1893. It must be emphasized that the odours resulting from such drainage problems meant much more to people then than it would now. It was widely believed that "however offensive these accumulations may be to our senses these effects represent but a trifling evil when compared with the result of their absorption in our bodies . . . in the air we breathe. . . . Among these [results are] want of energy, lassitude, headache, hot skin, thirst, diarrhea, and other intestinal disturbances. . . ." *Winnipeg Daily Times*, 10 March 1881.

7/H. N. Ruttan, "Report on Sanitary Condition of Winnipeg. . . ." It was estimated that in 1889 "not more than one-tenth of the houses are connected with either Water Works or Sewers. . . ." *MFP*, 29 Aug. 1889.

8/The Board of Health was established in 1893. See S.M., 1893, Chap. 28. Its formation had been urged by many Winnipeg residents in an effort to meet Winnipeg's sanitary needs. Indeed, in an apparent attempt to pass on the responsibilities of public health to another body, Council was one of its strongest supporters. See *MFP*, 13 Oct. and 9 Nov. 1892. The Board, however, served mainly to point out that Winnipeg City Council was very lax in health questions and urged, year after year, that that body set up an adequate civic health department. See Manitoba, *Sessional Papers*, 1897, No. 15, p. 250; ibid, 1900, No. 10, pp. 314–317.

9/R. Mitchell, "How Winnipeg Waged War on Typhoid," *Manitoba Medical Review*, Vol. 49, No. 6 (June–July 1969), pp. 166–167.

10/*City Council Minutes*, 19 Sept. 1904. The motion calling for the investigation reveals that Council still did not consider the matter too serious, as it referred to "the somewhat frequent occurrence of the typhoid" in the city.

11/*Council Communications*, No. 7362. A copy of this report also exists in Manitoba, *Sessional Papers*, 1905, No. 10, pp. 368–371.

12/Ibid. A distinction in the different types of outdoor toilets is important throughout the controversy. "Box-closets" were outdoor toilets made up of a wooden box situated on top of the ground and which was not necessarily watertight. "Pit-closets," which will be discussed later, were basically a hole in the ground running usually to a depth of four or five feet. This allowed for some soakage in the surrounding ground. Variations of this "pit-closet" included lining the pit with cement or galvanized iron pails. The reference to public wells was in areas where, lacking water service, people drew water from wells. The doctors had given the public water supply a clean bill of health but these wells were of doubtful purity.

13/*MFP*, 7 Dec. 1904; *WT*, 24 Nov. 1904, and *W. Telegram* 9 Jan. 1905. See also letter of Dr. Douglas to Board of Health, date 6 Dec. 1904, in Manitoba, *Sessional Papers*, 1905, No. 10, pp. 371–373.

14/*Council Communications*, No. 7362. The

lack of personal and political motivation at this early date is confirmed by the fact that the typhoid epidemic did not become a campaign issue in the 1904 civic elections. Mayor Sharpe and ten of twelve aldermen were returned.

15/*Council Communications*, Series II, No. 7468 and No. 7475; and Prof. A. Hazen, "Report on Sewer System and Water Supply for City of Winnipeg, Manitoba" (hereafter cited, respectively, as *Sharpe Report, Jordan Report,* and *Hazen Report*).

16/*Hazen Report.* As might be expected in a city where there was a considerable building boom, there were several sets of figures relating to the number of houses connected. For example, a report in the *WT* of 23 June 1905 gave the number of houses unconnected as around 4,200. See also Table 25, in Chapter 12.

17/*Jordan Report.* It is interesting to note that City Council took great pains to point out that many of the cases were from outside points. In other words, rural persons would come to Winnipeg for treatment and if they died in a city hospital the city was credited with the case. Without denying the validity of the argument in some cases, this sort of argument merely avoided the issue. Most cities would have the same problem and yet Winnipeg's death rate was still substantially higher.

18/*Ibid.* Maps drawn up for use in Jordan's report were later published in the *MFP*, 28 April 1905. They are useful for showing how the cases spread after October 1904 throughout the South End of the city.

19/*Ibid.* In the section of the report dealing with "other considerations" Jordan attempted to end the controversy that then existed among some medical authorities over whether or not "emanations from the sewers or from defective plumbing might in some way account for the prevalence of typhoid fever." He felt it was extremely unlikely that this could be a vehicle for the typhoid germ. However, he did add that "it might be remembered that the highly offensive stenches arising from decomposing matter in sewers have often been shown to exercise a depressing and weakening influence on human vitality. It is quite

within the realms of possibility that the noisomeness of the city sewers has thus played some part in rendering certain persons more susceptible to the attack of typhoid bacillus . . . by weakening his resistance. . . ."

20/The first class fire limits were detailed in bylaw 2737 (passed 4 May 1903). They included parts of wards 2, 4, and 5 and generally included the downtown business section. They covered an area of about 250 feet on either side of Main Street (from Broadway to Selkirk); Notre Dame (from Isabel to the Red River); and Portage Avenue (from Young to Portage and Main). In short, the area was not a very large one.

21/See *MFP*, 21 and 24 Nov. 1905; *W. Telegram*, 17 Nov. 1905.

22/*MFP*, 16 Nov. 1905.

23/See G. Rodrigue, "Typhoid Epidemic—Winnipeg—1904–06" (unpublished paper, Jan. 1970), p. 8.

24/*MFP*, 24 Nov. 1905.

25/City Health Department, *Annual Report* for 1914. The 1909 annual report is especially interesting since it contains numerous photographs of the various sorts of privies and water-closets used throughout the period. It illustrates most dramatically some of the problems faced by the health department.

26/*Ibid.*, reports for years 1908–14. It must be remembered that these figures, while as high as those in 1900–1903, took place in a city whose population had almost doubled.

27/*Comptrollers Reports*, 1904, 1905, and 1906.

28/In 1910 Winnipeg also established a publicly owned scavenging system. Prior to that date private citizens had to pay scavengers per load of refuse removed. Such a system was hardly satisfactory. See, for example, an account of the inadequacies in *WT*, 1 April 1893.

29/These programs are all mentioned in the Annual Reports of city health department. See also *W. Telegram*, 30 Jan. 1909; *WT*, 25 and 29 Sept. and 7 Oct. 1909; *City Health Committee Correspondence*, No. 189; and *MFP*, 30 April 1910 for information on

Sanitary Association of Winnipeg. This organization's efforts were largely directed toward city beautification; made up of the city's well-to-do, it hid behind the screen of Winnipeg's private charities. It rarely advocated the allocation of any of the city's tax monies for programs that would directly benefit the city's poor. Preventative steps were also taken during this period by the passage of a host of new health bylaws. See cw, *Bylaws of City of Winnipeg*, 1905–1914.

30/City Health Department, *Annual Report*, 1911.

31/Health *Bulletin*, August 1911.

32/Ibid., 1911 to 1914. See also *Annual Report*, 1914. In the 1914 report an analysis of the factors causing disease and death in infants observed that there were six major causes: pre-natal influences, ignorance or indifference of parents, poverty of parents, the later effects of neglected infantile conditions, insanitary conditions, and infectious diseases.

33/*City Health Department Correspondence*, Letter Book No. 12, p. 543. See also, "Report of Social Survey Committee," in *City Planning Commission Report, Council Communications*, Series II, No. 9700½, read 27 Jan. 1913. It records the infant mortality rates by wards as follows:

Ward 1 — 111.6 deaths per 1,000 births
Ward 2 — 134.8 deaths per 1,000 births
Ward 3 — 122.0 deaths per 1,000 births
Ward 4 — 211.5 deaths per 1,000 births
Ward 5 — 282.3 deaths per 1,000 births
Ward 6 — 214.9 deaths per 1,000 births
Ward 7 — 148.1 deaths per 1,000 births

It will be noted that the rate in Ward 5 is almost three times that of Ward 1.

34/*Annual Report*, 1913.

35/Health *Bulletin*, October, 1912. The fact that Winnipeg had over 6,000 horses and 1,000 cows within the city limits in 1909 aggravated the sanitary problem. See Bellan, "Relief in Winnipeg . . . ," pp. 56–57. A colourful discussion of these years when "Winnipeg ran on horse-power" is contained in Gray, *Boy from Winnipeg*, pp. 61–74.

36/*City Health Department Correspondence*, Letter Book No. 7, dated 4 November

1907, pp. 296–298. Commenting on the frozen plumbing problem in 1910, the annual report noted that there were 357 reported cases that year. But, the report went on, "we have reason to believe that not one-half of such instances are reported to the office, as many tenants are afraid to report them for fear of getting into trouble with their landlords. Most of the 357 cases mentioned were discovered by our own staff making house to house inspections. Particularly is this true of the north-end's so-called tenements, i.e., houses occupied by two or more families. Sometime the freezing is due to the neglect of the tenant to keep sufficient heat in the rooms, but in the majority of cases the freezing occurs below the level of the living rooms and is due to faulty and defective construction of the foundations of the cellars."

37/The value of building permits rose from $1.5 million in 1900 to $20.25 million in 1912. See *MFP*, 31 Dec. 1912. Since many of Winnipeg's "floating population" probably stayed in hotels the following comments from the Health Department annual report of 1910 are pertinent. In thirty hotels "various sanitary defects were found, consisting of defective drains, waste pipes . . . ; defective traps, water-closets, urinals, wash-basins, sinks, baths, laundry tubs and fittings connected therewith; foul and defective catch-basins, many of which were practically cesspools; closets and urinals situated in dark and ill-ventilated apartments; cellars and basements in filthy condition; mud and wood floors saturated with discharges from bar wastes and troughs in front of bars, containing matches, cigar-stubs and sputum; walls, floors, ceilings in filthy condition and generally dark and ill-ventilated . . . . The yards and surroundings of many of these premises were objectionable and conducive to unhealthy and unwholesome conditions."

38/See, for example, comments recorded in *WT*, 1 Sept. 1908 and 26 Feb. 1909. It must be emphasized that while the problem of overcrowding was most acute in wards 5 and 6, other areas of the city were not immune. Many of the large and resplendent homes in wards 1, 2, and 3 were taken over by unscrupulous landlords during these periods and were occupied by "from two to ten families without anything having been done to such houses in the way of alteration. . . ." City Health Department, *Annual Report*, 1912.

39/The figures for the average cost of housing are taken from cw, *Annual Reports of the Building Inspector*, 1908. See Appendix D for statistics on wages.

40/City Health Department, *Annual Report*, 1913.

41/Health *Bulletin*, August, 1911. Another example is in Woodsworth, *My Neighbour*. He cites a case where a landlady kept eleven lodgers in one room at five cents per night each.

42/City Health Department, *Annual Report*, 1910.

43/The word "tenement" had several meanings in this period. It was used to denote three different classes of buildings: old single-family dwellings inhabited by two or more families; new buildings designed as single-family dwellings and converted after construction; and buildings designed for

multiple-family use. It is the last category that is being considered here.

44/The medical health officer estimated that only one-third of the available lots in the city were built on in 1912. This factor, as well as Winnipeg's position on the "open prairie, wide and free," meant that the city, "unlike New York which was confined to a narrow neck of land of enormous values," was not plagued with "Colorado Canyons" of tenements. See Health *Bulletin*, February, 1912.

45/Ibid., May, 1914. See also photographs illustrating this problem in *Annual Report*, 1913.

46/Health *Bulletin*, July 1912.

47/Ibid., May 1913.

48/The annual reports of Health Department list all legislation affecting public health.

49/City Health Department, *Annual Report*, 1912.

50/Health *Bulletin*, December 1911.

51/Ibid., October 1912.

CHAPTER 14/*Red Lights in Winnipeg (pages 246–264)*

1/*City Council Minutes*, 16 March 1874.

2/See, for example, MFP, 18 Aug. and 7 Sept. 1875, 27 Nov. 1880. See also cw, *Report of Chief of Police*, 1881. In that year ninety-two charges were laid against "inmates of Houses of Ill-Fame."

3/It must be emphasized that labour in Winnipeg did not officially organize until 1884. See Robin, *Radical Politics and Canadian Labour*, p. 21. However, from the outset, organized labour took a strong stand on prostitution. See *The Voice*, 7 June 1901 and 23 April 1903.

4/*Winnipeg Times*, 9 April 1883.

5/Perhaps a typical example of the evangelical minister who became involved in social reform movement is presented by Rev. Dr. Salem G. Bland. See D. L. Butcher, "Rev. Dr. Salem G. Bland: A Study of His Activities and Influence in the Politics, Reform, Church and Society of Manitoba and

Western Canada; 1903–1919" (PAM, unpublished paper, February 1970).

6/*Winnipeg Times*, 9 April 1883. One minister blamed the social evil at least partially on "school directors who allow at school a common playground for boys and girls, and the too free intercourse between them. . . . In [this] way the evil seed is sown, and when the seed is sown it is no easy matter preventing a harvest." Ibid.

7/Ibid., 6 April 1883.

8/MFP, 30 Nov. 1880.

9/*Winnipeg Times*, 6 April 1883. Winnipeg's official policy of segregation was not, of course, announced publicly. This could have hardly been done since prostitution, besides being illegal under federal and provincial law, was expressly prohibited by city bylaw 25, passed in December 1874. Later evidence, however, indicates that segregation was the policy adopted by City Council.

10/*MFP*, 15 March 1883.

11/Gray, *Boy from Winnipeg*, p. 2.

12/See Chapter 8. It should be emphasized that this was not a new problem that suddenly appeared after 1900. During the construction of the CPR in the eighties many "workmen tried to escape to the flesh-pots of Winnipeg," and these men undoubtedly provided a major source of the prostitutes' business. See Berton, *The National Dream*, p. 294. The point is that after 1900 the problem was much more acute.

13/See PAM, *Royal Commission on Charges Re: Vice and of Graft Against the Police*, *Manitoba Sessional Papers*, 1911 (hereafter cited as *Vice Report*, 1911).

14/See L. Orlikow, "A Survey of the Reform Movement in Manitoba, 1910–1920."

15/J. W. Grant, *George Pidgeon: A Biography* (Toronto, 1962), p. 29. Quoted in J. Cooper, "The Red Light District in Winnipeg: An Issue in Civic Politics, 1903-1910" (PAM, unpublished paper, February 1970).

16/Ibid., p. 30.

17/See, for example, *MFP*, 8 Dec. 1910.

18/Orlikow, "Reform Movement in Manitoba," p. 18.

19/*WT*, 9 Oct. 1901; *W. Telegram*, 11 Oct. 1901.

20/*MFP*, 16 Nov. 1903; *WT*, 16 Nov. 1903. The latter's headline read "Pulpits Thunder Forth Their Denunciation."

21/Mayor Arbuthnot ended a long defence of the segregation policy by attacking the moral crusade launched by the City Ministerial Association in the following words: "Just to think that a man can get up and under the protection of the Church of God, deliver a so-called sermon, the language of which is simply disgraceful, is a shame and a disgrace. What he deserves is horse-whipping and the father of any of the young girls or the husbands of any of the women present would be perfectly justified in administering bodily chastisement. To think that our

innocent women should be subjected to such language makes my blood boil. What must be the nature of such a man who is capable of such a thing?" See *W. Telegram*, 17 Nov. 1903. The Board of Police Commissioners also defended the segregation policy in a public statement made in December. See ibid, 21 Dec. 1903; *MFP*, 21 Dec. 1903.

22/Sharpe was at the meeting of November 16 and made a speech supporting the anti-segregationists. See *WT*, 17 Nov. 1903.

23/It should be pointed out that during the mayoralty campaign of 1903 the segregation policy was only one of many issues, and Sharpe's election should not be construed as a direct result of his support of the Civic Social Purity Committee.

24/*WT*, 11 Jan. 1904; *W. Telegram*, 11 Jan. 1904; *The Voice*, 15 Jan. 1904. Under Mayor Sharpe Council even went so far as to change the name of Thomas Street to Minto, in an apparent attempt to erase the memory of the "old regime."

25/*Vice Report*, 1911.

26/Ibid.

27/*Royal Commission Hearings: Evidence*, Vol. 1. Accompanying the *Vice Report* are ten typed volumes of evidence.

28/Ibid.

29/Ibid.; *W. Telegram*, 1 Dec. 1910. The latter reference also states that John A. Gaynor of the Winnipeg Estate and Loan Company bought and sold four homes on the streets for a profit of $15,000.

30/*Henderson Directory*, 1909. It might also be mentioned that during the 1903 controversy, charges of more than just official "connivance" were made. It was reported in *MFP*, of 4 Dec. 1903 than an aldermanic candidate "named several prominent citizens as owning property and mortgage interests in the western colony." But this charge was never investigated.

31/*MFP*, 9 Dec. 1910.

32/*Royal Commission Hearings: Evidence*, Vol. 1.

33/Ibid., Vol. 2.

34/*WT*, 14 May and 15 June 1909; *The*

Voice, 18 June 1909; *MFP,* 5 May and 7 July 1909.

35/See *MFP,* 7, 12 and 17 July, 28 Sept. 1909.

36/F. B. DuVal, "The Problem of Social Vice in Winnipeg, Being a Reply to a pamphlet, entitled 'The attitude of the Church to the Social Evil' . . . ," PAM Winnipeg, 1910 (hereafter cited as DuVal, "Social Vice in Winnipeg"). Although essentially based on moral and religious arguments, the pamphlet also attacked segregation on more practical grounds. For instance, one of the arguments then being used by the pro-segregationists was that this policy had been recommended by the New York Committee of Fifteen. In 1903, the Police Commission had quoted this report as if it was "the latest important production on the subject by any Anglo-Saxon authority." Since the report stated that attempts to "suppress or stamp out the evil" were hopeless, the Police Commission felt their policy of "unofficial segregation," (i.e. a "change in the attitude of the law") was justified. The trouble with using the Committee of Fifteen as an authority, however, was that that group had specifically stated that segregation was unwise since the areas became "nests of crime" and, secondly, "segregation does not segregate." However, the Police Commission argued that while the committee did not recommend segregation for New York, they did admit it was the best policy. And since Winnipeg was "different" from New York (the "immoral population" was much smaller) it could be safely applied in Winnipeg. DuVal not only pointed out the fallacy of this sort of argument but he also said that the Police Commission had misinterpreted the report and, in any case, the Committee of Fifteen's recommendations had been denounced by many other authorities.

37/The exact meaning of the terms official and unofficial segregation are meant to distinguish between an open system of licensing as opposed to the system in force in Winnipeg. Thus, although the prostitutes paid a "licence" in terms of being fined quarterly, it was not openly accepting prostitution as legal since they were fined for practising their profession. The

difference seems minimal but it was felt to be a valid one by the Police Commission, if not by the Moral and Social Reform League.

38/*MFP,* 14 Nov. 1910.

39/Ibid., 12 Nov. 1910.

40/*W. Telegram,* 17 and 18 Nov. 1910.

41/*MFP,* 19 Nov. 1910.

42/Ibid, 21 Nov. 1910.

43/*City Council Minutes,* 21 Nov. 1910.

44/*MFP,* 21 Nov. 1910.

45/*WT,* 23 Nov. 1910; Toronto *Globe,* 24 Nov. 1910. Council's over-zealous action in regard to the Robson Commission led to some serious questioning of their motives by the *Tribune.* Under headlines such as "Do They Want The Truth?", it commented on such things as the fact that no meeting of the Lieutenant Governor-in-Council had been called but, rather, the setting up of the commission had been a personal decision of Attorney General Colin H. Campbell, in conference with Mayor Evans. Both were staunch Conservatives. To the Conservative *Telegram,* of course, the commission was of the utmost necessity in order to clear Winnipeg's name. See *W. Telegram,* 30 Nov. 1910.

46/See PAM, *Royal Commission Hearings: Evidence,* Volumes 1 to 10.

47/Considering Evans' well-known connection with the Conservative party, one might expect the Liberal *Free Press* to have supported E. D. Martin, an acknowledged Liberal. Yet the *Free Press* accepted Evans' view of the issue at stake and proceeded to give him at least nominal support. This action gives some indication of the power of the growth ethic. See *MFP,* 7 Dec. 1910. The *Tribune,* on the other hand, obviously supported the reformers but was not nearly as vigorous in its efforts as was the *Telegram.* Of course the labour newspaper, *The Voice,* was a sturdy supporter of the whole reform cause.

48/*MFP,* 5 Dec. 1910.

49/Ibid., 3 Dec. 1910. See also *W. Telegram,* 13 Dec. 1910.

50/*Canadian Annual Review*, 1910, p. 22. This number seems inordinately large since there were only 39,000 names on the voters lists, and even this figure represented many whose names were placed on the list as many as sixty-six times. See *WT*, 23 Dec. 1910 and Chapter 2.

51/*MFP*, 14 Dec. 1910. The charge was also supported by the *WT*. See 6 Jan. 1911.

52/E. Gurney to W. S. Evans, 9 Dec. 1910, PAM, *W. S. Evans Papers*.

53/The distinct connection between Premier Roblin and the *Telegram* is evident from the fact that in 1910 the paper received $26,000 worth of provincial government printing contracts compared with the $145.46 of the Liberal *Manitoba Free Press*. See Orlikow, "Reform Movement in Manitoba," p. 58.

54/*MFP*, 9 Dec. 1910. It has already been noted that Martin was a Liberal. James

Ashdown was also a supporter of the Liberal party and, even more important, the whole social reform movement of this period was generally allied with the Liberals. In other words, by supporting Evans and opposing Martin, the provincial Conservative party was also campaigning against the provincial Liberal party. See Orlikow, "Social Reform Movement in Manitoba," passim. Charges of "electoral corruption" were also made by *The Voice*, 16 Dec. 1910.

55/See, for example, *WT*, 24 March 1912; *The Voice*, 30 Aug. 1912; *MFP*, 13 Dec. 1912. See also, Gray, *Boy from Winnipeg*, p. 8. The presence of the prostitutes can be ascertained by checking the *Henderson Directory*. In 1915, for example, Minnie Woods still lived on Rachel (Annabella) Street.

56/*WT*, 6 Jan. 1911.

CHAPTER 15/*The Rise and Demise of a City Planning Movement (pages 267–280)*

1/*MFP*, 4 March 1892. The role of the *WT* in this campaign is described in an article in that newspaper on 18 Feb. 1950. See also PAM, Public Parks Board, *Historical Annual Report and Tables*, 1892-1905 (hereafter cited as Parks Board, *HAR*).

2/See "The Winnipeg Public Parks Board," in *Winnipeg's Diamond Jubilee*, pp. 177-180.

3/CW, Public Parks Board, *First Annual Report*, 1893.

4/The Parks Board, *HAR* contains descriptions of each of these parks. See also Map 2 which shows their geographical location; William Douglas, "Winnipeg Parks," *MHST Transactions*, Series III, No. 14 (1958–1959), pp. 61-65; and detailed *Annual Reports* of Parks Board in CW, *Special Committees File*. These latter documents cover in great length the improvements made over the years. The eight parks acquired in 1893 and 1894 were: Fort Rouge Park, Central Park, Victoria Park, St. John's Park, Selkirk Park, Dufferin Park, Notre Dame Park, St. James Park. The following public parks, squares, etc. were added prior to 1914. Fort Garry Gateway

(1900), Crescentwood Park (1903), Assiniboine Park (1904), Pembina Park (1905), Riverview Park (1905), Library Grounds (1905), Alexandra Square (1906), Exhibition Grounds (1907), City Hall Square (1907), Weston Park (1909), King Edward Park (1909), Elmwood Park (1909), Machray Park (1909), Clark Park (1909), Cornish Park (1909), Midwinter Park (1909), Logan Park (1909), Kildonan Park (1910), Sargent Park (1911), Kitchener Park (1911), and Seven Oaks Park (1914). By 1914 there were 580 acres of parks in the Winnipeg area (some of the parks, like the 282-acre Assiniboine Park, were a considerable distance outside the city limits).

5/Parks Board, *HAR*; and Public Parks Board, *Annual Report for 1900*.

6/See, for example, *MFP*, 4 Aug. 1906; *W. Telegram*, 12 May 1910.

7/It is interesting to note that even this prediction did not come true. Victoria Park was eventually sold to City Hydro and replaced by "a gigantic commercial building, smoke stacks, coal dump, smoke and soot." See Douglas, "Winnipeg Parks," p. 63.

8/*W. Telegram*, 13 May 1911.

9/See, B. McKelvey, *The Urbanization of America, 1860-1915* (New Brunswick, N.J., 1963), pp. 115-126; J. L. Hancock, "Planning in the Changing American City, 1900-1940," in Callow, ed., *American Urban History*, pp. 549-566; and C. Glaab, *A History of Urban America* (Toronto, 1967), pp. 259-263.

10/*WT*, 4 June 1909, carried a story on the growth of the European movement with special emphasis on Germany. A more complete review of the whole city planning movement is contained in an article by A. A. Stoughton, a Professor of Architecture at the University of Manitoba and one of the founders of the Winnipeg movement, in *MFP*, 23 May 1914. See also article in same edition by E. B. Reynolds, who was to become the honorary secretary of the Winnipeg Housing and Town Planning Association. These articles clearly reveal that the most active members of the Winnipeg movement were fully aware of developments in Europe and were influenced by them.

11/*Who's Who in Western Canada*, 1911, p. 307. See also article on town planning by Pearson in *MFP*, 30 May 1914; and "Movement for a Greater Winnipeg," *The Dominion*, Vol. 4, No. 10 (July 1913), pp. 82-83. William Pearson had moved to Winnipeg in 1899 and established a land and colonization society. He was a member of the WDIB and the Real Estate Exchange and belonged to the Masonic Order, the Carlton Club, and the Royal Colonial Institute. He was a Liberal and an Anglican and lived on Wellington Crescent.

12/See statement of hon. secretary of Winnipeg Town Planning Association in *MFP*, 23 May 1914.

13/*Canadian Annual Review*, 1913. The issue for 1914 describes the growth of the movement in Canada. See also, W. H. Atherton, "Review of Civic Improvement," *The Canadian Municipal Journal*, Vol. X, No. 2 (1915), pp. 62-63. Between 1909 and 1914 city planning commissions had been appointed in Calgary, Regina, Edmonton, Saskatoon, and Lethbridge,

while Toronto and Montreal had park commissions.

14/WDIB, *Annual Report for 1911*.

15/*W. Telegram*, 25 Feb. 1911.

16/*WT*, 10 June 1911.

17/F. J. Cole was appointed secretary of the Town Planning Commission in Oct. 1911. He had "practical experience in the work of laying out such British cities as Sunlight near Liverpool, Garden City, London, Woodlands near Doncaster, Earswick near York, and Hampstead near London," WDIB, *Annual Report for 1911*. Prof. Feather-Stonhaugh was an engineer and served on the Aesthetic Development Committee. Prof. Brydone-Jack was chairman of the Traffic and Transportation Committee and was the official representative of the University of Manitoba. Prof. Broderick was a citizen member of the Aesthetic Development Committee.

18/See Appendix to *The City Planning Commission Report*, Council Communications, Series II, No 9700½ read 27 Jan. 1913 (hereafter cited as *City Planning Commission Report, 1913*). See also CW, *Background for Planning*, prepared for the Metropolitan Planning Committee (Report No. 1), 1946.

19/*City Planning Commission Report, 1913*.

20/The membership of the various committees is recorded in the committee's report.

21/*City Planning Commission Report, 1913*.

22/See, for example, the view stated in *Western Municipal News*, Vol. 6, No. 7 (July 1911), p. 224.

23/*City Planning Commission Report, 1913*.

24/See reports of the conference in *The Canadian Municipal Journal*, Vol. VIII, No. 8 (August 1912), pp. 291-293, and, Vol. VIII, No. 9 (Sept. 1912), p. 338; *MFP*, 15, 16 and 18 July 1912; *The Western Municipal News*, Vol. 7, No. 7 (July 1912), pp. 217-219.

25/*The Voice*, 4 Oct. 1912.

26/Ibid., 1 Nov. 1912.

27/Ibid., 2 Aug. 1912. *The Voice* charged that "some institutions which look to the public for their finances . . . refuse point blank to supply the information which agents of the Commission are deputed to obtain." It did not elaborate on this charge, however.

28/*City Planning Commission Report*, *1913*. Interestingly, the key members of the housing and social survey committees were Doctors Douglas and Simpson, and William Pearson. In the course of their investigation these committees hired "competent investigators" and visited and examined 2,222 houses. They also studied the building codes and tenement bylaws of "a great number" of cities and used "for guidance and precedent" the recommendations of the National Housing Association of Great Britain and the National Housing Association of America. Finally, "the details of the chief Municipal Co-operative Housing and Heating Schemes, and Co-partnership Housing" were gathered and studied.

29/Ibid., The traffic and transportation committee did note, however, that the CPR tracks cut the city in half and not only caused a severe impediment to the smooth movement of traffic but created a social division as well. It recommended that either subways or bridges over the tracks should be immediately undertaken.

30/Ibid.

31/*Voice*, 31 Jan. 1913; *MFP*, 28 Jan. and 8 Feb. 1913.

32/*Council Communications*, Series II, No. 9738, read 3 March 1913. Other members of the executive were J. S. Woodsworth,

Dr. Simpson, Prof. Brydone-Jack, Dr. Douglas and F. J. Cole.

33/The members of this commission appointed by Council were J. D. Atchinson, chairman and member of Winnipeg Builders Exchange, Mayor Waugh, William Pearson, Prof. Brydone-Jack, C. D. Shephard, president of Real Estate Exchange, and J. W. Harris, city surveyor.

34/G. A. P. Carrothers, *Planning in Manitoba* (Winnipeg, 1956), p. 16.

35/*The Voice*, 1 Nov. 1912. See also issue for 2 Aug. 1912; and *Board of Control Papers*, No. 07190, dated 5 Oct. 1912. In the latter communication, which was a letter from F. J. Cole to the Board of Control, the former accused Council of "strange" actions. The letter read as follows: "From the Press I understand that City Solicitor has said, before the Board of Control, the amendment to the City Charter and also the by-laws relating to the Town Planning Commission is being misrepresented by the Commission, and from the start the Commission has not been doing the work it was appointed to do. . . . The Commission has certainly received no formal communication with reference to this matter, but as half the Commission is composed of Aldermen who have never attended the meetings, either of the Commission or its committees, he may have communicated his interpretation to one or more of these. If, as the City Solicitor is reported to have said, the Council all the time had the view that the Commission was not fulfilling its duty, it is strange that the members of the Council, who are members of the Commision, did not tell the Commission it was not carrying out the work called for in the by-law."

CONCLUSION/*The End of an Era (pages 283–286)*

1/See Bellan, "The Development of Winnipeg," chapters VIII and IX; and Morton, *Manitoba*, chapters 14 and 15.

2/*CAR*, 1912, Special Supplement, "Win-

nipeg, The Gateway of the Canadian West," pp. 89-90.

3/Bellan, "The Development of Winnipeg," pp. 486-487 and passim.

bibliography

MANUSCRIPT COLLECTIONS
Canadian Club of Winnipeg. *Papers, 1904–1914.* PAM.
Evans, W. Sanford. *Papers.* PAM.
Margaret Scott Nursing Mission. *Papers, 1904–1943.* PAM.
Western Canadian Immigration Association. *Papers, 1896–1908.* PAC.
Winnipeg Board of Trade. *Papers, 1874–1914.* PAM.
Winnipeg Development and Industrial Bureau. *Papers, 1907–1914.* PAM.
Woodsworth, James Shaver. *Papers.* PAC.

CANADIAN GOVERNMENT DOCUMENTS
Department of Agriculture. *Canada: A Handbook of Information for
      Intending Emigrants.* Ottawa, 1877.
————. *Census of Canada, 1880–81.* Ottawa: Maclean, Rodger and Co.
————. *Census of Manitoba, 1885–86.* Ottawa: Queen's Printer.
————. *Census of Canada, 1890–91.* Ottawa: Queen's Printer.
The Census Office. *Fourth Census of Canada, 1901.* Ottawa: King's
      Printer.
————. *Census of the Northwest Provinces: Manitoba, Saskatchewan,
      Alberta, 1906.* Ottawa: King's Printer.
————. *Fifth Census of Canada, 1911.* Ottawa: King's Printer.
————. *Census of the Prairie Provinces, 1916.* Ottawa: King's Printer.
Dominion Bureau of Statistics. *Sixth Census of Canada, 1921.* Ottawa:
      King's Printer.
————. *Seventh Census of Canada, 1931.* Vol. I, *Summary.* Ottawa:
      King's Printer.
Department of Agriculture Papers. PAC.
Department of Interior Papers. PAC.
Department of Public Works Papers. PAC.
House of Commons. *Debates, 1874–1914.*
Sessional Papers, 1874–1914.
Statutes, 1874–1914.
Kitto, F. H. *Manitoba: Its Development and Opportunities.* Ottawa:
      Department of the Interior, 1923.

PROVINCE OF MANITOBA DOCUMENTS
Department of Agriculture and Immigration. *Annual Reports,
      1886–1889.*

Goldenberg, H. C. *et al. Report of the Royal Commission on Municipal Finances and Administration of the City of Winnipeg.* Winnipeg: King's Printer, 1939.

Provincial Board of Health. *Annual Reports, 1895–1914.*

Sessional Papers, 1874–1914.

Statutes, 1874–1914.

Robson, H. A. *Report of the Royal Commission on Charges Re Vice and Graft Against the Police.* Winnipeg: King's Printer, 1911.

CITY OF WINNIPEG DOCUMENTS

Board of Consulting Engineers. *Report on a New Water Supply for the City of Winnipeg.* Winnipeg: Telegram Printing Co., 1907.

———. *Report on a Water Supply from Shoal Lake for the Greater Winnipeg Water District.* Winnipeg: Stovel Company Ltd., 1913.

Administration Board. *Aqueduct Construction Scheme.* Winnipeg, 1918.

Board of Control Papers, 1907–1914.

Building Inspector. *Annual Reports, 1900–1912.*

By-Laws, 1874–1914.

City Comptroller. *Annual Reports.*

City Council Minutes, 1874–1914.

City Engineer's Office. *Annual Reports, 1898–1914.*

Council Communications, 1874–1914.

"Documents in Reference to the Bridging of the Red River." City Engineer's Office.

Finance Committee Papers, 1874–1914.

Fire, Water, and Light Committee Papers, 1874–1914.

Health Committee Papers, 1905–1914.

Health Department. *Annal Reports, 1908–1914.*

———. *Report on Housing Survey of Certain Selected Areas.* Winnipeg, 1918–1921.

Letter Books, 1874–1914.

List of Electors, 1874–1914.

Market, License, and Health Committee Papers, 1874–1904.

Market, License, and Relief Committee Papers, 1905–1914.

Memo Re Taking over Winnipeg Electric Street Railway System. City Clerk's Office, 1925.

Miscellaneous Papers, 1874–1914.

Municipal Manuals, 1905–1970.

Public Parks Board. *Annual Reports, 1892–1914.*

Report of Marwich, Mitchell and Company on City of Winnipeg Finances. Winnipeg, 1908.

Special Committee Papers, 1874–1914.

Urban Renewal and Rehabilitation Board. *Urban Redevelopment Study No. 1: South Point Douglas.* Winnipeg, n.d.

———. *Urban Renewal Study No. 2: C.P.R. Tracks–Notre Dame Avenue–Main Street–Sherbrook Street.* Winnipeg, n.d.

———. *Urban Renewal Study No. 5: Selkirk Avenue–C.P.R. Yards–Salter Street–Main Street.* Winnipeg, n.d.

Water Power Committee Papers, 1903–1911.

Water Works Purchase Correspondence, 1892–1899.

Winnipeg Town Planning Commission. *Background For Planning: Report No. 1*. Winnipeg, 1946.

City Planning Commission. *City Planning Commission Report.* Winnipeg, 1913.

Elwes, R. G. *Winnipeg Water Works Company Report*. Winnipeg: O'Loughlin Bros. and Co., 1886.

Fanning, J. T. *Report on the Winnipeg Water Power of the Assiniboine in Manitoba*. Winnipeg: McIntyre Bros., 1889.

Greater Winnipeg Water Works District. *Papers, 1913–1921.*

Hazen, Professor A. *Report on Sewer System and Water Supply for the City of Winnipeg*. New York, 1905.

Henderson's Directories Limited. *Henderson's Directory of Winnipeg.* Winnipeg, yearly editions 1881–1914.

Hering, R. *Report on a Future Water Supply for the City of Winnipeg.* Winnipeg: McIntyre Bros., 1897.

Ruttan, H. N. *The Water Supply of the City of Winnipeg: Reports of 2nd March and 12th November, 1886*. Winnipeg: Walker and May, 1886.

————. City Engineer. *The Water Supply of the City of Winnipeg: Report of 8th April, 1887, on the Proposals of the Winnipeg Water Works Company*. Winnipeg: Call Printing Co., 1887.

————. *Report on Water Power and Navigation of the Assiniboine River*. Winnipeg: Phoenix Printing Works, 1888.

————. *Reports on the Sanitary Condition of the City of Winnipeg.* Winnipeg: Stovel Co. Ltd., 1893.

————. *Report on the Assiniboine River and Artesian Wells as Sources of Supply and on a System of Water Works for the City of Winnipeg*. Winnipeg: McIntyre Bros., 1896.

NEWSPAPERS AND PERIODICALS

The Canadian Annual Review, 1901–1914.

The Canadian Municipal Journal, 1905–1914.

The Daily Nor'Wester, 1894–1898.

Manitoba Free Press, 1872–1914.

The Manitoba Gazette and Trade Review, 1872–1874.

The Manitoban, 1870–1874.

The Manitoba Sun, 1886–1889.

Le Métis, 1873.

The Nor'Wester, 1859–1869.

Town Topics, 1898–1906.

The Voice, 1897–1914.

Western Municipal News, 1906–1914.

Winnipeg Daily Times, 1879–1885.

The Winnipeg Telegram, 1898–1914.

Winnipeg Tribune, 1890–1914.

CONTEMPORARY ACCOUNTS

Agnew, Dr. "Our Water Supply." *HSSM Transactions*, Series I, No. 2 (1883–1884), pp. 1–4.

Begg, Alexander and Nursey, Walter R. *Ten Years in Winnipeg*. Winnipeg: Times Publishing House, 1879.

Bowsfield, H. ed. *The James Wickes Taylor Correspondence, 1859–1870*. Altona: D. W. Friesen and Sons, 1968.

Brooks, G. B. *Plain Facts About the New City Hall*. Winnipeg: Walker and May, 1884.

Bryce, G. "Early Days in Winnipeg." *HSSM Transactions*, Series I, No. 46 (1894).

————. "The Five Forts of Winnipeg." *Transactions of the Royal Society of Canada*, Volume III, Section II (1885), pp. 134–145.

————. "A Great City Library." *HSSM Transactions*, Series I, No. 70 (1906).

————. "The Illustrated History of Winnipeg." *Manitoba Free Press*, 1905.

————. "Treasures of Our Library." *HSSM Transactions*, Series I, No. 64 (1904).

Bryce, Mrs. G. "The Charitable Institutions of Winnipeg." *HSSM Transactions*, Series I, No. 54 (1899).

Chapman, G. F. "Winnipeg: The Melting Pot." *The Canadian Magazine*, Vol. XXXIII, No. 5 (September 1909), pp. 409–416.

————. "Winnipeg: The Refining Process." *The Canadian Magazine*, Vol. XXXIII, No. 6 (October 1909), pp. 548–554.

The Clubs, Societies and Associations of Winnipeg. Winnipeg: Winnipeg Publishing Co., 1908.

Donald, W. J. A. "The Growth and Distribution of the Canadian Population." *Journal of Political Economy*, Vol. XXI (April 1913), pp. 292–312.

DuVal, F. B. *The Problem of Social Vice in Winnipeg*. Winnipeg: Moral and Social Reform Committee, 1910.

Elliott, G. B. *Winnipeg As It Is*. Winnipeg: Free Press, 1874.

Ewart, A. C. "The Municipal History of Manitoba." *University of Toronto Studies*, Studies in History and Economics, Vol II, No. 3 (1907), pp. 131–148.

Fitzgibbon, M. *A Trip to Manitoba*. Toronto: Rose, Bedford, 1880.

Ham, George H. *Reminiscences of a Raconteur*. Toronto: Musson Book Co., 1921.

Handbook to Winnipeg and the Province of Manitoba Prepared for the 79th Annual Meeting of the British Association for the Advancement of Science. Winnipeg: British Association, 1909.

Hill, Robert B. *Manitoba: History of its Early Settlement, Development, and Resources*. Toronto: William Briggs, 1890.

"How Winnipeg Welcomes the Immigrant." *The Dominion*, Vol. IV, No. 10 (July, 1913), pp. 15–16.

Macoun, J. *Manitoba and the Great Northwest*. Guelph: World Publishing, 1882.

"Movement For a Greater Winnipeg." *The Dominion*, Vol. IV, No. 10 (July, 1913), pp. 82–83.

Munro, W. B. "Boards of Control and Commission Government in

Canadian Cities. *Papers and Proceedings*, Canadian Political Science Association, Ottawa, 1913, pp. 112–123.

Murdoch, W. "The Red River." *HSSM Transactions*, Series I, No. 12 (1884), pp. 1–3.

O'Donnell, J. H. *Manitoba As I Saw It*. Winnipeg: Musson Book Co., 1909.

Parker, C. W. ed. *Who's Who in Western Canada*. Vancouver: Canadian Press Association, 1911.

Rowman, J. H. "The Red River." *HSSM Transactions*, Series I, No. 13 (1884), pp. 5-11.

Schofield, F. H. *The Story of Manitoba*. Vol. II. Winnipeg: S. J. Clarke, 1913.

Souvenir of the City of Winnipeg Presented to Members of the British Association for the Advancement of Science. Winnipeg, 1884.

Souvenir of Winnipeg's Diamond Jubilee, 1874–1924. Winnipeg: Civic, Social, and Athletic Association, 1924.

Steen, J. E. and Boyce, W. *Winnipeg, Manitoba, and Her Industries*. Chicago: Steen and Boyce, 1882.

Steen, J. E. *Winnipeg: A Historical Sketch of Its Wonderful Growth, Progress and Prosperity*. Winnipeg, 1903.

Thompson, W. T. and Boyer, E. E. *The City of Winnipeg*. Winnipeg: Thompson and Boyer, 1886.

"Tide of Winnipeg's Population Pouring Northward." *The Dominion*, Vol. IV, No. 1 (October 1912), pp. 13–16.

Tuttle, C. R. *The Civic Situation, Including a Brief History of the Corporation of Winnipeg from 1874 to the Present Time*. Winnipeg, 1883.

Wickett, M. "City Government in Canada." *University of Toronto Studies*, Studies in History and Economics, Vol. II, No. 1 (1907), pp. 3–24.

————. "The Municipal Government of Toronto." *University of Toronto Studies*, Studies in History and Economics, Vol II, No. 1 (1907), pp. 35–58.

————. "A Toronto Viewpoint." *Papers and Proceedings*, Canadian Political Science Association, Ottawa, 1913, pp. 131–135

Winnipeg Electric Railway Company Ltd. *Annual Reports, 1910–1915*. City Clerk's Office, City of Winnipeg.

————. *Historical and Financial Report Covering the Years 1892 to 1918*. City Clerk's Office, City of Winnipeg.

"Winnipeg—The Gateway of the Canadian West." *Canadian Annual Review*, 1912, "Special Supplement," pp. 1–90.

Woodsworth, J. S. *My Neighbour: A Study of City Conditions*. Toronto: Missionary Society of the Methodist Church, 1911.

————. *Strangers Within Our Gates*. Toronto: Missionary Society of the Methodist Church, 1909.

Young, G. *Manitoba Memories*. Toronto: William Briggs, 1897.

SECONDARY SOURCES

Armstrong, F. H. "Urban History in Canada." Urban History Group *Newsletter*, No. 28 (December, 1969), pp. 1–10.

Artibise, A. F. J. "Advertising Winnipeg: The Campaign for Immigrants and Industry, 1874–1914." *HSSM Transactions*, Series III, No. 27 (1970–71), pp. 75–106.

———. "The Crucial Decade: Red River at the Outbreak of the American Civil War." *HSSM Transactions*, Series III, No. 23 (1966–67), pp. 59–66.

———. "Mayor Alexander Logan of Winnipeg." *Beaver*, Spring 1974, pp. 4–12.

———. "Researching Winnipeg." *Urban History Review*, No. 2 (June 1972), pp. 14–18.

———. "The Urban Development of Winnipeg." *Urban History Review* No. 1 (February 1972), pp. 5–6.

———. "An Urban Environment: The Process of Growth in Winnipeg, 1874–1914." CHA, *Historical Papers*, 1972.

———. "Winnipeg and the City Planning Movement, 1910–1915." David J. Bercuson, ed., *Western Perspectives 1*. Toronto: Holt, Rinehart and Winston, 1974, pp. 10–20.

———. *Winnipeg: The Growth of a City*. Canada's Visual History Project, Series I, No. 1, National Museum, 1974.

——— and Dahl, E. *Winnipeg in Maps*. PAC, 1974.

Barber, P. "Class Conflict in Winnipeg Civic Politics: The Role of the Citizens' and Civic Election Organizations." PAM, unpublished paper, March 1970.

Belkin, S. *Through Narrow Gates: A Review of Jewish Immigration, Colonization and Immigrant Aid Work in Canada, 1840–1940*. Montreal: Eagle Publishing Co., 1966.

Bellan, R. C. "The Development of Winnipeg as a Metropolitan Centre." Ph.D. thesis, Columbia University, 1958.

———. "Rails Across The Red: Winnipeg or Selkirk." *HSSM Transactions*, Series III, No. 18 (1961–62), pp. 69–77.

———. "Relief in Winnipeg: The Economic Background." M.A. thesis, University of Toronto, 1941.

———. "Winnipeg, 1873–1914." Manitoba Society of Regional Studies, *Regional Review*, Vol. VI, No. 1 (April 1963), pp. 14–21.

Berton, P. *The Last Spike: The Great Railway, 1881–1885*. Toronto: McClelland and Stewart, 1971.

———. *The National Dream: The Great Railway, 1871–1881*. Toronto: McClelland and Stewart, 1970.

Bicha, K. D. *The American Farmer and the Canadian West, 1896–1914*. Lawrence, Kansas: Coronado Press, 1968.

Blake, Herbert W. *The Era of Streetcars in Winnipeg, 1881–1955*. Winnipeg: Hignal Printing Co., 1971.

———. *The Era of Interurbans in Winnipeg, 1902–1939*. Winnipeg: Bishop Printing Co., 1971.

Blyth, Jack A. *The Canadian Social Inheritance*. Toronto: Copp Clark, 1972.

Bradley, W. E. "History of Transportation in Winnipeg." *HSSM Transactions*, Series II, No. 15 (1960), pp. 7–38.

Bradwin, E. W. *The Bunkhouse Man: A Study of Work and Pay in the Camps of Canada, 1903–1914*. New York: Columbia, 1928.

Brown, C., ed., *Minorities, Schools, and Politics*. Toronto: University of Toronto Press, 1969.

Callow, A. B., ed. *American Urban History*. Toronto: Oxford, 1969.

Careless, J. M. S. "The Development of the Winnipeg Business Community." *Transactions of the Royal Society of Canada*, 1970, 4th Series, pp. 239–254.

——. "Limited Identities." *Canadian Historical Review*, Vol. L, No. 1 (March 1969), pp. 1–10.

——. "Nationalism, Pluralism and Canadian History." *Culture*, Vol. XXX, No. 1 (March 1969), pp. 19–26.

——. "Somewhat Narrow Horizons." CHA, *Historical Papers*, 1968, pp. 1–10.

Carrothers, G. A. P. *Planning in Manitoba*. Winnipeg, 1956.

Chiel, A. A. *The Jews in Manitoba*. Toronto: University of Toronto Press, 1961.

Clark, L., ed. *The Manitoba School Question*. Toronto: Copp Clark, 1968.

Clark, S. D. "The Prairie Wheat Farming Frontier and the New Industrial City." *The Developing Canadian Community*. Toronto: University of Toronto Press, 1962, pp. 99–112.

——, ed. *Social Development in Canada*. Toronto: University of Toronto Press, 1942.

——, ed. *Urbanism and the Changing Canadian Population*. Toronto: University of Toronto Press, 1961.

Comeault, G. L. "Archbishop Langevin, Schools, and Politics in Manitoba, 1895–1915." PAM, unpublished paper, February 1970.

Cook, Ramsay. "Stephen Leacock and the Age of Plutocracy, 1903–1921." John Moir, ed., *Character and Circumstance: Essays in Honour of Donald Grant Creighton*. Toronto: Macmillan, 1970, pp. 163–181.

Cooper, J. "The Red Light District in Winnipeg: An Issue in Civic Politics, 1903–1910." PAM, unpublished paper, February 1970.

Davidson, C. B. *et al. The Population of Manitoba*. Winnipeg: King's Printer, 1938.

Donnelly, M. *Dafoe of the Free Press*. Toronto: Macmillan, 1968.

Douglas, W. "The Forks Become a City." *HSSM Transactions*, Series II (1944–45), pp. 51–80.

——. "Winnipeg Parks." *HSSM Transactions*, Series III, No. 14 (1959), pp. 61–65.

Dyos, H. J., ed. *The Study of Urban History*. London: Arnold, 1963.

England, R. *The Colonization of Western Canada*. London: P. S. King and Son, 1936.

Feldman, L. D. and Goldrick, M.D., eds. *Politics and Government of Urban Canada*. Toronto: Methuen, 1969.

Ferguson, M. M. *A History of St. James*. Winnipeg, 1967.

Friesen, J. "Expansion of Settlement in Manitoba, 1870–1890." *HSSM*

Transactions, Series III, No. 20 (1963–64), pp. 35–48.

Fromson, R. D. "Acculturation or Assimilation: A. Geographic Analysis of Residential Segregation of Selected Ethnic Groups: Metropolitan Winnipeg, 1951–1961." M.A. thesis, University of Manitoba, 1965.

George, M. V. *Internal Migration in Canada: Demographic Analyses*. Ottawa: DBS, 1970.

Gibbs, J. P., ed. *Urban Research Methods*. Toronto: Van Nostrand, 1961.

Glaab, C. *A History of Urban America*. Toronto: Macmillan, 1967.

Glazebrook, G. P. deT. *A History of Transportation in Canada*. Vol. II. Toronto: McClelland and Stewart, 1964.

Gluek, A. C. *Minnesota and the Manifest Destiny of the Canadian Northwest*. Toronto: University of Toronto Press, 1965.

Gold, N. L. "American Migration to the Prairie Provinces of Canada, 1890–1933." PH.D. thesis, University of California, 1933.

Graver, A. E. *Public Health: A Study Prepared for the Royal Commission on Dominion-Provincial Relations*. Ottawa: King's Printer, 1939.

Gray, J. H. *Booze*. Toronto: Macmillan, 1972.

———. *The Boy from Winnipeg*. Toronto: Macmillan, 1970.

———. *Men Against the Desert*. Saskatoon: Modern Press, 1967.

———. *Red Lights on the Prairies*. Toronto: Macmillan, 1971.

Handlin, O., and Burchard, J., eds. *The Historian and the City*. Cambridge, Mass.: MIT, 1963.

Hansen, M. L., and Brebner, J. B. *The Mingling of the Canadian and American Peoples*. New York: Russell and Russell, 1970.

Hauser, P. M., ed. *Handbook for Social Research in Urban Areas*. New York: UNESCO, 1964.

Healy, W. J. *Winnipeg's Early Days: A Short Historical Sketch*. Winnipeg: Stovel Printing Co., 1937.

Hedges, J. B. *Building the Canadian West*. New York: Macmillan, 1939.

Henderson, A. M. "From Fort Douglas to the Forks." *HSSM Transactions*, Series III, No. 23 (1966–67), pp. 15–32.

Herstein, H. "The Growth of the Winnipeg Jewish Community and the Evolution of Its Educational Institutions." *HSSM Transactions*, Series III, No. 22 (1966–67), pp. 27–66.

Holt, W. S. "Some Consequences of the Urban Movement in American History." *Pacific Historical Quarterly*, Vol. XXII (November 1953), pp. 337–351.

Hosse, H. A. "The Areal Growth and Functional Development of Winnipeg from 1870 to 1913." M.A. thesis, University of Manitoba, 1956.

Huber, H. "The Winnipeg Board of Control, 1907–1918: Good Business or Progressive Municipal Reform?" PAM, unpublished paper, February 1970.

———. "Winnipeg's Age of Plutocracy: 1901–1914." Unpublished paper in possession of author.

Innis, H. A. *A History of the Canadian Pacific Railway*. Toronto: McClelland and Stewart, 1923.

Jackson, J. A. *The Centennial History of Manitoba*. Winnipeg: Manitoba Historical Society, 1970.

————. "The Disallowance of Manitoba Railway Legislation in the 1880's." M.A. thesis, University of Manitoba, 1945.

Johnson, J. K., ed. *The Canadian Directory of Parliament: 1867–1967*. Ottawa: Queen's Printer, 1967.

Kalbach, W. E. *The Impact of Immigration on Canada's Population*. Ottawa: DBS, 1970.

Katz, M. B. "Social Structure in Hamilton, Ontario." Thernstrom, S. and Sennett, P., eds. *Nineteenth-Century Cities: Essays in the New Urban History*. New Haven: Yale, 1969, pp. 209–244.

Kaye, V. J. "The Problem of the Ethnic Name." *Early Ukrainian Settlement in Canada, 1895–1900*. Toronto: University of Toronto Press, 1964, pp. xxiii–xxvi.

Kemp, H. D. "The Department of the Interior in the West, 1873–1883." M.A. thesis, University of Manitoba, 1950.

Klassen, H. C. "The Red River Settlement and the St. Paul Route, 1859–1870." M.A. thesis, University of Manitoba, 1963.

Kristjanson, N. *The Icelandic People in Manitoba*. Winnipeg: Wallingford Press, 1965.

Lampard, E. E. "American Historians and the Study of Urbanization." *American Historical Review*, Vol. LXVII, No. 1 (October 1961), pp. 49–91.

Lowe, Peter. "All Western Dollars." *HSSM Transactions*, Series II (1945–46), pp. 10–25.

Lower, A. R. M. *Canadians in the Making: A Social History of Canada*. Toronto: Longmans, 1958.

Lunty, A. J., and Hurley, K.C. *Armstrong's Point: An Historical Survey*, Winnipeg, 1969.

Lucow, W. H. "The Origin and Growth of the Public School System in Manitoba." M.Ed. thesis, University of Manitoba, 1950.

McCormack, A. R. "Arthur Puttee and the Liberal Party: 1899–1904." *Canadian Historical Review*, Vol. LI, No. 2 (June 1970), pp. 141–163.

MacDonald, Norbert. "Population Growth and Change in Seattle and Vancouver, 1880–1960." *Pacific Historical Review*, Vol. XXXIX, No. 3 (August, 1970), pp. 297–321.

Macdonald, Norman. *Canada: Immigration and Colonization, 1841–1903*. Toronto: Macmillan, 1966.

McEwan, G. *Between the Red and the Rockies*. Toronto: University of Toronto Press, 1952.

McFadden, M. "Steamboating on the Red." *HSSM Transactions*, Series III, No. 7 (1952), pp. 21–29.

MacInnis, Grace. *J. S. Woodsworth: A Man to Remember*. Toronto: Macmillan, 1953.

McKelvey, B. *The Urbanization of America, 1860–1915*. New Brunswick, N.J.: Rutgers, 1963.

McKillop, A. B. "Citizens and Socialists: The Ethos of Political Winnipeg, 1919–1935." M.A. thesis, University of Manitoba, 1970.

McMann, L. D. "Urban Growth in Western Canada, 1880–1960." *The Albertan Geographer*, No. 5 (1969), pp. 65–74.

McNaught, K. *A Prophet in Politics: A Biography of J. S. Woodsworth.* Toronto: University of Toronto Press, 1959.

Macvicar, M. *The Story of the Mission.* Winnipeg, 1939.

McWilliams, M. *Manitoba Milestones.* Toronto: J. M. Dent and Sons, 1928.

Marlyn, J. *Under the Ribs of Death.* Toronto: McClelland and Stewart, 1957.

Masters, D. C. "The English Communities in Winnipeg and in the Eastern Townships of Quebec." Mason Wade, ed. *Regionalism in the Canadian Community, 1867–1967.* Toronto: University of Toronto Press, 1969, pp. 130–159.

Mitchell, R. "Public Health in Manitoba." R. D. Defries, ed. *The Development of Public Health in Canada.* Toronto: University of Toronto Press, 1940, pp. 87–98.

———. "How Winnipeg Waged War on Typhoid." *Manitoba Medical Review*, Vol. 49, No. 6 (June–July 1969), pp. 166–167.

Morton, A. S. *A History of the Canadian West to 1870–71.* London: T. Nelson and Sons, 1939.

Morton, A. S., and Martin, C. *History of Prairie Settlement and Dominion Lands Policy.* Toronto: Macmillan, 1938.

Morton, W. L. *Manitoba: A History.* Toronto: University of Toronto Press, 1957.

———. *One University: A History of the University of Manitoba.* Toronto: McClelland and Stewart, 1957.

———. *The Progressive Party in Canada.* Toronto: University of Toronto Press, 1957.

Mott, Morris K. "The 'Foreign Peril': Nativism in Winnipeg, 1916–1923." M.A. thesis, University of Manitoba, 1970.

Newman, Peter C. *Flame of Power.* Toronto: McClelland and Stewart, 1959.

O'Gorman, K. "The Winnipeg Civic Elections of 1919 and 1920—A Comparison." PAM, unpublished paper, February, 1970.

Orlikow, L. "A Survey of the Reform Movement in Manitoba, 1910 to 1920." M.A. thesis, University of Manitoba, 1955.

Page, J. E. "Catholic Parish Ecology and Urban Development in the Greater Winnipeg Region." M.A. thesis, University of Manitoba, 1958.

Paquet, G., and Lithwick, N. H., eds. *Urban Studies: A Canadian Perspective.* Toronto: Methuen, 1968.

Pearce, W. G. *Winnipeg School Days, 1871–1950.* PAM.

Pettipas, K. "Margaret Scott and the Margaret Scott Nursing Mission, 1904–1943." PAM, unpublished paper, February 1970.

Phillips, A. D. "The Development of Municipal Institutions in Manitoba to 1886." M.A. thesis, University of Manitoba, 1948.

Plewman, W. R. *Adam Beck and Ontario Hydro.* Toronto: Ryerson, 1947.

Plunkett, T. J. *Municipal Organization in Canada*. Montreal: Canadian Federation of Mayors and Municipalities, 1955.

Porter, J. *Canadian Social Structure. A Statistical Profile*. Toronto: McClelland and Stewart, 1967.

————. *The Vertical Mosaic*. Toronto: University of Toronto Press, 1965.

Rea, J. E. "The Roots of Prairie Society." D. P. Gagan, ed. *Prairie Perspectives: Papers of the Western Canadian Studies Conference*. Toronto: Holt, Rinehart and Winston, 1970, pp. 46–57.

Regehr, T. D. "The Canadian Northern Railway: The West's Own Product." *Canadian Historical Review*, Vol LI, No. 2 (June 1970), pp. 177–187.

Reynolds, G. F. "The Man Who Created the Corner of Portage and Main (Henry McKenney)." *HSSM Transactions*, Series III, No. 26 (1969–70), pp. 5–40.

Rich, E. E. *The Fur Trade and the Northwest to 1857*. Toronto: McClelland and Stewart, 1967.

Robin, M. *Radical Politics and Canadian Labour, 1880–1930*. Kingston: Queen's University, 1968.

Rosenburg, L. *The Jewish Community in Winnipeg*. Montreal: Canadian Jewish Congress, 1946.

Russenholt, E. S. *The Power of a City*. Unpublished manuscript, City of Winnipeg Hydro Office.

Rutherford, P. F. W. "The Western Press and Regionalism, 1870–1896." *Canadian Historical Review*, Vol. LII, No. 3 (September 1971), pp. 287–305.

Ryder, N. B. "The Interpretation of Origin Statistics." *Canadian Journal of Economics and Political Science*, Vol. XXI, No. 4 (1955), pp. 466–479.

Schnore, L. F. ed. *Social Science and the City: A Survey of Urban Research*. New York: Praeger, 1968.

Sharp, P. F. *The Agrarian Revolt in Western Canada*. Minneapolis: West Press, 1948.

Silver, A. I. "French Canada and the Prairie Frontier, 1870–1890." *CHR*, Vol. L, No. 1 (March 1969), pp. 11–36.

Sinclair, A. M. "Internal Migration in Canada, 1871–1951." PH.D thesis, Harvard University, 1966.

Sisler, W. J. *Peaceful Invasion*. Winnipeg: Ketchen Printing Co., 1944.

Skelton, O. D. *The Railway Builders*. Toronto: Glasgow, Brook and Co., 1916.

Smith, A. "Metaphor and Nationality in North America." *Canadian Historical Review*, Vol. LI, No. 3 (September 1970), pp. 247–275.

Spigelman, M. "Bilingual Schools in Manitoba and Their Abolition." PAM, unpublished paper, February 1970.

Stanley, G. F. G. *The Birth of Western Canada*. Toronto: University of Toronto Press, 1960.

Stelter, Gilbert A. "A Sense of Time and Place: The Historian's

Approach to the Urban Past." Unpublished paper presented to CHA, Queen's University, June 1973.

Stone, L. O. *Migration in Canada: Regional Aspects*. Ottawa: DBS, 1969.

———. *Urban Development in Canada*. Ottawa: DBS, 1967.

Stuart, J. A. D. *The Prairie WASP: A History of the Rural Municipality of Oakland, Manitoba*. Winnipeg: Prairie Press, 1969.

Studness, C. M. "Economic Opportunity and the Westward Migration of Canadians During the Late Nineteenth Century." *Canadian Journal of Economics and Political Science*, Vol XXX (1964), pp. 570–584.

Syrnick, J. H. "Community Builders: Early Ukrainian Teachers." *HSSM Transactions*, Series III, No. 21 (1965), pp. 25–34.

Thomson, D. C. *Alexander Mackenzie: Clear Grit*. Toronto: Macmillan, 1960.

Thernstrom, Stephen. "Reflections on the New Urban History." F. Gilbert and S. R. Graubard, eds. *Historical Studies Today*. New York: Norton, 1972, pp. 320–336.

Thorlakson, T. K., and Mitchell, R. "James Kerr, 1848–1911, and Harry Hyland Kerr, 1881–1963: Pioneer Canadian-American Surgeons." *Canadian Journal of Surgery*, Vol. 9 (July 1966), pp. 213–220.

Turek, V. *The Poles in Manitoba*. Toronto: Polish Alliance Press, 1967. McClelland and Stewart, 1971.

Waite, P. B. *Canada, 1874–1896: Arduous Destiny*. Toronto: McClelland and Stewart, 1971.

Warkentin, J., and Ruggles, R. I. *Historical Atlas of Manitoba*. Winnipeg: Manitoba Historical Society, 1970.

Warner, S. B., Jr. "Cultural Change and the Ghetto." *Journal of Contemporary History*, Vol. IV, No. 4 (November 1969), pp. 173–187.

———. "If All The World Were Philadelphia: A Scaffolding for Urban History." *American Historical Review*, Vol. LXXIV, No. 1 (October 1968), pp. 26–43.

———. *The Private City: Philadelphia in Three Periods of Growth*. Philadelphia: University of Philadelphia Press, 1968.

———. *Streetcar Suburbs*. Cambridge, Mass.: MIT, 1962.

Winkler, H. C. "Early Manitoba Railroads." *HSSM Transactions*, Series III, No. 10 (1955), pp. 5–13.

Younge, E. R. "Population Movements and the Assimilation of Ethnic Groups in Canada." *Canadian Journal of Economics and Political Science*, Vol. X, No. 3 (1944), pp. 372–380.

Yuzyk, P. *The Ukrainians in Manitoba*. Toronto: University of Toronto Press, 1953.

Zaslow, M. *The Opening of the Canadian North, 1870–1914*. Toronto: McClelland and Stewart, 1972.

index